World Theories of Theatre

World Theories of Theatre expands the horizons of theatrical theory beyond the West, providing the tools for a truly global approach to theatre.

Glenn Odom identifies major debates in theatrical theory from around the world, combining discussions of the key theoretical questions facing theatre studies with extended excerpts from primary materials, specific primary materials, case studies, and coverage of Southern Africa, the Caribbean, North Africa and the Middle East, Oceania, Latin America, East Asia, and India. The volume is divided into three sections:

- *Theoretical questions*, which applies cross-cultural perspectives to key issues from aesthetics to postcolonialism, interculturalism, and globalization.
- *Cultural and literary history*, which is organised by region, presenting a range of theatrical theories in their historical and cultural context.
- *Practical exercises*, which provides a brief series of suggestions for physical exploration of these theoretical concepts.

World Theories of Theatre presents fresh, vital ways of thinking about the theatre, highlighting the extraordinary diversity of approaches available to scholars and students of theatre studies.

Glenn Odom is a senior lecturer in the Department of Drama, Theatre, and Performance at the University of Roehampton.

World Theories of Theatre

Glenn Odom

LONDON AND NEW YORK

First published 2017
by Routledge
2 Park Square, Milton Park, Abingdon, Oxon OX14 4RN

and by Routledge
711 Third Avenue, New York, NY 10017

Routledge is an imprint of the Taylor & Francis Group, an informa business

© 2017 Glenn Odom

The right of Glenn Odom to be identified as author of this work has been asserted by him in accordance with sections 77 and 78 of the Copyright, Designs and Patents Act 1988.

All rights reserved. No part of this book may be reprinted or reproduced or utilised in any form or by any electronic, mechanical, or other means, now known or hereafter invented, including photocopying and recording, or in any information storage or retrieval system, without permission in writing from the publishers.

Trademark notice: Product or corporate names may be trademarks or registered trademarks, and are used only for identification and explanation without intent to infringe.

British Library Cataloguing in Publication Data
A catalogue record for this book is available from the British Library

Library of Congress Cataloging in Publication Data
Names: Odom, Glenn, 1975- author.
Title: World theories of theatre / Glenn Odom.
Other titles: World theories of theater
Description: Milton Park, Abingdon, Oxon ; New York, NY : Routledge, 2017. | Includes bibliographical references.
Identifiers: LCCN 2016049113| ISBN 9781138822559 (hardback) | ISBN 9781138822566 (pbk.) | ISBN 9781315742496 (ebook)
Subjects: LCSH: Theater--Philosophy.
Classification: LCC PN2039 .O35 2017 | DDC 792.01--dc23
LC record available at https://lccn.loc.gov/2016049113

ISBN: 978-1-138-82255-9 (hbk)
ISBN: 978-1-138-82256-6 (pbk)
ISBN: 978-1-315-74249-6(ebk)

Typeset in Sabon
by HWA Text and Data Management, London

Contents

Preface vii
Acknowledgments ix
Publishers' acknowledgements xi

1 Introduction: world, theatre, theory 1

PART I
Theoretical questions 13

2 Aesthetics 15
   2.1 Selections from *On the Art of Nō Drama:* Zeami Motokiyo, translated by Thomas Rimer 27
   2.2 Selections from the *Natyasastra*: Bharata Muni translated by Manomohan Ghosh 37
   2.3 Selections from "Drama and the African World-view" in *Myth, Literature and the African World:* Wole Soyinka 43

3 Theatre and politics 54
   3.1 Selections from "'The revolution as Muse': Drama as surreptitious insurrection in a post-colonial, military state": Femi Osofisan 65
   3.2 Selections from *Towards a Revolutionary Theatre*: Utpal Dutt 74
   3.3 Selections from "Manifestos for a New Arab Theatre": Saadallah Wannous 78

4 Decolonization, hybridity, postcoloniality, interculturalism, and globalization — 101
   4.1 "Theatre and Culture": Enrique Buenaventura, translated by Joanne Pottlitzer — 111
   4.2 Selections from "What the Twilight Says: An Overture": Derek Walcott — 120
   4.3 Selections from *It Shall Be of Jasper and Coral:* Werewere Liking, translated by Irene Assiba d'Almeida — 128
   4.4 Selections from "Performing for Aboriginal Life and Culture: Aboriginal Theatre and Ngurrumilmarrmiriyu": Maryrose Casey — 136

5 Identity / The actor — 152
   5.1 Selections from *Theatre of the Oppressed:* Augusto Boal, translated by Charles A. and Maria-Odilia Leal McBride — 160
   5.2 Selections from "Human Experience and the Group": Suzuki Tadashi, translated by Thomas Rimer — 167
   5.3 Selections from "On Directing": Jiao Juyin, translated by Shiao-ling Yu — 176

6 Modernity and theatre — 184
   6.1 Selections from *Introduction to Theater:* Hirata Oriza, translated by Hiroko Matsuda — 190
   6.2 "The potential of theatre": Gao Xingjian, translated by Mabel Lee — 200

7 Toward a theorization of gender in world theatre — 209
   7.1 Selections from "A Maori Point of View: The Journey from Anxiety to Confidence": Roma Potiki — 217
   7.2 An Interview with Poile Sengupta: Anita Singh — 220

PART II
Cultural and literary history — **227**

8 Latin America and the Caribbean — 229

9 Sub-Saharan Africa — 246

10 North Africa and the Middle East   254

11 Australia and New Zealand   262

12 East Asia   270

13 India   277

PART III
Practical exercises

14 Theory and practice   285

    References   294
    Further reading   296
    Index   302

Preface

I am a white man who was raised in Texas in the late 20th century. I have lived many places around the world and visited even more. I have a decent reading knowledge of several European, Asian, and African languages, although I am only fluent in English. I am a lover of theatre in all its forms. I approached first African and then Asian theatre as a novice in my late 20s. During my first trip to Nigeria, I became fascinated by the things I was being taught that required me to completely abandon my current modes of thinking. The idea that there were other worlds of thought, other ways of seeing the world, and, indeed, other worlds out there was humbling and exhilarating. After endeavoring to think in and through these other worlds, I became equally fascinated by the collisions between worlds.

As the above should make clear, I have an emotional investment in writing this book. Throughout my career as an academic, I have often felt that I needed to spend too much space in an article explaining the "foreign" material to my readers. More importantly, I have found that it is far easier to be published if I present the material as "foreign." The more comparative my work with African and Asian theatres becomes, the more difficult it is to find an audience for it. It is my intention to join a growing group of academics and practitioners trying to shift the culture of the Western academy broadly and in Theatre Studies specifically. I hope my enthusiasm is apparent throughout the text and I encourage my readers to enter with an open mind.

Prior to its publication, portions of this book have been read by several dozen people. Based on their invaluable comments, I want to emphasize a few points that come up in the book. First, this book only briefly discusses theatre theory from Europe and the U.S. That theory is readily available and well-known. Several readers suggested that this book would only be of interest to people in Asia and Africa. I want to emphatically challenge this suggestion!

Is European theatre theory universal? Did it somehow crack the theatrical code and become relevant to all societies at all times? Is it the one "right" perspective? If not, then other perspectives might have something to say about "theatre" in addition to "African Theatre" or "Latin American Theatre."

To assume that European theatre theory is complete unto itself and capable of explaining "theatre" as a whole is dubious on philosophical grounds and it ignores theatre history. Most scholars point to Greece as the foundation of theatrical practice in the West. Dionysus is associated with this practice, and most Dionysian cults trace the Greek god of theatre to either Africa or Asia. The god of Western theatre is not Western. Moving quite beyond mythology, Peter Brook was inspired by India and Africa, Bertolt Brecht by China, and Artaud by Bali. The great names of Western theatre theory knew the value of looking at other theatrical traditions.

To be sure, we could retrace their steps, looking at the same half-dozen theorists and practices from around the world that these theatrical giants encountered. We could claim that only these few figures are "important" to theatre. This, however, would ignore the cultural contexts of the figures who inspired Brook, Artaud, and Brecht.

These theories are certainly useful in studying theatre from Africa, Asia, Australia, and Latin America, but I encourage my readers to consider the fact that our contemporary Western theatre has been shaped by influences beyond the Anglo-European. Each of the theorists in this book contributed to theatrical development in their own countries. Most are known regionally and many have international reputations. The fact that they are currently unknown to many Western readers is NOT an indication of their importance. It is an indication that there is a whole world of exciting possibilities that many Western scholars have yet to explore.

Acknowledgments

Without the encouragement and support of the staff and University of Roehampton, this book could not have been written.

As I suspect I will say with everything I publish in my career, the shape of this book owes a great deal to Jane Newman who has continued to be my advisor a decade after graduate school ended.

The students and professors and the Institute for World Literature provided the inspiration for starting this task.

Theo D'haen and David Damrosch offered insight into the world of publication.

Ben Piggott and Kate Edwards have been the most supportive editorial team I could have hoped for.

Cody Poulton stepped in and generously offered help with a last-minute translation.

Thanks to my students Sabrina Corral and Ojas Patel who offered their perspectives.

Also my thanks to the hundreds of you who took a few moments out of conferences to comment on this work and offer suggestions on potential inclusions, who have spent decades working all over the world bringing wider attention to materials, and who have written so brilliantly and in such detail on these texts. The book would never have been possible without your work.

Publishers' acknowledgments

The publishers would like to thank all those included in *World Theories of Theatre*, and acknowledge the following sources for permission to reproduce their work in this volume:

Excerpt from Liking, Werewere. *It Shall Be of Jasper and Coral* and *Love-across-a-Hundred-Lives*, translated by Marjolijn de Jager, pp. 25–40. Translation © 2000 by the Rector and Victors of the University of Virginia. Reprinted by permission of the University of Virginia.

Excerpt from *Natyasastra*, translated by Manomohan Ghosh. Varansi: Chowkhamba Sanskrit Series, 1987. Reprinted by permission of Chowkhamba Sanskrit Office.

Excerpt from Maryrose Casey, "Performing for Aboriginal Life and Culture: Aboriginal Theatre and Ngurrumilmarrmiriyu," *Australasian Drama Studies*, October, 2011. Permission granted by Maryrose Casey.

Excerpt from "What the Twilight Says: An Overture" from *Dream On Monkey Mountain and Other Plays* by Derek Walcott. Copyright © 1970 by Derek Walcott. Reprinted by permission of Farrar, Straus and Giroux, LLC.

Excerpt from Femi Osofisan "'The Revolution as Muse': Drama as surreptitious insurrection in a post-colonial, military State", *Theatre Matters, Performance and Culture on the World Stage*, 1998 © Richard Boon and Jane Plastow 1998, published by Cambridge University Press, reproduced with permission.

Excerpt from Wole Soyinka, "Drama and the African World-view", *Myth Literature and the African World*, 1990 © Wole Soyinka 1990, published by Cambridge University Press, reproduced with permission.

Enrique Buenaventura and Joanne Pottlitzer, "Theatre and Culture", *TDR/The Drama Review*, 14:2 (Winter, 1970), pp. 151–156. © 1970 by New York University and the Massachusetts Institute of Technology.

"Manifestos for a New Arabic Theatre" ("Bayanat li Masrah 'Arabi Jadid", first published in Arabic in 1970), © Saadallah Wannous, 1970. This excerpt is published with permission from the Wannous estate.

"An Interview with Poile Sengupta", by Poile Sengupta and Anita Singh, *Asian Theatre Journal* 29:1, pp. 78–88, 2012. Reproduced with permission of University of Hawai'i Press.

The Way of Acting: The Theatre Writings of Tadashi Suzuki by Tadashi Suzuki. Translation copyright © 1986 by J. Thomas Rimer. Originally published in Japan as *Ekkyō suru Chikara,* © by Tadashi Suzuki. Published by Theatre Communications Group. Used by permission of Theatre Communications Group.

Theatre of the Oppressed by Augusto Boal. Translation copyright © 1979 by Charles A. and Maria-Odilia Leal McBride. Originally published in Spanish as *Teatro de Oprimido* in 1974 © by Augusto Boal and in English by Urizen books in 1979. Published by Theatre Communications Group. Used by permission of Theatre Communications Group.

"Finding Gems", *On the Art of the Nō Drama: The Major Treatises of Zeami*; translated by J. Thomas Rimer and Yamazaki Masakazu © Princeton University Press, 1984. Republished with the permission of Princeton University Press.

"The Potential of Theatre", *Gao Xingjian: Aesthetics and Creation* pp. 41–63. Republished with permission of Cambria Press.

Every effort has been made to contact copyright-holders. Please advise the publisher of any errors or omissions, and these will be corrected in subsequent editions.

Chapter 1

Introduction
World, theatre, theory

This book is both an anthology of and a guide to world theatre theory from Asia, Africa, Australia, New Zealand, and South America. This book has pedagogical aims, seeking to introduce material that will often be unfamiliar to a Western audience. It will be most useful for scholars trying to expand their breadth, although it does provide ample suggestions for further readings as well. This book could not have been written without the brilliant work done by scholars who have devoted their lifetime to study and practice within the regions and nations discussed here – and, as an overview, it can never hope to do justice to the richness of their arguments. I do hope, however, that this book provides one ground for fostering conversations between and among these specialists and their students.

What do artists, directors, actors, and academics from these regions have to say about the way theatre works and about the relationship between theatre and society? Each of these regions provide a diverse array of historical and contemporary performances, theatrical practices, and theories about literature and theatre. The West has offered a number of theatrical theories which are frequently used to explain, interpret, and analyze theatre from these other regions. This guide provides a starting point for utilizing the theories of a wider range of locations as a means of understanding theatre. Before providing a further rationale for such a guide, it is important to define the terms "world," "theatre," and "theory."

World

There are two notions of "world" at play in the text. First, there is "world" as a marker of breadth – theories from multiple locations around the world. The volume unapologetically uses the word "world" to signify that portion of the world which is not Europe, Russia, or the U.S. – which is to say, most of the world. For decades, "world" anthologies have unapologetically included only these regions that I exclude. Many of these anthologies have been expanded to include one or two samples from "other" locations but still give precedence to Western materials.

If the point of this anthology is to bring together theories from parts of the world traditionally underrepresented in Western collections, why call this a "world" anthology rather than choosing another term? The phrase "non-Western" implies that the West is the definition and other places are "not" meeting this definition. The phrase "Third World" comes out of Marxist terminology and implies parts of the world which are neither communist nor capitalist. "Postcolonial" implies that each of the locations in question was subjected to colonial dominance at some point in the past, which is not the case. "South American, Australian, Asian, and African" is specific yet cumbersome, and it tends to reinforce the idea that the continents are homogenous locales. "Global East and South" is the best currently used option, but it is closely linked to postcolonial studies and again implies homogeneity. "World" in this context refers to a scope and diversity of possible theories.

I have chosen the word "world" to suggest the diversity of possibilities in theatre from the regions in question, but the word has a second meaning as well: the idea that there might be an interconnection, a commonality, or a value to considering exchange. Maybe there is something to the idea of theatre as a world phenomenon. Perhaps there is something different that can be learned about the whole subject when placed in this larger context. In order to determine if this idea of an interconnected world is of value, we must first understand the parts of the world on their own terms (recognizing that these terms are frequently informed by generations of intercultural contact).

This idea of an interconnected world beckons tantalizingly from the theatre: for instance, Neloufer De Mel (1999) explores a Sri Lankan theatre's production of Wole Soyinka's (Nigerian) *Opera Woyonsi*, which is an adaptation of both John Gay's (British) *The Beggar's Opera* and Bertolt Brecht's (German) *Threepenny Opera*, which is itself an adaptation of Gay's work. At least four different cultures and countries collide in this intercultural production. While examining each region, nation, or group individually yields results, contemporary theatre also travels, both metaphorically and literally. This anthology is structured in such a way as to provide two necessary approaches to productions like the one De Mel describes: first, this production must be understood in terms of each of its separate theatrical traditions; second this production must be understood in terms of the blending of these various traditions and theories of theatre.

The word "world" here signals crossing boundaries and circulation – theatre in motion, touring theatre, intercultural and transnational theatre, and theatre texts being read in new locations. This "world" denotes fields that deal with similarity and difference, with a balance between breadth and depth, with new notions of textuality, and with new notions of reading. I stand behind the choice to couch this project in terms of "world" precisely because I want to raise those issues: new theories both present and require new ways of accessing texts.

This idea of "world" is not without its problems. The contents of this anthology are diverse – they do not point to one, single type of theatre, but rather to many different conceptions of what theatre is and does and looks like. The word "world" could wrongly imply a universality – that there is a single definition of theatre that has variations around the world. In this definition of world, which is not the one at stake here, differences are reduced to window-dressing over the core of similarity. As Chinua Achebe (1997) points out, the word "universal" is often code for "Western." This anthology gives equal weight to both similarity and difference in both local and global contexts. The "world" here is a world where ideas are created locally, transmitted globally, and then reinterpreted in new local contexts.

The idea of theory being produced "locally" raises its own set of problems with the definition of "world." Presupposing that theory emerges from particular parts of the world places focus on the identity of a given author. In our current globalized world, it is commonplace in academies around the world to encounter people of a range of nationalities. Is an American who has taught in Nigeria for 25 years then writing "Nigerian" theory? What sort of theory is an Indian writing about India from within the U.S. academy producing? Rather than claiming the ability to distinguish some sort of cultural authenticity, which would be a dubious claim indeed, this book classifies theory according to its explicit intended audience, the author's own explicit self-identification within the work in question, and the specificity of the matter being discussed. Thus, something like Wole Soyinka's (1976) exploration of theatre-qua-theatre from his explicitly Nigerian perspective for a world audience fits (see Chapter 2), while something like Kanika Batra's (2010) feminist comparative approach to the theatres of India, Jamaica, and Nigeria, written in the neutral voice that characterizes Western writing for an academic audience, does not (despite the cultural heritage of the author herself). This is not a judgment of the quality of the theory in question, merely of the stated aims of the author and whether these aims reveal the piece to be non-Western theatre theory (as in the case of Soyinka) or a theorization of non-Western theatre (as in the case of Batra). "Local" here means either a nation, an ethnicity, or a region, depending on how the author contextualizes the work and is a matter of critical judgment on my part.

The above classification system is not absolute, particularly as it approaches edge-cases that exist in multiple modes of discourse at once. For instance, William H. Sun, under several names, has written pieces for Western audiences, pieces for Chinese audiences, and pieces for both audiences. He writes on an array of topics and was educated in both China and the U.S. Labeling such a writer as either belonging to the West or the world does not work. South African theatre theorists are particularly difficult to classify with this system as their work is often received quite differently in the U.S., the U.K., and within South Africa itself. With a limited amount of space, I have generally opted for writers who position themselves further from the Western academy as such writers are more likely to be new to the audience of this book.

This returns us to the global part of the definition of "world." At various points in history, large portions of the world have been connected culturally and economically. The idea of a nation-state is still relatively new. The structure of this book emphasizes the possibility of connections between regions (including the West) even as it points out the specificity of theory from each region. Except for the very earliest theorists discussed here, all the writers, Western or world, explicitly reference the theatre and / or theory emerging from at least one other region somewhere in their extended writings. Once the Western academy gains more familiarity with theories emerging from the world and begins to incorporate such theories on an equal footing with Western theatrical theory, there is certainly space for further examination of the intercultural nature of modern theatre theory.

Theatre

In the context of world theatres, the definition of theatre often ends up reinforcing a divide between ritual and theatre and / or between performance and theatre, but this will not be the case here. In these commonplace divisions, "theatre" is a text-based phenomenon, usually taking place in a custom-built playhouse under the supervision of a director. This sort of theatre is performed to promote culture, to educate, or to provide entertainment. "Performance" in this definition refers to actions that follow a different set of rules from everyday life, but generally excludes theatre. Storytelling, sporting matches, holiday celebrations, circuses, and religious observances are some common examples of performance. "Ritual" is a subcategory of performance that is, unfortunately, most regularly used to refer to performances of religious or social significance in non-Western parts of the world ("non-Western" is the appropriate term here because the intention is to signal that these locations are being treated as different from the West): African masked dances or Buddhist prayers are common examples of "ritual."

The issue with the above definitions is that they assume that "real" theatre looks like it does in one vision of Western theatre, and this is simply not the case in the rest of the world (or even always in the West). What does one do with highly narrative forms of dance like the Indian Kathakali, which clearly tell stories but don't have scripts in the same way as Western theatre? What about performances like Werewere Liking's in the Ivory Coast which are clearly scripted but are also intended to enact a ritual and change something in society (see Chapter 4)? Diana Looser (2011) provides a host of examples of Pacific Island performances that can be considered theatre if we broaden our definition. On the other hand, considering everything to be "theatre" decreases the power of the term as an analytical device.

How then should one choose what counts as "theatre" and what does not? This anthology defines theatre locally rather than globally. I selected materials not based on their ability to match a preconceived notion of theatre, but on the topic they addressed. As with defining where a given theory comes from, defining whether or not something is theatre depends on whether or not the critic in question, from within the local context, considers it to be theatre. This allows for movement between religiously inflected theatres like those of Bharata and Liking, text-based theatre like Wole Soyinka's, and theatre that moves between text and physicality like Gao Xingjian's. Part of what is at stake in these theories is precisely how one defines theatre at that given moment in that given context.

This definition is problematic inasmuch as it does exclude a number of performance traditions that clearly inform theatrical practice. For instance, egungun is a masked dance (performed by several ethnicities in Nigeria) designed to bring a community together. It also features prominently in a number of Nigerian plays. It is absolutely not thought of as theatre in Nigeria, although its "theatrical" nature is recognized. These types of performance are addressed in other anthologies. This anthology focuses on theatre as defined in each given context.

Theory

In the Western academy "theory" is the use of a series of ideas to open up new ways of understanding texts or the world in which we live. In this common usage, theory is spread in written forms and often grows out of the analytical philosophers (like Kant or Hegel) or resistance to these philosophies. Theory also is often preceded by an adjective that suggests a political nature: Marxist, feminist, or postcolonial.

As a number of Western critics have pointed out, theorization – generation of new ideas – can happen during performance, in narratives, in dialogue, and in a number of other forms. Broadly speaking, this is referred to as "practice-based" theory. This anthology includes a number of case studies and physical activities as an effort to recognize the vitality of such practice-based theory. One issue with such theory is that it can be difficult to transmit its results to a wider public in writing given that they were discovered physically. Most of our academic knowledge is consumed in written form, so practice-based theory often ends up as written theory that had its roots in practice. Certainly, many of the printed pieces here fall into this category. Other pieces were initially published as part of novels, religious texts, or interviews. These styles of writing fall outside the "norm" of theory in the West, but are clearly engaging with the creation of ideas about how theatre and the world work.

Despite the fact that much theatre theory emerges from practice, there is currently a division in many parts of the Western academy between practice and theory. While it is far beyond the scope of this book to prove this point, the hostility between practice and theory is detrimental to theatre. In its most virulent form, theoreticians can argue (or appear to imply) that practitioners are not rigorous or haven't thought through their work. Practitioners can argue (or appear to imply) that theoreticians are too abstract and out of touch with the reality of theatre. In fact, these two approaches are not mutually exclusive. I have never met a practitioner, however hostile to theory, who didn't, in fact, theorize their own work in some fashion. Without practitioners, theoreticians would have nothing to write about. The inclusion of a "practical" section at the end of this book encourages readers to think about the ways in which these theories might be enacted and embodied. Indeed, a significant percentage of the theories contained here make explicit reference to the relationship between practice and theory.

The two adjectives in "world theatre theories" have already been defined, but it is important to note that the ideas of similarity and difference contained in "world" applies to the plural version of the word "theory" as well. There are multiple theories presented here, each of which can stand on its own. These theories do share a common concern with broadly defined theatre and as such, some similarities emerge between various theories presented, although no single similarity is present across all the theories in question.

Why read (or write) this book?

Over the course of the past year, I have encountered the word "Brechtian" used in a variety of contexts. Two of these stuck out to me, not because they are unique, but because they are deeply problematic and quite common. The first was a description of a piece of modern Chinese theatre as Brechtian. The second was a description of traditional Zulu performance as Brechtian. One problem here is temporality: traditional Zulu performance predates Brecht. The problem in the first case is slightly more complex. A modern Chinese playwright might well have been influenced by Brecht, but Brecht characterizes a major portion of his theory as having come out of the Chinese tradition. It is not uncommon to find such ahistorical, non-situated analyses in theatre studies, and their prevalence points to limitations in both our current theoretical vocabulary and the accessibility of world theories of theatre.

The definition of theory provided above suggests that theory enables us to see the world or theatre in new ways. Western theory provides a set of specific vantage points and can generate certain types of knowledge. Every theoretical system comes from a specific vantage point and every system has its blind-spots and limitations alongside its strengths. The type of knowledge generated by the thoughtful application of Western theory to world materials is not wrong, but it is limited. The more theoretical vantage points we have, the stronger our understanding of theatre practice will become.

The above statement is somewhat utopian. Theories exist in a globalized society that is strongly influenced by power dynamics. While there is nothing inherently wrong about applying Western theatre theory to world texts, this application is damaging when it is done at the expense of the other theories in question. Theories emerging from the world are treated as derivative of Western theory, just as theatrical practices from other parts of the world are often read as derived from Western practice. This becomes a habit of thought that is so deeply engrained that attempting to change things is met with resistance.

There is another reason for creating such a volume, which is curiously almost the opposite of the first. On one hand, there are critics who want to read everything in terms of the West. On the other hand, there are people who insist on the radical specificity of their own fields of specialization. These scholars insist that their ten years of theatre from their one region of one nation must be examined and contextualized within the period and region – they argue that the distinctiveness of the moment makes comparison irrelevant.

As with the use of Western theory, examining various moments of theatre in their narrowest contexts provides interesting results, and this approach has strengths and weaknesses. These locally-centered examinations can often unintentionally suggest that the local material is only relevant locally, for instance implying that Western theory has a global reach, but Chinese theory is only applicable in Chinese contexts. Not only does this keep the rich array of knowledges offered by area specialists separate from mainstream academic theatre discussions, it also limits our ability to discuss transnational and intercultural movements by assuming radical difference.

This book, then, needs to be written to bring the rich work of area specialists into contact with other area specialists and to remind all of us that Western theories are not universally applicable.

Selections

It is a big world – not everything could be included. I wanted to cover each of the major regions and, when possible, multiple major subgroups within these regions (francophone, French-speaking, and anglophone, English-speaking sub-Saharan Africa, for instance). For some regions, there are multiple samples which display the range of theories available, and for others, like the Middle East, there are fewer anthologized pieces. This ratio roughly corresponds to the number of available pieces of theory in each region. I have aimed for a range of old and new material. I have likewise selected several well-known pieces and several pieces that will only be known to specialists in a given region. I have tried (with somewhat limited success) to find a balance in gender of the theorists. While there are a number of female artists, there are far fewer female theorists in the regions in question. I have also specifically included pieces not previously available in English. In short, while this anthology is not comprehensive, it is representative of the spread of theories, although no single theory in here should be read as codifying all of "African," "Asian," or even a given national theatre.

Structure

The heart of this book (Part I) is an anthology of world theatre theory contained within a series of chapters (2–7) devoted to the treatment of issues of aesthetics; politics and structure; colonization, interculturalism, and nationalism; identity; modernity; and gender. Since theory can be abstract, most of these chapters begin with a specific case study that presents some details from theatre performances or texts. These performances help to introduce the types of questions that the theory texts deal with. When possible, I have provided links to recordings of these productions. These case studies are designed to get at questions in their general form and not to provide detailed analysis of the texts in question. The chapters move on to consider the multitude of definitions of the key concepts that emerge from theories of theatre around the world. These chapters are focused on showing the range of available theory.

These chapters are structured in terms of a series of major questions raised by the diversity of world theatre theory. These questions and the subjects of each of the chapters are explicitly from the theories themselves. As such, while they may overlap with Western theoretical concerns, there are many questions that Western theory considers important that are not explored (this is particularly true in the gender and colonialism sections), and there are questions explored that Western theory either has never addressed or does not currently address. Again, Western theory is readily accessible and heavily researched – readers who wish to bring Western theory to bear on the theoretical discussions raised in the book will find adequate resources to do so elsewhere. Each of these questions is elaborated on in each of the contexts in which it appears, paying particular attention to how this elaboration relates to and differs from similar questions in Western theatre. Framing these theoretical debates in terms of core questions provides an outline of the approaches one might take when analyzing theatre in light of these theories. It also emphasizes the degree to which no one theory in this book should be taken as representative of larger groups – these theories ask questions, and sometimes these questions overlap. The answers to these questions are far less likely to be similar, given the vast differences between the contexts considered here. While there are certainly connections that can be drawn between chapters in this section, I have only highlighted these connections when the theories themselves did so. I urge my readers to consider each theory in isolation and in contrast with the other theories dealing with the same topic before (or instead of) trying to create an overarching theory of "world theatre."

Part II is a historical and cultural overview of Southern Africa; North Africa and the Middle East; the Caribbean; India; East Asia; Latin America; and Australia and New Zealand, focused on the fluctuating, interlocked socio-political events and philosophies of each region. Chapters 8 to 13 emphasize the diversity of ideas emerging from the region while also noting commonalities where present. Each of the history chapters (8–13) is intended to give a brief overview of significant names, events, and literary movements within each region. Obviously, in such a short amount of space, this is not an exhaustive history. Think of it, instead, as a guide to further reading and a general contextualization of the material in this book.

The book concludes with a short chapter (Chapter 14) devoted to providing pragmatic instructions for actually physically engaging with the various embodied techniques discussed in the theories. Theatre is a living form and the ideal way to engage with world theatre is to travel the world and see performances. The theories contained here are, at times, only written traces of theory-as-practice executed by actors and directors around the world. The physical exercises suggested here are a blend of the actual practices by some of the theorists in question and pedagogical techniques designed by Western practitioners that highlight certain aspects of the theories in question.

There is also a guide to further reading and a bibliography, which is particularly important inasmuch as this book has explicitly left out most Western secondary criticism. There is a multitude of Western scholars not represented here who have made fascinating, insightful critiques of the theories in this anthology. There was not space to do them justice, but the further reading list does acknowledge their contributions to the field. The list also includes histories of each region; theatre histories; additional works by the playwrights, theorists, and critics anthologized here; and an array of related theories on gender, postcolonialism, and class that don't address theatre directly. A separate list of references of works cited in the text is also provided.

Common questions

Why isn't person X included?

Names from the theatre world like Athol Fugard and Mohan Rakesh seem strangely absent from the anthologized selections. Theatre scholars like Martin Banham and Yvette Hutchinson are likewise absent. Names from postcolonial theory like Gayatri Spivak are similarly not represented in the anthologized selections. There are two issues at stake here. No anthology will be comprehensive, and people with specialisms in a given region will doubtless be aware of "missing" figures. I have included many of these additional theorists in the further reading. The second issue, however, is that I stuck closely to the guiding principles laid out above. Figures like Banham are writing for Western audiences from within Western institutions. Spivak and others are theorizing about things other than theatre, however useful their work might be in analyzing theatre. Neither Athol Fugard nor Mohan Rakesh have published extended pieces of theory on theatre, despite their prominence as theatrical figures. Their embodied theatrical practice certainly is a mode of theorization, but it is one that cannot be anthologized in the same fashion. While this book includes case studies and a section of "active" theoretical work, it could not hope to offer an exhaustive study of world theatre practice alongside a (non-exhaustive) study of world theatre theory.

Given that a premise of this book is that a Western audience is not regularly exposed to world theatre theory, it is hardly surprising that I, as a Western writer, will have missed at least a few important figures from around the world. This book has changed based on the feedback of hundreds of scholars already, and I encourage readers to send me any citations that I have omitted, provided they meet the above criteria: all anthologized pieces must be *theatre theory* originating in *world* contexts (not just addressing world theatre). The further reading guide also serves as a record of names that have been suggested that didn't quite fit with the above criteria – work that is absolutely relevant to this discussion, although not the sort of primary source found in this book.

Why isn't issue X included / Why is issue X included?

I started this project by accumulating all the world theatre theory I could find (and having it translated where needed). The issues raised in this volume grew out of this reading of world theatre theory. That is to say, the issues here are specifically, explicitly *not* the same ones that would be raised in an anthology of Western theatre theory. The brevity of the final section where I discuss gender is a result of the relative concentrations of world theatre theory around given issues.

Isn't your use of national categories problematic?

The world is becoming increasingly globalized. Nationalism is often linked to state violence and xenophobia. The category of nation has been critiqued by scholars the world over as a decaying left-over of European modernity. To impose nation as a category is to reinscribe European modernity and the carving up of the map that Europe enacted.

Yes. All of the above is true.

This does not stop scholars from around the world from regularly referring to and identifying with national categories. Often these same scholars discuss a universalized notion of "theatre" that transcends these categories, while simultaneously differentiating between Asian theatre, African theatre, and / or Western theatre. Given that I found more world scholarship on theatre that identified primarily with a region, I have attempted to highlight regional connections without collapsing local and national difference.

Recalling that a primary goal of this book is familiarizing an audience with a set of material that is often not readily available in the Western academy, it made sense to lay out this material in a straightforward way – and this meant falling into some of the patterns of Western scholarship.

As such, I strongly urge readers to question and challenge the idea of the nation and the specter of the nation that this book absolutely reinforces at times. What would it mean to read world theatre theory from a global perspective? What perspective on the idea of nation, globalization, or the world emerges in the anthologized selections? How would one use this theory differently in a global context? Is there new theory to be written for our globalized world from a globalized standpoint?

Doesn't including Western material as an explanatory device reinforce a Western hegemonic view of what theatre is? And furthermore, doesn't your definition of key terms favor Western practices?

Diana Looser (2011) has written about the fact that many Western critics dismiss the existence of pre-colonial Pacific Island theatre. Her argument is that this theatre can only be ignored if we take an overly-narrow definition of theatre from the West and attempt to apply it to other locations. She argues against the idea that something is not theatre just because it doesn't look like Western theatre. While many of the issues raised in this anthology resonate with Western theatre theory, the specific chapters are devoted to the ideas that emerged most strongly in world theatre theory (with the already noted exception of gender). Not only did the issues themselves emerge from an examination of world theatre theory, but the definitions of these key terms are likewise based on world theories. These definitions stay at a fairly general level, allowing for the diversity of theorizations of a given concept that emerge around the world, but they are coherent enough to see the connections between these materials as well.

The Western material is included as a guide for readers – a way of recognizing the specificity of the anthologized material. Given the intended audience of this anthology will likely not be familiar with all, or perhaps most, of the theories presented here, the references to the West provide a first step in further exploration. Once I begin to explain a given local theory, I specifically do not read this theory through any Western framework (e.g. postcolonial studies).

Why doesn't this text engage more regularly with the issues raised by postcolonial studies?

Scholarship on those parts of the world that were formerly colonized by Europe follows a specific set of practices that, together, are referred to as postcolonial theory. This set of practices is designed to deal with the diversity of specific issues that emerge as a result of colonization. This is currently the Western academy's primary way of thinking about the non-Western world.

This anthology specifically turns away from the practices of postcolonial studies partly because not all theatre from the non-Western world is postcolonial. Some of the earlier work in this anthology is pre-colonial. Some of it is from nations that were never formally colonized. Even amongst the former colonies, the differences between colonial experiences make a blanket application of postcolonial theory inappropriate.

Aside from these historical issues, the point of this book is to pluralize our theoretical approaches. Postcolonial theory is but one theory among many, and, at times, its concerns are shared by the authors in question here. At other times, the authors treated here chart out new theoretical terrain. The application of postcolonial theory runs the risk of creating exactly the same sort of hegemony it seeks to dismantle. This text engages with postcolonial issues in the terms set out by the theory contained within the anthology.

Part 1
Theoretical questions

Chapter 2

Aesthetics

> A beautiful thing is never perfect.
> Egyptian proverb

Case study

The information for this case study was taken from various video and audio archives alongside published editions of these play scripts. This case study looks briefly at three different operas from China. First is *The Legend of White Snake* (a 1957 version revived regularly), performed in a highly stylized traditional Chinese form called *jingju*, which is often referred to as "Beijing Opera" in the West. The second is *The Legend of the Red Lantern* which is one of the politically-charged operas produced during the Cultural Revolution (1966–1976) under the rule of Mao Zedong: labeling this production "Chinese Opera" is indicative of the fact that Mao wanted to create a national (as opposed to regional) revolutionary art with realistic tendencies. The final production is *Snow in August*, an opera written by Nobel Prize winner Gao Xingjian (b. 1940), which was inspired by *jingju* and Western opera. The first two were remarkably successful, whereas the third was not well reviewed. As one would expect for a country as large as China, with such a diverse history, Chinese theatre contains many, many different performance traditions. The relationship of these is generally not developmental. As forms grow and change, they maintain their unique identities, rather than rejecting what has gone before to claim a wholly new practice (in the U.S. and the U.K. we talk about the avant-garde as a rejection of parts of realism, for instance, in contrast to the parallel development of many styles of performance in China). China has many different theatres that have developed along their own routes. This case study puts three important Chinese productions –

each containing traditional operatic elements – next to each other and looks at the differences and similarities. In short, the question here is how to evaluate these productions given how vastly different they are. What makes them good? Is it beauty? Technical skill? Political impact?

There are many versions of *The Legend of White Snake* in poetry, prose, and opera in China dating back to the 1300s. The fantastical legend involves a series of related vignettes dealing with the transformation of animal spirits into humans, immortality pills, magic, and love: it is certainly more complex and lengthy than something from Grimm's fairy tales. Various versions have focused on moral or spiritual lessons one might learn from the story, but generally the fairytale love story is central. The version in question here is a 1957 *jingju* opera by Tien Han. This text has been revived every few years (with a hiatus during most of the Cultural Revolution) and toured both Europe and China successfully. The Chinese Central television broadcast of a recent revival are available on Youtube.[1] As is immediately apparent upon viewing, even recent revivals of this opera use traditional costumes and instrumentation (with some technical and regional variations). The costumes and makeup are exaggeratedly elaborate and do not reflect the way such characters might have dressed or looked in reality at any period. These costumes accentuate the movements and facial expressions of the actors, allowing for a number of dramatic effects. Similarly, the singing is highly specific to the characters, with several of the roles producing a higher-pitched keening that is not duplicated elsewhere in Chinese musical traditions, and is more stylized than the singing in contemporary Western musicals. The libretto is not highly poetic; indeed, most of it is prose, albeit prose intended to be sung. Many recordings of the opera focus on a few favorite scenes, which is easy to do given that the plot is episodic. Each scene can stand alone, but together they grow to a climax. The cast of at least fifteen members is smaller than many Chinese Operas, but still substantial.

This type of opera has a set of specifically defined categories of role: the old man, the young man, the soldier, the old woman, and so on. Actors would train their entire careers to play a specific type of role. Each role had a set of gestures and a style of specific movements associated with it. For instance, part of an actor's training would include learning appropriate ways to sit, appropriate ways to draw a sword, appropriate ways to walk, or appropriate ways to move a fan. These movements were further subdivided depending on the mood communicated by the movement (e.g. how does one reach for a sword when in a different mood; after reaching for the sword, how does one grasp it?)

While *White Snake* has been around in various forms for generations, *The Legend of the Red Lantern* is a far more recent addition to the Chinese Opera scene. Its story contains no magical elements and, instead, focuses on one family's noble sacrifices for the revolution. This production was one of eight operas that the Cultural Revolution endorsed. In other words, during a good portion of the twentieth century, the government officially stated that this opera was artistically good, appropriate for the revolution, and edifying for people. During the Cultural Revolution, one could hear recordings of this opera being played publicly and regularly in urban settings, and, to a lesser extent, in rural sections of China. It is difficult to gauge how much of the popularity of the piece was government enforced. Arias (sections of music) from the opera are still performed, however, which suggests that at least some of the merits of this piece were its own rather than governmentally enforced. As can be seen on a clip on Youtube[2] this opera updated the instrumentation (including a piano) and the costumes of traditional operatic styles. It kept the singing style roughly similar to that exhibited in *White Snake*. Like *White Snake*, it is primarily prose-based. The libretto is less episodic than *White Snake*'s, but popular arias are still regularly excerpted. *The Red Lantern* was slightly unusual relative to traditional opera characterizations in China inasmuch as it focused on the lives of three females, with the primary male role playing a relatively small part. The text of the libretto, which can be found in the *The Columbia Anthology of Modern Chinese Drama* (Chen, 2014), provides a reasonably exciting story, although, in both translated and original form it is not as prosodically stylized as many of the rest of the works in the same anthology – it is straightforward speech.

While Gao Xingjian has emigrated to France and now writes in French, when he wrote *Snow in August*, he was specifically attempting to create a modern opera using Chinese and Western traditions. *Snow in August* was initially performed in Taiwan in 2002 and was not a critical success. Much of the original production is available online through various video aggregators,[3] and an English translation of the text of the libretto with extensive photographs and production notes has been completed by Gilbert Fong. Gao's work uses many of the stylistic elements of *jingju's* musical scores, a more Western singing style, less stylized costumes than *jingju*, various types of acrobatics, and an abstract set reminiscent of various styles of Chinese painting – specifically Buddhist meditative drawings. Gao's plot is a series of vignettes relating to the life of a Buddhist patriarch. There are multiple possible moral lessons to be drawn from the performance, but few of these are stated directly. Indeed, the text of this performance is complex and nuanced, with its craft shining through even in translation. Unlike the two previous operas discussed, *Snow* was not critically successful (although it has been restaged several times). Some critics noted that they were not certain what Gao was trying to do by mixing traditional and modern elements into the same piece.

One of the questions posed by this chapter is how we evaluate, appreciate, and analyze these three performances. In simplest terms (albeit terms that do not apply to these productions), we probably wouldn't critique a tragedy for not making us laugh – nor would we critique a comedy for not containing enough tragic elements. We might, however, say of both comedy and tragedy that the acting choices didn't seem to fit with the scenic design.

What then are the criteria by which we can decide whether something like these three operas are good? There are obvious differences and similarities between these three productions. Some aspects of each performance might appeal to some individuals and not to others, but can we say that one performance is "better" than the other? Perhaps fidelity to "tradition?" Perhaps innovation? Maybe each production needs to be judged relative to what it tried to accomplish? Are there some purposes that are "better" than other purposes? What elements are needed in the theatre to make it successful at doing what it is supposed to do? Should theatre be evaluated in terms of its content, its form, or its effect? Perhaps a combination of these factors?

Is *White Snake*'s success due to its fidelity to a well-known, much-loved legend? Is it a masterful example of the ideal form of *jingju*? Is it the combination of the story and style that makes this opera work? Are we supposed to appreciate technical skill or beauty? Are these the same thing?

Did *Red Lantern* work because of its communist sentiments? Because it was dominated by women? Because the performers had mastered the technical skills necessary to perform? Because the performers altered the precise traditional modes of performance? Was this production supposed to make people feel a certain way? Was it just supposed to be a pretty spectacle?

When placed next to *Red Lantern*, how should we gauge Gao's work? The plot is more complex, with many more events. The characters are more complex and do not correspond easily to types. The movement, while acrobatic and stylized, was more varied and didn't follow a set template. Are these things good or bad? Does Gao's work only make sense when in the context of stylized Chinese Opera, or can it be appreciated on its own merits? How do we gauge a performance that is explicitly supposed to be changing conventions?

White Snake focuses on beauty, *Red Lantern* on communist thought, and *Snow in August* on artistic innovation. None of these three productions are primarily focused on spiritual enlightenment, which is something that many aesthetic theories address. None of them seem particularly concerned with direct fidelity to life (with what we might broadly call "realism"), although the political realities of *Red Lantern* can't be ignored. Some aesthetic theories suggest that theatre should be judged on its ability to represent life "accurately." Of course, it could be argued that these three operas represent some aspect of life more "truly" or "deeply" than realism ever could.

As with all of the questions posed in this book, these questions have some sort of answer or answers within the Western tradition. The questions get more complex when focused on theatre from around the world. This chapter explores the ways in which both the answers and the questions shift in various world contexts: as importantly, however, this chapter finds commonalities – shared questions, concerns, and vocabulary that can serve as a point of departure into deeper explorations of specific aesthetic systems. One inescapable conclusion in this comparative approach is that there cannot be an overarching theory of aesthetics that can deal with the diversity of world theatre – using the West, or indeed any individual location as a point of departure, shapes and limits the sorts of questions and answers one might find. This chapter points out some of those limitations by showing the radically different starting points that various aesthetic theories have found.

Introduction

All of the world's earliest theatrical theory deals with questions of the form and function of theatre – with aesthetic questions. Aesthetics, broadly speaking, is the study of what makes something beautiful and / or pleasing and / or good. Indeed, it is almost impossible to imagine discussing theatre without considering these questions: certainly all of the pieces anthologized here deal with aesthetics in one way or another. The questions posed above are vital to theatre. Theatre is performed for some reason. Sometimes this reason is entertainment, sometimes it is the creation of beauty, sometimes it is praising a supernatural entity, sometimes it is uniting a community, sometimes it is protesting a social or political injustice, sometimes it is convincing people to think in a certain way, sometimes it may be a combination of all of these (or something not included in this list). As art, theatre is always participating in some sort of aesthetic system – whether or not the aesthetics are clearly articulated. Aesthetic theory is often prescriptive – telling theatre what it should do. Whatever the purpose of a given theatre might be, people need to know how the theatre might best accomplish that purpose. While in a

Western sense the word "aesthetic" is most often associated with ideas of beauty, when we turn to the global sense of the word, other concepts emerge as well.

The foundational texts of aesthetic theory are often part of the almost mythical golden eras of culture – eras during which the arts flourished. Early aesthetic theory often tends to describe things in detail, without always providing the rationale or justification for these descriptions (in stark contrast to some later aesthetic theory like Emmanuel Kant's *Critique of Judgment* which is more concerned with abstract ways of determining aesthetic value). This makes early aesthetic theory remarkably open to interpretation. This chapter will lay out some of the more common interpretations of aesthetic theory from around the world, each of which serves a particular purpose at a particular time.

A definition of aesthetics

In order to judge the appropriateness of such a move, we need to start with one more interpretive move – articulating a definition of aesthetics. If this were a book devoted to one particular period in one particular nation, the concept of aesthetics would be far easier to define. In broadest terms, the field of aesthetics involves all aspects of art, architecture, and literature that might be perceived of as beautiful, right, or good. At times in history, aesthetics has been limited to visual arts. At times "beautiful" is replaced by "useful" or "spiritually uplifting." At times aesthetics is in conflict with form or with content, and at times form and content are the location of aesthetics. We can see the idea of aesthetics at work any time a critic of a piece of art says "I didn't like it, but I recognize the skill used to create it." This commonly heard idea raises another contentious point about aesthetics: this field is an attempt to give a concrete set of non-subjective guidelines for what "counts" in art. At several periods, artistic movements have insisted on the radical subjective nature of their art – its beauty lies precisely in the eye of the beholder and not in a set of abstract guidelines.

All of the above definitional difficulties lie in the concept of aesthetics. The debate can grow even more contentious when trying to decide how to further define any given idea of aesthetics. In other words, even if we agree that aesthetics is the visually perceivable beauty of something, and that this beauty serves the purpose of elevating the human soul, we can still disagree about whether that is best served by simple elegant columns or by elaborately ornate spires.

There are two issues at stake here. First, the question of what gives art or theatre value. Simply by relating theatre to art there are several suppositions we make that world theories of theatre challenge, chief among them the idea that theatre doesn't "do" anything, but exists in the same category as Western classical sculpture – pretty and edifying to look at (at least this is one idea of one style of "art," albeit an idea that is readily open to challenge). In the Yorùbá faith in Nigeria, sculptures are used to connect with gods, as part of theatrical rituals designed to generate concrete changes in society. This is a wholly different idea from the attempts to perfect forms practiced by the Neoclassicists in France in the nineteenth century as they sought to bring order and balance to theatrical features in order to create a model of a perfect work of art. While they are wholly different ideas, both are answers to the same question: What gives art or theatre its value?

The second issue arises after the first is dealt with: what is the best mode for theatre to reach its goals? There are two broad answers to this question. The first is an idea that the theatre must be ordered and balanced and therefore beautiful / useful / spiritual because of its balance. Questions of how many acts, how many characters, how many subplots, the relationship between plots, the existence and location of a climax, and even the appropriate types of characters and plots fall into this category. This extreme idea of order as creating value tends to list precise things that theatre must or must not do. The second extreme is the idea that theatre presents a mode of chaos – a disruption of balance – and therefore reaches its goals by destabilizing and shifting social patterns around it. This second idea celebrates experimentation and often looks more at function than at form. There is all manner of positions between these extremes.

In short, then, this chapter uses the word aesthetics to refer to questions of theatrical form in relation to theatrical purpose. This definition fits with traditional Western ideas of aesthetics – balance and unity create beauty and beauty allows theatre to show the world as it might be (or, in the case of some varieties of modern art, to be beautiful simply for the sake of artistic beauty). It also fits with theatres that are more directly and immediately tied to religion, ritual, politics, or spirituality – certain forms, or the various challenges to these forms, are more appropriate for communicating with higher powers or for changing the world.

This definition leads to a set of questions that are reasonable to ask of theatres from around the world. These questions are the more general form of the questions raised by the case study. To what extent is theatre involved in the formal creation of beauty? Is the form of theatre secondary to some other potential project (political, social, ritual)? How rigid are the aesthetics of the theatre? Do they change as the world changes or are they treated as timeless? Are the theatrical aesthetics guidelines and principles or specific rules? Which elements of theatre are most regulated by aesthetic concerns? How does this pattern of regulations reflect the purpose of the theatre in question?

The above questions emerge from some of the suppositions shared by various world aesthetic theories. Considering the differences between these theories allows us to discuss what a given theatre is "supposed" to do. If any given theatrical context (e.g. late Elizabethan England) has a set of rules and guidelines, there is a "normal" theatre in this period. There will always be a few plays that epitomize these rules, but there will be many that break the rules. By figuring out what a theatre is "supposed" to look like – and how these formal elements relate to the purpose of the theatre – a researcher should be able to hypothesize about what purpose any deviations from the normal model might serve. While aesthetic theory always postulates a normal (or a range of possible normals), theatre is constantly evolving. This evolution is often specifically shaped by resistances to what a given aesthetic theory expects.

Western foundations

The West has no shortage of aesthetic debates. Some of these are distinctly theatrical and others emerge from the visual arts and architecture. Within the theatre world, Aristotelian aesthetics and Neoclassicist aesthetics have proved to be among the most enduring ideas – although their endurance is partly due to the frequency with which they have been critiqued, especially in modern times. Aesthetic theory is not like scientific theory – it can't be proven or disproven. It can be accepted or resisted – but it is hard, within the Western context, to imagine completely replacing a given aesthetic theory with something that is wholly new. In the twentieth century, many Western theatre artists turned to other parts of the world in order to explore alternative aesthetic modes, although many of these experiments ended with foreign elements incorporated into frameworks that still echoed with their Aristotelian roots.

What is Aristotelian theatre? Aristotle (384–322 BCE) was a Greek philosopher and scientist who wrote about everything from zoology to aesthetics. His *Poetics* is often considered to be the foundation of Western theatrical theory. Aristotle provides a model for tragedy, discussing the necessary components of a play and the various forms these components should take. Aristotle's formal discussion of theatre is based on the idea that theatre should act to inspire fear and pity and, through this fear and pity, encourage people toward more virtuous lives.

To understand Aristotelian aesthetics, it is thus useful to consider Aristotle's idea of virtue alongside his idea of theatre. Aristotle privileges action above other theatrical elements. "Action" in this case refers to plot – concrete things done by the characters in the play. The fact that he places action as more important than emotion or other elements is not surprising, given that his theory of virtue is also active. Virtue is not just a quality that people have – virtue exists when it is in action: virtue is what you do (and to some extent who you are – the fragments of Aristotle that survive have been interpreted in a variety of ways, and the extent to which Aristotle relates the internal psyche of a person to virtue has historically been subject to debate). In addition to talking about virtue of action, one of Aristotle's most often cited concepts is the "golden mean" – the idea that virtuous action is balanced action. He gives the example of the virtuous quality of courage. Too little courage and you are a coward, never taking action and therefore not improving yourself or the world. Too much courage, however, is just as bad – you will throw caution to the wind and rush headlong into dangerous situations. The golden mean is not the halfway point between too much courage and not enough courage – it is actually slightly on the side of excess.

Aristotle describes his ideal theatre as creating this sort of virtue in his audience, and to this end, he focuses on the ways in which formal aspects of theatre (construction of plot, character, etc.) can generate fear and pity in the audience, which leads to catharsis (emotional purging), which, in turn, empties the human to be refilled with the virtue taught in the tragedy. Aristotle discusses not wanting to violate the unity of his representation in any way, and mentions keeping plots simple (action), not jumping between locations (place), and not skipping around in time (time). The Neoclassicists establish these as the "three unities", and open up debates about whether or not theatre can represent the entirety of a single day or whether it must be limited to representing only the amount of time that actually elapses within the play. Can the stage space be divided to represent multiple settings? Can the setting actually change between scenes (from the outside to the inside of a building, for instance – generally Neoclassicists and their followers wouldn't allow more dramatic shifts in setting)? If theatre is going to inspire fear and pity in the audience, it must take a form that the audience can accept, and in the case of Aristotle to some extent – and the Neoclassicists to a greater extent – this meant keeping all of the elements of the play unified into a coherent system.

The rules that Aristotle, and later the Neoclassicists, outlines for representation are directly related to the virtue that his theatre seeks to create and to the audience's ability to follow the play. Later chapters of this book look at some resistances to Aristotle.

World foundations

The idea that theatre might entertain as well as instruct also becomes a part of the discussion – and some of the results of this discussion can be seen in the large-scale Broadway and West End musicals that are an economic, if not always artistic, engine driving theatre. The insertion of the phrase "if not always artistic" into the above sentence displays a bias that is peculiar to Western theory – namely the assumption that entertainment, art, and education are separate enterprises. Western notions of culture can divide popular entertainment from art. While Western theatre history certainly has its intersections with religion – and has at various times sought to emphasize its ritual roots – these intersections have not been readily visible in much of Western theatre since the sixteenth century. Indeed, there is academic skepticism about the ritual roots of Greek tragedy. While religion is certainly a topic in many pieces of Western theatre, it is far less common to find theatre being used as religious observance or as part of ritual practice (with the obvious exception of several modern intercultural theatre practitioners like Richard Schechner who turned to the rest of the world to consider the place of ritual practice in theatre).

In many cultures – like China's – ideas of art, spirituality, entertainment, and politics mix much more freely in aesthetic theory. One of the earliest Chinese works to theorize dramatic effect is actually a book explaining religious practices. The *Book of Rites* (early second century BCE) discusses the merger of music and action for dramatic and spiritual effect. This book was used in governmental contexts, and the rites contained therein also display a connection between performance and politics. This material is echoed in Li Yu's 1671 theoretical exploration of theatre, which is found in *Casual Expression of Idle Feeling*. *Casual Expression* is a comprehensive guide to conduct, discussing all aspects of a balanced, appropriate life. In the sections dealing with theatre, Li Yu elides the moral with the natural, and, in doing so, emphasizes the spiritual nature of the practical aspects of theatre.

China is not alone in this insistence on maintaining close connection to the ritual roots of theatre. Dhanamjaya's *Dasarupa, Treatise on Hindu Dramaturgy* (tenth century) and Bharata's work discussed below both trace the connection between artistic form, spirituality, and entertainment in the Indian context. In Africa, contemporary writers like Wole Soyinka and Femi Osofisan debate the relationship of artistic practice, ritual, politics, and life in Nigeria. Each of these distinct sets of aesthetic theories presents its own criteria for evaluating theatre's ability to fulfill these various functions, and their own prioritizations of these various functions.

While many theatres around the world retain their ritual roots, and connections between theatre and spirituality are more common in the world than the West, there are secular world theatre aesthetic theories as well: it would be grossly incorrect to label Western theatre as purely secular; and world theatre as purely spiritual. Within twentieth-century China, Mao Zedong writes about socialist theatre and its ability to promote revolution. In Japan *The Actor's Analects* collects seventeenth-century thoughts on the aesthetics of Kabuki theatre. This extensive series of fragments of diaries and instruction manuals seldom directly references religious ritual, although it retains a pervasive sense of decorum. Similarly Ngugi Wa Thiong'o and Augusto Boal (whose work is in Chapter 5) write about theatre from a secular standpoint, promoting community performance.

These disparate examples bring up another thread in the aesthetics of world theatre – the idea of popular and / or community performance. To some extent, this intersects with major moments of Western theatre history – certainly Shakespeare's Globe theatre had its moments for the general populace, Italian *commedia dell'arte* and even medieval British Christian theatrical events were similarly accessible to wide audiences. To what extent is theatre meant for the elite and to what extent is it meant for the general public?

Bringing up the idea of ritual and the idea of communal or popular participation in theatre does not exhaust the possibilities of world theatrical aesthetics. The questions posed by world aesthetics do have certain commonalities, but the specific content is radically different.

Zeami and the Flower of Theatre

It would be difficult to overstate the importance of Zeami Motokiyo (circa 1363–1443) in theatre history. He was a prolific playwright and is credited with having founded a school of nō drama (a highly stylized Japanese theatrical mode), which shaped more than 600 years of art. He also produced one of the most extensive actor handbooks of the classical world through his many treatises on drama. While a majority of Zeami's books were initially intended to be the secret training manuals of his school, within a generation his theoretical and practical work on theatre had spread well beyond Zeami's immediate circle.

Zeami was a court favorite during much of his career and received an education far beyond that normally afforded to actors. While the details of his life remain a mystery, he was exiled to a small island during the turbulent Ashikaga years for reasons lost to time. When he returned, his son, who was supposed to take over Zeami's theatre school, died (potentially under mysterious circumstances) and the school went to a nephew (likely against Zeami's wishes).

Perhaps little record of the details of Zeami's life survives because of the turbulence of the period. After generations of emperors had succeeded one another, the military became increasingly directly involved with the governance of Japan. This involvement threw off the balance between the great houses of Japan and the emperor. Zeami's father passed away while Zeami was in his twenties, and thus Zeami took control over a theatre during a period in which the long-time stability of Japan was shaken and the future was unclear.

Zeami's allegiances were clear, however, and he was commissioned by the court of the shogun, Ashikaga Yoshimitsu. To this end, Zeami developed a training system for his actors and a theory of theatrical aesthetics. Thomas Rimer (who, along with Ramazaki Masakuzu, published the translation of Zeami contained here) points out that Zeami's aesthetic theory is distinct from Aristotle's inasmuch as Zeami is particularly concerned with the relationship between the theatre and the audience. Zeami imagines his theatre as a live production with live actors, in front of real people. Aristotle, on the other hand, writes about the technical elements of a theatrical script, with considerably less focus on production. Rimer argues that this split between two foundational works of theatrical aesthetics accounts for the West's tendency toward a logocentric (word-centered) focus on text and Japan's continued focus on performance and production.

Aside from a general focus on audience, there are several other striking features of Zeami's work. Chief among these is his penchant for poetry. He describes theatre with the metaphor of a flower, with the actor's aura roughly corresponding to the scent of the flower. Zeami's ideas about nō are incredibly precise. He states adamantly what should and should not happen at moments in the production. The fact that his treatises also contain metaphors that can only be "roughly" explained suggests that part of theatre remains a mystery – or at least remains mysterious enough to defy easy explanation. Whereas the Aristotelian aesthetic seeks to precisely define exactly what components make a perfect theatrical text, Zeami's aesthetic is content to leave space for mystery (a mystery that he says might take 40 years of training for an actor to come to appreciate).

Across many theories of aesthetics, the discussion of beauty focuses on what is consistently good and pleasing. It is curious that Zeami insists that nō theatre shows all aspects of the human existence, and the stage must balance these aspects. Beauty isn't found through an excess of goodness, but, instead, through a balance of competing impulses, good or bad. Zeami also suggests ways in which the actor might modify the performance for different audiences – and while nō remains a theatre that rewards careful study, Zeami's idea of aesthetics can shift depending on the audience. Unlike Aristotle who assumes a homogenous audience, Zeami assumes the audience will change.

While Zeami's aesthetic shifts with the audience and contains rough elements, he insists that the actor's performance itself should never be coarse. The beauty of theatre's flower lies in its ability to genteelly present all aspects of life to all people. Zeami uses theatre to elevate both his audience and his surroundings. Several terms, which appear in the translation of Zeami below, have very specific meanings within the Japanese context, and these are useful in understanding Zeami's aesthetic values. Thomas Rimer, the translator of the excerpt below, provides extensive notes on words that do not move easily from Japanese to English. Zeami discusses 砕動 (saidō), which is translated as "delicacy within strength" but literally refers to a crushing movement. Zeami contrasts this with 力動 (rikidō) or rough / forceful movement, a style of movement of which Zeami disapproves. The distinction between these two types of violent movement is simple on one level: one contains the violence within a larger pattern of graceful movement while the other does not.

A complication emerges when trying to determine what this means in terms of performance. Clearly this is not a directly representational theatre – the actor should not duplicate the violence of the world. On the other hand, Zeami speaks disparagingly of 無主風 (mushufū) translated as "externalization," a term which refers to an actor who, while technically performing the craft, has no internal connection to the work. This is not a theatre entirely built on externals or internals. It is neither fully representational nor fully presentational. This is symptomatic of Zeami's general idea that beauty is found in the unity of disparate elements. He takes binary ideas and finds ways of unifying them in one theatre.

Extract 2.1 Selections from *On the Art of Nō Drama*
Zeami Motokiyo, translated by Thomas Rimer

Finding Gems and Gaining the Flower (Shugyoku tokka)

1. Question:

Concerning the presentation of sarugaku, suppose that an actor has rehearsed and learned his art in accordance with his own development and has studied his art in every detail, and, with the value of experience, has reached the limit of his capacities. Why is it then that, although he neglects nothing, it may well occur that some of his particular performances are successful and some are not? What is the reason for this?

Answer:

[...] The reason that the same actor who performs with the same highly developed skill will achieve different results from different performances may well be because, depending on the occasion, the balance between yin and yang may not be in harmony [with the rhythm of his performance]. Conditions vary because of the four seasons, day and night, morning and evening. The nature of the audience itself changes. Sometimes it is made up of the nobility, sometimes commoners. The playing spaces, too, range from large to small. If the first sound made by the actor after sensing this changing atmosphere is inappropriate, or if the pitch of the music is not suitable, the performer and the audience will not be in harmony. Therefore, the actor must put himself thoroughly in accord with the atmosphere of the occasion so that his chant will suit the situation and cause the spectators to issue cries of appreciation. Such is the way to begin a harmonious performance.

Then again, there are variations due to warm and cold weather, day and night, morning and evening. The sound of the music must harmonize with those factors for good results. Cold weather is related to yin, and warm weather to yang; appropriately, therefore, bright music should be performed to balance cold weather, and melancholy music played to counteract the warm weather. Concerning the matter of harmonizing bright and melancholy, if the atmosphere at the place of performance is gloomy, because of the weather, and the mood seems somehow forlorn, the actor should grasp the precise nature of this condition and use a bright voice, which might be described by the following poem:

> The moon is serenely reflected on the stream,
> The breeze passes softly through the pines,
> Perfect silence, reigning unruffled—
> What is it for?

He should blend it with a relatively easy and lengthy melody, so as to obtain a proper vocal synthesis. He can thus bring about a regulation of the atmosphere, and when this is achieved, the actor and audience share the same feelings. When this musical atmosphere is reflected in the visual aspects of the performance as well, the audience will be stimulated to find the performance truly moving. When the musical elements can completely unite the feelings of an actor and audience, the presentation will achieve genuine success.

On the other hand, when the atmosphere of the performance seems basically bright, the breath used in the actor's vocal production should be well controlled, and he should choose as the basis for his performance a dark voice, which might be described by the following poem:

> In the midst of the night
> The raven, tinged with snow,
> Flies off.

He will thus achieve a mutual harmony and appeal to the feelings and senses of the spectators, thereby demonstrating the effectiveness of his musical art. On an occasion when the performance is held on a fall evening, or during the winter, although the sun may be bright and the assembled audience remains excited and bustling and does not quiet down, the actor should use a voice containing both bright and dark elements so that the immediate mood of the spectators can be matched. The musical atmosphere created by the *shite* — will come to move the audience and reinforce the visual aspects of the performance. As the actor continues to chant, the spectators will be drawn to the performer's physical appearance, producing a powerful effect. If the audience is as one person in praise of the beauty of the emotions shared with the actor, an ideal performance will truly have been achieved. The fundamental principle for such a success involves the transfer by the actor of the musical atmosphere that he first creates to the visual aspects of his performance. [...]

2. Question:

Now I can certainly understand that the success or failure of a performance depends on the atmosphere of the occasion. In our art, I can see that in the case of an artist who has practiced for many years and has finally reached a level of wide fame, he can present a performance that moves his audiences on the basis of his long experience. On the other hand, a beginner who has merely learned the Two Arts can excite the interest of his audience as well through the charm of his childlike appearance. Can it be said that the nature of this fascination the audience finds in a mature performer is the same? I am unclear about this.

Answer:

I have written about this matter elsewhere. I have compared the nature of this artistic attraction to a Flower, which gives rise to a sense of profound novelty. The knowledge of this process at its highest development means to "know the Flower." This is described in the Teachings on Style and the Flower.

In general it can be said that a flower shows its beauty as it blooms and its novelty as its petals scatter. A certain person once asked, "What is the spirit of Transiency?" The answer was, "scattering blossoms, falling leaves." Then came another question. "What is the meaning of Eternity?" The same answer, "scattering blossoms, falling leaves" was returned. Indeed there can be different interpretations of one single moment that are of profound interest. One who can create such feelings of enjoyment in any of the performing arts is truly gifted, and if he can sustain this ability to create interest during a long career, he is truly a master. The fact that an actor can develop and maintain this skill to the end of his career can be likened to the constancy of "scattering blossoms, falling leaves." Then again, there are artists who merely manifest an ordinary level of talent. Now, as concerns the Nine Levels, it goes without saying that the Flower is manifested in the upper three levels, yet in the middle three and lower three levels of our art as well, insofar as they possess elements of interest, there are appropriate Flowers for them as well. For example, if farmers and rural people find the flowers of wild trees beautiful, then such is the viewpoint of uneducated persons. Those who are moved by the three highest levels share the viewpoint of those who are highly cultivated. Actor and spectator alike will show a level of discernment depending on their own level of cultivation. Let me attempt to explain what I mean. Let us imagine two general categories, the fundamental

Changeless Flower and a second, its manifestation, the Changing Flower. The Changeless Flower represents the upper three levels of the nō and can be compared to the cherry. Such is the level appropriate to a highly cultivated audience. The highest level of the middle rank can be referred to as the True Flower and can be represented as the cherry also. Still, a bloom on this level can be compared not only to the cherry but to the plum, the peach, or the pear. The red and white appearance of the plum in particular is especially elegant. [...]

Those with cultivation, however, as they have wide powers of observation, do not despise the Changing Flowers. An actor, too, must adopt the same attitude. He should have wide learning, so as to master all the Nine Levels of accomplishment without exception. There is a famous Zen koan that states the following. "The various truths of the phenomenal world are manifestations of one Essence; the one Essence only exists in various manifestations found in the phenomenal world." In the same fashion, the Changing Flowers can be seen as manifestations of the essential Changeless Flower, and so the various levels of accomplishment can be seen as various kinds of Flowers, each with their appropriate beauties. In any case, as concerns any doubt over the differences in the kind of fascination the audience may find in the novelty of a child's performance as against that of a mature actor, the matter can be explained by the difference between the Changing Flower and the Changeless Flower.

3. Question:

How should the term Fascination (omoshiroki) be elaborated? The word is often explained by making a comparison with a flower, but that word in turn serves only as a metaphor. Yet the sensation is felt before any comparison is articulated. What constitutes the essential nature of this sensation we call Fascination?

Answer:

In order to grasp the essential nature of the term Fascination, one must of course grasp the nature of the Flower and the deepest truths of our art. Before, I spoke of Fascination, I spoke of the Flower, and I spoke of Novelty. All three represent different names for the same conception. In fact, Peerless Charm, Flower, and Fascination, although they are in fact separate, spring from the same emotion. They too can be ranked as high, middle, and low. Peerless Charm surpasses verbal expression and lies in the pure realm that lies beyond the workings of consciousness.

When this realm is given visible expression, the result is the Flower. A conscious appreciation of this beauty constitutes Fascination.

The word omoshiroki came about as follows: delighted by the dances of the gods at sacred Mount Kagu, the goddess Amaterasu opened the heavenly stone doors and first saw the bright faces of all the gods. Thus the word "face-fair" (omoshim) came into being. Actually, however, in such a brief instant of time there would surely not have been the time necessary for the goddess to actually make such an observation. The word omoshiroki was thus created through a consciousness of those sensations. What word could possibly have been used to describe such sensations even before they came into consciousness?

When relating this matter to the highest levels in our own art, it can be said that this moment of Fascination represents an instant sensation that occurs before the rise of any consciousness regarding that sensation, a Feeling that Transcends Cognition. [...] After the goddess Amaterasu had shut the great stone door, the world and all its territories became dark. Then the light suddenly appeared. The reaction of all creatures must have been that of unreflecting joy. It resembles the instant when a vague smile without self-awareness [appeared on the face of Kagyapa]. At the moment when the heavenly doors were shut and the world was plunged into darkness, the situation may be compared to that of Peerless Charm that transcends words; the sudden brightness can be compared to the Flower; and the moment of consciousness concerning that brightness might be compared to Fascination.

[...]

5. Question:

In all the arts, one speaks of Fulfillment in performance. Is the meaning of the term merely on the surface? Or does it harbor some profound significance? What is the real meaning of the term?

Answer:

The term Fulfillment is made of two characters that mean "to become" (成) and "to settle in place" (就). As concerns the art of the nō, the word seems to explain the process by which an audience comes to feel that Fascination I spoke of before.

Fulfillment is related to the process of jo, ha, and kyū. This is true because there is in the composition of the word Fulfillment itself a suggestion of the process that involves a sense of completion. If this natural process toward completion is not carried out, no feelings of

Fulfillment can arise. It is that instant of Fulfillment in an artistic work that gives the audience a sensation of novelty. The proper sequence of jo, ha, and kyū provides the sense of Fulfillment.

Thinking over the matter carefully, it may be said that all things in the universe, good and bad, large and small, with life and without, all partake of the process of jo, ha, and kyū. From the chirp of the birds to the buzzing of the insects, all sing according to an appointed order, and this order consists of jo, ha, and kyū. (Indeed, their music surpasses any question of mere skill and represents an unconscious Fulfillment.) Their singing creates a pleasing musical sensation and gives rise to feelings of a Melancholy Elegance. Still, if Fulfillment is not achieved, even if those natural sensations are pleasing, they do not create a mood of Melancholy Elegance. In the play Takasago, there is a chant that states how the forest in the spring is moved by the east wind, and how the insects of fall sing in the cool dew. All their music takes the form of waka. All the sounds of nature, from the sentient and nonsentient alike, are expressed in poetry and show the auspicious feelings of Fulfillment in accordance with the principles of jo, ha, and kyū. Grasses and trees alike are wet with rain and dew in this rhythm of jo, ha, and kyū, just as flowers and fruits appear at the proper season. The voice of the wind and the sound of the water as well follow the same design.

[...]

Various Items Concerning Role Playing

It would be impossible to describe in writing all the various aspects of Role Playing. Yet as this skill forms the fundamental basis of our art, various roles must be studied with the greatest care. In general, Role Playing involves an imitation, in every particular, with nothing left out. Still, depending on the circumstances, one must know how to vary the degree of imitation involved. For example, when it comes to playing the part of a ruler or a high official, it is extremely difficult to perform with the necessary detail, since the actor cannot know the real way of life of the court nobility, or the bearing appropriate to a great lord. Still, he can study carefully their way of speaking, observe their circumstances, and ask the opinion of those noblemen who watch the performances. Next, he must imitate down to the smallest detail the various things done by persons of high profession, especially those elements related to high artistic pursuits. On the other hand, when it comes to imitating laborers and rustics, their commonplace actions should not be copied too realistically. In the case of woodcutters, grass cutters, charcoal burners, and salt workers, however, they should be imitated in detail insofar as they have traditionally been found congenial as poetic subjects. In general, men of lowly occupation should not be imitated in any meticulous fashion, nor shown to men of refined taste. Should they see such things, they will merely find them vulgar, and the performance will hold no attraction for them. The need for prudence in this matter can be fully understood. Thus the degree of imitation must vary, depending on the kind of role being performed.

Women's Roles

In general, a young *shite* is the most suitable actor to play the part of a woman. Nevertheless, playing such a part represents a considerable undertaking. If the actor's style of dress is unseemly, there will be nothing worth watching in the performance. When it comes to impersonating high-ranking women of the court, such as ladies-in-waiting, for example, since the actor cannot easily view their actual deportment, he must make serious, detailed inquiries concerning such matters. As for items of clothing such as the kinu and the hakama, these too cannot merely be chosen on the basis of the actor's personal preference. The actor must make a proper investigation concerning what is correct. When it comes to impersonating an ordinary woman, however, the actor will be familiar with the appropriate details, and so the task will not be difficult. If the actor dresses in an appropriate kinu or kosode, that will doubtless suffice. When performing kusemai, shirabyoshi, or mad women's roles, the actor should hold a fan or a sprig of flowers, for example, loosely in his hand in order to represent female gentleness. The kinu and the hakama, as well, should be long enough to conceal his steps, his hips and knees should be straight, and his bodily posture pliable. As for his head posture, if he bends backward, his face will appear coarse. If the actor looks down, on the other hand, his appearance from the back will be unseemly. Then too, if he holds his neck too stiffly, he will not look feminine. He should certainly wear a robe with long sleeves, and he should avoid showing the tips of his hands. His obi should be loosely tied. The fact that an actor takes great care with his costume means that he is truly anxious to perform his role as well as possible. No matter what the role, bad costuming will never be effective, and, in the case of a woman's role, proper dressing is essential.
  [...]

Question:

In the common language of artistic criticism, the term Bending is often used. What does the term mean?

Answer:

The term is almost impossible to explain in writing. No explanation can capture its beauty. Nevertheless, such an artistic element certainly does exist. Such beauty can grow only after the actor's own Flower is well established. If one examines the matter closely, it can be seen that Bending is hard to grasp through rehearsal and difficult to manifest through any particular means of performance. To manifest Bending, one must first grasp the extremity of the Flower.

Therefore, an actor who has truly identified one aspect of the Flower, even though he has not mastered every form of Role Playing, may be able to grasp the beauty of Bending. Indeed, this quality can be said to exist at a stage even higher than that of the Flower. Without the Flower, Bending has no meaning. Without the Flower, the effect of Bending is merely gloomy and grey. The Bending of a flower in full bloom is truly beautiful. Yet how can the Bending of trees without blossom attract any interest? The crucial element to master is the Flower; then, on top of that, one must master the beauty of Bending. To give an example of this quality is not easy.

An old poem says:

> [...]
> In the thin mist,
> Morning flowers wet
> On the bamboo hedge:
> Who was it who said
> Autumn evenings are best?

Then again, there is another poem:

> Find mutability
> In that being which alters without fading
> In its outward hue—
> In the color, looks, and the deceptive flower
> Of the heart of what this world calls man!

Such feelings are doubtless those that must be expressed in Bending. One must look into the heart of these poems for the meaning of such things.

Bharata and the concept of rasa

As noted in Chapter 13, many of the documents associated with Indian history have a literary / mythological / spiritual style to them. Providing background on Bharata Muni must take three forms. First, the portions of his life that fit with traditional Western definitions of history; second, the narrative of his life that he himself offers, and third, the meditations on spirituality. The Western category of "theory" immediately breaks down when confronted with the richness of Bharata's writing. Indeed, these three aspects of Bharata's writing mirror a larger trend in Indian culture in which reaching the goal of self-realization requires knowledge of the abstract theory of the Upanisads, the logical approach found in the Brahmasutras, and the practical advice of the Bhagavad Gita.

According to later sources that provide a variety of dates, Bharata wrote the *Natyasastra* (*natya* meaning music, dance, and theatre; *sastra* meaning guidebook or scripture) sometime between the third and first century BCE. Alexander the Great had marched into India in the waning days of the fourth century BCE, and retreated in 324. The earliest Buddhist texts refer to the Maurya family who founded an empire after Alexander left. This empire controlled a large percentage of the world's economy and still ranks among the most populous empires in history. The golden age of India, which is marked by a rise of Hinduism, increased tolerance, renewed interest in intellectual pursuits, and a flourishing of the arts, began 600 years later, but, given that so little is known of the period, the Mauryas and the next 1,500 years is known collectively as the middle period or classical period despite the many dynastic changes. So, while we don't know anything about Bharata himself – even his existence as a single person is in doubt – we do know that the *Natyasastra* is not only India's first surviving work of theatre theory, but also an important precursor to India's golden age of artistic advancement.

Bharata himself tells a very different story. Indeed, part of the confusion about authorship with the piece is due to the fact that Bharata tells the story of composition as if it was happening to someone else. The sages came to Bharata and asked Bharata to tell the story of the composition of the *Natyasastra*. He responds that the Brahma (Hindu god of creation and creator of humankind) asked him to compose something that would teach while being pleasing to the spectators. Brahma goes on to specify that he wants for this new thing to be appropriate for general consumption and not limited to priests and those of the highest caste. Bharata begins to prepare, training his sons to perform with him. Indra and other gods pitch in to help, adding grace to the qualities Bharata sought. His first production, played before the gods, is a rousing success, but the story he tells angers the demons who were watching. The gods agreed to protect the theatre. Bharata pacifies the demons by saying that there is nothing in any of the worlds that would not be included in his theatre. The *Natyasastra* does not explain why the demons would have been pacified by this idea, but they apparently were. Bharata also asks the gods to perform a sacrifice on the stage to inaugurate this venture.

From these two accounts, we can extract several ideas that are useful in understanding Bharata's work. First and foremost, as a *sastra*, this text is scriptural – it deals with gods and is itself holy. The instantiating moment of Indian theatre is tied directly and clearly to the gods. While Greek theatre (may have) emerged from various rites and rituals, Aristotle is not writing about spiritual matters and certainly does not cast his text as holy. What does it mean to predicate an art form on contact with the gods? Bharata clearly says that this form is also supposed to provide entertainment and pleasure, which means this theatre isn't exactly what the West might label a ritual. On the other hand, its close connection with the gods means that its purpose is substantially different from most Western theatre. Bharata serves as a reminder that the lines we draw between religion and art or between religion and entertainment are not the same lines drawn in other contexts. There is a concrete, tangible quality to Bharata's religion, and thus his theatre, with its religious connections, accomplishes a wide array of purposes.

The rigidity with which Bharata lays out the various patterns of the stage and the various emotions portrayed on the stage might well relate to the spiritual purpose of his theatre. The gods might demand things in a precise form. Equally possible, however, as India was reformed into a new empire, Bharata might have been inspired to create a theatre that could lend structure to this new and confusing order of things. The instruction provided by his theatre might have been a way of formally indoctrinating people into the ways of the new empire. If this is the case, it also makes sense to have a precisely structured theatre – all people should learn the same lesson in the same way to be part of the same empire. An empire, by definition, pulls together a diverse group of people with diverse beliefs.

Of all the concepts in Bharata's work, the idea of *rasa* (which can be loosely translated as taste or flavor) has attracted the most attention from critics around the world. It is the subject of a considerable amount of debate, and theatre artists like Richard Schechner have taken the concept and adapted it to new theatrical purposes, which provides a further profusion of possible definitions. *Rasa* is certainly related to the emotional content or mood of certain works, and Bharata has outlined a number of different emotional qualities from the works. *Rasa* is not just the mood established onstage, however. It is also the way in which the audience internalizes this mood – it is the experience of specific emotions in a specific context. The rigid organization of the stage serves a spiritual purpose, but it also appropriately positions the audience to experience / embody / imbibe the *rasa*: each *rasa* is a precise combination of a multitude of "flavors" which can only exist when properly executed. These emotional categories exist independently of the human experience of them to some extent – they are set categories.

What purpose does *rasa* serve? Aristotle argues that fear and pity can lead to catharsis, which, in turn, can generate virtue. Like Bharata's *rasa*, Aristotelian catharsis exists – within contemporary criticism – in an odd space between and among the actor and the audience. Unlike Aristotelian catharsis, however, the experience of *rasa* is an end unto itself – it is not designed to do anything beyond allowing the audience to experience the specific flavor.

What does it mean to have a rigid aesthetic framework that has "taste" as one primary goal? How would a theatre based on the gustatory sensation of emotion be different from a theatre based on visual beauty? How can such theatrical modes be identified in text or in performance? Is this a way of understanding all theatre through its emotional content, or is *rasa* a distinctive feature of Indian theatre? What is the relationship between taste and the spiritual aims with which Bharata opens his work? Essentially Bharata asks us to consider what value our lived experiences have – and how we might begin to think about such experiences in a theatrical context.

Extract 2.2 Selections from the *Natyasastra*
Bharata Muni, translated by Manomohan Ghosh

With a bow to Brahma […] I shall relate the Canons of Drama, as these were uttered by Brahma.

Once in the days of yore, high-souled sages such as Atreya and others who had subdued their senses approached the pious Bharata, the master of dramatic art during an intermission of studies. He (Bharata) then just finished the muttering [of Mantras] and was surrounded by his sons. The high-souled sages who controlled their senses, respectfully said to him, "O Brahmin, how did originate the Natyaveda similar to the Vedas, which you have properly composed? And for whom is it meant, how many limbs does it possess, what is its extent and how is it to be applied? Please speak to us in detail about it all."

Hearing these words of the sages, Bharata spoke thus in reply about the Natyaveda: "Get yourselves cleansed, be attentive and hear about the origin of the Natyaveda devised by Brahma. O Brahmins, in the days of yore […] people became addicted to sensual pleasures, were under the sway of desire and greed, became affected with jealousy and anger and [thus] found their happiness mixed with sorrow, […] the gods with the great Indra as their head, [approached] Brahma and spoke, to him, "We want an object diversion, which must be audible as well as visible. As the [existing] of Vedas are not to be listened to by those born as Sudras, be pleased to create another Veda which will belong [equally] to all the Colour-groups (*varna*)."

"Let it be so," said he in reply and then having dismissed the king of gods (Indra) he resorted to yoga and recalled to mind the four Vedas. He then thought: I shall make a fifth Veda on the Natya with the Semi-historical Tales (*itibasa*), which will conduce to duty (*dharma*), wealth (*artha*) as well as fame, will contain good counsel and collection [of traditional maxims], will give guidance to people of the future as well, in all their actions, will be enriched by the teaching of all authoritative works (*Sastra*) and will give a review of all arts and crafts.

With this resolve the Holy One from his memory of all the Vedas, shaped this Natyaveda compiled from the four of them. The recitative (*pathya*) he took from the Rgveda, the song from the Sama[veda], the Histrionic Representation (*abhinaya*) from the Yajur[veda] and Sentiments (*rasa*) from the Atharvaveda, [and] thus was created the Natyaveda connected with the Vedas principal and subsidiary, by the holy Brahma who is omniscient.

After the creation of the Natyaveda, Brahma said to Indra, "Semi-historical Tales have been composed by me; you are to get them [dramatized and] acted by gods. Pass on this Natyaveda to those of the gods who are skillful, learned, bold in speech and inured to hard work."

At these words of Brahma, Indra bowed to him with folded palms and said in reply, "O the best and holy one, gods are neither able to receive it and to maintain it, nor are they fit to understand it and to make use of it; they are unfit to do anything with the drama. The sages who know the mystery of the Vedas and have fulfilled their vows, are capable of maintaining this (Natyaveda) and putting it into practice."

[...]

[Bharata says] "O Brahmins, I then prepared to give a performance (*prayoga*) in which was adopted the dramatic Styles (*qui*) such as the Verbal (*bharati*), the Grand (*sattvati*), and the Energetic (*arabhati*). I then went [to Brahma and] after bowing, informed him [of my work]. Now Brahma told me to include the Graceful (*kaisiki*) Style also [in my performance], and he asked me to name materials conducive to its introduction."

[...]

Now when the performance relating to the killing of the Daityas and Danavas began, the Daityas [devils] who came there [uninvited] instigated by the Vighnas (malevolent spirits) with Virupaksa as their leader, said, "we shall not see in this manner this dramatic performance come forward". Then the Vighnas (evil spirits) together with the Asuras resorted to magical power and paralysed the speech, movement as well as memory of the actors.

[...]

Having noticed these attempts caused by the insult of the Daityas I, along with my sons, approached Brahma [and said], "O holy one and best of gods, the Vighnas (the evil spirits) are determined to spoil this dramatic performance; so enlighten me about the means of its protection."

"O the high-souled one," said Brahma then to Visvakarma, "build carefully a playhouse of the best type."

[...]

Brahma called the evil spirits and said, "Why are you out for spoiling the dramatic performance?"

Questioned thus by Brahma, Virupaksa together with the Daityas and the Vighnas, said these conciliatory words: "The knowledge of the dramatic art which you have introduced for the first time at the desire of the gods, has put us in an unfavourable light, and this is done by you for the sake of the gods; this ought not to have been done by you who is the first progenitor of the world, from whom came out alike gods as well as Daityas."

These words being uttered by Virupaksa, Brahma said, 'Enough of your anger, O Daityas, give up your grievance (lit. sorrow) [...] The drama as I have devised, is a mimicry of actions and conducts of people, which is rich in various emotions, and which depicts different situations. This will relate to actions of men good, bad and indifferent, and will give courage, amusement and happiness as well as counsel to them all.

The drama will thus be instructive to all, through actions and States depicted in it, and through Sentiment arising out of it.

[...]

Description of the Playhouse

There are three types of playhouse devised by the wise Visvakarma [...] Their sizes vary [...]: The length (lit. measurement) of these [three types] fixed in terms of cubits as well as Dandas, is one hundred and eight, sixty-four or thirty-two. They should [respectively] have [sides] one hundred and eight, sixty-four and thirty-two [cubits or Dandas] long. The large playhouse is meant for gods and the middle-sized one for kings, while for the rest of people, has been prescribed the smallest [theatre].

[...]

After it has been laid, walls should be built and this having been completed, pillars within the playhouse should be raised [...] In the beginning, the ceremony in connexion [sic] with the Brahmin pillar should be performed with completely white articles purified with ghee and mustard seed [...]

General Principles of Distribution of Roles

After considering together their gait, speech and movement of limbs as well as their strength and nature, the experts are to employ actors to represent different roles [in a play]. Hence the selection of actors should be preceded by an enquiry into their merits. The Director (lit. the master) will not feel difficulty in the choice [if such procedure is followed]. After ascertaining their natural aptitudes, he is to distribute roles to different actors.

The Role of Gods

Persons who have all the limbs intact, well-formed and thick-set, who are full-grown (*vayonvita*), not fat or lean or tall or large, who have vivacity, pleasant voice and good appearance, should be employed to take up the role of gods.
[...]

The Role of Kings

Actors of the best kind who have beautiful eyes, eyebrows, forehead, nose, lips, cheeks, face, neck, and every other limbs beautiful, and who are tall, possessed of pleasant appearance, dignified gait, and are neither fat nor lean, and are well-behaved, wise and steady by nature, should be employed to represent the role of kings and princes (*kumara*).
[...]

The Final Benediction

What more should I say? Let the earth be full of grains, and be free from diseases for all time. Let then peace for cows and Brahmins, and let the king protect the entire earth.

Wole Soyinka – a transitory, eternal, distant, near, holistic aesthetic: "The Fourth Stage" and "Drama and the African World-view"

Friedrich Nietzsche's *The Birth of Tragedy* remains one of the most enigmatic pieces of theatre theory in the Western canon. Nietzsche argues that one of the great problems with Western art is the separation between Dionysian and Apollonian elements. A large portion of the text is devoted to defining precisely what he means by these terms, but, essentially, Apollonian art is the "plastic" or static recreation of beauty, while Dionysian art is a more chaotic, mobile, fluid representation of beauty. Nietzsche finds both competing impulses in Greek tragedy, and therefore praises tragedy for its ability to pull together these two concepts of beauty.

Like Nietzsche's, Soyinka's version of aesthetics is as mystical and mysterious as Aristotle's is mathematical and measured. Unlike Bharata, whose work is also explicitly metaphysical, Soyinka and Nietzsche are both modern writers. Soyinka was an established playwright by the time Nigeria gained its independence in 1960. At a time when the Negritude movement, which celebrated the distinctive qualities of African arts (see Chapter 9) was gaining prominence, Soyinka was considered the *enfant terrible* (the terrible child) of the African theatre movement. He famously said "A tiger doesn't sit around talking about its tigritude, it just pounces," which suggests his impatience with his senior colleagues in the African theatre world. Soyinka's play, *A Dance of the Forests*, was commissioned for the national independence festival, but was then shut down by the government who felt that the play sent the wrong political message. Soyinka's work continued to send political messages, and he was jailed shortly after Nigerian Independence for two years during the Nigerian Civil War. After his release, he continued his work as both a playwright and a human rights activist (he regularly met with government officials, often at their request, to discuss political issues, as documented in his multi-volume autobiography). He won the Nobel Prize in 1986, making him the first African to win the literature prize, but by this time his relationship with the government had further soured. One year after Sani Abacha took control of Nigeria, Soyinka fled the country. Shortly thereafter, Abacha declared a death sentence on Soyinka, supposedly bragging that he would be the first head of state to put to death a Nobel Laureate.

In a single word, Soyinka's aesthetics is about holism – holism of actors and audience, holism of spiritual experience, holism of man and gods, and holism of theatrical elements. Both his 1973 essay, "The Fourth Stage," and his 1976 book, *Myth, Literature and the African World*, in which he devotes a chapter to African drama, begin by making some comparison between African and Western aesthetics.

Soyinka claims that Western theatre changes its mind on a regular basis and redefines its aesthetics, whereas Yorùbá aesthetics are timeless. Soyinka conflates the Yorùbá, one ethnic group in Nigeria, with all of Africa for the purposes of his argument (in keeping with his holistic take). He eschews divisions between things, but inasmuch as his pieces reference specific Yorùbá deities, like Ògún, his claims of universal African concepts may be questionable. What does it mean to have a timeless aesthetics? For Soyinka, this aesthetics relates to man's place in the cosmos. Man and gods are separated by a cosmic gulf; man is, at times, separated from community; and even some of the gods are separated from other gods (and in several Yorùbá myths, gods are cut up / divide themselves). Curiously, this perpetual experience of division is what calls into being the holistic aesthetic – the aesthetic in which things come together.

Several Yorùbá deities are significant in Soyinka's pantheon, and his versions of these deities – while perhaps not fully unique – certainly are distinctive. The Yorùbá creation story states that, while there is a supreme being, Olòrún (alternately Olódùmarè), it was Obàtálá, a deity associated with purity, who actually created a habitable earth and the forms of man. While there are several variations of the creation story, in most Obàtálá gets drunk while shaping some men, which leads to physical deformities in the world. Many attribute this drunkenness to Èṣù, (among other things) the god of crossroads, trickery, the messenger of the gods, and the god who allows for understanding of divination. Either as a result of the drunkenness or as part of the divine plan, Obàtálá creates the form of man, but Olòrún gives these forms life. Soyinka characterizes Obàtálá as a god of static representation – of the plastic arts – inasmuch as his creations remained lifeless.

Soyinka's characterization of Ògún is harder to trace back to Yorùbá stories. The Ògún from Yorùbá faith is violent and hyper-masculine. He is supposed to have cleared space for both the gods and mankind on the earth, using his iron machete. Ògún is the god of war, of iron, of hunting, and of blacksmiths. As with all Yorùbá deities, he has multiple aspects, and, as with all Yorùbá deities, one of these aspects involves creation: references to the creative work of Ògún are challenging to find prior to Soyinka's work, however. Soyinka claims the god of iron is a god of restorative justice, merging the beauty of static art, the potential for change in the fluid arts, and the potential for novel creation and innovation. Soyinka labels this combination as tragic inasmuch as Ogunian mysteries exist just beyond the reach of humanity. Aside from moments when the "communicant chorus" and the tragic actor serve as "a mouthpiece for the god," the potential of Ògún cannot be reached.

The Yorùbá aesthetic, then, is about a quest for an unreachable unity – a desire to merge that which has been separated. In the moment of the creative impulse – the moment before the art is committed to physical form and still exists in the mysterious, chthonic (demonic, primal) realm – humanity feels the unity, but it is a fact of creation that it brings a fixity, always moving from the impulse to create a completed creation that exists in one form. Transition and the transitory nature of art are the second most important concepts in Soyinka's version of Yorùbá aesthetics. Beauty can only be found in the temporary and not in the permanent. Art must consistently move toward something that it can never reach. Stasis robs art of its beauty.

While Soyinka's work might share the mystical impulses of Zeami and Bharata, it specifically rejects their formal listing of the properties of beauty. The mystical realm, for Soyinka, is neither fully distant, fully unknowable, nor eternally fixed. The holistic and transitory aesthetics Soyinka outlines simultaneously suggests the immanence of the mystical realm and its distance; the eternal yet fluid nature of the Yorùbá metaphysical world.

**Extract 2.3 Selections from "Drama and the African World-view" in *Myth, Literature and the African World*
Wole Soyinka**

First, let us dispose of some red herrings. The serious divergences between a traditional African approach to drama and the European will not be found in lines of opposition between creative individualism and communal creativity, nor in the level of noise from the auditorium – this being the supposed gauge of audience-participation – at any given performance. They will be found more accurately in what is a recognisable Western cast of mind, a compartmentalizing habit of thought which periodically selects aspects of human emotion, phenomenal observations, metaphysical intuitions and even scientific deductions and turns them into separatist myths (or 'truths') sustained by a proliferating super-structure of presentation idioms, analogies and analytical modes. I have evolved a rather elaborate metaphor to describe it; appropriately it is not only mechanistic but represents a period technology which marked yet another phase of Western man's comprehensive world-view.

You must picture a steam-engine which shunts itself between rather closely-spaced suburban stations. At the first station it picks up a ballast of allegory, puffs into the next emitting a smokescreen on the eternal landscape of nature truths. At the next it loads up with a different species of log which we shall call naturalist timber, puffs into a halfway stop where it fills up with the synthetic fuel of surrealism, from which point yet another holistic world-view is glimpsed and asserted through psychedelic smoke. A new consignment of absurdist coke lures it into the next station from which it departs giving off no smoke at all, and no fire, until it derails briefly along constructivist tracks and is towed back to the starting-point by a neo-classic engine.

This, for us, is the occidental creative rhythm, a series of intellectual spasms which, especially today, appears susceptible even to commercial manipulation. And the difference which we are seeking to define between European and African drama as one of man's formal representations of experience is not simply a different style or form, nor is it confined to drama alone. It is representative of the essential differences between two world-views, a difference between one culture whose very artefacts are evidence of a cohesive understanding of irreducible truths and another, whose creative impulses are directed by period dialectics. So, to begin with, we must jettison that fashionable distinction which tends to encapsulate Western drama as a form of esoteric enterprise spied upon by fee-paying strangers, as contrasted with a communal evolution of the dramatic mode of expression, this latter being the African. Of far greater importance is the fact that Western dramatic criticism habitually reflects the abandonment of a belief in culture as defined within man's knowledge of fundamental, unchanging relationships between himself and society and within the larger context of the observable universe.

Let us, by way of a paradigmatic example, take a common theme in traditional mask-drama: a symbolic struggle with chthonic presences, the goal of the conflict being a harmonious resolution for plenitude and the well-being of the community. Any individual within the 'audience' knows better than to add his voice arbitrarily even to the most seductive passages of an invocatory song, or to contribute a refrain to the familiar sequence of liturgical exchanges among the protagonists. The moment for choric participation is well-defined, but this does not imply that until such a moment, participation ceases. The so-called audience is itself an integral part of that arena of conflict; it contributes spiritual strength to the protagonist through its choric reality which must first be conjured up and established, defining and investing the arena through offerings and incantations. The drama would be non-existent except within and against this symbolic representation of earth and cosmos, except within this communal compact whose choric essence supplies the collective energy for the challenger of chthonic realms. Overt participation when it comes is channelled through a formalised repertoire of gestures and liturgical responses. The 'spontaneous' participant from within the audience does not permit himself to give vent to a bare impulse or a euphoria which might bring him out as a dissociated entity from within the choric mass. If it does happen, as of course it can, the event is an aberration which may imperil the eudaemonic goals of that representation. The interjector whose balance of mind is regarded as being temporarily disturbed is quietly led out and the appropriate (usually unobtrusive) spells are cast to counter the risks of the abnormal event.

I would like to go a little deeper into this ritualistic sense of space since it is so intimately linked with the comprehensive world-view of the society that gave it birth. We shall treat it first as a medium in the communicative sense and, like any other medium it is one that is best defined through the process of interruption. In theatrical terms, this interruption is effected principally by the human apparatus. Sound, light, motion, even smell, can all be used just as validly to define space, and ritual theatre uses all these instruments of definition to control and render concrete, to parallel (this is perhaps the best description of the process) the experiences or intuitions of man in that far more disturbing environment which he defines variously as void, emptiness or infinity. The concern of ritual theatre in this process of spatial definition which precedes, as we shall discover, the actual enactment must therefore be seen as an integral part of man's constant efforts to master the immensity of the cosmos with his minuscule self. The actual events which make up the enactment are themselves, in ritual theatre, a materialisation of this basic adventure of man's metaphysical self.

Theatre then is one arena, one of the earliest that we know of, in which man has attempted to come to terms with the spatial phenomenon of his being. Again, in speaking of space, let us recognise first of all that with the advancement of technology and the evolution – some would prefer to call it a counter-evolution – of the technical sensibility, the spatial vision of theatre has become steadily contracted into purely physical acting areas on a stage as opposed to a symbolic arena for metaphysical contests. The pagan beginnings of Greek theatre retained their symbolic validity to dramaturgists for centuries after the event, so that the relative positions of suppliant, tyrant or deus ex machina, as well as the offertory or altar, were constantly impressed on their audience and created immediate emotional overtones both when they were used and by their very act of being. (I do not, for the purpose of this essay, wish to debate whether the fixity of these positions did not, contrasted with the fluid approach of African ritual space, detract from the audience's experience of cosmic relations.)

Medieval European theatre in its turn, corresponding to the religious mythology of its period, created a constant microcosmos by its spatial correspondences of good and evil, angels and demons, paradise, purgatory and hell. The protagonists of earth, heaven and hell enacted their various trials and conflicts in relation to these traditional positions, and the automatic recognition of these hierarchical situations of man created spiritual anxieties and hopes in the breasts of the audience. But observe, the apprehended territory of man has already begun to contract! Cosmic representation has shrunk into a purely moral one, a summation in terms of penalties and rewards. [...]

Ritual theatre, let it be recalled, established the spatial medium not merely as a physical area for simulated events but as a manageable contraction of the cosmic envelope within which man – no matter how deeply buried such a consciousness has latterly become – fearfully exists. And this attempt to manage the immensity of his spatial awareness makes every manifestation in the ritual theatre a paradigm for the cosmic human condition. There are transient parallels, brief visual moments of this experience in modern European theatres. The spectacle of a lone human figure under a spotlight on a darkened stage is, unlike a painting, a breathing, living, pulsating, threateningly fragile example of this paradigm. It is threatening because, unlike a similar parable on canvas, its fragility is experienced both at the level of its symbolism and in terms of sympathetic concern for the well-being of that immediate human medium. Let us say he is a tragic character: at the first sign of a check in the momentum of a tragic declamation, his audience becomes nervous for him, wondering has he forgotten his line? Has he blacked out? Or in the case of opera will she make that upper register? Well, ritual theatre has an additional, far more fundamental anxiety. Indeed, it is correct to say that the technical anxiety even where it exists – after all it does exist: the element of creative form is never absent even in the most so-called primitive consciousness – so, where it does exist, it is never so profoundly engaged as with a modern manifestation. The real unvoiced fear is: will this protagonist survive confrontation with forces that exist within the dangerous area of transformation? Entering that microcosmos involves a loss of individuation, a self-submergence in the universal essence. It is an act undertaken on behalf of the community, and the welfare of that protagonist is inseparable from that of the total community.

[...]

Ritual theatre, viewed from the spatial perspective, aims to reflect through physical and symbolic means the archetypal struggle of the mortal being against exterior forces. A tragic view of the theatre goes further and suggests that even the so-called realistic or literary drama can be interpreted as a mundane reflection of this essential struggle. Poetic drama especially may be regarded as a repository of this essential theatre; it expands the immediate meaning and action of the protagonists into a world of nature forces and metaphysical conceptions. Or, to put it the other way round, powerful natural or cosmic influences are internalised within the protagonists and this implosive factor creates the titanic scale of their passions even when the basis of the conflict seems hardly to warrant it. (Shakespeare's Lear is the greatest exemplar of this.) Indeed, this view of theatre sees the stage as a constant battleground for forces larger than the petty infractions of habitual communal norms or patterns of human relationships and expectations, beyond the actual twists and incidents of action and their resolutions. The stage is created for the purpose of that communal presence which alone defines it (and this is the fundamental defining concept, that the stage is brought into being by a communal presence); so, for this purpose, the stage becomes the affective, rational and intuitive milieu of the total communal experience, historic, race-formative, cosmogonic. Where such theatre is encountered in its purest form, not as re-created metaphors for the later tragic stage, we will find no compass points, no horizontal or vertical definitions. There are no reserved spaces for the protagonists, for his very act of representational being is defined in turn by nothing less than the infinite cosmos within which the origin of the community and its contemporaneous experience of being is firmly embedded.

Drama, however, exists on the boards; in the improvised space among stalls in the deserted or teeming market, on the raised platform in a school or community hall, in the secretive recesses of a nature-fringed shrine, among the push-buttons of the modern European stage or its equivalents in Africa – those elegant monstrosities raised to enshrine the spirit of misconceived prestigiousness. It is necessary always to look for the essence of the play among these roofs and spaces, not confine it to the printed text as an autonomous entity.

[...]

Our first example, *Song of a Goat*, a play by J. P. Clark, has the advantage, for this exercise, of fitting into the neat category of tragedy in the European definition. It was first performed in Europe at the 1965 Commonwealth Festival of the Arts in London; its reception was not of the best, and for very good reasons. First, the production was weak and amateurish. An inexperienced group playing on a London stage for the first time in their lives found that they could not match the emotions of the play with the technical demands of the stage and auditorium. The staging of the play was not particularly sensitive, in addition to which there were the usual unscripted happenings which seem to plague amateur productions everywhere. A rather lively goat, another practical mistake, tended to punctuate passages of intended solemnity with bleats from one end and something else from the other. The text itself (we may as well get over the critical carps at once), written in verse, betrays a self-conscious straining for poetic effect, leading to inflated phrasing and clotted passages. For a company which was not wholly at home in the English language, the difficulties were insurmountable. In an English audience it created resistance, even hostility.

[...]

I have touched on some of the technical reasons why, unlike some African audiences before whom this play has since been staged, the European audience found itself estranged from the tragic statement. One other reason was voiced by the newspaper critics; this had nothing to do with the fortuitous events of stage presentation but rather chose to limit, in far more general terms, what areas of human unhappiness may contain the tragic potential. It underlined yet another aspect of the essential divergences of the European cast of mind from the African: that, on the one hand, which sees the causes of human anguish as viable only within strictly temporal capsules, and the other whose tragic understanding transcends the causes of individual disjunction and recognises them as reflections of a far greater disharmony in the communal psyche. The objection was this sexual impotence [of the protagonist] was a curable condition in modern medicine (or psychiatry). In addition, child adoption provided one remedy, among others, for sterility; therefore sexual impotence or sterility were outside the range of tragic dimensions for a European audience.

There was something familiar in that plaint. I had heard it some years earlier after a London production of Ibsen's *Ghosts*. Syphilis, asserted a critic or two, was no longer an incurable disease. Ibsen's play had consequently lost any tragic rationale it might have had in the mercury days of venereal science.

[...]

The socio-political question of the viability of a tragic view in a contemporary world has preoccupied schools of social vision since the preliminary clashes of the empirical stance against metaphysical (religious) orthodoxies. This has become crystallised in, I suggest, two main attitudes. One, represented by the Marxist view of man and history, denounces the insidious enervation of social will by the tragic afflatus. The other is the rear-guard action of crumbling defences. It speculates that there has been a decline in tragic understanding (i.e. the referential basis from which man is convincingly projected in confrontation with forces beyond his remedial understanding). From this basis of suspicion and a related awareness that this represents a quite unnecessary loss in creative territory, an almost comprehensive list of major twentieth century dramatists have felt compelled, at one time or the other, to rifle and re-present [sic] Greek tragedy as containing statements of relevance even to post-Marxian times.

[...]

George Steiner observes, in his diagnosis of the decline in tragic grandeur of the European dramatic vision, a relatedness between this decline and that of the 'organic world view and of its attendant context of mythological, symbolic and ritual reference.' The implication of this, a strange one to the African world-view, is that, to expand Steiner's own metaphor, the world in which lightning was a cornice in the cosmic architecture of man collapsed at that moment when Benjamin Franklin tapped its power with a kite. The assimilative wisdom of African metaphysics recognises no difference in essence between the mere means of tapping the power of lightning, whether it is by ritual sacrifice, through the purgative will of the community unleashing its justice on the criminal, or through the agency of Franklin's revolutionary gadget. What George Steiner effectively summarises is at some stage of intellectual hypothesis, at some phase of scientific exploration, at each supposition by European man about the possible nature of things, that architectonic unity which is the basis of man's regulating consciousness (of which the most personalised expression is his art) suffers the same fate of redundancy as the assumptions and theories themselves. For cultures which pay more than lip-service to the protean complexity of the universe of which man is himself a reflection, this European habit of world re-definition appears both wasteful and truth-defeating.

We must return to the stage manifestation, to the dramatic expression which confronts its audience with such human revelations as breed an awareness of a play of forces which contradict a technologically remediable world, this being the most easily isolated challenge of the tragic intrusion. It becomes necessary to examine the nature of the concrete event which, when successfully mirrored, dislodges the technological rationale with which the healthy, well-adjusted audience is conditioned to ward off penetration of the 'pathetic fallacy'.

And the most significant discovery, or more accurately, recognition is that we encounter in such plays a complete, hermetic universe of forces or being. This is the most fundamental attribute of all true tragedy, no matter where geographically placed. In *Lear* for instance, the world of the court, the world of Old Man Frost in the disordered community of wind and heather is rounded and entire. The relationship of seemingly disparate entities such as Court and Nature is established through character transition – Lear, Kent, Edgar and Clown, out from one and into the other environment and back again; then the progressively vixenish daughters in near physical transformation. Such is the spatial architecture of the play that the specialised world of cronies, villains, principles of inheritance and courtly protocol becomes accessible to and paralleled by whatever world the audience inhabits, with its own laws, norms and values. The universe of *Hamlet* is wrapped in a similar envelope; so are the haunting habitations of John Synge, Gay, Lorca, even Wedekind at his most uncompromising interiority. Encapsulation of these exclusivist spheres of existence within which all action is unravelled appears to be the first prerequisite of all profound drama, and tragedy most specifically. Its internal cogency makes it impervious to the accident of place and time.

[...]

The death of an individual is not seen as an isolated incident in the life of one man, nor is individual fertility separable from the regenerative promise of earth and sea. The sickness of one individual is a sign of, or may portend the sickness of, the world around him. Something has occurred to disrupt the natural rhythms and the cosmic balances of the total community.

Major issues raised: aesthetic questions to ask when reading theatre from around the world

What is the purpose of theatre?

Aristotle is frequently understood to privilege the moral education theatre can provide over its entertainment value. The contrast between education and entertainment or between education and artistic expression seems to have shaped a good deal of the discussion of the purpose of the theatre in the West. The next chapter examines the potential political purposes of the theatre. Discussions of the beauty of theatre often turn into discussions of how one might best appreciate theatre, which is, in turn, closely related to the idea that theatre should have some sort of an effect on its audience. It is not unusual, then, to find discussions of the purpose of theatre mixed in with discussions of aesthetics. In short, to know if theatre is "good" or "correct," it is useful to know what the theatre is supposed to be accomplishing. For example, theatre designed to shock might purposefully not contain crafted poetic phrases, an elaborate, balanced set, or the other aspects associated with Western classical ideas of theatrical beauty, and, while that doesn't stop us from making our own judgments about the degree to which we "like" such theatre, an educated critique of this theatre needs to contain an understanding of what the theatre set out to do.

For Zeami, the question of aesthetics and the question of the purpose of theatre seem to be almost identical. The theatre presents beauty and the audience must learn to appreciate this beauty. Zeami does not discuss the potential ramifications of this learning to appreciate beauty. The idea is that the beautiful and the good are nearly, if not entirely, interchangeable. Zeami is not as directly moralistic as Aristotle – he does not talk about virtue as extensively, but he does discuss beauty elevating the human spirit. Zeami's idea of beauty is quite specific, so it would be logical to ask whether the elevation of spirit achieved by such beauty is likewise specific.

The idea that beauty can be found in understatement is a Buddhist principle, but Japanese Buddhism contains many, many distinct sects, some of which made rather grandiose statues and images. The idea of a simplicity of spirit – an emptying out of desires – is common to most sects of Buddhism, and thus the idea of the "good" might be more consistent; unless, of course, one considers that Japan is also shaped by Shinto and Confucian beliefs. Similarly, Zeami's school of nō theatre was one of many – Japanese culture had variations in technique, but the focus remained on these technical manifestations of beauty. All this being said, Zeami insists on his theatre having grace 幽玄 (yūgen). This is a cornerstone of Japanese aesthetics more broadly, but, as Rimer points out in his translation notes (Zeami, 1984), this word comes from Chinese philosophical texts where it also means mysterious. So, Zeami's theatre works in a technical way to create a specific idea of beauty which, in turn, will create a specific good in society in a mysterious way.

The use of the word "technical" raises a second issue with "beauty" as the primary purpose of theatre. As any connoisseur – be it of opera, of nō, of wine – will tell you, knowledge of the subject enhances the experience of it. Zeami's beauty elevated the audience, but also expected the audience to be sufficiently able to grasp the basic precepts – to recognize beauty when they saw it. Bunraku – a puppet theatre – appealed to the popular masses in a way nō did not (nō theatre was often performed for the upper echelons of society). The beauty of nō theatre elevates society, but society must be sufficiently elevated to appreciate the beauty of nō theatre. Indeed, a literal translation of "nō" suggests a skills-based theatre – a theatre of craft.

This is a notion of aesthetics as judgment, as discernment: it is possible that elevation by Zeami's theatre requires such discernment. This notion stands in stark contrast to Soyinka's idea of a spiritual aesthetics. Soyinka's notion of theatre is that, at its best, it creates a metaphysical situation in which the actors and the audience participate. If nō theatre is metaphorically a fine wine to be sipped, discussed, and evaluated from a position of education, then Soyinka's theatre is ... simply different. Its purpose is different and so the methods used to evaluate it must be different. Soyinka focuses on form rather than on effect (see form vs content debates below).

Whereas nō theatre tends to evoke one moment, one mood at a time, Soyinka's aesthetic focuses on a journey. His theatre is transitional and in motion, and the audience is encouraged to take this journey along with the production. Soyinka's aesthetic suggests that we might critique theatre for being too static, for a lack of growth of the characters. This is precisely the opposite of the aesthetic of Zeami's nō, which would consider growth and change of characters as cluttering an otherwise clear expression.

Whereas Soyinka focuses on a specific sort of spiritual experience, Bharata explains theatre in terms of the variety of experiences it can offer to the audience. Like Zeami's idea of beauty, these experiences in some way elevate those watching the theatre, but, unlike Zeami who equates a single notion of beauty with a presumably singular notion of the good, or Soyinka who insists upon a singular view of the metaphysical condition of humanity, Bharata's range of *rasa* is wider – there are many possible experiences, and mixing and matching these creates the richness of theatre.

So, when sitting down to watch a performance, what questions should one ask? Is the performance designed to create a diversity of experience or a singular experience? Is the performance focused on the beautiful and the good, on the journey to reach the beautiful and good, or on something else entirely? Is it about what you see, what you feel, or what you experience? To understand aesthetics is to understand what the theatre in question has set out to do, and, as the other anthologized pieces in this book will display, there is a wide range of theatrical purposes, and even theatres with similar purposes will develop their own particular styles.

Structure vs content

Aesthetics is the study of beauty, but some aesthetic theories insist on moving beyond the physical characteristics and the structure into the content of theatre. Is it the form of theatre that makes it beautiful or the ideas that lend beauty to the form? Perhaps it is a combination of form and content?

Zeami refers to this conflict in terms of substance and function. He claims that all the mechanical aspects of nō – all the carefully designed and executed hand-gestures, all the physical training, and all the beautiful costumes – are part of the "function" which he refers to as the smell of the flower. The substance – the flower itself – is the spirit behind this function. What makes nō beautiful – subject to the appreciation of the connoisseurs of the art – is the substance, which is specifically not grasped through the eyes, but, instead, through the spirit.

This is odd, given that nō is a highly structured, formal mode of theatre. Zeami talks about training actors from childhood onward. He goes on the say that the function – the physical representation – will only display a portion of what is going on inside the mind of the performer. It is this moderation of raw substance that Zeami praises. The external form should be an understatement of the true substance behind the form. This, again, is a suggestion that Zeami's theatre is for connoisseurs, for an elite audience who can figure out what is left unsaid.

Soyinka's diatribe against the formal paradigm shifts in Western theatre could be read as his dismissal of form in favor of spiritual content. Certainly, Soyinka's work moves through a variety of different forms. At times, as with *Madmen and Specialists* (1970), Soyinka writes in a realistic style. *A Dance of the Forest* (1960), on the other hand, might be classified as surrealism inasmuch as animals, spirits, gods, and plants speak. Characters are transported around the stage as if in a dream. *Trials of Brother Jero* (1959) borders on slapstick comedy at moments. Despite this diversity in forms and styles, Soyinka remains committed to his aesthetic statements. There may be many appropriate forms for expressing the same spiritual journey.

This diversity of forms stands in marked contrast to the opening section of Bharata's work, which specifies down to precise measurements exactly what a theatre should look like. On the other hand, within the somewhat rigid boundary of form, Bharata insists his theatre can express a variety of contents.

After ascertaining the purpose of the theatrical event, the next step is to consider what part of the production one is looking at to fulfill this purpose. Is it the form, the content, or some combination of the two?

Unity and balance

The above questions suggest dividing theatre up into a number of distinct segments. Bharata, Aristotle, and Zeami, which is to say classical aesthetic theorists, all discuss their theatres as unified, with all parts working together to create a whole. It is interesting to consider which ideas remain stable from classical aesthetics to the present, and which ideas emerge across a variety of different cultural ideas of aesthetics. Some notion of unity transcends cultural and temporal boundaries. Soyinka's theatre creates a single metaphysical effect, despite the diversity of elements he might include. Even postmodern bricolage, a collection of many disparate elements, creates a sort of unity. While the idea of unity-as-beauty may be shared, the constituent parts of this unity are quite different in different settings.

With the exception of Aristotle, unity does not imply homogeneity. Aristotle insists on a unity of time, place, and action (although the nature of these unities becomes more static after the French Neoclassicists revive interest in Aristotle in the eighteenth century). His theatre takes similar pieces and combines them for a single effect. While Zeami's nō theatre presents a single experience – one moment, one mood – it does so by finding a unity of difference. Zeami specifically praises the ability to see difference and to find ways of making this difference fit into the pattern. For Zeami, the contrasts serve to even out a character. If moderation is good and extremes bad, one way of finding the center is by combining disparate elements from the poles.

Bharata's work combines flavors, but might be considered pluralism rather than unity. In other words, all the elements work together, but they remain separate from one another. Each taste can be discerned, and they are better for the combination.

Soyinka insists on the unity of the spiritual world that forms the basis for the metaphysics of his plays, and upon the unity of the effect of his plays, but places no special emphasis on the unity of elements within the plays. The idea of completeness might usefully be substituted for the idea of unity within Soyinka's work. His plays seek to display both physical and metaphysical realms – to give the entirety of a journey. This journey may not be unified, but it should have some sort of completion, even if that completion is failure.

This discussion reminds us that we have to consider the ways in which elements of a production fit together as an aesthetic question, but that one notion of "unity" cannot be applied across different aesthetic systems.

Notes

1 www.youtube.com/watch?v=DIB0N6ZkoGI
2 www.youtube.com/watch?v=Fp67HEavPwc
3 For example, www.youtube.com/watch?v=Lo0fKwOWiN8

Chapter 3

Theatre and politics

Right through rehearsals we try to evolve a method whereby the petty-bourgeois alienation of the actor can be hammered at to help him acquire a proletariat standpoint. [...] The actor's art is thus made to relate closely to the world where it grows, and his artifices, devices, tricks of the trade, can no longer be crowned with a halo of absolute theories – things like Poor Theatre, Total Theatre, Physical Theatre, Transcendental Theatre, Therapeutic Theatre, and other such absolutist absurdities [...] theatre is part of a social process, there can no more be one immutable Theory of theatrical production, than there can be one true religion, or one true God, or one true Aryan race

Utpal Dutt, *Towards a Revolutionary Theatre*

Case Study: Badal Sircar's 1973 production of *Spartacus*

All of the information in the case study that follows is taken from Badal Sircar's own writing about his work. This chapter explores the ways that theatre can be political, and this is the question posed by the case of *Spartacus*. What is it about the content, form, or style of this production that audiences and performers alike would consider to be political?

While economic and social inequities can be found in every country, India's caste system formalized these inequities along hereditary and ethnic lines. For more than sixty years, India has worked to dismantle the damage done by the caste system and to provide opportunities for the formerly disadvantaged castes. This has proved a slow process and the old caste boundaries are still apparent in Indian society. India has no national language: more than one hundred different languages are spoken within India's borders. Each language represents a cultural identity. In the cities, these languages and cultures interact with each other, sometimes succumbing to pressures of larger languages. In rural areas, where exposure to multiple cultures and access to education are more limited, differences between languages and among cultures can be quite pronounced. India gained independence from Britain in 1947, but remnants of British culture are easily found throughout the country. India is a country of diversity, and this diversity is sometimes sharply divided and sometimes hybridized into new forms. Broadly speaking, folk performance and theatre in India tends to construct simple narrative through dance and music with limited spoken content, but the balance of these elements, their styles, and balance between ritual and theatre shift from form to form. A diverse set of cultures will, of course, have a diverse set of theatres.

It is to this society that Badal Sircar (1925–2011) directs his Third Theatre. As is true with many of the writers in this volume, the social problems in India when Sircar wrote were pronounced and immediate: with poverty, a newly forming government, and a state approved caste system clearly visible, it makes sense that Sircar insists that his writing is not theoretical. He explains his ideas about theatre through examples taken from his theatrical practice. Unlike Osofisan, who asks for intellectual discussion, Sircar's theatre and his theory suggest active intervention.

Sircar's Third Theatre blends traditional rural theatrical practices with contemporary urban practices. Both the rural and urban practices are, themselves, already hybridized, as one would expect in a country with the cultural diversity of India. Nonetheless, Sircar sees a stark line between urban and rural. He argues that effective theatre must reach the masses – that it must be accessible. To this end, he taps into the open-air folk dances and music common in rural theatre. He also argues that traditional folk theatre, while beautiful and interesting, is ill-equipped to deal with the social problems facing society. He thus imports the thematic concerns of urban theatre into the vibrant structures of traditional performance

Many of Badal Sircar's plays were designed to be performed in Anganmancha (roughly translated as "Space Theatre.") This theatre was really just an empty 850 square foot room with only enough space to put in 75 spectators. The audience seats that Sircar brought into the room could be rearranged into any pattern he saw fit, and his productions often shifted the audience around. Sircar commented that he didn't want the audience sitting in chairs, which he claimed would "separate" them from performers. Instead he had wide backless benches that he referred to as "levels." These benches were never more than three rows deep and some were wide enough that an actor could walk along the back if audience members were sitting. Rather than using theatrical lighting, Sircar employed traditional light bulbs. To stop echoes in the empty space, Sircar hung heavy curtains around all the walls.

Spartacus was the first production specifically written for this space and it premiered in January 1973. *Spartacus* is the story of a slave revolt in the first century BCE in Rome. Spartacus was a gladiator – a slave forced to fight for the amusement of Romans. The revolution was unsuccessful and Spartacus' army was defeated, but, as Sircar notes, the sentiments that this war stirred up never faded in Rome and the slaves continued to find ways to rebel.

Sircar's production was almost entirely physical, with musical accompaniment. In other words, the actors did not speak very often – they conveyed the story through action. The music was produced entirely by singing actors (there were no instruments). Despite not having any words, Sircar notes that the plot of the play was relatively complex. There were a number of different characters, each taking a series of actions. Sircar notes that the actors had to work extremely hard due to the physical nature of the piece – he specifically, proudly notes that they sweated a great deal.

The show eventually transferred to a public park. After the show – with a running time of 80 minutes in the park and 110 minutes in the theatre – Sircar invited audience feedback. The audience uniformly said that they had "felt the direct impact" of the play. Sircar also notes that the rough pebbles on the ground of the park caused several of the actors to bleed during the performance.

So, this production tells a story about Roman slaves to an Indian audience in a small, open theatre. The play was more active than verbal, involving the actors' blood and sweat more than their words. The spectators were seated in small groups throughout the playing space. In the park the audience consisted of whoever happened to be passing by (and those who had intentionally come, presumably, although Sircar does not mention this). At this production, the audience sat on the ground rather than on benches. Sircar specifically states that he finds the mode of theatre in India prior to this production to be on the wrong side of the violent class struggle: he specifically criticizes the overly simplistic, melodramatic nature of the theatre popular in rural areas. He was happy with the revolutionary impact of this new theatre.

The question posed by this chapter is "why?" What is revolutionary about this particular production? Is it the plot of the production? The fact that the plot was complex? The fact that the audience didn't sit in a traditional format? The fact that the play was active and movement-based? The fact that the play used few words? The fact that the actors literally bled? The fact that there were not elaborate lights? The fact that the audience was encouraged to discuss the play afterwards?

If any of those factors, or some combination of those factors, made this theatre political, were these factors distinct to the situation in India in 1973 (perhaps the large numbers of under/uneducated rural poor moving into cities during this period)? Would other social and political situations require radically different theatrical approaches? Are there certain things revolutionary theatre should do? Are there certain things theatre can't do if it wants to be revolutionary? Are there multiple types of revolutionary theatre or have various places around the world come up with wholly different theatres of revolution? For that matter, how do we gauge the political effect of revolutionary theatre? At the broadest level, each of the theorists below, and, indeed, most of the theorists presented in this volume, are intent on making both political and artistic statements. This chapter explores the techniques they use to do this.

What is the political?

The commonplace definition of the political is too narrow to encompass the projects of world theatre.

Some theatre (e.g. South African protest theatre) is directly, explicitly designed to speak to government policy. This theatre frequently directly stages social problems and often makes a very clear case for solutions. In South Africa, under apartheid, the government prevented the black population from advancing economically in a variety of ways, like limiting the extent to which black people could leave their own townships. A typical South African protest piece might stage the struggle of a black man to find work under this confining system, and then it would have one of the characters directly articulate the fact that the government was keeping this man from finding a job.

In regions where such theatre exists, its political intentions are abundantly clear. When theorists from around the world write about political theatre, they frequently focus on types of theatre that interact with the political world in less direct ways. The term "ideological" is useful when considering this mode of theatre. Ideology refers to all of the patterns of thought, all of the practices, all of the laws, and all of the interactions that work to keep all societies running smoothly. Louis Althusser's definitions of ideology suggest that there is nothing that is not subject to ideology. Althusser's definitions grow out of the work of Karl Marx, who argued that all parts of a given society are built to maintain the current class system. While Marx was German, his philosophy was extensively discussed by artists and political figures in Africa, India, the Caribbean, and China (Marx's work also shows up in Japan and the Middle East, but not to the degree that it is present in the other locations). It is challenging to find a theorist of political theatre anywhere in the world (post-1900) that does not mention Marx. Each region developed its own unique version of Marxism, but each version shares some basic principles. The idea of an omnipresent ideology that shapes all aspects of society is one such shared idea.

Ideology is not just something that is spoken from a pulpit or an Oval Office; even acts that appear trivial can actually serve the state. Ideology is the complete set of social norms in which we are being trained on a daily basis. Ideology works to reinforce all the social, political, and economic behaviors we take for granted. These behaviors range from our consumption of various products, to our voting patterns (and indeed the idea of voting itself), to what types of clothing we wear (and the fact that we wear clothing), to what range of political views we might hold. In minute ways, we are being trained in everyday life – for example, trips to the grocery store, commercials on television, standing in lines, songs on the radio – to value specific types of behavior and thought. In Althusser's definition of ideology, these day-to-day occurrences are far more effective at keeping society under control than armed soldiers or other more repressive methods.

Ideology is neither a good nor a bad thing. It is always a limitation, but society can only function if we have certain agreed upon limitations. This chapter's discussion of the political impact of theatrical structures, then, considers not only overtly political moments like the passing of a law, but also, and more importantly, the ideological critique that theatre can level. Radical theatre can make us aware of the ideological conditions under which we live.

One of the many substantially different ideas of the ideological structure of the world comes from the Yorùbá people in Nigeria, and this concept is part of a cultural tradition that predates Marx (although it has been connected with Marxism in Yorùbá philosophy repeatedly). Yorùbá philosophers discuss a concept of ìfọgbọ́ntáayése,which suggests that all knowledge is working together for the pragmatic good of society. Like ideology, this concept is all-encompassing – there is no outside. On the other hand, while ideology is not inherently positive or negative, ìfọgbọ́ntáayése suggests a positive, if homogenous, change through greater knowledge. If knowledge is working to better society, then theatre's political resistance might take a more educational form in this case. While ideology remains the best English term for a range of concepts dealing with the ways in which social structures are related to politics, the discussion below explores the differences in conceptions of what is problematic in / about ideology and how theatre might address these problems. Some theatre might resist certain policies, some might resist certain aspects of an ideology, and some might resist the homogeneity implied by *any* ideology.

This diversity of modes of resistance is important to remember, given the diversity of political situations, ideologies, ideas about politics, and theories of ideology in the world. The Yorùbá people are one of over 250 different groups in Nigeria, and many of these 250 groups have their own philosophies of the nature of politics, political action, and ideology. The concepts of ìfọgbọ́ntáayéṣe and ideology are, themselves, by definition ideological. The Yorùbá people have held a good deal of power in Nigeria since 1960, and, indeed, many leaders – both good and bad – have considered themselves to be Marxists. Thinking about politics in terms of ideology is thinking about politics in a certain way – a way that groups in power think about politics. If the idea that ideology shapes all aspects of our lives in order to keep the current social system strong is true, then it logically follows that the *idea of ideology* – the idea supported by powerful groups – is, itself, part of this power structure. Thinking about politics in terms of ideology is reinforcing some part of ideology. This sort of logical trap – the idea that any system could be part of an ideology – explains some of the extreme, radical efforts of political theatre to violate theatrical conventions: any vestiges of the old system might carry the old ideology with them.

Should revolutionary theatre directly interact with politics in the manner of South African protest theatre? Should it attempt to draw attention to ideology in order to change it? Should it attempt to change the way we think about what is political? Different theorists and practitioners from around the world have come up with different answers to these questions.

What is structure?

The above questions deal with what revolutionary theatre should do. This section deals with how theorists from around the world design their theatrical practices to meet these goals. As with ideology, which is a major concept that many theorists employ, the concept of structure is an almost inevitable part of theorizations of political theatre around the world. The basic, repeated sentiment is that the content of political theatre is only a portion of this theatre's political force. While discussions of theatrical structure are incredibly common in the theoretical works of theatre practitioners around the world, the secondary criticism written by Western academics often focuses more on content than on structure. A focus on content certainly yields interesting results, but given that structure is something that the writers, producers, theorists, and performers around the world focus on, the relative absence of structural considerations in secondary criticism is striking. The rest of the political aspect of theatre comes from its structure: the way theatre is put together reflects the ideology of the society that creates it, and therefore putting theatre together in new ways can reflect the possibility of new ideologies.

When speaking in the literary and theatrical world, structure is deceptively easy to define. Structure refers to the basic components without which a given type of theatre or performance could not exist. Structure includes things like the Aristotelian elements of tragedy, with emphasis on plot and character which are found in the script itself. Theatrical and performance structures include an audience. Structure includes basic mechanisms of representation: what do you see on stage and how is what you see related to plot, character, or reality? Structure can also refer to the ordering of scenes and the relationship among these scenes. Structure can refer to the number of different "movements" a piece of theatre has: some nights at the theatre include acrobatics, dance, and several short plays, for instance.

The problem with this definition of structure, however, is that it makes it very difficult to determine what is important in a given piece: there are so many structural elements that have to go into each production. In Western theatre we can determine what structures are worthy of comment through the application of Aristotelian theory (or resistance to this theory). Aristotle gives us a list of what makes good theatre. We can determine where the structures of a given theatrical event differ from Aristotle and then we can analyze these differences to figure out what structural interventions the theatre is making. If we have a "normal" structure and structure is ideologically meaningful, then changing this normal structure must have meaning. This concept works acceptably when dealing with Western theatre, because the West is used to thinking of theatre in Aristotelian terms (even when it sharply resists these terms). When moving into the rest of the world, there are often sharply competing modes of "normal" theatre – there is not one "normal" Asian theatre or even Chinese theatre. Without an examination of the theories from various regions of the world, it can be difficult to determine which structures of a play are most open to analysis in each context.

In what follows, each of the theatre theorists in question recognizes this problem and discusses some aspects of "normal" theatre and life in their respective countries or regions and then discusses how the structures of their theatre work against this "normal" theatre. Of course, these theorists are being selective – they are making an argument about what they see as normative in their contexts. Remember, ideology is the political force that structures society – and theatre – in certain ways. The repeated idea below is that revolutionary theatre must change the normal structure of theatre so that it can change the normal structure of society, but what counts as "normal" and what gets changed is radically different in each setting. Also, remember that, while this statement about normal structures and revolutionary theatre is *generally* found in theatre theory around the world, this is not the only way to think about political theatre – and the theorists below each depart from this general model in one way or another.

Western structure and politics

At varying periods, the theatres of the world have each engaged directly with political issues. At times this engagement took the form of parody or satire; at other times, realistic protest theatre restaged the conflicts of the day. Modern and contemporary Western theatre theorists have discussed the ways in which the actual structures and formal elements of traditionally-staged theatre reinforce social conditions. In this argument, things like the relationship of the audience to the stage, the linear structures of traditional plots, and the "realistic" portrayal of character all communicate a certain attitude toward individuality, independent thought, and human agency (the ability of individual humans to make choices and take actions that impact the world). By this line of reasoning, if you sit quietly in the audience and observe what is happening on the stage, you will, similarly, sit quietly and observe the political situation: you will not intervene in either. In most basic terms, in order to be political, many theorists in the West have argued that theatre must violate theatrical conventions – a radical theatre for a radical politics.

In the West, Bertolt Brecht and Antonin Artaud have argued for radical shifts in theatrical structures which would lead to equally radical shifts in the audience's experiences of theatre and ultimately of life. Brecht argues for an intellectual and politically-charged, non-realistic "epic" theatre. Artaud articulates the parameters of a "Theatre of Cruelty" that communicates experience directly to the audience without intermediary forces. If an audience can be made to think (Brecht) or to have deep, real experiences (Artaud) in the theatre, then the theatre becomes a challenge to the social structures that are reinforced by traditional staging. This is a structuralist argument – all structures have meaning and therefore changing the structure is also meaningful. "Old" structures are associated with the way things are. Avant-garde or "new" structures attempt to change how things are or to reflect the changes that are taking place.

For example, Bertolt Brecht is very direct in his desire to create immediate, tangible political change, and he starts by looking at what structures of theatre must be altered to fit with alterations in society. In *On Form and Subject Matter*, Brecht explains that he is not creating a set formal aspect for all performance, but allowing for the necessities of the subject matter to dictate form:

> [t]he proper way to explore humanity's new mutual relationships is via the exploration of the new subject-matter ... simply to comprehend the new areas of subject-matter imposes a new dramatic and theatrical form ... petroleum resists the five act form.
> (Brecht 1964, p. 29)

Brecht moves fluidly from talking about theatre to talking about petroleum. He believes that social structures and theatrical structures are linked. New moments in society necessitate formal changes in theatre: to say that petroleum resists the five-act form is to say that shifts in social structures require shifts in theatrical structures. Brechtian theatre, while precise, is able to alter itself to account for these new conditions in ways that a traditionally structured five-act realistic drama cannot.

In "The Modern Theatre is the Epic Theatre," Brecht explains that this "new subject-matter," the condition of modern life, calls for a "radical *separation of* elements" (Brecht 1964, p. 69). Theatrical structures no longer work together to create an illusion or representation of a location or action: Brecht suggests that "illusion is sacrificed to free discussion," but the elements of illusion, the individual theatrical pieces such as lights, props, make-up, etc., still exist on the Brechtian stage. He removes them from their traditional context, however, and makes the familiar strange in order to promote discussion. He might have actors carry on their own lighting sources, for instance, or have actors move slowly through a series of naturalistic poses. An actor making the theatricality of theatre visible to the audience is a means of violating convention for Brecht – it is a rupture of theatrical structure and, potentially, of ideology.

This is not to say that the audience is detached from the performance, merely that the point of the performance is not to create a shared experience for actor and audience: "[T]he spectator, instead of being enabled to have an experience, is forced as it were to cast his vote" (Brecht 1964 p. 39). For Brecht, all this is an attempt to bring drama back to its "social function." This function is recognition of current situations: "To discuss the present form of our society, or even of one of its least important parts, would lead inevitably and at once to an outright threat to our society's form as such" (Brecht 1964 p. 41). Epic drama is politically resistant drama, and this resistance does require the intervention of the spectator, however alienated.

While Brecht is only one example of a Western theorist who focuses on theatrical structures in order to make political change, his work exhibits a common understanding of the relationship between theatrical structure and ideology. Traditional theatrical structures reinforce traditional political ideologies.

World structure and politics

Theatre theorists from around the world have expressed similar sentiments about theatrical structure and ideology, for instance:

> The dramatic heritage available to us has simply proved inadequate. And it is not only that the machinery provided by the old society for dealing with chaos has lost its capacity for total effect, it is also that the very metaphysical raison d'etre of that machinery has been eroded with the advent of a new sociopolitical philosophy.
>
> (Osofisan, 1982, p. 72)

In this moment, Femi Osofisan's rallying cry for Nigerian theatre echoes similar sentiments expressed by Brecht and other Western theorists: he is lamenting that neither traditional Nigerian theatre nor contemporary European theatre can cope with the problems of the contemporary Nigerian state. Society has changed and so theatre must change to be relevant. At the same time, a changing theatre may change society. These changes take place at a structural level.

In parts of the world that were subjected to colonialism or semi-colonialism, the question of theatrical structure becomes even more political. Each of these cultures had its own theatre and/or performance traditions with their own distinctive structures. Before, during, and after colonization, these cultures also had access to Western theatrical structures. Theatre theorists in these cultures were left with the difficult task of figuring out which of the range of theatrical structures corresponded to their political projects: to their desire to create a postcolonial or anti-colonial theatre, and to create theatres that spoke to local political concerns. While Brecht and Artaud were responding to a single system, world theatre theorists are generally responding to at least two contrasting systems. In other words, Brecht and Artaud can be revolutionary by pointing to a prior moment in European theatre and distinguishing themselves from it. World theatre theorists had to establish their relationships with their own theatrical pasts, the European theatrical past, and potentially the European theatrical present. Both Brecht and Artaud utilized formal elements and techniques from other theatres – specifically Asian theatres – and thus their alteration of theatrical structure is, to some extent, hybrid. For modern theatre theorists in formerly colonized locations, blending and hybridity is itself a powerful political statement. If a group of people conquers a country and oppresses its people while simultaneously offering access to some of the amenities of the modern world then, as numerous postcolonial critics have pointed out, the oppressed people will often experience contrasting ambivalent desires to mimic and destroy their oppressors. Theatre is a potent force of cultural transmission – Europe exported its theatre along its colonial trade-routes. Part of colonialism's success depended on convincing the colonized populations that European culture was valuable, and theatre was a perfect tool for this. To resist European theatre was to resist colonization: to adopt a portion of European theatre was to imitate some aspects of the colonial power. In broad terms, Western structures carry with them Western ideas.

Aside from colonial issues, which will emerge more fully later in this book, world theatre must also deal with the relationship of its theatrical structures to the material conditions of life in various countries. Life in India is not the same as life in China and is different again from life in the U.S. If theatre is to have meaningful political impact, it must, in some fashion, relate to the specific lives in question. While Western theories of structuralism (particularly in structuralist anthropology) tend to seek universal structures, parts of the rest of the world localize even their most hybrid and intercultural structural experiments. Both Brecht and Artaud claim to be writing about *theatre* in a universal sense, and don't insist upon a specific historical contextualization of their work. The theories in this chapter, on the other hand, tend to focus on creating theatres for specific sets of political situations, while still exploring more general notions of what constitutes theatre. This chapter explores the ways that world theatre theorists have experimented with local structures of plot, character, audience relationships, and acting techniques to generate political results.

The three anthologized pieces that follow are written by Femi Osofisan, from Nigeria; Utpal Dutt, from India; and Saadallah Wannous, from Syria. Their theatrical practices and political concerns vary widely. Osofisan's theatre is aimed at the educated classes and experiments with levels of audience involvement; Dutt's work speaks passionately of (and sometimes to) the working class and adopts many characteristics of realism; Wannous' theatre takes a variety of forms and shifts constantly to meet the needs of communication of any given audience at a particular moment. Despite this variation, each theorist discusses the ideological impact of theatrical structures in terms of audience, realism, and cultural specificity / traditional cultural forms.

In exploring these areas of theoretical tension, the discussion that follows makes reference to a number of other theorists and practitioners, some of whose work is contained in this book. Even this broader range cannot account for all possible structural modes of political resistance. There are many societies in the world and these societies continue to change. This change allows for an ever-shifting set of innovative theatrical possibilities. In this chapter, it is important to recognize the common, shared assumptions about structure and the shared structures of political theatre around the world *and* to recognize the different arguments made about these structures in different locations.

Osofisan's theory of "surreptitious insurrection"

While Wole Soyinka remains the most well-known Nigerian playwright, many Nigerian critics locate his theatrical work in a prior generation that spans from the late colonial era (1950s) to the Biafra War (1967). This generation of writers includes Ola Rotimi, J.P. Clark-Bekederemo, and Amos Tutuola. This is a generation of hope and exploration that is perhaps characteristic of a nation on the cusp of independence. With the Biafra War clearly marking the failings of the First Republic of Nigeria a short seven years after its inception, a new generation of playwrights emerged, most notably Femi Osofisan, Wole Oguntokun, Kole Omotosho, and Bode Sowande. It is significant to note that, with the exception of Zulu Sofola and Tess Onwueme, all of the major figures in the first and second generation of Nigerian playwrights are of Yorùbá heritage (and male, for that matter). Power in the First Nigerian Republic was concentrated in the heavily Islamic, Hausa-controlled northern sections of the country. The Biafran War was an attempt by the Igbo people of the East to declare independence. Yorùbá politicians, from the West, have held various positions of power in multiple later iterations of Nigeria, notably Olusegun Obasanjo who was both a military ruler in the 1970s and a democratically elected president from 1999 to 2007. However, in what remains a deeply divided populace, the North has held power more consistently than any of the groups in the other sections of the country. The continual jockeying for power after independence led to a number of military dictatorships (although the precise count is, itself, a point of political contention), and it is to these dictatorships that Osofisan's development of a new poetics responds. The fact that so many of these leaders were hostile both to social change and to Yorùbá political activity shapes the ways in which Osofisan responds: he is creating a theatre that can speak to the ever-changing political situation in Nigeria.

"Surreptitious Insurrection" provides a theatrical concept that allows us to consider the structural interventions theatre might make in the political world. Aside from political allegory, the idea of performance, audience, tragedy, and theatre in general carry a context-specific political charge. Osofisan magnifies this political effect through heightening and then violating the theatrical spectacle: the increased theatricality acts as a mask for the political interventions Osofisan's plays make so that the audience can see things that the censors cannot. The production Osofisan describes in the anthologized material draws toward a conclusion, but stops before completion. The actors then ask the audience what the appropriate conclusion is. In this way, Osofisan can avoid censorship and engage the audience without losing the vibrancy of the initial story. The audience reaches the conclusion, and, more importantly for Osofisan, debates and considers the conclusion. It is a central tenet for Osofisan that discussion of current social problems is an important step in finding a solution for these problems. Depriving the audience of a ready-made conclusion leads to such discussion, but only if the audience is engaged with the theatricality of the initial story.

Extract 3.1 Selections from "'The revolution as Muse': Drama as surreptitious insurrection in a post-colonial, military state"
Femi Osofisan

> . . . the only safe place I've ever known is at the centre of a story, as its teller.
>
> (Athol Fugard)

> We might say then . . . that Osofisan's play is, ultimately, a celebration of the Revolution as Muse.
>
> (Abiola Irele)

I

Except by surreptitious tactics, the voice of protest in a one-party state cannot be pressed to the public ear. When the state in question is, in addition, under the iron grip of military dictatorship, and one too that is stridently intolerant of criticism and opposition, protest in whatever form becomes a gamble with danger, unless formulated with especial cunning. In particular, in the field of drama, a recourse to ruse becomes de rigueur, if only because, in theatrical performance, the fate of several persons is involved; hence the artist must accept it as a primary obligation to proceed through such strategies of enlightened guile that will ensure that his or her collaborators do not become the careless victims of official thugs. Happily, however, against the inert silence which autocrats seek to impose upon their subjects, the dissenting artist can triumph through the gift of metaphor and magic, parody and parable, masking and mimicry. With this gift, properly deployed, the terror of the state can be confronted, demystified. But it has to be a conscious tactic of deployment, one that has also to be constantly re-tuned and re-honed to the particular moment, a covert and metamorphic system of manoeuvring which, for want of a better term, I have summarised as 'surreptitious insurrection'.

How does this system operate? To answer this question, we must first take a rapid tour through the history of my own country, Nigeria, in order to understand the turmoil which constructs my plays, and against which my plays are constructed. Nigeria became 'independent' from a century of British colonialism in 1960. But in reality, like everywhere else from where the British departed, ours was no more than a 'flag independence', a situation where economic control remained in London, while the local leaders left behind were stooges carefully selected from among members of the elite sympathetic to British interests. These were people who had accepted to serve as agents for the British policy of 'indirect rule', and so enjoyed a privileged status under colonialism.

Thus, in Nigeria political leaders from our conservative, Muslim north, who had resisted western education and missionary influence, and had even initially opposed the granting of independence, came to power. And the southerners, who had embraced western education, who had even travelled to Britain or to America to acquire knowledge of western systems, and so were to a large extent deeply westernised in their outlook, were not loved at all nor trusted by the duplicitous Britons, and ended up in the opposition parties.

Thus the stage was set, in our 'independent' country, for conflict, if not chaos. Since our new rulers had scant understanding or sympathy for parliamentary systems, the government was soon mired in ineptitude and corruption, and became embroiled in a bitter war with its more voluble and more aggressive opponents. Then came the rigging of federal elections in 1964, which proved to be the final straw for the fragile democracy. All hell broke loose. The western section of the federation in particular – that part controlled by the opposition party – reacted in an orgy of looting and arson, and political homicide.

This state of anarchy provided the excuse for a section of the army, under some effervescent young idealists, to seize power, killing the prime minister and several of his ministers, who happened to be mostly from the north. (The army rebels were mostly southern Christians and Igbo.) The victory of the progressive forces if 'victory' indeed it was – lasted only a couple of months. A savage reprisal followed from northern officers, accompanied by the massacre in the north of Igbo people. The latter were thus forced to flee to their homeland in the east, where they finally declared a secession from the Nigerian federation. But the incipient 'republic of Biafra' which they announced was doomed from the first to failure – a federal onslaught under the government of General Gowon brought the rebellion to an end in 1970.

It was thus a nation which had undergone a terrible bloodbath, and was now subsumed under military might, that provided the backdrop for the work of my generation when we came to young adulthood and began to write seriously in the early 1970s.

It was a nation of myriad paradoxes, in a time of paradoxical riches. Peace had been won on the battlefield but, on the home front, a different kind of war was just beginning. The nation yearned for freedom, for the impulse to liberate its enormous potential for creativity, and put its muscles behind the wheel of modernisation. But the soldiers were everywhere with their guns and bayonets, haughtily feathering their own nests alone, stifling initiative with their decrees. Power for them was merely an excuse to line their own pockets, and all the noisy programmes of 'development' announced with tedious frequency and fanfare became convenient drainage pipes through which national wealth was greedily siphoned into private bank accounts. Incredible wealth was flowing into the nation's coffers from the discovery of oil and the prodigious revenue it brought. Yet for the majority of the people misery and squalor formed the dough of their daily life. The more money the nation earned, the more the official corruption pullulated, and the worse grew the impoverishment of the common folk. Amazingly, against all the euphoria of Independence, the gap widened even more distressingly between the haves and the have-nots, and our nation, even in the midst of its oil, sank further down the list of the world's poorest. Now and then public anger over these accumulated grievances, ferried by a sympathetic press, exploded into violence, but these protests were always scattered and random – pockets of striking workers here, a farmers' uprising there – and never anything at all like 'the great revolution' expected. Indeed, each outburst only helped the soldiers, for in its wake would come another *coup d'état*; a more brazen sector of the military would replace the previous one, and business would be resumed again as usual.

This has been the repeated scenario of political life in Nigeria, this game of musical chairs of military regimes and abortive civilian revolts which has led us to our present entrapment in the snare of the IMF–World Bank Structural Adjustment Program (SAP).

Clearly, if we are to escape from this wasteful and tragic cycle, there must be a revolution: the soldiers must be made to climb down from the saddle of power; the lower classes empowered; and an enlightened leadership, composed from all sectors of the population, must be created to replace the present usurpers. And, in the light of market developments in the post-communist era, an honest, patriotic and committed middle class must be assembled, gifted enough to lead the urgent work of repair and raise the investment necessary for industrialisation and the building of infrastructures.

Obviously, it is quite easy to make these prescriptions; what is hard is to say how to bring them to fruition. It is clear however that not all revolutions have to be violent or bloody. And, in my opinion, one vital prerequisite for the task of salvaging our country is a committed educated class. As I see it, of all of the various 'communities' which make up Nigerian society it is the educated community, armed with a proper ideological consciousness, that can successfully undertake the building of a dynamic modern economy, towards which we yearn to stir our country. Hence the really vital battle, I believe, is to be waged by the educated class – which in our country does not necessarily constitute a privileged elite, at least not since the advent of SAP.

Now I know that the received wisdom in radical circles is that any properly progressive work is one carried out with/among the masses, or at least in the circle of the dispossessed. And in our environment, this would mean the peasants, who form the majority of the population, or the urban wage-earners, who are clearly the subaltern class in our cities. I know of course that among the peasants some valuable work has been going on under the rubric of the Theatre for Development. Nevertheless, while I recognise the potential usefulness of this kind of work, and have on some occasions participated in it, my feelings remain that in the age of marauding multinationals, and in our peculiar circumstances as a fledgling, neo-colonial state trapped at the periphery of world capitalism, these approaches are not enough by themselves. They are not only riddled with self-contradictions but are fundamentally insufficient to provoke the desired change to the macro-society without some additional kind of intervention.

In any case, because of the dissonant heterogeneity of our country it is impossible at the moment to find a common language to address the 300-plus ethnic groups of peasants, a fact that opens them to exploitation by tribal tin gods and wily politicians. To reach them at all, and unite them behind a common ideal, we would still have to pass through the members of the educated class. In a similar manner, the workers' population is relatively thin and confined to only a few cities: at important moments, it is to those educated among them that leadership is normally entrusted. Thus the educated class spreads into every group and every community: properly mobilised, they can form a decisive revolutionary army that will arrest the present drift of our society and, in the manner of the Asian Tigers, transform it into a flourishing modern and industrial economy. While Theatre for Development projects continue at various micro-sites, a simultaneous battle must also be waged at the larger, but intangible, level of consciousness.

So what is the role of the playwright in all this? My argument so far has been that the educated class is at the core of development in any modern economy, and that the failure of our society in Nigeria, and in other African countries, is to be traced to the lamentable decadence of that class.

As a playwright, therefore, it is this question that obsesses me. Almost all of my plays, since I became a self-conscious dramatist, have been passionately devoted to it, and dominated by it. In some works, I am trying to expose this class failure and probe its causes. In others, I am denouncing its corrosive agents, while in others I am ridiculing its antics. And still in others I am trying to stir the class out of its customary apathy into combat, provoking it into anger and active resistance. Sometimes I am trying to do all these things in the same play. I am constantly, ceaselessly pounding at the educated class, trying to lance, and heal from within, that abscess which Fanon so presciently identified long ago as our distorted consciousness, and which shows itself in collective amnesia and inertia, in cowardice, and an inordinate horror of insurrection. Deliberately, I put pepper on the open sore of the educated class's consumer mentality, its limp mimicry of foreign cultures. I insist again and again that this class, to which I myself belong, has a historical responsibility to lead society from misery into prosperity, from the darkness of under-development to the dawn of technological modernity. I attack its criminal complicity in the betrayal of our people, showing how it is because of the willingness of certain of its members to form an alliance with the military that the democratic movement remains unborn. Likewise, I reveal how it is that because some elements of the military have learnt how to insinuate themselves into the class, and manipulate it with cynical opportunism, the rest of society has been successfully co-opted or cowed, as a result of which corruption has grown to become the national ethos. In the quest for an alternative to all this parasitism, I turn official historiography and mythopoesy on their heads, insisting on their hidden partisan agenda, and offer a dialectical counter-narrative, in which history is seen from the lower side, from the perspective of those who are society's victims. This is why female heroes are so prominent in my plays, since the empowerment of women is crucial to this prospective programme of liberation and modernisation.

All the same I divide this class into two – between those whose ideas are already formed, whose positions are therefore already secure on the social ladder, and those whose minds are still in formation, but who will be potential recruits into the class. And it is to the latter, mainly, that I direct my work. Unlike the situation in the developed countries perhaps, students in our higher institutions occupy a unique place on the train of social formation, which no doubt explains the phenomenon of student power in Third World politics. Students are young and dynamic, alert to injustice and wrong, capable of compassion, quick to learn or unlearn. They are just old enough to be excited by the competitiveness of opinions and the selectivity of choice, but not old enough to be saddled yet with the burden of family or other responsibilities. This means that they can readily be summoned for 'instant action', advantageous for those causes requiring protest marches or agitprop activity (though disadvantageous for those needing more reflective response). Assembled from disparate backgrounds and cultures, they comprise the various ethnic, gender and social types and, along with the army, are the ones who most truthfully constitute a 'nation' in more than just the geographical sense. Furthermore, and perhaps most important of all, students are also ideologically pliant and hence neutral, not yet frozen within the theology of any particular camp or cult. For me, therefore, this is the ideal moment to reach them as growing citizens. One year afterwards is already too late. By then the student has graduated, and turned into someone else – a banker, a journalist, an accountant, a lawyer, an army officer – an established member of the professional middle class, in whose hands directly or indirectly the destiny of our nation has been trapped since

Independence. Henceforth, it is these ideas the student has imbibed from the campus that will largely guide his future life and decide the manner of his intervention in public life. The committed dramatist who is able to reach that undergraduate student before s/he fully matures therefore, while his or her allegiance is still fluid, is obviously taking a more than decisive step in the work of communal rehabilitation.

Still it must not be imagined that this work, even when clearly elucidated, is easy to accomplish. The state obviously has a stake in the formation of its citizens. A corrupt state, in particular, has an interest in seeing that its subjects do not become enlightened for, as it knows, knowledge is the first weapon of freedom. To the slave-master, any initiative that aims to break the chains of the slave is subversive, and must be suppressed. So with the dictator, for whom the progressive artist is always a target. Hence the playwright who pursues the kind of agenda I have outlined above must be ready for official reprisal in the form of censorship or even direct elimination. Especially under a military regime, whose laws are capricious and vindictive, and where even death sentences against opponents can be backdated, the dramatist who wants to survive and still keep doing his work is obliged to operate with the tactics of a cultural guerrilla. And it is in such a context that playwriting becomes an act of surreptitious insurrection.

Furthermore, the committed playwright must remember that it is not only the antagonism of the state that he needs to anticipate; there is also the potential hostility of the audience. Most of those who come to the theatre come in search of entertainment, for 'relaxation' from the agonising realities of their life through a momentary escape into the fabulous world of illusion. Nothing would horrify them more therefore than to be called upon to 'think' at such outings. Hence a play that seeks to win attention cannot afford to present itself like a political tract or a religious sermon. Besides, if the ideas on stage push against prevailing popular positions or currently accepted norms and practices, as they must, response from the spectators cannot be expected to be spontaneously warm or sympathetic, unless the playwright takes care to package his play, cleverly, through the furtive masks that art itself can furnish. These strategies will differ of course from play to play, and from occasion to occasion, depending on the particular crisis the playwright has chosen to confront, as well as the circumstances of performance, and so on. In the remaining part of this chapter I will try to illustrate my own procedures with one concrete example.

For me, then, as I said earlier, so absorbing has been the post-colonial experience of anomie that I have been unable to divorce my work from it, or from the urgent need to change it. Each week, at least since the coming of the soldiers and the discovery of oil, our life in Nigeria has been marked by unending crisis, a situation which, from a certain grey perspective, is paradoxically propitious to the creative imagination. Thus, virtually all my plays have taken their inspiration from one immediate crisis or other, to the extent where it is rare that I choose a theme to write on. Rather, it is the theme that chooses me. When, for instance, at the end of the civil war the government of General Gowon grew monumentally corrupt, the need to confront it publicly prompted me to *The Chattering and the Song,* in which I found metaphors to explain why the regime had to go and in what way social justice could be established in its aftermath.

[...]

It was not because we as a people were more disposed than other societies towards criminality, but simply because in the kind of society we had fabricated for ourselves, crime had become an obligatory practice in the rites of survival. And so robbers were not an aberration, but were a creation of the society itself, which such unconscionable measures as public execution would not eliminate but instead aggravate. It was we ourselves who manufactured our own robbers, and the solution therefore lay in a more sobering prescription – altering our social and political set-up, creating a more equal society, and democratising our polity, starting with the removal of soldiers from powers

Fine enough – but how should these ideas express themselves on stage? Given the controversial nature of the topic, and the sensitivity towards it of both the rulers and ruled, conventional drama in the western sense of it – as for instance in the Shavian tradition – was obviously inappropriate. By experience I had learnt already the inadequacy, for our audience, of the form of conventional western drama, based as it is on the primacy of words. The drama which our people savour is still one in the mould of 'total theatre', that is, a multi-media production, in which dialogue is no more important than other paralinguistic signs. There must be music and song, dance, colour and spectacle. The only problem here, however, is that unless the playwright exercises control, the message can be subsumed by the theatrical game itself.

Hence, in search of an appropriate form, the wise thing was to turn back to our traditions. How, I pondered, did our predecessors proceed to deal with sensitive issues without incurring the wrath of the rulers, or the antagonism of their audience? In Africa, we are no strangers to art forms that are designed to entertain, as well as instruct or condemn. And one tradition that immediately came to mind was the folk tale in performance. For not only do these tales combine entertainment and instruction, but they also have the kind of techniques to shelter the outspoken artist from official harm. As many observers have noted, oral performers are able to voice trenchant criticism, even while keeping their audience amused, and even when the target of their barbs sits on the throne. The theatrical elements of the genre make it the most popular art from in the community, but are these adaptable to the modern stage with paying spectators? One can isolate its elements: a protean one-man cast, with or without the accompaniment of musicians, who narrates *and performs;* a story located in *fabu*-land, whose protagonists are frequently non-human figures with, in particular, the trickster figure of the Tortoise as hero; the antiphonal chants; and, finally, a moral that summarises the play's didactic purpose.

Utpal Dutt and the alienated man

While Badal Sircar and Utpal Dutt (1929–1993) lived through the same parts of Indian history, their writing styles and general world-views are strikingly different. Sircar's Third Theatre offers a hopeful picture of a hybrid theatre inspiring people to social change. Dutt offers a cynical critique of what is broken in Indian theatre and India more broadly. Dutt is explicit in his connections to Western Marxist theory, stating that man has become alienated from the material conditions of life – man no longer knows how he relates to the world around him. Dutt brings up large-scale conflicts like the Indo-Pakistan War of 1971, which led to the independence of Bangladesh (East Pakistan) from (West) Pakistan; Mahatma Gandhi's independence movement; the various military conflicts and trade disputes with China from the 1960s to the 1980s; and Indira Gandhi's election rigging. Dutt repeatedly states that knowing history is vital to revolution and that knowledge is change (which is reason enough for the history chapters in this book). Curiously, neither Dutt nor Sircar speak of the history of India before the twentieth century (prior to colonization), although Dutt's history expands from India to include the uprisings in Paris in 1968 and some details of Russia's communist history. While he is writing for the Indian conflict, the people's struggle in other countries is also worthy of note. At a time when many in India were denigrating the Chinese because of the multiple conflicts, Dutt offered continued reminders that the People's Republic of China was, itself, engaged in a Cultural Revolution – in a revolution that espoused a particular brand of Marxist thought. His interest in Russia and Paris, although less controversial, can be explained in the same way. In Russia, the Czars had been overthrown and a communist government had taken over. In Paris, wide-scale protests by the people led to the collapse of de Gaulle's government (although de Gaulle shortly returned to power). For Dutt, history is the history of the people and the people's revolution. Like Brecht and Artaud, and unlike Sircar, Dutt sees his project as universal.

Like Sircar, Dutt is skeptical of urban life, because this life removes man from connection with the earth, with heritage, and with community. Dutt, as a Marxist, refers to this separation as "alienation." The word alienation is often used in a Brechtian context in English translations. For Brecht, theatre could cause alienation and thereby give the audience a necessary distance from which they could intellectually engage with what is going on. The alienation that Dutt seeks to combat is a more profound and fundamental alienation. People have forgotten who they are, what they are, and how they fit within the universe. Dutt's theatre valiantly seeks to end this alienation.

Dutt is painfully aware, however, that acting itself is a process of alienation – that theatre is not reality. Furthermore, he is aware that his audience and actors are alienated individuals. While he experimented with traditional *jatra* (singing and storytelling) and with Western avant-garde techniques, Dutt's theatre generally directly staged social problems in a predominately "realistic" mode. For Dutt, realism involved presenting complex heroes – fallible people struggling to be better. He strove for accurate performances from his actors, insisting the actors understand the motivations of the characters they played. He also considered it his job as a director to train his actors in a revolutionary mindset. His experimentation with form was always in the service of content: "form is worthless if it is not the form of its content" (1982, p. 197). His plays incited anger and political action in equal measure. Dutt was jailed as a result of the political response to his plays.

Extract 3.2 Selections from *Towards a Revolutionary Theatre*
Utpal Dutt

The first lesson we try to impart therefore during rehearsals is not literature, nor theatrecraft, but Marxism-Leninism. Right through rehearsals we try to evolve a method whereby the petty-bourgeois alienation of the actor can be hammered at to help him acquire a proletarian standpoint, a proletarian world-view. This makes him a better actor.

Why is the proletariat in a privileged position in his view? Why does the proletarian point of view lead to Truth, and all other class-standpoints end in God, Idealism, Metaphysics and other disguised lies?

[...] The proletarian explanation of the world is the only true one, because the proletariat feels himself as an object of production, before he can think of the world. His quest for truth begins with consciousness of himself and his labour as a commodity, and therefore he understands himself, in the words of Frederic Jameson (1971, p. 187) as "a moment in production, a process". To the serene, "objective", "scientific" petty-bourgeois, commodity is something to be consumed, its origin quite unimportant. To the worker, the world which he comprehends through his consciousness of himself as a commodity is nothing but a process of production. He has thus already arrived at the truth of constantly changing phenomena, of constantly changing production-relations as the basis of the world. To him, reality is a process, not an immutable present, from which all other classes begin their deduction.

Thus, this view of the world makes the actor conscious of theatre also as a process, as the constantly-changing reflection of social-relations, as a point-of-view in class-struggle.

The actor's art is thus made to relate closely to the world where it grows, and his artifices, devices, tricks of the trade, can no longer be crowned with a halo of absolute theories—things like Poor Theatre, Total Theatre, Physical Theatre, Transcendental Theatre, Therapeutic Theatre, and other such absolutist absurdities one hears bandied about. Since the theatre is part of a social process, there can no more be one immutable Theory of theatrical production, than there can be one true religion, or one true God, or one true Aryan race.

But within the narrow world of his artifices too, the actor becomes better and better as an actor, as he acquires the proletarian viewpoint of constantly-changing phenomena, interacting on one another, a world of contradiction and unity of opposites. [...] It teaches him to approach a part, not as something immutably fixed, but as a person, richly sensuous and constantly-altering, from good to bad to good again, with his great ideals, and common fads, his nobility and his meanness. [...]

We, therefore, begin our rehearsal by [noting that] nothing is final. The actor must grow with the part, not learn to be one. In nature nothing is quite identical with anything else. In nature x is not equal to x. A pound of rice is "not really equal to a pound of rice; if only one took the trouble to count the grains on both sides, he would discover a difference of a few hundred units. Therefore, it is ridiculous for the actor to try and remember exactly what he did in the last rehearsal. Each rehearsal is a new experience towards the realisation of a character. Each day's labour with text and movement is to bring oneself closer and closer to the play and to the character—and through them to society, to a social act, that will for a period unite the players with the people.

> [...] Participation in political struggle does not by itself lead to overcoming of alienation, but it is the only valid precondition for it in a country like India. [...] When all social activity is alien to man, the subversion of this society is, the only way to conquering alienation, everything else will further deaden the mind and make the artist's alienation deeper and stronger. [...] The creation of an ideal in a theatrical production also creates a need for it in society and its consumption is appropriated by individuals. Furthermore, these political ideals create in their producer the need to create more and more in close relation to larger and larger masses of consumers. Dedication to political ideals, i.e. overthrow of alienated society, inspires the dramatist, the regisseur, the actor and the audience to battle alienation itself. The theory of Alienation presupposes a possible society without Alienation. To work for that society through his own medium is precisely the task of a conscious artist, and it stands to reason therefore that the world itself will lead the artist to consciousness of alienation. All men are alienated in this society, but most are unconscious that they are. Political struggle makes man conscious of his own alienation from production, society and nature and equips him for battle against Alienation.

Saadallah Wannous and audience-based structures

Syria gained independence from France in 1946, although various political negotiations for independence had begun in the 1920s. Compared to the Algerian War of Independence (1954–1962), the Syrian transition to independence was relatively non-violent, tending more toward protests than to armed struggle. This relative non-violence did not continue through the latter half of the twentieth century, during which Syria and its neighbors saw a variety of conflicts, many of which are ongoing in 2016. Syria shares a border with Israel, and in 1967, the Six Day War broke out between the two countries. In 1978, the Camp David Accords – a set of talks in which the boundaries of Israel were determined by the U.S., Israel, and Egypt – determined Israel's new relationship with Palestinians living within and near its borders. This accord was reached without Palestine's participation and Palestine, Syria, and the United Nations condemned the new agreement. Syria itself had a series of constitutions and military coups, culminating with the formation of the United Arab Republic (1958–1961), which combined Egypt and Syria. This unity proved short-lived and Syria reasserted its independence which brought about another series of coups and an affiliation with communist Russia. From 1970 until 2000, Hafez Al-Assad served what was initially to be a seven-year presidential term. His son, Bashar Al-Assad, succeeded him upon his death. Under Hafez's term as president, Syria officially became a socialist state and officially recognized Islam in the new constitution.

As with Dutt and Sircar, Wannous is concerned with the twentieth-century developments. His theatre addresses the present moment. With the various conflicts and coups, it would be logical to expect that the Syrian people had strong opinions about the direction(s) in which their country was moving. Wannous argues, however, that the people seem uninvolved and uncommitted to political change. He characterizes them as passive. Wannous' theatre seeks to use communication to establish the ability to think critically about contemporary events and his manifesto discusses the ways in which theatrical structures might be rethought in order to bring this about. Like Soyinka, Wannous rejects formal innovation as an end unto itself and insists on contextualizing all theatre in terms of its intended audience, stating that the intended audience of Arabic theatre should, for the time being, be the masses. As such, Wannous turns away from Absurdism and other abstract theatrical movements in favor of a concrete, pragmatic theatre with immediate effects.

He argues that democracy is open communication among people, that theatre is inherently democratic, and that all acts of theatrical communication are resistant to what he views as the ongoing tyranny of the Arab world. Democracy is communication. Democracy fights tyranny. Theatre is communication. Therefore theatre fights tyranny. After becoming frustrated with the inability of theatre to communicate on the profound level he desired, Wannous took a thirteen-year break from theatre to work directly toward the solution of social problems. Both before and after his hiatus, Wannous spoke in absolutes. His theory is polemical, leaving no middle ground. For instance, at moments he states that the patterns of Islamic thought stultify democracy by limiting communication. He offers theatre as an antidote to this, not as a replacement for Islam, but as a replacement for what he views as the poor implementation of Islamic practice. This is a provocative statement, which is echoed in Wannous' theatre. Wannous laments, however, that his audiences do not seem to hear or absorb his message.

As with many polemical writers, Wannous is at his strongest when dealing with big ideas. The details of his system are not always clear. His desire, however, is to create a theatre that promotes communication, critical thinking, local examinations of local problems, and a re-examination of tradition. This theatre will engage the public in authentic issues. Wannous insists that his communicative strategies must consistently shift – his theatre must always be "experimental": he talks about it in terms of a progressive series of ever-improving failures that it will learn from. Some of his productions are almost entirely in the mode of Western realism, while others, like the one discussed below, are explicitly metatheatrical with the actors and the director commenting on the possibility of performance. Rather than advocating a single style of performance, Wannous advocates any style of performance that will communicate in a given context.

It is difficult to find a reference to Saadallah Wannous that does not lament the fact that he remains virtually unknown in the Western academy.

Very few of his plays have been translated, and this anthology is the first publication of an extended translation of his theoretical work. While audiences of Wannous' work certainly benefit from knowledge of Syrian history, his focus on communicating the ability to think critically extends far beyond the Syrian borders. The fact that he is not read widely in the West is deeply ironic considering that Wannous' primary concern is with the communicative aspects of theatre.

Extract 3.3 Selections from "Manifestos for a New Arab Theatre"
Saadallah Wannous, translated by Eyad Houssami

1. Starting from the Audience

Plain and simple: the entry to a conversation about theatre, its evolution and the solutions to its problems, is the *audience*. Here, I attempt to turn inside out the formulas of traditional research methodologies of Arab theatre, of its problematics and its so-called "crisis" or "difficult birth." I can say and with no exaggeration that these very same problematics still arise in every critical debate, theatre conference, or roundtable: questions of identity, authorship, language, deficiencies in text, and financial means with the recent additions – and high time! – of *iltizam* (commitment and obligation to society) and of expressing the realities of our environment.

[...] And so we turn these formulas inside out in an attempt to enter the problem from, as we see it, the right and natural way: from the audience. For what distinguishes theatre among all other cultural activities and phenomena is that it is at its essence a *social event*. It has been since it arose and still is today even though this understanding diminished in the bourgeois Italianate theatre. Because it is a social event, when we dwindle *theatre as phenomenon* to literary study, to aesthetic pronouncements that deploy elements of theatre production in isolation or neatly aligned alongside each other, this belies an ignorance and furthermore leads to the falsification of its social content and perversion of the role it should play in our lives.

[...]

Firstly: so long as theatre is a social event, meaningful only if performed before or among spectators, then we must start by asking: who are these spectators? Indeed, determining the audience of the theatre that we want to establish or develop is the first issue that we must confront because determining its identity – its social makeup and cultural circumstances, its problems and images of suffering – will subsequently fix the grounds and define the parameters of our work. It is also the first step in determining the particularities of theatrical expression that befit this audience, no longer a throng of ghosts with likeness and face, their inner concerns reflected in the lineaments, hidden by the darkness of the hall.

Secondly: after we designate our audience and distinguish its sociocultural makeup, the following question on which hinges outcomes of far-reaching consequence springs forth: what do we want to say to our audience? No doubt, addressing this question is intertwined first and foremost with how we address question one. For determining the audience implies, one way or another, our stance vis-à-vis this audience, what we want to convey provided we understand its needs, and our awareness of theatre's capacity for change and action. We choose the audience inasmuch as we take an intellectual and social stance, which will dictate the content of our work, the ideas that we want to stage and to highlight their dynamics.

Thirdly: then comes the question that unites the two prior issues and draws them together in one relationship, at its core the *theatrical relationship*. The question concerns how to connect with the audience. What means should we use to bring about definitive interaction with spectators? Or what form coincides with the givens of the previous two questions and fastens them in an unbreakable and rich relationship, free of subjugation?

"To determine the audience" is neither a term for consumptions nor a slogan for political or intellectual hypocrisy; rather, it is a project and way of thinking through which we can really figure out the kind of audience that theatre makers face. When they choose the spectators, they choose their problems and ambitions, whereupon they form an opinion and thereafter explore their own way to express it. Taking stances: they concatenate then intertwine to merge and form *theatre as phenomenon*, hence its value and efficacy.

In this consists a clear and practical basis to evaluate all the works we see around us. Should we wonder about either the audience theatre addresses, the content's engagement with this audience, or the harmony between the form of expression and between, on the one hand, the cultural horizons of the spectator and, on the other, the content; we have before us an impressive crop of inferences and gauges to analyze the work and to bring to light the extent of its authenticity or falsity, by virtue not of theoretical abstractions but rather of practical diagnosis grounded in socio-political and aesthetic values.

Maybe now's the time to ask: how do we envision the birth and growth of a theatre movement starting from the point of departure we set prior? And how does that lead, practically speaking, to devising unequivocal responses to the issues that have long troubled our Arab theatre?

We're going to start with question one and actually designate the audience among whom we want to pitch our theatre. We respond immediately: we want a theatre of audiences, that is for the people, the toiling class. Inasmuch as this response seems convenient and hackneyed, we are placing it in a context that is inconvenient and offers no concessions for pronounced slogans. To be more precise, our response has no value and is incomplete if we do not pass from it to an in-depth study of the condition of these classes, of their lived circumstances and problems. Only then do we have scientific knowledge based on the actual experience of living together and reasonable analyses rather than clichés and in-stock reproductions. This knowledge replaces the prefab formulas, or in other words the easier path to creating a theatre experience, composite because it is daily interaction with audiences on a variety of levels: political, social, intellectual, and artistic. It is an interaction of reciprocity. It learns from experience and improves. Its starting point, the actual land we live on. Its purpose, to create with these spectators a theatrical idiom that involves cultivating awareness, in addition to pleasure, and deepening comprehension of their shared fate, their problems and lot in society. That is getting back to basics. We discard the available models because they don't matter. We don't make theatre solely to prove that we can keep up with civilized culture. And to prove that we know the swan song of theatre. Were it our only purpose, then it wouldn't be worth all this trouble. We make theatre because we want to change and develop mentalities, together to deepen our collective awareness of historical destiny. This being our purpose – and I'm honing in on it in this reportorial style despite my knowledge that most do not depart from such an understanding of theatre, it would be worth starting from the people with and for whom we will work. Those in the middle of and before whom we will stand as we speak our speech. Situated like so from the beginning, we cannot but present works that touch and resonate with people, effecting them favorably; we will moreover build our self-awareness of the hollows of ignorance and fantasy and of the facile ideas accumulating in our minds, like a diaphragm between us and reality. It will break down in the process of coexistence, of rubbing shoulders, and we will awaken to urgent realities, to how people think, the way they understand things ... giving rise to dialogue. This dialogue will generate formulas and stances; then begins the authentic experience of a popular theatre, springing from and closely united with the people, with efficacy to boot.

What needs to be said out loud will spring spontaneously from such an experiment, and this speech will take on its suitable form. This is certainly not a mechanical or quantifiable process, its every dead end inevitably leading to the next. I contend that we have the talent, the cultural context, and that both the zeal and devotion are there. The process of interaction that we envisage will enrich and heighten further yet these givens. Bit by bit, we will find ourselves driving a theatre movement with solid underpinnings, deeply rooted in the ground of reality, the veritable ground of audiences for all theatre. It is, for that reason, distinguished by fantastic characteristics that feed its growth, development, and continuity – a living dialogue between theatre and audience. By virtue of its points of departure and underpinnings, it might be able, after first scraping away the prefab theatre formulas, to return to the prefab formulas and, with a coherent critical stance, to take them on, provided that international theatre trends do not remain the Sunna of Allah and His Prophet and that they are not placed on another level and treated with the same old rituals of academic deference and cultural deflection. Rather, the movement that we're talking about has – due to its awareness of its foundations, reality, and understandings of culture – what it takes to be delivered from getting lost between formulas and schools of theatre, for it does not consider them mere fashions, the choice among them a matter of taste, not of discussion, because it knows that schools of theatre are schools of thought and that form is an expression of specific political and social stances. Its stances vis-à-vis these schools cannot be but critical; otherwise, it will betray its points of departure, implanted in reality above all else.

Through this process, one of the confusing vortexes, in which our Arab theatre strays, will end our Arab theatre that seems still like the child, breath taken away, bewildered, standing before a vitrine packed with all sorts of models and not knowing how to choose. That model or that one. That toy or the other.

Considering that the theatre movement in question departs from the reality of the audience and aspires to put into effect the highest degree of connectedness with the audience and also to leave the greatest impression, it must undertake serious daily study of its own experience in theatrical expression and on style and language and form. It may experiment with known forms or may invent its own unique forms – and no doubt it will arrive at the moment of formalistic innovation – but in both cases what determines the trend we choose is living, practical experience and, in that same vein, the harvest of daily interaction with the audience: knowing where they're at culturally, how they think, and how they respond.

The harvest of failure and studying failure. Of success and analysis of the reasons behind it.

A form, both suitable and evolved, will gradually come to crystallize for an efficacious theatre, for the public. The horizon of options and experiments, awaiting this movement, are wide. So too does it possess a rich heritage of forms and modes of popular expression from which it might benefit. It will definitely benefit from and employ them in a more effective and sounder way than those who apply them to build a culture on folklore either to compensate for a cultural and civilizational deficiency by restoring and developing folklore or to pay heed only to superficial reasons for renewal and formal experimentation. For folklore, in our movement, has another value and different purpose. It is possible to benefit and to employ folklore to the extent that it coheres with the content and manifests in a better way that content's reach to the minds of spectators. Using it otherwise, as an inspiration for superficial formalistic reasons, is unacceptable.

Many questions about language, form, folklore's inspiration, and so on – often posed in an amputated, cut off manner – burden Arab theatre. And clearly, the process of seriously exploring an authentic form – one conducive to communicating with the audience, with the process starting from the audience – guarantees relief from this burden. Suitable solutions to all these issues will emerge decisively. No longer will the question of language be discussed around roundtables or televised symposia; rather, it will be tested against daily practice, and its problematics will undergo analysis through this practice. So too for all the other issues, including theatre architecture.

We forecast a theatre movement distinguished by a final feature: it is a process of ongoing interaction between theatre and its audiences. It learns from its audiences as it comes to know them. It gives and takes in a lively debate that enriches its contents and widens its limits every day. No doubt, therein we will restore the impetus and initial muse of theatre as phenomenon, the impetus and muse from when it was a celebration. On top of all that, we will restore its initial efficacy, its originality and social orientation.

Indeed, a theatre movement distinguished by these attributes – it alone can pull Arab theatre out of its wasteland. It alone can analyze what is real among the problems and pass over the counterfeit among them. It springs from its audience. It drinks from and gives to it. It dialogues with the audience; they enrich each other. And that is when an authentic theatre is born. Whatever its setting, it sets off a social event, fertile dialogue, and a collective awareness of reality and destiny.

The Healthy Beginnings of Arab Theatre

[...]
Theatre productions at that time [mid-nineteenth century], in all that they comprised – elements emerging organically and colors of popular arts as well as improvisation and intimacy as well as topics springing from problems of the local environment or those pivoting around them, until they are in harmony with them – theatre productions at that time were veritable social events, in a period when society was yawning, awakening from a long rest. So then theatre accompanied this awakening and opened its eyes to the limits of own possibilities just as it contributed to them.

And in my opinion, we direly need to revisit these periods and study them well to discover to what degree such beginnings were teeming with health and to what degree the first pioneers realized, even instinctively, the nature of theatre as a social phenomenon that grows among people and extends among their ranks. For that reason, they – despite their departure from prefab formulas of theatre as it is in Europe – did not get muddled in these formulas; they didn't hold them up with pedantic sanctity. Rather, they subjected them, with much wit and perspicacity, to their own unique sense of their audience – its circumstances, particularities, and problems. They commanded astonishing creative spontaneity that overcame the rigor mortis rules and drew their own forms and expressive visions from the people themselves.

[...] They also would improvise scenes or allow unexpected occurrences to drive the production somewhere new. In this sense of impulse and in this ongoing daily dialogue (despite the fact that it disgusts the great minds of sophisticated, ritualistic theatre), and in the utilization of elements foreign to theatre making with the purpose of freshening things up, and in warming up the spectators to the intimacy of their presence together as a group before the stage – in all this, we observe signs of health and a deep understanding of theatre. Theatre, not as it is known in the conservatory books, not that I hold any grudges against them, but rather as it was at its origins in truth: theatre that syncopates both the group and the stage, which concerns the group because it springs from and is about them, and further that delights them.

The spectator integrates with the group, and the presence of the theatre game wholly engages the group so long as it isn't strange or foreign in its makeup and content vis-à-vis their life circumstances and cognizance of them. There may have been among the first pioneers a firm sentiment toward adaptation of international plays instead of presenting them verbatim – this also caused contempt of these pioneers among modern dramatists. They accused them of defaming international heritage and of inanity. They may have known that theatre's value lies in its expression of an environment and its interweaving with the threads of this environment; for that reason, therefore, presenting international plays will make these plays seem strange and walled in by barriers prohibiting an Arab spectator – and particularly in that period – from finding them favorable or from taking their example to stir up his interest, however over-determined the structure of absorbing the events.

[...]

From the beginning, the oppressing authorities sensed the danger of theatre as a work that wrecks the prevailing status quo and that shakes up its old, inveterate values.

[...]

And what is truly noteworthy in the experiences of those pioneers, bearing in mind the major ordeals that they had to face, is that the means they had to make their shows unsettling events was not the text, and all that it does to critique prevailing values and the shameful status quo, but rather, above and beyond, that the performance itself was an unsettling event. And with these means that we have mentioned prior, they succeeded in bringing a number of people together who before long were entering a phenomenon of all-encompassing estrangement and transcending the distance between the stage and the audience – and of intimacy, improvisation, and sometimes performance participation – and who feel the sense of their collectiveness and shared grievances, who to a further extent theatricalize together.

Theatre is a Group Work

[...]

In truth, group work cannot be a matter of gathering up individual efforts; rather, it is the emergence of a new mode of creation: it has the fertility of groupness, the richness of ongoing dialogue, and the indefatigable, serious sense of exploration. What we have before us is a collective interaction of energies in the context of a collaborative creation that is grounded, coherent, rich, and full of individuality in its groupness. As we likened the first understanding with a series of disengaged links, we shall liken the project of the second understanding to a chemical interaction whose elements give all they can – changing, altering, transforming each other. All this in a process pressured by a charge that leads in the end to a remodeled and surprising makeup composition. We do not intend the dissolution or effacement of the individuals. On the contrary, we want to set off their possibilities to give as much as they can in this supreme fertilization, to purge themselves of the stains of narrow individualism and of the impediments of personal anxieties.

Therefore, what we mean by "theatre is group work" is the emergence of a collective of individuals who have some sort of likeness, clarity of vision, sincere enthusiasm, and persistent capability to dig and to explore. The collective immediately enters a new type of experience, breaking from the leash of the traditional project, and sets off as a group not individuals in the construction of theatre that manifests its original inspiration. That is, a group uprises in a stagnant environment. And in this collective, there will be a writer, director, actor, and others; however, they will never work individually or in isolation from the others. The project will remain an ongoing dialogue of two complimentary directions together. A dialogue within the collective itself that clarifies and deepens ideas, that designs and builds the work. And another dialogue between the collective and the spectators, or the audience they aim at. The two dialogues move together, inevitably. They each reflect on the other in a debate that makes theatre blossom in beneficence.

It is a collective brimming with capacities, not with in-stock ideas and fixed forms of working. Through daily practice, creative effort, and continuous dialogue, their potential will explode as will the potentiality of their context. It will create a theatre clamoring with life and vitality that grows day by day – because it won't stiffen in molds or die in stagnant frameworks – because the only aim is for theatre to shake its spectators, to unsettle their peace of mind, and to heighten their awareness as if by electric shock.

In such a group movement, in which a larger group – the audience – also merges, we will have the ability and the strongest of fronts to awaken and embody our shared fate together, actors and spectators. In that, the greatest ambition of theatre is made manifest: to break out of our freeze to unite in a group, to awaken afterward to our shared destiny and its calculus as a group.

We Must Charge Not Discharge

Theatre arose politically, and it still is political. This is true even when it seems indifferent to politics and avoids getting involved in its problems. Try as it might to steer clear of politics' anxieties and vortexes, it expresses a political stance and serves a political purpose, which is, in brief, to divert the people from attending to their matters of destiny and to turn their attention toward thinking about their life circumstances and models for changing them. That is the essence of theatre – and maybe of culture generally, in every place and time. And all that these pages put forth departs from and confirms this truth.

Thus, the collective that will anchor the rules of a theatre movement will have among its individuals the requisite awareness of their political role as a collective and the capacity to watch for the pitfalls lying in wait for them as they perform this role. The collective certainly knows, due to its constitution and the authenticity of its link to its environment, the nature of the struggle that its theatre will reflect: a social struggle of the highest degree. So too does the collective realize the truth of destiny, a sense that it wants to be shared: a political and historical destiny above all else.

But despite this clarity that seems to simplify the issue greatly and to lead to certain results, there are many pitfalls that might lead to totally contrary results. Theatre's role and what it can do in its environment is a complicated and difficult question; and if we don't have the awakened keenness of mind at all times, then we may forever pervert this role or betray it. Many are the theatre works we have seen these last years that in the end lead to the opposite of what they want to say, works that, in this, become yet an additional factor of delusion and deceit.

We are certainly not building castles in the air about what theatre can do in any given society. As Brecht says, "Theatre cannot make a revolution just as it cannot replace the foundations of society." We know that theatre is one aspect of this daily, long-term effort that paves the way for a modest possibility among possibilities for change. When this change occurs, it will not depart from a theatre venue or a theatrical setting. Nevertheless, theatre plays a role, a role in the periods of pervasive repression and systematized apoliticization during which it can be a brilliant remedy. For by virtue of its groupness, daily practice, and its present and direct relationship with the people, it offers the false impression of being a political activity. We cannot help ourselves: we are struck by magnificent power when we see ourselves shaking, even partially, the metal walls of apoliticization. Throughout all this, it is important to bear in mind the complex and difficult peculiarity of theatre. It is a double role. It is a delicate balancing act: starting with its awareness of the truth of ongoing struggles all around, it must clarify these struggles, uncover them, and determine their nature. To educate the audience, to reflect his life circumstances and then to analyze and shed light on what lies beneath. So too must theatre, departing with a cognizance of the indeterminate nature of political fate, a nature that is always receptive to change when possibilities for change ripen and the people pursue them, to incite people to work, to impel them to pursue the mission of changing their current fate – and at the same time. The Arab theatre that we want is one that realizes its double role as such: to educate and to incite the spectator. It is a theatre that does not put the spectator at ease or relieve him of his sorrows. On the contrary, it is theatre that unsettles him, that makes his blood rush, and over the long run prepares him for the pursuit of changing fate. As I said before, there are many pitfalls in this uphill mission; for if theatre does not reveal truth or errs in its analysis of the status quo, it turns into a tool of ignorance and delusion. If it can't develop a project and use every tool and means it has to inject the spectator and to incite him to work, it transforms into an inducer of discharge, purging spectators of resentment, anger, or concern and that empowers the direness of their situation. In the end, it numbs them and fortifies the reigning status quo, solidly and deep-rootedly.

How fine and delicate a line between two endings, one that charges and the other that discharges! I could have catalogued the many examples of plays and performance that weren't able to discern this line, so they ended, despite their intense intrepidness, up with anesthetizing results. They ended, and they served, despite their claims, what they wanted to criticize. In all of these cases, spectators left with cheer on their faces, exhaling silently and sighing with joy, as if they left their held up burdens on the chairs before leaving. What a finale! It makes the theatre collective that we envisage to spend the rest of the night holding itself accountable and questioning the hidden reasons of its falling short or its mistakes. As to those who are glad with this success, those who wait backstage waiting for the influx of well-wishes to come and take them by the hand, to express their relief and delight in the evening that passed, they don't matter. They remain far from realizing the mission of theatre that we want and need.

Requested of the Audience

[...] There is no doubt that the spectator can take on a major positive role in theatre's direction, and it's up to us to teach him how to take on this role and to encourage him to excel in it in an effective way until he is actually examining theatre's direction and evaluating its foundations.

For the spectator to take on this role, he must himself change and rehearse his role as spectator in a new and different way unlike what we know.

Firstly: the spectator must be aware of his importance in any theatre performance. Everything that happens on the stage is aimed at him, and it addresses him. That is to say, the value of this performance is subject to the stance taken by the audience toward it.

Secondly: the passivity of the spectator must come to an end. So too must his placid state facing the stage and all that happens there. He must well realize that all that happens before him implicates and concerns him, and it's up to him to take a stance toward it.

Thirdly: the spectator must feel a sense of responsibility and that the stance he takes toward any work of culture in general or any play in particular has significant and dangerous consequences, both for him and for his country.

For this reason, it is requested of the spectator to change first and foremost the school-like way he sits in the theatre. And also his surrender to his chair and acceptance to all that is presented to him. It is requested that he bears in mind his importance as a spectator and that he rejects being exploited or deceived. The spectator must pay careful attention to what is spoken and to what happens on the stage before him and to be wary of falling into the trap of liars, imposters, inanities.

It is requested of him to intervene with honesty when he glimpses a lie or to bring to light inanity and deceit.

It is requested to break from those trying to anesthetize him, or to keep away from fundamental problems and issues. If he doesn't see himself on the stage, he should intervene and teach the spectators a lesson about the society they live in. If he finds his own image to be counterfeit, he should prohibit its display. To stop it. To scream in the face of counterfeits.

It is requested ... It is requested of him to remember forever that what happens before him concerns him and that he has no right to condone lies, deceit, or inanity for the benefit of social conduct or to maintain appearances with fatuous academic reverence. The spectator is not a student in primary school, and it's up to him to pay attention to all that falls upon his ears, with total calm and receptivity. The spectator is the fundamental half of any theatre performance – he is the object of the performance and is responsible for it too. For that reason, it's up to him to exercise fully his rights and to play his role in a positive, unrestricted way. It's up to him to carry his load in every theatre activity, to accept and to deny, to force together with and to break off from the performance. To say what he wants and to rectify what is told to him. In brief, not to be a passive participant that takes whatever is placed before him without any objection or examination. Does this mean that he should be impertinent?

Yes. It is requested from the spectator to be aware and impertinent. In that alone, many of the inanities and lies will collapse, and theatre will become a socio-cultural activity that draws together the stage and the venue in a rich and solid debate, a relationship.

This is but a digest of vast topics to which we will return, again and again.

Structural questions to ask when reading theatre from around the world

Theatre of which people? For which people? By which people? Questions of audience

Theatre requires an audience, at least one performer, someone or some group serving as an author, and someone or some group serving as a director. Political theatre often encourages us to examine power. There are a number of hierarchies contained in the idea that an author has written something which a director leads actors to faithfully reproduce for an audience who absorb this entertainment. The (hypothetical) basic requirements for theatre – the actors, audiences, director, and author – raise the first set of questions political theatre addresses. Political theatre has experimented with making the audience more active or even demanding full participation by eliminating the idea of the audience entirely. Political theatre has challenged the authority of the author by experimenting with improvisation, with collaborative writing, and with adaptation of works by well-known authors. While the director as a single individual guiding the production is subject to less contention than the idea of the audience or the author, directors vary from relatively authoritative to relatively collaborative. Beyond the question of audience participation, there is a question of who such an audience might be. Political theatre often addresses issues of class, race, gender, and education, and considerations of these same demographic categories shape the audience to whom the play is directed.

Should revolutionary theatre be written for the masses or for the educated?

It is a fundamental ideological premise that, within any ideology, someone benefits and therefore is invested in reproducing that ideology. If the current system is working for you, you are less likely to want to change the system. Based on this simple idea, Karl Marx and many other revolutionaries have insisted that revolution can only come from the oppressed or from the working classes. These are the classes that have something to gain by altering the structures of society. Other revolutionary thinkers, like Gayatri Spivak, herself a committed Marxist, have pointed out that, by definition, those without power in a given ideology are going to have difficulty gaining power. In this regard, it makes sense to think that revolution must require participation of the educated, the elite, or the powerful. Major communist leaders have debated this subject, and Mao Zedong famously changed his stance as he led China through the Cultural Revolution. If theatre is to effect political change, this change must involve people. Political theatre must determine its audience.

Osofisan's theatre targets the educated class – an audience he recognizes has not historically been the target of politically-minded theatre, and he demands that this class directly, pragmatically engage with the political implications of his work. Osofisan writes in English, which is the national language of Nigeria, but is, at the same time, a language associated with access to education. He argues that the choices presented in his plays – the morals or messages – are best implemented by people already in power. They can change the social structure and allow further political revolution to happen.

This is dramatically different from the Theatre for Development movement and the community theatre movement in Africa. Ngugi Wa Thiong'o (Kenya) and Zakes Mda (South Africa) both have practiced a type of theatre that is not only aimed at the general population but is actually co-created by the proletariat (in this case, economically disadvantaged, mainly rural, undereducated villagers). Ngugi acted as a facilitator to help the village of Kamirithu create a piece of theatre. This wasn't just theatre for the community; it was theatre by the community and theatre that created community. The positive effects on the community, as discussed by Dale Byam, are unmistakable, and they certainly drew the attention of those in power: the Kamirithu Center was bulldozed and Ngugi was jailed.

While the sides of this debate between an audience of the elite and an audience of the oppressed are clearly drawn, some artists, like Sircar, attempt to adopt a theatre that would appeal to both the educated elite and the working masses. Such theatres often are hybrid forms that take a variety of song, dance, and speech from different theatrical traditions. This type of hybridization in theatre suggests the possibility that new audiences might be created: Sircar's theatre can educate the oppressed and connect the elite to their rural roots. By Sircar's logic, if a given theatre targets one section of the population, this targeting could act as a reinforcement of the existence of that segment of the population: theatre directed at poor, marginalized groups reinforces the idea that these groups are poor and marginalized. The creation of a new type of theatre allows for us to imagine a new type of audience.

All three of these modes exist side-by-side in the world theatre theory. In contrast, both Brecht and Artaud assume a certain homogeneity to their audiences (a relatively elite homogeneity), even while they challenge the place of the audience within the performance. The question of audience composition arises with a greater degree of regularity in world theatrical writings.

What should the audience do / think / feel during the performance?

The question of who should be in the audience for a given piece of theatre blends quickly with the question of what part the audience plays in the production: spectators, direct participants, spiritual participants, students, something else, or some combination of these. While they differ in terms of class, both Osofisan and the community theatre movement make clear statements about the relationship between formal elements of African theatre – specifically actor / audience relationships – and political change. As a general principle, political theatre requires *something* of its audience: the audience are the people who will eventually make the change happen.

Outside of the African context, Boal's Theatre for Development – also aimed at peasant classes – functions by breaking down theatrical illusion and making spectators into "spect-actors" who actively create the theatre. Boal's theatre might occur guerrilla-style, on a street corner with no warning. The "audience" in this case is free to respond to the scene unfolding before them "in real life." Both in these guerilla settings and in more traditional theatre venues, Boal invites the audience to step inside the action and take over roles. He engages them as active participants in solving the problems of oppression presented in his scripts. The logic here is straightforward – if you want to encourage your audience to take action, your theatre should help them be active. In this case, spectating is the opposite of being active. While Brecht wants his audiences to think while in the theatre, and then use this thought in the outside world, Boal insists on audience members taking action while still in the theatre setting.

Aside from class, Osofisan differs from Boal's concept of Theatre for Development with regard to the spectator. Osofisan says:

> I want desperately to get close to the spectator, to each and every one I have trapped in the darkness or half-light, to penetrate very close and intimate, like a knife in the ribs. I want to make that spectator happy but uncomfortable. I want to turn him open, guts and all, spice him, cook him in the filthy, stinking broil of our history. I want him washed inside out, in the naked truth, and then I sew him back again a different man. I believe that, if we wound ourselves often and painfully enough with reality, with the reality all around you, if we refuse to bandage our sensitive spots away from the hurt of truth, that we can attain a new and positive awareness.
>
> (Awodiya, 1993, p. 18)

Osofisan's spectator is the recipient of the action. While Osofisan demands that his spectators think and consider, he does not encourage his audience to co-create his theatre. The discussion happens after the theatrical event. In this case, Osofisan has a lesson he wants to impart: he is in control "sewing" his audience back together after they have been reformed by the theatre.

The contrast between Boal and Osofisan is clear, but there are other issues that arise in world theatre when considering the role of the audience. Wannous discusses the audience in terms of alienation (in a discussion that parallels Dutt's discussion of the actor). Alienation, here, refers to the Marxist concept that workers have been cut off from their means of production. In Wannous' case, his audience has been trained to answer all questions through *turath* (a general term for tradition that also can indicate a set of cultural documents passed down generationally – *turath* might be thought of as a canon of cultural judgments). For Wannous, relying on tradition is a form of silence – and, of course, democracy is found in communication so silence is undemocratic. Wannous captures the despair he feels at this sort of tradition-inspired silence in the audience in a brief piece in a Lebanese daily *al-Safir*:

> I wanted to say "No." And I search for my tongue but find only a foam of blood and fear. From my severed tongue the defeat started, and the funeral procession set out … from my suppressed "no" the enemy got through, as well as the separation, the poverty, the hunger, the prison, the torturer, and the contemporary Arab collapse …[t]he "no" citizen is, for the Arab thrones, a bigger danger than the Israeli danger, and a conspiracy worse than the imperialist conspiracies.
> (Kassab, 2010, p. 26)

While this piece is specifically about the Camp David Agreement, it addresses the general issue of audience's willingness to accept the way things were or the way things are as the way things should be. Wannous repeatedly talks about separation, severance, and isolation. The audience cannot speak because they are not connected to the concrete realities of their world, to each other, or to themselves: and part of the reason they are cut off is the over-reliance on *turath*. Focusing on tradition separates the audience from the present; being separated from the present, the audience cannot speak to the present; and, without speech there can be no democracy.

The audience must be retrained so that they can critically respond to the theatre and to events around them. Passively sitting by, suppressing their dissenting opinions, is a form of death. After several attempts to engage the audience through other structures, Wannous wrote a play *An Entertainment Evening for June 5th* that dramatizes the audience's role within the theatre. In the play, the lights come up on a stage dominated by a chalkboard that briefly recaps Israel's June 5th attacks (a.k.a. the Six Day War) and then says that this attack shows "even more clearly our need to see ourselves, to look into our mirrors and ask: Who are we? And Why?" (Kassab, 2010, p. 27).

For Wannous the question of audience participation is not a question of actively participating or passively spectating: instead he focuses on the patterns of thought that the theatre should seek to change in the audience, and, indeed, that the audience must change in order to engage with the theatre more fully. Unlike Osofisan, who has definite lessons in mind, Wannous wishes to encourage the audience to question everything. Unlike Boal, Wannous gives primacy to thought rather than action – although he certainly discusses concrete political engagement enough that the connection between thought and action is clearer than it is in Brecht.

The audience composition question has a sharply-drawn line between the elite and the oppressed, and the debates over these sides are contentious. In contrast, there is general consensus around the world that political theatre must in some way shift the traditional audience role. While there is also a sharp line between active and passive theatrical audiences, political theatre requires that its audience be active to some extent. The precise nature of these activities is the grounds for debate. While the question in the prior section was whether the theatre focuses on elite, oppressed, or some combination thereof, the question here is a broader one: what precisely is the audience expected to do during and after the performance?

What is the place of "realism?"

Is political theatre best accomplished with realistic or non-realistic staging techniques? Which parts of the production should be realistic? The characters? The plot? The setting? Everything? If the production is not realistic, what is the relationship between the production and reality? What is "reality"?

The concept of realism varies widely from tradition to tradition. In the early part of the twentieth century, "realistic" portrayals of Shakespeare in China involved prosthetic noses and heavy blue eye-shadow in an attempt to appear European. For purposes of clarity, this chapter uses "realism" to refer to photo-realistic staging practices where sets, costumes, and acting style all attempt to visually and emotively duplicate life in all its physical detail. Revolutionary theatre theorists from Brecht, Artaud, and Grotowski to Soyinka, Osofisan, Sircar, and Wannous have rejected this style of realism for one reason or another, although several types of protest theatre celebrate realism as the one path to political resistance.

Curiously, one of the most common moves in discussions of political theatre and realism is to challenge the idea that realism is an accurate representation of reality. Osofisan, Artaud, and Soyinka reject realism for its inability to get to the heart of the matter, the "real" conditions outside of the theatre: realism is, for them, an inadequate representation of reality. The stage can never be "real" – realism will always fall short of reality, and thus there is a desire to create a theatre that is more real than realism, a theatre that moves beyond appearances to get at the heart of things. Osofisan, Soyinka, and Artaud each accentuate or exaggerate aspects of their staging in order to get at the heart of reality: the things happening on the stage may not look like the things happening outside the window, but looks can be deceiving.

Each of these theorists has argued that the reality presented on their stage shares "real" core issues with the outside reality. For instance, when a giant hand falls from the sky in one of Artaud's plays, this is obviously not realistic, but getting crushed by a giant hand might evoke the same feeling in the audience as being overwhelmed by life. This example raises the question posed above: what counts as real?

Three (of the many) definitions of realism

I. Reportage/reproductive realism

One very logical way of defining realism is to say that realism consists of the accurate reporting / reproduction of actual events in detail as they actually happened using the actual words that were spoken in the moment based on actual records. This form of political performance is often referred to as "documentary theatre." John Kani, a black man who lived through apartheid, collaborated with Athol Fugard on several important pieces of South African theatre and wrote and starred in an autobiographical play that traces major developments of his life. The documentary impulse can be seen in the works of Western artists like Anna Deavere Smith who constructs one-woman plays from interview material. Smith's work explores marginalized communities and communities in crisis. Similarly, the Laramie Project is a piece that utilizes the details of an actual murder case to draw attention to hate crimes and gay rights. Culture Clash and Luis Valdez both deal with some documentary material in their plays while exploring American Latino identity. It is worth noting that all of these examples of documentary theatre in the U.S. involve underrepresented or marginalized groups in some fashion. While there are counter-examples, documentary theatre frequently does focus on telling stories that would not otherwise be heard as they "really" happened. Since official documents, statistics, and histories often leave out the voice of the marginalized, documentary theatre seeks out these stories and presents them.

While documentary theatre insists on primary sources – on direct access to the people and the documents involved, the staging of this work is not always traditionally realistic. The "real" in this theatre is in the events it documents, and not, necessarily, in the way that it is staged. Dalia Basiouny (Egypt) mixes newsreel footage with autobiographical work and political commentary. In this instance, her staging practice is non-illusionistic – it does not recreate a photograph of the life of the people involved – but nonetheless lays claim to "reality" through its insistence on connections to documented events. Similarly, Yael Farber's early work collected stories of torture and oppression from the apartheid era in South Africa. As she was collecting these stories, she often worked with the people involved to create the theatre piece. They were "acting" in a sense, but they were also re-enacting traumatic moments from their past. Farber's work was not photo-realistic either. In one play, sheets hang from the stage and these sheets are at once laundry and props that can be used in non-naturalistic ways – wrapping a character in the sheets, for instance. Farber has her actors / interviewees keep dream journals during the rehearsal process, and many of the symbolist moments in Farber's work come from these dream journals. Farber's work is also a kind of realism – what is real for Farber are the stories and the individual's response to these stories. Finding an effective stage mode for communicating this reality may or may not involve photorealism.

What does documentary theatre do politically? Farber's work is certainly telling stories that might not otherwise have been heard, and South Africa is invested in such storytelling, as seen by its lengthy truth and reconciliation hearings in which the whole country was given the chance to speak about their experiences under apartheid. The speaking of truth was intended to unite a country that had been deeply divided. This type of speaking is powerfully cathartic for the person telling a story to an audience. The simple but profound idea here is that speaking the truth will force those in power to change what they are doing.

Potentially the more "real" or "true" a performance is the more political effect it can have. It doesn't matter how this truth is presented, as long as it is heard. The documentary theatre movement draws its power from its concrete, direct, structural relationship to actual historical events and the people who participated in these events. This "reality" also has a potential downside. Of course, retelling or recreating an event is bound to be different in some fashion from the event itself. Even this most "real" of realisms is still a representation – a story being told after the fact. Farber says that she was always careful not to exploit the stories that her interviewees shared. In making a private event into a public representation, there is always a danger of misrepresentation and even psychological harm to the "owner" of the story.

II. Mimetic realism

While the idea of documentary theatre makes the argument that political effects are encouraged through a relationship with reality, a number of nations in the developing world have high poverty rates: reality is harsh and this harshness is easily visible. If revolutionary theatre is designed to change this reality, then the idea of "realism" is a bit strange. If realism is mimetic, and the reality it has to imitate is harsh, then the realism itself could turn into a harsh reinforcement of already existing social conditions. Nonetheless, if theatre is to change reality, it must interact with the real in some fashion. Some theatre artists turn away from realism entirely in order to generate their effects: and the basic logic in these cases is that theatre has the potential to inspire – to show new possible worlds, and not the current reality. Showing possibilities outside of the harsh reality can, in turn, inspire people to make changes.

Badal Sircar's theatre is the most "unrealistic" of any of the theatres discussed in this chapter. It is struggling to bring about a new reality, which necessarily means imagining things outside of the old reality. Sircar laments that theatre faces harsh financial realities, and he suggests that these are made worse by theatre's desire to compete with cinema. Theatre, he argues, cannot be as effective at realism as cinema, but cinema is also limited to realism. For Sircar, theatre has the potential to be more fantastic. Sircar's theatre with its dance and signing is avowedly non-realistic, and based on his statements about cinema, perhaps even anti-realistic (Sircar, 1978).

Sircar does note that he wants his actors to perform "honestly," which implies that, however non-realistic the performance, being grounded in the bodies of the actor will create a reality based on a given set of circumstances. Sircar says theatre is inherently a "concrete" form as compared to the abstract appeal of music, painting, or sculpture. "Concrete," for Sircar, seems to be associated with narrative elements. Theatre tells a story, and this story is tied directly to the living actors onstage, even though these actors are singing and dancing: Sircar is concerned with the immediate embodiment of the story in living bodies that are not mediated by a camera.

The ability to tell fantastic stories frees Sircar's theatre to generate the world it imagines: it is not bound to show the world as it is in a realistic fashion, it can move toward the world that might be. This theatre is connected to reality through the real bodies of the actors performing, not through the specific staging techniques.

Sircar discusses the ritual nature of theatre as a way of explaining the power of his fantastic performances. Sircar discusses "magic" moments in which theatre causes groups to come together. Rituals may take place in the real world, but they generally point outside themselves to ideas, beings, or power sources that exist in other states of reality. Rituals grow from the real world and their effects change the real world, but – at least in Sircar's reading – their power comes from somewhere unexplainable, somewhere "magic." Non-realistic theatre, then, can be a tool of resistance precisely because it is free of the bonds of reality but is, of necessity, still connected to reality in some fashion. The magic of creation can extend not just to social groups, but to reality itself. Since Sircar's theatre is not realistic and since it relies on fantastic creations and the bodies of the actor, it is difficult to directly theorize. Sircar's theoretical work is full of examples that provide a faint glimmer of the rich experiences of his theatre. To some extent all theatre must be experienced to be understood, but this is particularly true in the case of artists like Artaud and Sircar who attempt to move further away from textually-based, realistic theatre.

III. Socialist realism

Yet another mode of realism combines Osofisan's concern for reality of conflicts with documentary theatre's concern with the reality of the individual. Dutt's realism must reconnect people with their pasts, with their languages: what is real for Dutt is individual people and their individual lives. While Dutt is a staunch Marxist, his version of realism is different from the realism advocated by Mao Zedong or other Chinese and Russian advocates of socialist realism. Socialist realism is by no means a unified type of theatre, but, in Maoist China, official, state-endorsed theatre was limited to a small handful of model operas and ballets – and these model pieces certainly considered themselves to be part of socialist realism. This brand of socialist realism is characterized by starkly drawn characters, e.g. the noble worker, the corrupt manager, the heroic rebel, the morally bankrupt occupying force. The plots were also extremely straightforward. Curiously, given that these productions were operas, socialist realism does not include a realistic performance style. In Russia, socialist realist artists debated the importance of the interior realities of characters: Stanislavski revolutionized the way actors approached their roles by helping actors ask questions about characters' psychological motivations.

Dutt states that his work differs from socialist realism, and by this he means that his actors should not be the heroic figures seen in Maoist model opera where good and evil are clearly delineated in different characters. Dutt, while recognizing that right and wrong are still absolutes, argues different social classes perceive right and wrong differently, and that any given person will be torn by conflicting impulses. Dutt's realism focuses on the complexity of these competing impulses.

In order to return people to themselves, to de-alienate society, he must remind people of who they are, what they know, and what they have experienced: he must portray divided people. Wannous sought to end the audience's alienation by making them consider social problems from a variety of angles. Dutt's theatre actually stages this consideration of problems in order to de-alienate the actors and thus present a more realistic, un-alienated theatre – a theatre that will generate social change precisely because the audience will finally be able to recognize themselves in the characters presented.

Each of these three types of realism focuses on a different part of reality (psychological, material, or historical) and a different part of the performance. The goal is always to generate a political effect – a change in the real world – but there are many paths to this goal. While political theatre must navigate its relationship to reality, these relationships are incredibly varied and there is no overarching pattern. The big questions to ask in this regard are as follows: What is the relationship of theatre to reality? What counts as reality?

The question of language

What language should theatre be in? Any given language has several different ways of speaking it. Parisian French is different from Québécois French, which is different again from the French spoken in Senegal. Within any given country, the same language shifts its form with class and region. If political theatre is intended to bring the nation together, then some form of a national language might be appropriate – either as a means to encourage more people to adopt such a language or as a means to unite those who already speak it. In many of the formerly colonized countries in the world, European languages are used for official communications and for higher education. At the same time, some of these countries contain several hundred native languages within their borders. Writing in native languages might reach a portion of the population in a way that a European national language could not. Some revolutionary theatres have decreased the importance of text in performance and instead rely on the languages of music and dance. If the intended audiences are indeed the working class, and the working class is largely undereducated, then theatre must find "languages" appropriate to this audience.

Badal Sircar poses just such questions:

> When I try to talk about the language of theatre, the first question I have to face is – who am I? That includes series of questions – where do I come from? Where do I belong in this complex social structure in the complex world? What are my times? What is my language? What is my theatre? What is the language of my theatre?
>
> (1978, p. 26)

Language is a question of identity. The language that you speak can define who you are. Language is also, obviously, the shared vehicle by which we communicate with the rest of the world. Revolution is communication for both Dutt and Wannous. Dutt laments the fact that people have been "driven into their burrows of merely private existence" (Dutt, 1982, p. 3). Dutt goes on to comment on the nature of language. He says, quoting Marx, that language arises from need. When the need to have replaces all other needs, meaningful communication dies. The need to have is directed inward, language and communication are directed outward. Dutt notes that the city gradually kills off the individual language of the people who move there, and in saying this, he says that these people are separated from their pasts. Language is identity and identities change as people change. While change can be good, Dutt is also concerned that too much change will lead to a loss of identity and / or language. Dutt's theatre seeks a language that is unique, communicative, revolutionary, and connected to the past. This is a tall order for any one language given the apparent contradictions in these terms: how can a unique, specific language still communicate to a larger group? How can a language stay connected to the past and still be revolutionary? The case study that began this chapter avoids the language issue by shifting the focus to music and action. Boal encourages his spectators to generate their own unique languages. Osofisan and Soyinka write primarily in English: Osofisan's writing tends to be plain-spoken while Soyinka's writing tends to be very ornate. Wannous writes in a highly-educated Arabic. When reading political theatre around the world it is important to consider which language is being used, how that language is being used, and how much of the performance is based in language. The answers to these questions will vary radically, and the same questions will emerge again in Chapter 4.

Questions of nation and community

In what ways can theatre promote nationalism or create / shape nations? In what way is revolutionary theatre the product of larger global forces like the needs of the workers? In other words, is political theatre political in a national or a world context?

All four of the theatre artists in this chapter use theatre to address specific social issues in their respective environments. That being said, Wannous specifically discusses the ways in which his theatre is Arab, uniting people across a variety of nations. In contrast, Dutt discusses his theatre as the theatre of the workers. While he may address the specific problems of Indian workers, his related reference to theorists from elsewhere unites these workers with workers all over the world. Sircar discusses an Indian theatre: the theatre of a single nation. Osofisan discusses a theatre for the educated in Nigeria: a theatre for a portion of a single nation designed to change the whole nation. These varying degrees of broadness can be thought of as creating communities and connections around the world or within a nation.

National theatre might refer to a theatre created by a nation – a reflection of the qualities of that nation. National theatre might also refer to a theatre designed to create a new image of what the nation might be. These ideas exist in a tension with one another: either the theatre speaks to the nation that exists or it speaks to the nation that might be. Sircar is at once taking the current nation into account and building a theatre that will shift the rural population of the nation into a new mode of political interaction. Sircar's theatre is trying to unite various communities within the nation into a new, hybrid community.

Similarly, when Jiao Juyin (see Chapter 5) writes about the creation of national Chinese theatre, he is also writing about a unification and celebration of Chinese culture. China's boundaries shifted dramatically over the course of its history, and the Qing Dynasty, which ruled until the early part of the twentieth century, was Manchurian. The Manchus were sometimes allied with China and sometimes allied with the Mongols (the force that the Great Wall was built to protect against). In other words, China's last dynasty had come from the outside with a new set of customs. Shortly after the fall of the Qing Dynasty, Japan forced China to sign unfavorable peace treaties. China was a state in need of national unity.

Jiao Juyin proposed a nationalizing of spoken theatre (Western-style theatre) as a cultural representation of the new type of Chinese identity he and others hoped for. Jiao's new national theatre was to be spiritual, but this spirituality was always to be connected with the physical. Jiao insists on the audience and the actors co-creating the theatre. He also discusses the place of poetry, traditional theatrical techniques, a focus on action, and the search for "truth" in his new theatre. While Jiao never finished the essay where he most clearly discusses the nationalization of drama, the outline that remains suggests that Jiao is picking the best elements of both Western and Chinese theatres in order to generate a new, distinctly Chinese, culture. Even in an explicitly nationalist piece of theory, hybridity has a place.

Sometimes the communities formed by political theatre are even broader than the nation. Wannous' theory moves fluidly between the category of nation and the idea of an Arab world (which, like Soyinka's statements about Africa or even Jiao's notion of China, is always going to be incomplete representations of the complexity and diversity of these groups). For both Syria and the Arab world, Wannous is discussing a theatre that will change people. His theory does not focus on exactly what these changes will lead to, but it is clear that he is desperately dissatisfied with the passivity he sees around him. He sees a group united by a cultural heritage, and he envisions a theatre that can overcome the negative portions of this cultural heritage.

Political theatre will establish or reinforce some community. The scope of this community is an important question to consider when analyzing theatre around the world.

Conclusions

If ideology informs everything we do, then all theatre is political. This chapter addressed world theatre theories that specifically discussed their place in the political spectrum. In the essays discussed here, Wannous and Dutt talk about the form of theatre secondarily and about its political impact first. Sircar focuses on a new hybrid form, while Osofisan describes a more general theatrical innovation. At other points, these writers express other portions of their theatre philosophies and focus on different aspects of the questions raised above. These authors do agree on the fact that political theatre is situated theatre – that it must, in some way correspond to the specific ideological situation in which it is created.

This specificity acts as a caution. When attempting to determine what the political impact of a given piece of world theatre might be, it would be easy to use Brecht or another familiar theorist as an explanatory device. Certainly, a Brechtian analysis would provide interesting information, but theory is, itself, ideologically shaped. Brechtian theory grows out of the same ideological milieu as Brechtian theatre. To place another theatre into the Brechtian ideology would be to perform an alienation – to cut the theatre off from its own ideological context. Certainly, there will be similarities – the strong Marxist tendencies that run through much of the political theatre in the world suggest a world-wide proletariat if nothing else, but each political project is taking a distinctive form for a distinctive reason within a distinctive ideology. Nonetheless, issues of language, social class, national identity, colonization, hybridity, traditional theatre, and notions of realism suggest that there are substantial differences both among world theatres and in the theories behind these theatres. Each of these different structural debates relates directly and clearly to theatre's attempt to change or reinforce current ideologies.

Chapter 4

Decolonization, hybridity, postcoloniality, interculturalism, and globalization

> French directors were sent to Africa to teach Africans how to do good theatre [...] Africans who succeeded in putting up shows opted for forms with song and dance, which were considered 'authentically African' and were the only theatre that could be exported to a Europe still hungry for exoticism. The result: Young Ivorian writers and directors lost their 'mirrors' [...] most of my plays don't try to demonstrate how Ivorian I am. Identity is not a given but a shifting notion
>
> Koffi Kwahulé, "This New Eurafrique Magic"

Case study: Aime Cesaire's 1969, *A Tempest*

The latter half of the twentieth century saw a profusion of adaptations of Shakespeare performed around the world. One of the most famous of these adaptations was Aime Cesaire's *Une Tempête*, an adaptation of Shakespeare's *The Tempest* set in Haiti. While most of the case studies in this volume focus on a single production, this case study will use Cesaire's published script and the stage directions contained therein as evidence of many productions of the same show. As a writer of the Negritude movement (see Chapter 9), Cesaire had strong ties to France, the Caribbean, and Africa. His 1969 play came near the end of a wave of decolonization in Africa and more than a hundred years after Haiti gained independence through the world's only successful slave revolt.

Cesaire's adaptation keeps the basic plot of Shakespeare's work largely intact. Prospero, an exiled former duke, uses magic to sink a ship carrying his brother – the current duke, the king, and the prince. Prospero's servants / slaves, Caliban and Ariel (natives to the island that Prospero now claims), confuse and trick the castaways. Prospero's daughter Miranda falls in love with the prince, and Prospero consents to allow the two of them to marry. In Shakespeare's version, Prospero renounces his magic and leaves the island with the king and the newly-married couple, leaving his servants behind. In Cesaire's version, Caliban and Ariel, who figure much more prominently, are both black, in contrast to Prospero who is white. This Prospero sets Ariel free but continues to live on the island with Caliban. Another significant difference in Cesaire's version is the presence of Eshu, a Yorùbá deity associated with seeking wisdom and, more prominently in Cesaire's text, with disruptive trickery.

Cesaire's text shifts Shakespeare's story to make its colonial undercurrents clear. Caliban hates Prospero, and reacts violently when Prospero suggests that he has provided civilization in the form of language: this matches the criticism of the idea that the colonized world was a savage place that Europe needed to save. Caliban criticizes Ariel for willingly serving Prospero, a parallel to the colonial criticism of those who attempted to serve the Europeans. On this level, Cesaire's text provides a passionate, straightforward attack on neo-colonial attitudes, showing directly and clearly the damages caused by colonization and the insidious patterns of thought that remain after colonization ends.

While the overall thrust of Cesaire's work is clear, several aspects of this work raise questions: remember, in the last chapter, theatrical structure frequently carried with it political ideas. If the object of Cesaire's critique is European colonialism, why use Shakespeare to level this critique? The Negritude movement is a celebration of the uniqueness of African culture. How can one of the most important texts written by a Negritude author use Shakespeare? Is this text a copy of Shakespeare? Is it an attack on Shakespeare? Is it using the tools provided by Shakespeare? Is it something different entirely that just happens to make reference to Shakespeare? Are there any elements of this text or performance that are not European – any indications of native theatre traditions?

Curiously, Cesaire's text opens with a metatheatrical moment in which the various actors discuss which roles they play. The director steps in and assigns some roles and allows actors to choose others. We see actors putting on costume pieces. Why is this reminder of the idea of "performance" present in an anticolonial play? What is being said about cultural identity? About the roles colonialism creates? About freedom?

Introduction

As the last chapter suggested, some models of thought consider everything to be political. In the context of theatre theory from around the world, culture is certainly politicized. The world is a connected place – trade routes, wars, conquests, colonization, alliances, and even tourism have shaped global interaction for millennia. Our current definition of globalization may be new, but global exchanges are not. Culture is shared, exchanged, imposed, defended, attacked, sold, assimilated, rejected, and otherwise interacted with as various groups around the world meet.

We see some concern with circulation and cultural contact in the discourses about "purity" of culture in Thucydides, in fourteenth-century Spain, and in contemporary Europe. Desire for cultural purity in several of these contexts has provided justification for extreme, often immoral acts, but it has also led to movements to preserve various languages and celebrate various cultures. These concerns, however, are largely political and not artistic, even when the immediate point of reference is art or literature.

When concerns over cultural exchange (as opposed to preventing cultural exchange) and interaction do come to the forefront of Western theatrical theory in the twentieth century, the *general* thought is that the world provides a rich tapestry of theatrical traditions that can be studied and used to improve upon European theatre. For example, Euro-American theatre chose to study Asian theatre in order to figure out different modes of considering representation: they chose to create a hybrid theatre that blended different cultures together, which is a distinct contrast to fears about keeping a culture "pure." The Globe to Globe Festival held at Shakespeare's Globe Theatre in London in 2012 was a stunning example of this sort of exchange. Each of Shakespeare's plays was performed in a different language by representatives from different countries. The exuberant description of this event on the Globe's website[1] nicely encapsulates the optimism of the Western idea of cultural exchange as choice:

> Many of the world's greatest directors, over six hundred actors from all nations, and audiences from every corner of our polyglot community, will assemble to celebrate the stories, the characters and the relationships, which are etched into all of us. Shakespeare is the language which brings us together better than any other, and which reminds of our almost infinite difference, and of our strange and humbling commonality. And above all there are the plays themselves, plays which have travelled far and wide, and which on their travels have midwifed new theatre cultures, spread light and laughter, and helped nations, new and old, to define themselves.

Cultures choose to define themselves (with the help of Shakespeare), come together, form a community, respect differences, and generally enrich us all through the sharing of stories.

The word "chose" in the prior sentence is significant here. Meetings between various societies in the world are seldom balanced. While the Western powers may have some degree of choice in what parts of world culture they take in, other nations, particularly those subjected to colonization (e.g. Latin American, African, India, Korea, and Caribbean nations), were often forced to adopt parts of other cultures. Even when, as in cases like China, there was no formal colonization by the West, the economic and military power the West deployed put (and continues to put) cultural pressure on other nations.

Outside of the West, the *general* pattern is different: this is not a matter of choosing elements that might improve a theatre. In this model, the dominant cultural mode is often associated with power – which means both that European theatre is associated with oppression and with being powerful / modern enough to resist oppression. On the other hand, native / indigenous / local / traditional theatre is associated with both resistance to Europe *and* potentially with anti-modern ideas that are keeping the formerly colonized nation from advancing. Formerly colonized nations feature a mix of cultures, some indigenous, and some imposed from the outside: colonization has been discussed as the desire to spread European culture to "uncivilized" people (who the Globe Theatre suggests can learn about their own nations through Shakespeare), which completely ignores the already extant cultures of these people. As these cultures mix and blend – sometimes harmoniously and often through conflict – new cultures are created. These cultures reflect a different sort of hybridity than the culture of choice described above. Intercultural, blended, and hybrid theatres are the product of cultural interaction: these interactions look dramatically different and are theorized dramatically differently depending on which side of the power divide you are on.

The questions posed by the material in this chapter are as follows: Should cultures – and theatre specifically – remain pure and attempt to preserve the culture in question? How would one go about defining a pure culture in any case? If cultures mix, how do power imbalances change this mixture? Should theatre reflect mixed cultures? What elements of theatre should transfer between cultures? Can ritual and tradition be used to resist colonial influences? Are ritual and tradition keeping countries from advancing? Can the thoughts / feelings / stories / philosophies of nations be expressed if the theatrical techniques used are from other nations? These are all questions about the nature of culture and its interactions with power: in other words, these are questions about how people live and the amount of choice they have in this matter. Few areas in art and literature around the world are as hotly contested as this one.

The above questions are slightly different from those posed by many of the chapters in that there is general consensus around some of the answers. "Preserving" culture, for instance, has generally been critiqued, in recent scholarship, as a false project that assumes a singular cultural form rather than an evolving culture. It takes something that should be a living, breathing, evolving project and makes it into a museum relic, albeit a well-preserved relic. While this is the current general consensus, it hasn't always been, and thus exploring the logics that allow us to reach this conclusion is worthwhile. Such exploration of possibilities allows us to more fully grasp the project of different types of cultural practice.

Definitions

The materials from this chapter have generated a profusion of terms, and the definitions of these terms shifts depending on the context around the world. The brief definitions that follow are the usages that are most common in U.S. academic texts. Several of the theorists anthologized below provide their own definitions of these words – and these definitions are often quite contentious. It is useful to know the definitions against which these theorists are writing.

The definition of the word "colonial" is not subject to a great deal of debate. Colonization was the process of one nation formally taking away the political autonomy of another nation. Some colonies were "settled" by their colonizers – colonizers moved to these places en masse. Other colonies saw only the occasional government official, missionary, or businessman from the colonizing power. Colonization has a political dimension, but it also impacts culture and society at all levels. The colonizing power frequently viewed the colonized nation as an economic vehicle – the colonizer grew rich while those colonized were exploited. While this definition is uncontroversial, figuring out exactly which nations or groups were subject to colonization proves more difficult, and terms like semi-colonial have come into existence to discuss nations (e.g. China) that never formally ceded the entirety of their political power, but who, it is argued, lived as de facto colonies regardless. Some nations like Japan were involved in both sides of semi-colonial and colonial relationships through their history (and, in the case of Japan, potentially simultaneously). Most often, when colonization is discussed in the Western academy, it refers to African, Caribbean, and Indian colonies formed in the late nineteenth and early twentieth centuries, but Latin America, North Africa, and Asia have their own histories with colonization as well (some dating back to the fourteenth century and some continuing into the twenty-first century). While the U.S. started as a series of colonies of the European powers, even after independence, the former colonists remained on land that had initially been settled by other groups – but the U.S. is seldom included on the side of the colonized (although it is often implicated as a colonizing or semi-colonizing influence elsewhere). Anticolonial refers to forces in the colonized nation that opposed colonization.

"Postcolonial" refers to the status of a nation after formal colonization ends, and, as with colonization, this term is most often applied in the African, Caribbean, and Indian contexts. Some nations like the U.S. that were once colonies are seldom described as postcolonial. The idea in labelling something "post" colonial is that the colonization is still somehow having an impact on the current functioning of the nation. Sometimes this takes the form of the postcolonial nation adopting languages, cultural elements, parliamentary systems, economic systems, or models for international relations from their former colonizer – and in many cases, to the borders (and existence) of the nation-state in question. Colonization also tended to leave the colonized nation in poor economic conditions, and these conditions were made worse by the racial (racist) policies that tended to be the direct or indirect legacy of colonial rule. Postcolonial is both a term of resistance and something to be resisted. It marks that the legacy of colonization must be carefully considered and fought against, but, on the other hand, it marks the current close connection between the former colony and the colonizer.

"Multicultural" refers to one of the ways that governments or societies choose to respond to the diversity of cultures contained within a given community's boundaries. There are many, many different forms of multiculturalism, but the term generally refers to a stated desire to treat and represent all cultures equitably. Multicultural is most often a pluralistic impulse – an idea that multiple cultures can coexist independently of one another in the same society.

Some modes of multiculturalism also consider the possibility of cultural blending. One term for this, a term that is most often deployed in artistic contexts, is "intercultural." The multitude of intercultural movements generally attempt to combine cultural elements from two or more cultures into a single artistic product. The various cultural elements are still visible and potentially distinguishable from one another.

If the elements blur together to the extent that they cannot be told apart, this is often referred to as "hybridity" – and this term is applied in artistic, political, and social spheres. It is a common postcolonial argument to note that the postcolonial individual is always hybrid, and that the goal of postcolonial society should not be to attempt to undo this hybridity. This common line of argument often continues to note that the hybrid belongs to both worlds, but also doesn't fully fit in either world. The "cosmopolitan" is one particular type of hybrid – one who has adapted elements of multiple cultures in order to fit in one of the world centers. The imagination of the cosmopolitan person is one who moves fluidly between multiple languages, is fluent in current social developments, and can fit equally well in London, Paris, New York, Shanghai, or Tokyo. To be cosmopolitan implies wealth, education, and at least some degree of power.

One extreme form of hybridity is globalization. Globalization is the idea that the planet is linked economically, culturally, and (less often discussed in the literature and theatre worlds) environmentally. Forces like the International Monetary Fund promote certain types of development. Inexpensive instant communication paired with faster travel means that the connections between distant parts of the globe are, indeed, becoming stronger. Globalization's advocates suggest that these closer connections will help economically disadvantaged areas of the world. Globalization's opponents point out that colonization also claimed that it would help the economically disadvantaged, and that globalization is a means of exerting control over other countries.

All of the above terms refer to ways in which cultures might interact. Each of the above terms has variations within it and all the terms are different from one another. "Intercultural theatre" and "postcolonial theatre" are categories of study that include much of the diversity of ways in which cultures might interact. With each theory discussed below, it is useful to ask what manner of cultural interaction is being assumed or argued for. What are the power relationships involved? What is the degree of separation between the cultures? What is the degree of blending between the cultures? What is the intended outcome of the meeting of cultures? Is there an implied or stated universalism? Is there an implied or stated particularity to each culture?

Western interculturalism

U.S. theatre theorists do not frame their work in terms of colonial resistance. While the 1990s and 2000s in Britain saw a profusion of plays concerned with immigration, immigrants, and cultural diversity, this discussion and the issues raised are simply not the same as discussions of migration in the rest of the world. Power dynamics shape every question in this book, but in this chapter, power dynamics preclude the West from directly experiencing the full range of questions explored in other contexts (although postcolonial theory does pose these questions). In other chapters, similarities and differences were treated as neutrally as possible, but in this case pointing out the contrast between Western theories and the rest of the world will, almost of necessity, act as a critique of the Western theories.

The West absolutely has intercultural theatre, but this theatre looks very different from intercultural theatre created elsewhere: the one small piece of overlap lies in the idea that interculturalism might be used to create art – that interactions between cultures can create an interesting product.

For example, Eugenio Barba (who has devoted his life to theatrical practice and makes no claims to a unified theory for his work – in fact, he describes all his work as deeply idiosyncratic) adopts movement practices and formal elements from Asian and European theatre not usually in the mode of Western realism, and often privileges the physical over the linguistic. Indeed, one of Barba's best-known, if most enigmatic, concepts is the pre-expressive – the ways of moving that humanity shares before any cultural interventions or complications. Barba and Savarese's *A Dictionary of Theatre Anthropology* (1991) is an attempt to document and categorize the pre-expressive. As implied by its title, Barba considers this to be a scientific study, albeit one that leads to an amazing artistic practice.

This branch of theatre practice starts with premises about the possibility of universally shared theatrical characteristics, and sometimes even universally shared human characteristics. This theory then moves to questions about the differences among cultures, be these differences surface-level or deeper. Barba takes as foundational the idea that some aspects of culture are translatable / transferable despite cultural difference. There are physical, artistic, or social principles that are basic enough to transcend individual cultures, and these elements can move between cultures.

Barba seeks to find a universal beneath the surface differences. Barba's pre-expressive provides a means of understanding how shifts in body weight create certain effects and a means of figuring out portions of other techniques that can be instructive in the actor's own practice. Within the context of an actor's work, which is squarely where Barba places it, this idea is unproblematic, if difficult to implement. However, the idea of the pre-expressive has long since left the space of theatrical practice and entered into the theoretical world, where it becomes more problematic. Hunting for the shared basic movement principles of humanity can easily turn into a search for a primitive, unspoiled, pure, original human. Inevitably, such searches turn away from Europe and toward the former colonies, reinscribing racist ideas about cultural superiority even as they place value on "the primitive." To be clear, this is something that is done with Barba's theory; Barba's own practice focuses on cultural exchange. He "barters" his theatre for other theatres on what he characterizes as a relatively equal playing field.

In terms of what separates cultures, Barba says:

> [t]oday the very word 'comparison' seems inadequate to me, since it separates the two faces of the same reality. I can say that I 'compare' . . . traditions only if I compare their epidermises, their diverse conventions, the many different performance styles. But if I consider that which lies beneath those luminous and seductive epidermises and discern the organs which keep them alive, the poles of the comparison blend into a single profile.
>
> (1996, p. 218)

In other words, Barba believes that cultural differences are only skin-deep. While Barba is referring to Eurasian theatre here, his general point has certainly influenced critical approaches to understanding the relationship between African and Western theatre. "Culture" in this case is the shell we put around our core, universal humanity. Barba also says, however, that in reading theatre "there are analogous principles because they [the theatres] are born of similar physical conditions in different contexts. They are not however homologous, since they do not share a common history." For Barba, saying that differences are only skin-deep does not necessarily invalidate the idea that context can radically alter similar concepts.

Barba does not directly discuss the power dynamics at play in this negotiation between universal and specific, an issue that becomes readily apparent in Western intercultural theatre's discussion of "choice." Western intercultural theatre is generally predicated on a model of interested artists choosing to collaborate across cultural borders. At times this shifts to the idea of Western artists studying and then adapting / adopting / appropriating the cultural practices of other artists, but generally Western interculturalism is collaborative. Collaboration implies choice and equality. Critics of interculturalism broadly, and Western interculturalism specifically (e.g. Rustom Bharucha), refer to this idea of choice as (false) "volunteerism." The power dynamics of colonization prevent a totally "free" choice.

Eugenio Barba's idea of a cultural barter exemplifies the idea of interculturalism as a choice. The basic concept is that groups will meet and share performances with one another, paying for the privilege of being a spectator with the work of being a performer. Sometimes these barters culminate in some sort of cultural blending where Barba or one of his company members melds individual performances into a unified spectacle for an additional audience. At other times, the barter would end after the last performer had completed a performance. I participated in a barter during August 2011 at the Odin Teatret in Denmark during an acting workshop. The other participants in the workshop came from around the world and the first step of the barter consisted of a number of individual performances by these artists. On this barter day Barba discussed his notion of culture. He said culture was always an individual thing. He said, "I believe in friends, not cultures." When I asked why the barters almost always contained people of multiple nationalities, if not multiple cultures, he said that theatre groups were micro-cultures. Any group, any community forms its own culture. In his initial barters, he was less concerned with *Italy* in 1974 and more concerned with finding the older songs and dances from the particular town he was in. The idea of friends from around the world sharing what makes them unique and thereby creating works of art is the beautiful vision of Western interculturalism (and with all beautiful visions, it focuses on certain things and willfully ignores others).

Western intercultural theatre certainly has political implications, but the practitioners of this form often focus instead on the artistic implications of this theatre. There is a strong underlying assumption that art, being linked to culture, will impact society and create political change, but, aside from Brecht's intercultural work, this assumption goes largely unrecorded.

While it renounces the political in favor of the artistic, Western interculturalism spends a good deal of time trying to determine precisely what "culture" is – as seen in Barba's discussion of micro-culture. If an element of staging practice, a mode of speaking, a style of dress, or a dance step is taken out of its original context and put in a new context, has intercultural theatre been achieved? Is the culture contained in the plot and the message of the theatrical piece? Is culture a network of signs, constantly being reread? Trying to locate culture often leads to the assumption that culture is a static object that can be located. While Western theory allows for culture as a performed aspect of society – something that people do in addition to something that they are – it nonetheless can also define other cultures relatively narrowly (e.g. Chinese theatre is conflated with Chinese Opera, which is conflated with Beijing Opera, which is, itself, a mixture of a number of local and regional forms). Culture is reduced to a list of items that can be enumerated and analyzed. Western intercultural theatre then often characterizes itself as an apolitical experimentation with artistic forms in order to negotiate various definitions of cultural interactions in order to find the relationships between the universal and relative parts of culture.

World foundations

When focusing on the place of culture in modern world theatre practice, the issue of resistance to Western colonial and imperial power looms large. Aime Cesaire, Wole Soyinka, Tawfiq al-Hakim, Kateb Yacine, and Ama Ata Aidoo all write plays that deal with the damage done by colonial powers.

Colonization and intercultural theatre are not the only places that the idea of culture emerges in relationship to world theatre. In Chinese history, the regional variations between opera styles openly accentuated intracultural difference, and Mao Zedong attempted to meld all of these into a single, orthodox style that could stand in for a unified China. In this case, "culture" is a marker of unity and difference within a single country. In South Africa, John Kani, Athol Fugard, and Lewis Nkosi used theatre as a form of cultural and political resistance to apartheid. In this case, theatre was a marker of ways in which culture could be used by a majority to resist the rule of a minority. In Kenya, Ngugi Wa Thiongo's community-based theatre served a Marxist goal – providing the mass of under-educated, impoverished villagers with confidence in their ability to express themselves. When one looks beyond the modern world, the possible relationships between theatre and culture become even more diverse (and considerably less accessible to Anglophone scholars).

More than any other chapter in the book, the theories that follow represent only a tiny fraction of what could be said about the relationship between theatre and culture. Each excerpt below raises its own set of questions. Since the question of who has the authority to speak on behalf of cultures is central to much of world theatre, I will forgo my usual introductory set of questions here and let each of the critics below pose their own questions on their own.

Buenaventura and anti-culture

Enrique Buenaventura (1925–2003) describes his own career as eclectic. He formed his own theatre troupe, Teatro Experimental de Cali (TEC) in Colombia in 1955. The theatre persevered through the various armed conflicts that have been part of Colombia's history since the 1960s. These conflicts have varied from riots and protests in cities to guerrilla fighting to open conflict between armed members of conflicting political parties. Culturally, Colombia contains a mix of African, Spanish, native Latin American, U.S., and Middle Eastern people and customs. As with much of Latin American, Spain conquered Colombia and held it as a colony. The African influence comes largely from the slave trade.

Buenaventura defines culture in a different way from the other theorists discussed here, who use culture to mean the customs, lifestyle, and art of a given set of people, e.g. Chilean culture is different from Cuban culture. For Buenaventura, the contrast is between high and low culture – those who adopt the markers of status and consider themselves "cultured" and those who do not. Buenaventura raises a common critique of this deployment of culture, namely that a great deal of what counts as high culture comes from Europe and the U.S. He laments the fact that theatre in Colombia has trained people to believe that they cannot be cultured unless they know what Europeans know. While there are certainly moments of active cultural imperialism in history – moments when a dominant power instilled its religious, artistic, and cultural standards on other people in order to maintain a power structure – there is a more insidious type of pressure that Buenaventura notes.

Unlike Wole Soyinka and Femi Osofisan who fight over the place of tradition and ritual in contemporary theatre, Buenaventura articulates lines existing between culture and politics, between mechanical and human, and between rejecting or accepting colonial history. With every binary he presents he finds a way to make the theatre a middle ground between these forces. "Middle ground" here does not signal compromise, but, instead, the creation of a new space in which new possibilities open: not precisely a hybrid, but rather a new species entirely.

Buenaventura talks about a poor theatre that is outside of the system. What are the specific characteristics of such a theatre and what are its aims? How is it different from the other theatres Buenaventura critiques?

Extract 4.1 "Theatre and Culture"
Enrique Buenaventura, translated by Joanne Pottlitzer

At a 1967 symposium in Montreal, I, along with other colleagues, had to answer the question: "What kind of theatre should we do?" Throughout almost my entire professional life, I have been asked that same question and with each new stage of my life I responded differently. But when I heard it in that foreign country, where the only thing familiar to us Latin Americans were the Indian reservations, I suddenly felt I was on another planet, stunned. I don't remember what I answered. I said something vague and unrelated—"anti-culture"— and I realized I was again entering a new stage.

At this time I had just finished *Documents from Hell*, which was staged by Danilo Tenorio of TEC (Experimental Theatre of Cali), my own theatre in Colombia, and was the most serious attempt we at TEC had made to become involved in the life of our people. Previously we had worked to build a "cultural" theatre—with certain conflicts and occasional attempts at liberation. I have never cared much for the vague word used for everything, the word "culture." My hostile attitude was not one to boast about, it was something like a rebellion against one's father. Yet I was a "man of culture," living and working in it, defending it, and speaking in its name.

What does "culture" mean for a theatre worker in Latin America? Look at TEC, when it was an "official," established theatre. It was a modernist company, that is, a company that had ended the star system in its staging and ensemble work; generally, it reserved the star system for the director, who felt it was necessary to be up on plays currently produced in Europe and the U.S. These, together with a few classics, formed the repertory.

Little by little my innocent distrust of "culture" became a conscious rejection of the dramas prepared and elaborated in Europe and the U.S. for us to sell here. In theatre, the product comes with instructions for unpacking and displaying. It is necessary to travel abroad—naturally!—to see plays and acting techniques, to keep up to date.

Our most serious problem is clientele. The need to consume those theatrical products—created for totally different people who are accustomed to them—is not felt by our potential customers. It must be created. Movies and television have satisfied their basic need to "spend" the dead time between work and sleep, and all our theatre can do is try to lure audiences away from them. Our urban theatre-goers are those who, having more time between work and sleep, become interested in "culture." They know something about European, American, and new Latin American authors; this select nucleus of initiates little by little wins over a few sensitive professionals and the bourgeoisie who have "traveled."

In the large Latin American capitals this process sometimes creates a solid theatrical institution with producers, backers, connections, authors' rights, actors' unions, etc. Of course it is subject—and increasingly so—to violent, cyclical attacks of barbaric Latin-Americanism, military landslides which do away with all art out of simple self-defense. The situation is the opposite of what many people think: the current battle of the CIA is to stabilize, to institutionalize the Latin American "intelligence" forces. Sometimes the CIA finds itself caught between two opposing forces: those of order, which in many countries consider art a kind of disorder, and those of disorder, the students, who fight to turn the cultural resources we get from Europe and the U.S. into something digestible by "corrupting" the product with an infusion of politics. Many Latin Americans who belong to the international republic of arts and letters resolve this contradiction by making a radical separation between art and politics. As artists, their fundamental concern is art; their only objective is good art. As men they are politicians and commit themselves to all kinds of declarations. The best way to do this is to live in Europe and support Cuba. I am not making any accusations—I consider that position deeply honest.

I traveled for five years throughout my continent, to ports, cities, and villages, my contacts with culture only occasional. Except in Recife, Pernambuco, and in Buenos Aires, where I was with theatre people, I didn't have enough money to go to plays or movies. Once, in Recife, I went by the Santa Isabel theatre and I saw that an Italian opera was playing (with Brazilian singers). I continued walking and a few blocks away I came upon a "Bumba meu boi," a kind of popular dance/opera/pantomime. How can they call either one "culture?" I told some Brazilian friends that instead of the opera there should be a "Bumba meu boi" at the Santa Isabel. Today, with even folklore sucked into "culture," I wouldn't make the same suggestion. In Bahia and in Haiti there was once a culture which united marketplace and ritual, the sea with the port, the city with the peasant who comes to sell his products. It had nothing to do with folklore, that is, with those remains of an exotic life shown to the tourist, but dealt with organic relationships. But the system has penetrated even the farthest corners of these places, corrupting them. Political bosses like Duvalier use these forms for electioneering, giving them local and racial "color," perverting them: such is the tragic case of Haiti.

We artists are not going to decolonize culture by ourselves. We alone are not going to achieve a fusion of the European and North American elements which—although the folklorists and indigenists protest—are imbedded in us. We are not able to join those elements with the timid—because colonized—culture of the majority. The abyss between the two, like the abyss between productivity and misery, can begin to be closed only by revolutionary violence, and only new forms of society born out of revolution can heal the split permanently.

A director-actor-playwright, a "comedian" as one says too aptly in Spanish, does his job with his whole organism, and transmits experience through a form that is direct, alive—and ephemeral. He cannot pack up his way of life and memories and go off to set them down in a tranquil place without soldiers, without guerrillas, without starving proletarian masses, without students. I confess that I regret very much that I am unable to escape, that every day I have to make an almost mystical effort not to run away. My commitment, fortunately, is not just a personal attitude nor has it been an individual decision. It encompasses the story of TEC.

We have been an official theatre, pampered by the government and the press, invited to the Theatre of Nations. We have sold the cultural product like more or less honest merchants. Yet without really knowing how, without anyone suggesting it to us, the need to develop our own work with our own raw materials and to show it here led us to confront the system structurally. The challenge inherent in the kind of independence that is not proclamation, not manifesto, not folklore nor nationalism, willy-nilly ends up questioning the system. This challenge cannot be absorbed, it is not culture, it uses art for subversive ends. The system doesn't accept it. The trouble is that we don't accept it totally either. To believe that we are outside the system when we only have serious differences with it is self-deception. To shake loose entirely from established institutions requires a solidarity and experience that we do not have. Many Latin American theatre people find themselves in a similar trap. In our country, however, especially in university groups, there are ways out of the dilemma. The most common has been to do "political" theatre, to use the theatre as a form of political agitation. That way you can kick and scream, you can scratch the skin of the system—but you continue to be its prisoner, you remain in its power.

To let yourself be forced to either the pole of commercialism or that of agitprop only leads to eliminating any possibility of true artistic subversion, of undermining the system in its essentials: the consciences and conduct of its victims.

The only possibility is to become the owners of our own means of production, to develop our product and communicate among ourselves directly, even to exchange the product directly—in large zones of our community—for other things that we do not produce. Such exchange at the margin of the system is extremely difficult, not only because the system attacks us from the outside, but because its mechanisms within us, the mechanisms of moral and psychological "order," paralyze us constantly.

TEC is being thrown out of the system. What we are trying to learn is where we are landing and what we can do there. Can we continue doing theatre? And so I have returned to the question that was asked me in Montreal. There are other groups—the Living Theatre and the Bread & Puppet Theatre among them—who share our situation. What differentiates us from them is the society in which we work, the audiences to whom we direct ourselves. I think that the insistence on "giving" and "giving of oneself," on giving love, on reaching the audience, on hurting them, shaking them up, even frightening them, is imposed on those groups by an audience from big cities, obliged to consume everything. The fear of being consumed, being directed, obliges these groups in turn to produce something so irritating—or so pure—that it cannot easily and harmlessly be digested by the consumer.

Our people in Colombia do not consume. They are consumed and they are avid, in great need of something to consume. Of course, with things presented in such a simplistic way, our work seems cut out for us. Those who don't consume are apathetic because immediate and primary needs do not give them rest; they barely have time for anything else. Besides, they are on the margins of society. They are used by the system, but the system keeps them separated. They are a "reserve army;" they are the only ones who need to destroy the system to survive. Many of them don't even have the timid and secret "folk" culture I spoke of before, which still flows—like underground rivers—beneath certain isolated rural zones. The language of these outcasts needs deciphering, and we must learn it in order to establish communication. For a long time TEC has been involved in the language of books and magazines, in the language of "culture," in the problems of theatre as an institution. And it isn't easy—unless we cease to be theatre people, unless we stop doing our work in theatre as well as we can so that it will be more effective—for us to succeed in this new form of communication. Yet each day the system obliges us more to be what we have to be. We can only thank it for pushing us by its total opposition to men, opposition to life.

Now, we could have deduced from all this that we had to dedicate ourselves to what is usually called "popular theatre" or "theatre of the masses," a theatre for a fixed audience and about a specific set of problems. Yet this is just another trick of the system, as elementary as nationalism, folklore, or agitprop. Because the system has cast out the exploited, should you create a product for them that is no more nutritious than the food surpluses it leaves them? Some maintain that the exploited don't want anything else, that they don't have the capacity to participate in the full and complex diversion of a real theatrical production. These people have degraded the notion of "popular art" and have put it on the farcical level of our democratic vote. To accept that we must do low quality theatre at the outset in order to be able to "elevate" the level of the people, is to enter wholly into the system. It is to say that the people are not yet mature enough for freedom and that the system, through its artists and technicians, will have to prepare them little by little for it.

Then there are the demagogues who maintain that all true art is popular, that art has always come from the people and that it is necessary to dispense with "decadent forms" and use "popular forms." But "decadent forms" are nothing more than attempts at self-expression made by the outcast artist, the artist isolated by the system but condemned to sell his work in the market of the system itself. His only resort is to use a personal code, to perfect and refine his technique, or, as a lone witness, to make a pop-inventory of the reasons for fighting against dehumanization. In Latin American countries the avalanche of imperialism, the great colonial adventure, has caused and continues to cause cultural genocide. Destroying the indigenous cultures (which, in the original great American empires, were not "popular," but as refined and aristocratic as were those of China and India), it created a mestizo people that had barely begun to crystallize its way of life, when it was destroyed by the second and third imperialist avalanches—by capitalism and the United States, which with the help of the gentle poets of the agrarian idyll (generally landowners, in reality or nostalgia) killed mestizo art and converted folklore into archeology.

(What we need for the revolution is to be able to use freely the colonizers' conquests in science and art in developing our peoples' buried tradition, their experiences as outcasts and workers—exactly as Vietnam uses modern arms, engineers, doctors, heavy industry, planes to defend its right to live in accord with its cultural tradition.)

There is an even worse demagogy: to make the exploited believe that through their marginal position they automatically acquire an aware proletarian mentality. Such populism is fascist at root.

TEC doesn't do theatre for the masses. We do not consider theatre an adequate means of information nor do we want to propagandize anyone. We direct ourselves to the men and women whom exploitation wants to reduce to an amorphous mass, to the lowest common denominator. We believe that theatre's objective is not to jell the masses around a few minimal aims, but to present maximal aims, of great complexity, so that the condition and conscience of class is a transitory means of accomplishing those aims. We are looking for communication basically in the relationship between play and audience. That is why our work and style are not directed solely to workers or peasants, but also to the bourgeoisie and students: colonial deformation concerns us all in different ways. By making different classes aware of their role, we can divide the public, confront it with a demystified, unroutinized reality. But we need to go still further. The colonized man must be divided within himself, to show him how, at the level of habit, conditioning, morality, he continues to carry within him the exploiter against whom he is fighting. And the exploiter must be shown that all charitable ways of soothing his conscience or of calming the wrath of the exploited will not last long, because they are resting on a radically false foundation.

In this period of "impersonal," mechanized power, of neo-capitalism "without proprietors," theatres should create plays not about machines but about dehumanized beings with concrete privileges and interests, with ridiculous little stories—and also about the hands which operate that gigantic backdrop, the mass media. That is why communication in the theatre is for us not a problem only of emoting, of creativeness, of empathy. It is not a problem of "objective research," not a demonstration of ideology. It is an action which is taken apart, piece by piece, impinging on all our means of perception, touching the experiences of the actor and the spectator, and finally, is put back together for us to criticize.

In my play *Documents from Hell*, several episodes about violence showed some decomposing social classes, made up of vague, amorphous people. A play about violence should have involved us with all the documentation existing on that problem in Colombia. But the production was based fundamentally on stage images, on improvisation. It is a mistake to think that within us are all characters, and it is a mistake to think that the images improvisation creates on the stage reveal by and of themselves the weakness or the intensity of the play's contradictions. The images of improvisation, if we are able to let them happen through objective, concrete stimuli in the actions we are representing, can dig out the gestural and spatial styles implicit in the text and can define behavior, but they can also turn into a chain reaction of magical associations, that is, of associations whose causality resides in other associations and not in the things happening on stage. A minute establishment of fact from the most exhaustive documentation is the only thing that can guarantee us true creative freedom. It is necessary to understand that creating is not inventing. We and the audience are re-creating a model reality, and only through that reality, in active proof of it, are we revealing ourselves to ourselves and to the public, just as we reveal the public to ourselves and itself.

Our task in the theatre is to begin to synthesize the two Colombian cultures. And we must begin now, because in this period of acute and increasing contradictions we can weigh the life of imported art against the resistance from our buried cultural elements, we can see and show their traumatic cross-assimilation. If we do not work now to discover a truly artistic and truly revolutionary style, the problem of art in a future, different society will he reduced to vulgarizing the synthesis at the level of shallow "popular art."

> In TEC's work we have prepared for a profound attack on our basic situation. We have dispensed almost entirely with scenery, lighting effects, and other purely technical resources, for two reasons. First, we live in an underdeveloped environment and are, in the true meaning of the word, a poor theatre. Second, we think that the theatre should be one means of avoiding enslavement by the mechanical and to mass media. That doesn't mean doing away with the media, but setting down a clear boundary line between the direct oral and gestural communication of man to man, and propaganda. The forms of direct communication, man to man, exist among our people and they must be studied and used.

Derek Walcott and hybridity as ending

In the introduction I noted that this volume is concerned with written theatrical theory and therefore does not directly address the rich variety of other modes of theorization, specifically embodied theorizations. Derek Walcott's piece is certainly written and is undeniably theoretical, but it is also poetic and narrative. It doesn't look or feel like the other theories in this volume. If the notion of ideology presented in the last chapter is accurate, then even the way we write theory (and write about theory) is ideological. Walcott's radical poetic practice clearly suggests alternative ways of approaching the questions posed by theatre around the world. In approaching these questions not only from a distinct standpoint in the West Indies, but also with a distinct methodology, Walcott's work has the potential to reach conclusions that would not otherwise be reachable.

Unfortunately, inasmuch as Walcott's theory is also poetry, the level of interpretation necessary is much higher than that required by most of the other theorists in this book. All reading is, of course, interpretation, but poetry invites a wider array of interpretations than analytical prose, which generally articulates and supports a series of arguments for a reader to follow. There are certainly things that Walcott's texts undeniably states – and the discussion below will bring up these topics. In places where Walcott's poetic theory opens itself to a range of interpretations, the discussion will focus on the questions raised by this array of possible interpretations and not on selecting a "best" interpretation.

Walcott (b. 1930), a Saint Lucian Nobel Prize winner, is known for his poetry and his plays. As with most of the Caribbean, Saint Lucia was contested by the British, the French, and to a lesser extent, the Spanish. For much of its colonial history, the small island of Saint Lucia was considered to be a "dependency" of Martinique (roughly a colony that didn't warrant its own governor so was the responsibility of the governing body of its larger neighbor). While Saint Lucia did not gain full independence until 1979, it had functioned relatively autonomously since the mid-twentieth century. It did briefly align itself with the West Indies Federation, which was an attempt to create a unified political body out of the Caribbean islands. Walcott's work discusses the extreme poverty of the islands, the desire to please the former colonial power, the desire to destroy the former colonial power, the transformation of rebel heroes into tyrants, the problematic status of language in the colonial context, and the place of art in all of this.

Walcott is critical of the government for attempting to celebrate a false version of the past – a re-enactment of rituals for tourists. His critique here mirrors the common critique of the search for "pure" culture I mentioned above. He notes that the African rituals to which the Caribbean might lay claim were practiced with belief in Africa, and that practicing them as art significantly changes these rituals. By the same token, he notes that feeble mimicry of Europe is always doomed to be a pale, needy imitation whatever else it might accomplish. In this regard he makes a similar point to Buenaventura, but, whereas Buenaventura seeks to create an art outside of the system, Walcott specifically says that his practice emerges from the impoverished nature of the system. In this sense, Walcott argues that the Caribbean does not have full access to either cultural heritage. He makes a similar argument with regard to language. The Caribbean lays claim to so many languages, but no language seems to belong to it – it is a land between things, a land of twilight.

While Walcott's work undoubtedly expresses anger at the former colonial powers, he also lightly mocks his earlier Manichaeism – his division of the world into two parts. Not only is Walcott's artist stuck between a new nation and an old colonial power, he is torn by class alliances. For Walcott, this in-between space is challenging and difficult, although the artist must accept the space to produce theatre. Walcott's artist is educated and therefore, almost by definition, not completely impoverished – education costs money, even if just the money lost from not earning a salary while in school. On the other hand, Walcott's artist wants to speak to the nation, and much of the nation is poor. Walcott articulates this as another intractable problem facing theatre in the post-colonial world. It must always be a hybrid of classes as well as a hybrid of cultures. It is constantly pulled between competing forces.

One of the biggest interpretive questions with Walcott is determining how much of his essay is describing things, how much is critiquing things, and how much is advocating for new things. What are the goals of Walcott's theatre? What kind of world is it creating or what kind of world has created it? Is Walcott's notion of culture fluid or static? In that the world Walcott describes is impoverished, where does the potential for change lie in Walcott's work?

Extract 4.2 Selections from "What the Twilight Says: An Overture"
Derek Walcott

> But I see what it is, you are not from these parts, you don't know what our twilights can do. Shall I tell you?
>
> *Waiting for Godot*

I

When dusk heightens, like amber on a stage set, those ramshackle hoardings of wood and rusting iron which circle our cities, a theatrical sorrow rises with it, for the glare, like the aura from an old-fashioned brass lamp is like a childhood signal to come home. Light in our cities keeps its pastoral rhythm, and the last home-going traffic seems to rush through darkness that comes from suburban swamp or forest in a noiseless rain. In true cities another life begins: neons stutter to their hysterical pitch, bars, restaurants and cinemas blaze with artifice, and Mammon takes over the switchboard, manipulator of cities; but here the light makes our strongest buildings tremble, its colour hints of rust, more stain than air. To set out for rehearsals in the quivering quarter-hour is to engage conclusions, not beginnings, for one walks past the gilded hallucinations of poverty with a corrupt resignation touched by details, as if the destitute, in their orange-tinted backyards, under their dusty trees, or climbing to their favelas, were all natural scene-designers and poverty were not a condition but an art. Deprivation is made lyrical, and twilight, with the patience of alchemy, almost transmutes despair into virtue. In the tropics nothing is lovelier than the allotments of the poor, no theatre is as vivid, voluble and cheap.

Years ago, watching them, and suffering as you watched, you proffered silently the charity of a language which they could not speak, until your suffering, like the language, felt superior, estranged. The dusk was a raucous chaos of curses, gossip and laughter; everything performed in public, but the voice of the inner language was reflective and mannered, as far above its subjects as that sun which would never set until its twilight became a metaphor for the withdrawal of Empire and the beginning of our doubt.

Colonials, we began with this malarial enervation: that nothing could ever be built among these rotting shacks, barefooted backyards and moulting shingles; that being poor, we already had the theatre of our lives. So the self-inflicted role of martyr came naturally, the melodramatic belief that one was message-bearer for the millennium, that the inflamed ego was enacting their will. In that simple schizophrenic boyhood one could lead two lives: the interior life of poetry, the outward life of action and dialect. Yet the writers of my generation were natural assimilators. We knew the literature of Empires, Greek, Roman, British, through their essential classics; and both the patois of the street and the language of the classroom hid the elation of discovery. If there was nothing, there was everything to be made. With this prodigious ambition one began.

If, twenty years later, that vision has not been built, so that at every dusk one ignites a city in the mind above the same sad fences where the poor revolve, the theatre still an architectural fantasy, if there is still nothing around us, darkness still preserves the awe of self-enactment as the sect gathers for its self-extinguishing, self-discovering rites. In that aboriginal darkness the first principles are still sacred, the grammar and movement of the body, the shock of the domesticated voice startling itself in a scream. Centuries of servitude have to be shucked; but there is no history, only the history of emotion. Pubescent ignorance comes into the light, a shy girl, eager to charm, and one's instinct is savage: to violate that ingenuousness, to degrade, to strip her of those values learnt from films and books because she too moves in her own hallucination: that of a fine and separate star, while her counterpart, the actor, sits watching, but he sits next to another hallucination, a doppelganger released from his environment and his race. Their simplicity is really ambition. Their gaze is filmed with hope of departure. The noblest are those who are trapped, who have accepted the twilight.

If I see these as heroes it is because they have kept the sacred urge of actors everywhere: to record the anguish of the race. To do this, they must return through a darkness whose terminus is amnesia. The darkness which yawns before them is terrifying. It is the journey back from man to ape. Every actor should make this journey to articulate his origins, but for these who have been called not men but mimics, the darkness must be total, and the cave should not contain a single man-made, mnemonic object. Its noises should be elemental, the roar of rain, ocean, wind and fire. Their first sound should be like the last, the cry. The voice must grovel in search of itself, until gesture and sound fuse and the blaze of their flesh astonishes them. The children of slaves must sear their memory with a torch. The actor must break up his body and feed it as ruminatively as ancestral story-tellers fed twigs to the fire. Those who look from their darkness into the tribal fire must be bold enough to cross it.

The cult of nakedness in underground theatre, of tribal rock, of poverty, of rite, is not only nostalgia for innocence, but the enactment of remorse for the genocides of civilization, a search for the wellspring of tragic joy in ritual, a confession of aboriginal calamity, for their wars, their concentration camps, their millions of displaced souls have degraded and shucked the body as food for the machines. These self-soiling, penitential cults, the Theatre of the Absurd, the Theatre of Cruelty, the Poor Theatre, the Holy Theatre, the pseudo-barbarous revivals of primitive tragedy are not threats to civilization but acts of absolution, gropings for the outline of pure tragedy, rituals of washing in the first darkness. Their howls and flagellations are cries to that lost God which they have pronounced dead, for the God who is offered to slaves must be served dead, or He may change His chosen people.

[...]

To believe in its folk forms the State would have to hallow not only its mythology but re-believe in dead gods, not as converts either, but as makers. But no one in the New World whose one God is advertised as dead can believe in innumerable gods of another life. Those gods would have to be an anthropomorphic variety of his will. Our poets and actors would have not only to describe possession but enact it, otherwise we would have not art but blasphemy and blasphemy which has no fear is decoration. So now we are entering the "African" phase with our pathetic African carvings, poems and costumes, and our art objects are not sacred vessels placed on altars but goods placed on shelves for the tourist. [...]

Since art is informed by something beyond its power, all we could successfully enact was a dance of doubt. The African revival is escape to another dignity, but one understands the glamour of its simplifications. Listen, one kind of writer, generally the entertainer, says: "I will write in the language of the people however gross or incomprehensible"; another says: "Nobody else go' understand this, you hear, so le' me write English"; while the third is dedicated to purifying the language of the tribe, and it is he who is jumped on by both sides for pretentiousness or playing white. He is the mulatto of style. The traitor. The assimilator. Yes. But one did not say to his Muse, "What kind of language is this that you've given me?" as no liberator asks history, "What kind of people is that that I'm meant to ennoble?", but one went about his father's business. Both fathers. If the language was contemptible, so were the people. [...]

Our writers whined in the voices of twilight, "Look at this people! They may be degraded, but they are as good as you are. Look at what you have done to them." And their poems remained laments, their novels propaganda tracts, as if one general apology on behalf of the past would supplant imagination, would spare them the necessity of great art. Pastoralists of the African revival should know that what is needed is not new names for old things, or old names for old things, but the faith of using the old names anew, so that mongrel as I am, something prickles in me when I see the word Ashanti as with the word Warwickshire, both separately intimating my grandfathers' roots, both baptising this neither proud nor ashamed bastard, this hybrid, this West Indian.

[...]

III

> I am thinking of a child's vow sworn in vain,
> Never to leave that valley his fathers called their home.
>
> Yeats

To be born on a small island, a colonial backwater, meant a precocious resignation to fate. The shoddy, gimcrack architecture of its one town, its doll-sized verandahs, jalousies and lacy eaves neatly perforated as those doilies which adorn the polished tables of the poor seemed so frail that the only credible life was nature. A nature without man, like the sea on which the sail of a canoe can seem an interruption. A nature with blistered aspects: grey, rotting shacks, the colour of the peasant woman's dress, which huddled on rocky rises outside the villages. But through nature one came to love the absence of philosophy, and, fatally, perhaps, the beauty of certain degradations.

In that innocent vagabondage one sought out the poor as an adventure, an illumination, only to arrive where, rooted like a rigid articulation of the rocks, the green and blue enamelled statue of the Virgin leaned from her niche, facing a green and blue Atlantic, like the peeling figurehead of a slave ship (in her various shrines her age could change from decorous matron to eager postulant), and where, back in the bleached, unpainted fishing village streets everyone seemed salted with a reek of despair, a life, a theatre, reduced to elementals. The acrid, shuttered smell of the poor was as potent and nocturnal as the odours of sex, with its intimacies of lowered Virgin lamps and coconut-fibre mattresses until it seemed that a Catholic destitution was a state of grace which being part-white and Methodist I could never achieve. That life was measured as carefully as broken shop-bread by its rituals, it had dimpled the serene smile of Our Lady of the Rocks by its observance of five o'clock mass, rosaries, scapulars, coloured prints, lampions with perpetual flame floating in oil, vespers, fasts, feasts and the shell-bordered cemeteries by the village river. The race was locked in its conviction of salvation like a freemasonry. There was more envy than hate towards it, and the love that stubbornly emerged showed like weeds through the ruined aisle of an abandoned church, and one worked hard for that love, against their love of priest and statue, against the pride of their resignation. One worked to have the "feel" of the island, bow, gunwhales and stern as jealously as the fisherman knew his boat, and, despite the intimacy of its size to be as free as a canoe out on the ocean.

That apprenticeship would mean nothing unless life were made so real that it stank, so close that you could catch the changes of morning and afternoon light on the rocks of the Three Sisters, pale brown rocks carious in the gargle of sea, could catch the flash of a banana leaf in sunlight, catch the smell of drizzled asphalt and the always surprisingly stale smell of the sea, the reek that chafes in the guts of canoes, and the reek of human rags that you once thought colourful, but, God give you that, in rage, a reek both fresh and resinous, all salted on the page, that dark catalogue of country-shop smells, the tang of raw, fine powdery cod, of old onions drying, of the pork-barrel, and the shelves of faded cloth, all folded round the fusty smell of the proprietor, some exact magical, frightening woman in tinted glasses, who emerged from the darkness like history. [...] It smelled strong and true. What was its truth?

That in the "New Aegean" the race, of which these fishermen were the stoics, had grown a fatal adaptability. As black absorbs without reflection they had rooted themselves with a voracious, unreflecting calm. By all arguments they should have felt displaced, seeing this ocean as another Canaan, but that image was the hallucination of professional romantics, writer and politician. Instead, the New World Negro was disappointingly ordinary. He needed to be stirred into bitterness, thence perhaps to action, which means that he was as avaricious and as banal as those who had enslaved him. What would deliver him from servitude was the forging of a language that went beyond mimicry, a dialect which had the force of revelation as it invented names for things, one which finally settled on its own mode of inflection, and which began to create an oral culture of chants, jokes, folk-songs and fables; this, not merely the debt of history was his proper claim to the New World. For him metaphor was not a symbol but conversation, and because every poet begins with such ignorance, in the anguish that every noun will be freshly, resonantly named, because a new melodic inflection meant a new mode, there was no better beginning. It did not matter how rhetorical, how dramatically heightened the language was if its tone were true, whether its subject was the rise and fall of a

Haitian king or a small-island fisherman, and the only way to re-create this language was to share in the torture of its articulation. This did not mean the jettisoning of "culture" but, by the writer's making creative use of his schizophrenia, an electric fusion of the old and the new.

So the people, like the actors, awaited a language. They confronted a variety of styles and masks, but because they were casual about commitment, ashamed of their speech, they were moved only by the tragi-comic and farcical. The tragi-comic was another form of self-contempt. They considered tragedy to be, like English, an attribute beyond them.

IV

The future of West Indian militancy lies in art. All revolutions begin amateurishly, with forged or stolen weapons, but the West Indian artist knew the need for revolt without knowing what weapons to use, and just as a comfortable, self-hugging pathos hid in the most polemical of West Indian novels, so there was in the sullen ambition of the West Indian actor a fear that he lacked proper weapons, that his voice, colour and body were no match for the civilised concepts of theatre.

[...]

The pride of the colonial in the culture of his mother country was fiercer than her true children's because the colonial feared to lose her. The most conservative and prejudiced redoubts of imperialism are in those who have acquired that patina through strenuous reverence: her judges and, ironically enough, her artists. My generation since its colonial childhood had no true pride but awe. We had not yet provided ourselves with heroes, and when the older heroes went out of fashion, or were stripped, few of us had any choice but to withdraw into a cave where we could scorn those who struggled in the heat. Change was too subterranean for us to notice. Our melodramatic instincts demanded sudden upheavals, and found nothing in the Roman patience of legal reforms. We became infuriated at the banal demands of labourer and peasant. We romanticised the poor. But the last thing which the poor needed was the idealisation of their poverty. No play could be paced to the repetitive, untheatrical patience of hunger and unemployment. Hunger produces enervation of will and knows one necessity. Although in very few of the islands are people reduced to such a state, the empire of hunger includes work that is aimed only at necessities. It's inevitable that any playwright, knowing that this is his possible audience, will not be concerned with deprivation as his major theme. So the sparse body of West Indian theatre still feeds on the subject of emaciation and what it produces: rogues, drunkards, madmen, outcasts, and sets against this the pastoral of the peasant. Its comedy begins with the premise that all are starved or deprived, or defend themselves from being further deprived by threats. Hunger induces its delirium, and it is this fever for heroic examples that can produce the glorification of revenge.

Yet revenge is a kind of vision. The West Indian mind historically hung-over exhausted, prefers to take its revenge in nostalgia, to narrow its eyelids in a schizophrenic daydream of an Eden that existed before its exile. Its fixation is for the breasts of a nourishing mother, and this is true not only of the generations of slaves' children, but of those brought here through indigence or necessity, in fact, through the threat of hunger. But the communities maintain a half-brother relationship threatened by jealousies and suspicion. There is more romance in anthropology than there is in ordinary life, and our quarrels about genealogy, our visionary plays about the noble savage remain provincial, psychic justifications, strenuous attempts to create identity; yet there is nothing atavistic about our desires except that easy nostalgia which Hearne has described. Once we have lost our wish to be white we develop a longing to become black, and those two may be different, but are still careers. "The status of native is a nervous condition introduced and maintained by the settler among colonised people with their consent" says Sartre, introducing Fanon, and the new black continues that condition. His crimes are familial, litigious, his hatred is turned inward. The law is all he can remember of his past. Slaves, the children of slaves, colonials, then pathetic, unpunctual nationalists, what have we to celebrate? First, we have not wholly sunk into our own landscapes, as one gets the feeling at funerals that our bodies make only light, unlasting impressions on our earth. It is not an earth that has been fed long with the mulch of cultures, with cycles of tribalism, feudalism, monarchy, democracy, industrialization. Death, which fastens us to the earth, remains pastoral or brutish, because no single corpse contributes to some tiered concept of a past. Everything is immediate, and this immediacy means over-breeding, illegitimacy, migration without remorse. The sprout casually stuck in the soil. The depth of being rooted is related to the shallowness of racial despair. The migratory West Indian feels rootless on his own earth, chafing at its beaches.

Werewere Liking and Marie-Jose Hourantier: tradition as solution

Werewere Liking, a Bassa, was born in 1950 in Cameroon and moved to the then-vibrant artistic scene of the Ivory Coast in 1978 (during this time, the Ivorian economy was among the strongest in Africa). She collaborated for many years with French anthropologist Marie-Jose Hourantier, who directed much of Werewere Liking's early work. They founded the Ki-Yi Mbock (ultimate knowledge) movement and the Ki-Yi Performance Village in order to promote their particular idea of ritual theatre. Specifically, Werewere Liking says that her theatre creates meaningful, effective rituals that will have concrete effects on the world around her. After the two parted ways, Liking continued her work in the village, shifting its focus to helping African youth use theatre to change their lives. Liking relates this shift in focus to the deteriorating conditions in the Ivory Coast after the death of Félix Houphouët-Boigny who had led the country from 1960 to 1993. Since that time there has been a coup and two civil wars.

The excerpted section of Werewere Liking's novel, *It Shall be of Jasper and Coral* (2000), challenges several aspects of this anthology even while it clearly theorizes many of the same issues. First, it is a novel written in a poetic form that contains moments of dialogue written as if for theatre (which is in some ways similar to Walcott's theory albeit with different effect). Neither poetry, theatre, nor novel are generally thought of as forms in which theory is disseminated (although Plato's dialogues certainly challenge this notion as well). By writing in this hybrid form, Liking emphasizes the extent to which she is addressing issues and controversies in theatrical and artistic practice rather than presenting answers to these problems. She describes both of her speakers as participating in increasingly frequent masturbation over the course of the novel. This is a clear indication that their ideas should not be taken at face value. The questions they raise are important, but their answers are potentially less so. The form Liking adopts also emphasizes the hybridity of the modern African nation by allowing multiple voices to be present within a single narrative. Even the main narrator phrases her speech as a series of questions rather than as a firm "authorial" guiding voice. This novel, containing theory within itself, is not sitting outside of the situation it describes, passing judgment from a distance. It recreates the situation. It recognizes its own messy, cluttered, fragmentary nature and challenges the reader to discover the beauty and value that exist despite, or perhaps because of, this messy fragmentation.

Liking introduces the whole novel by inviting the reader to play a game with her and try to imagine a way out of the bleak circumstances that plague her imaginary setting of Lunai (and she explicitly connects Lunai to Africa). Much of the first section of the novel is a debate between a Westernizing impulse and a desire to return to a mythical African past. The two speakers, Babou and Grozi, change their minds often and frequently go over-the-top, exposing the cruel, dangerous undercurrents of their arguments. In the excerpt below, Babou and Grozi begin to discuss their ideal village, interrupted occasionally by a narrator whose words appear in italics.

By the time the characters begin to discuss theatre in the main excerpt below, they have agreed that they must form a new culture of sorts. To do this they must form a new language and a new way of conceiving of language. The "Masks" that they refer to are part of a number of traditional African rituals in both East and West Africa in which the spirits of ancestors of gods become visibly present, embodied in the masked forms of human dancers during ritual events. The extent to which the god is "represented" by the masked form, is present within the masked form, or "is" the masked form, varies from location to location in Africa. Whatever the variation, these sorts of rituals are one of the most recognizable, frequently seen connections to Africa's mythical past. When the characters in Liking's novel debate what they should do with the masks, they are returning to the question of the place of Africa's past within the contemporary society. On the other hand, the masks are disguises and they have the potential to change or hide the identity of the wearer. By leaving the double-meaning of "mask" in place, Liking questions the extent to which holding on to old rituals changes or hides the identity of a new Africa.

What is Werewere Liking suggesting about the nature of language? What is the relationship of this language to theatre? Is there a definition of art that emerges from her work, or merely definitions she rejects? The ending of this section of the novel is clearly functioning on a level that we might call "mystical." What is the place of this type of thinking in the theatre Liking

---

Extract 4.3 Selections from *It Shall Be of Jasper and Coral* Werewere Liking, translated by Irene Assiba d'Almeida

BABOU: Well then, how will we speak, what will we hold a dialogue with?
GROZI: They'll be speaking with a well-placed look one that grasps
A hand that knows and holds on
A tone that gives direction
A sound that assembles
They will be shape within speech Action within meaning
Rhythm within idea
They will speak the original tongue They will find the lost Word again They will have a dialogue with open heart and full mind.
They will have a dialogue with the breath of life. . . .
BABOU: With the same repetitive words, the same old worn-out phrases?
GROZI: Nobody will find it absurd anymore that languages and forms evolve together with people. The zombie troops will no longer be there to ask them at the edge of a dream: "For which trend school are you registering?" and they will exclaim: "Oh but ... That's not

traditional! Oh but ... That's not African! Yes but . . . No but . . ." To prevent them from creating, from living. . . .

BABOU: That's why there is no echo anymore in Lunai. The word no longer conceals reality for the one who gives it. His truth no longer lies in these words. And here we are forced to seek a new language that might adjust itself to the situation we are in as an old race out of step and putrefied. . . .

GROZI: A copious language that can address itself to all our senses at the same time, attack us like an octopus from every angle to clean us out, shake us until the crust of indifference, of old age is completely gone. . . .

[...]

Goddam! I fell asleep again!!! Where was I? Ah yes.. . Dedicated to...

My problem is that Grozi and Babou talk too much. . . . If they'd act according to what they say I wouldn't have any qualms about dedicating my golden logbook to them and I'd be in much better shape. . . . Nailed to a pillory
Hanging in a precarious balance
In which my only wrong was to be the wife of the other
In the depths of the waves limbo lies spying on me
With broken arms I hang here
Since I've been hanging .. .

Never mind! . . . I'm dreaming that their ideas encounter the Echo-that-moves-to-action! And me, I may still be there to see the living example. . . .

[...]

"It shall be of jasper and coral
It shall be of breath and fire. . . ."
And so be it.

On page two I want to write an epigraph. A strong word a word-of-strength that will have to undress the reader carefully and profoundly cleanse him before he lays a finger on me on my private self. . . .

Fine! page 2. Epigraph. . . .

What would be the most interesting subject?

It will have to embrace everything in one line concern everybody. . .

Let's see. . . .

At this moment in Lunai every Tsetse is interested in art in the idea of art.

In the streets all you hear is rambling and raving about art everybody is talking at the same time unequivocally wanting to impose his most recent invention.

"Art is a commitment"

"Art is a message"
"Art is the power-idea"
"No, not at all! Art is truth. . . ."
All day long. . . .
And woe to the artist if what one thinks the "message" is does not support the speeches of the powers-that-be: ideologies moralities often just fashionable class struggles and thus automatically of a passing nature. . .
[...]
"Art is . . . It is a pastime a poverty-concealer a death-dodger nothing else. . . ."
"Art is . . . Mystification manipulation . . . With a hyphen between mani and pulation, please, Maud. . . ."
"Film is . . . It's the abbreviated thread of a picture story in full color. . . ."
"Painting is ... It's a garbage dump of old pictures to keep memory going, it's ... Eh ... Painting. Ah but ... It's not African! Africans aren't familiar with either paint or brushes!"
"Yes, but . . . What about the Tassili?"
"No, that wasn't really painting! . . ."
"Music, now that's African! It's rhythm syncopated a thousand times to wiggle and sway to and not to have to think. Music is the message of today's African!"
"Sculpture . . . Oh yes, that's African!"
"Oh yeah, why . . . ?"
"You know, form. . . . Yes, you know the African form. What, is that like the African form?"
Well, twisted of course. . . ."
"So it would be enough to twist every art form for it to become African."
"Eh . . ."
"And theater . . . That's not African."
"Of course! No! . . . Yes, it is!"
"In Africa there were only rituals and rites are not theater." "Yes, they are! No!"
"African theater is dance music song poetry. It's total you see."
"No! Yes! Total theater everywhere. Besides the word theater comes from theatron you know the Greeks. . . ." "But the Greeks came to Africa before . . ."
"No! Yes!"
"Maud, write! . . . all night long. . . ."
"What is Art? What is African Art?"

GROZI (to himself, in a dream): Grandfather was trying to explain this to me, the night before he died. His voice was clear and melodious. What he was saying seemed true to me but I didn't really understand its meaning too well. . . .

[...]

"And the shapeless memory not bound by time becomes the power-idea in the conscience or through the consciousness-raising of its two creators: the Artist and the Public. . . . And the power-idea becomes the shape of a sound, the shape of a word, of a color, the shape of a rhythm, of a space. . . ."

BABOU: But since I did register, I should go all the way to the end and here I am forced to cram those pontificating formulas in my head again, "art is the power-idea."

GROZI: "And form becomes art again. . . . And Dambala the snake swallows its own tail." Ah! but his voice. . . .

BABOU (exasperated): You idiot! What are you jabbering on about? You don't really want me to start up again about the old quarrels on form and content? That's as old as the hills! And me, I tell you this: I'm looking for a thesis, you understand? A new idea!

GROZI (coming out of his dream in a bit of a stupor): What? What are you talking about?

BABOU: Don't worry. I can see we're not on the same wave-length; in any case I need to give some very serious thought to African art. What is African art, what is not? Is there just one African art?

GROZI (thinking more clearly again): Of course there's an African art, or rather there have been African arts just as elsewhere there has been Byzantine art, Flemish art, and all the rest. But that was in the time when space hadn't really been conquered yet: the universe was ... split up into thousands of little closed worlds. . . . Do you hear them talking today about French painting, English sculpture when they're alluding to what's being made now?

BABOU: First you'd have to know who is English and who is French these days. . . . They'd be talking about movements and that has nothing to do with race, with nationality. . . .

With broken arms
I'm hanging here ever since I've been hanging
And limbo is spying on me. . . .

GROZI: So you understand that it is difficult to talk about African art today without falling back into the old clichés again. We can go on copying the ancient African arts or we can be inspired by them if we feel the need. Those arts surely deserve that much, don't they? But the African Artist of today cannot, must not repudiate himself nor repudiate his duty to create as a man: a man in a "sidereal era" who experiences "live" the launching of the Apollos and other Soyuz rockets, a soccer game in Venezuela, the shooting of Christians in Lebanon and in Ireland, who suffers and shares the rise of the price of oil and the fallout of the neutron bomb, and who expresses this through his own particular sensitivity.

BABOU: That kind of art obviously can no longer limit itself to the garish colors of women's pagnes as they pound grain in their mortars, to sunsets over fishermen's huts, and to small dugout boats! It can no longer be satisfied with reproductions of statues, masks, and meaningless dances.

GROZI: And rightly so. . . . The poorest fisherman dreams of a fine motor-driven canoe. The lowliest of peasant women envisions purchasing a mixer and dreams of a white villa where miraculous ovens no longer blacken the sides of her pots. . . . Besides, isn't it natural to want to free yourself from thankless tasks in exchange for others that are more exhilarating? Aren't movement and change essential to life? The blender instead of the mortar, the skyscraper and villa instead of the mud hut, and the quest for a personality that is better adapted to this new environment, are they not also the African reality of today? Why then should artists be consigned to small dugouts mud huts and mortars that nobody else wants anymore, why then pontificate: "The Artist bears witness to his time. . . ." And at the same time ask him to be the museum of an "Africanity of days gone by." ...

Hanging in a precarious balance
In which my only wrong was to be the wife of the other I hang here since I've been hanging. . . .

BABOU: But what then makes the African artist different from any other? Aren't we risking too much uniformity, too much standardization even where Art is concerned?

GROZI: Me, I believe that only the form the Inner Vision and the techniques of its approach truly create the distinction between one person and the other. Everyone can't approach the divine by the same methods, by the same paths. And it surely won't be computer science and its machinery that will make any changes here, and in any case that wouldn't be anytime soon. . . .

Consequently, art will continue to be diversified, of this I have no doubt. . . .

BABOU: They even say that "geoclimatological" sensitivity by itself is sufficient to disclose a thousand nuances of the sky. . . . That should reassure both the xenophobes and the claustrophobes. . .

[...]

There was a time in the "land of the heart-shaped cradle" when the different gods decided to keep knowledge to themselves: men didn't know how to make use of it. . . . Every time it was given to them they would abuse it degrade it throw it off balance and again the gods would have to wear themselves out by gluing the broken pieces together again. They'd had enough! After all a man seemed happy enough when no effort at all was asked of him no attempt to move beyond his instincts no self-censorship at all. . . . It was sufficient to leave him with just his survival instinct so that he could vegetate as would ruminants or wild beasts in the animal world for the rest of eternity. That seemed to be his "sweet sin."

But Hilolombi who had created mankind and had placed great hopes in him took a negative view of this half-life lethargy even though he recognized his creation-creature was far from perfect. So he decided to send him a whole group of Masks whose mission it was to civilize him.

The other gods took umbrage at this generosity that would automatically lead to a new deliverance they were sure of it but out of respect for Hilolombi who was their elder they gave in once again and the civilizing Masks swooped down upon the "heart-shaped cradle" and their primary purpose was to initiate men into wisdom that is to say into knowledge and its appropriate use. . . .

They would appear here and there to children women to the eldest ones they would appear the Masks. . . .

The Masks created associations brotherhoods they pro-claimed laws rights they defined and assigned duties to everyone they organized they cultivated.

There were Initiates and Great Initiates. Hilolombi regained confidence in himself as well as in his creature and one morning he showed him the view into the sixth heaven the heaven of choice.

That same evening mankind chose to become god and Hilolombi sighed with relief and went off to get some rest: the road toward Evolution lay clearly marked and wide open mankind could manage nicely all by itself the civilizing Masks had accomplished their mission. All the gods burst out in songs of joy: they had done well to listen to Hilolombi the Eldest. From now on they too would be freed from their mission as Masters of conscience and they could try their hand at creating. They all deserved a vacation. . . .

But when they woke up at the dawn of a new cycle they were taken aback at the sight of mankind floundering around awkwardly in the animal world!

They were enraged and terribly disappointed. In Unanimity, they decided to condemn these cretins of men to vegetate in the animal

> *world chewing their cud or hunting prey and too bad if it was for all eternity and so it was done.*
>
> *But some civilizing Masks had contracted a dangerous virus: compassion for mankind! They were the ones who came to the gods to plead for another chance for men but the Eldest One would hear nothing of it anymore. . . .*
>
> *One day Urn, one of the most fanatic ones to plead man's cause, decided to try something on his own. He stole a bit of knowledge and went off to the "heart-shaped cradle" where he hid in a hole waiting for someone to pass by who would be able to take it from him without burning himself without setting life on fire. . . .*
>
> *Alas, not one single male felt like doing anything at all nor would he have dreamed of going in search of anything at all in the heart of the earth and especially not in search of knowledge. There he is, poor Urn, tormented by the fire of knowledge [...]*
>
> *I am the primordial atom that could never be content with a masculine rib in order to Exist.*
>
> *I am the Matrix Mother in which Ideas and Forms and Breath of life are in gestation so that all may be because I am. And everything is.*
>
> *I am woman of men and of women who come from woman. I walk ahead and I am.*
>
> *I walk behind and I precede.*
>
> *I am everything that moves ahead and advances toward the divine.*
>
> *I am the woman of the day and the night.*

creates? What is the relationship of the argument about theatre being made and the form Liking writes in?

Maryrose Casey and framing performance

Maryrose Casey is one of the leading Australian scholars on theatre and performance, particularly when it comes to indigenous performance. The majority population in Australia has traditionally ignored the indigenous population for the most part, aside from the occasional "exotic" performance described by Casey below. Australian history is generally written about as starting with the settlement. Casey is one of the scholars responsible for reinserting indigenous voices into the general consciousness. Her work is divided between research on the history of indigenous theatre – which contains an insistence that such a history exists – and the theorization of performance practice. In all her work, she is attentive to what she has referred to as issues of framing. Rather than thinking about theatre in its direct links to culture as do many of the other theorists discussed above, Casey looks at the performance context, including the audience and herself as a critic. In its most basic sense, the idea of framing is straightforward. Theatre is staged in a particular way and all of the elements of this staging add to or detract from the performance. Was the performance advertised in youth-oriented magazines? In women's magazines? Were discounts offered to school groups? What sort of space is it being performed in? Who has access to this space? These questions can be relatively straightforward in some contexts, but Casey explores the richness of the idea of frame in a location with such a complex history of colonial settlement and aboriginal culture. The differences between various possible audiences and various locations for theatres can be extreme in this context. The final part of Casey's frame is the critic, who is reframing the performance for yet another audience, and Casey staunchly insists that the critic recognize his or her own unique position relative to the material. In the interest of following her admonition here, I am writing about her theory as an interested, white outsider to Australian theatre having seen and / or read the greatest hits – the theatrical canon, read much of the scholarship surrounding this work, and also done some focused reading on indigenous performance and theatre. As such, my "framing" of Casey's theory could potentially pull it toward contexts where I have greater expertise (i.e. Africa). Since Australia has a distinct history and Australian scholars have repeatedly argued that Postcolonial Studies as a discipline provides inadequate heuristics for the Australian case, I will resist that impulse and encourage my reader to do the same.

In the excerpt below, Casey is particularly interested in the way that indigenous performance practices are staged for colonial audiences. Given that one of the performances she discusses is entitled *Aboriginal Theatre*, one might expect a discussion of the boundary between theatre and performance. While the existence of theatre as distinct from performance was an issue at the inception of white Australian theatre history in the mid-twentieth century with Ray Lawler's work, contemporary scholarship within Australia generally moves between these categories without apology, and thus I will not try to locate the point at which the reframing of performance makes it into theatre, the point at which dance and theatre meet, or the point at which intercultural adaptation of theatre into other performance modes makes the modes theatre (if such points exist).

Casey uses the idea of framing to critique the discourse of "authenticity" that surrounds indigenous performance practices. In the white Australian imagination, Aboriginal culture, when it figures at all, is figured as a static, primitive thing that existed before white people settled in / colonized Australia. Aboriginal culture might be valued as a museum piece – a marker of the way life was. The first of the two performances described was explicitly attempting to preserve a dying culture for later generations to appreciate in such a fashion.

The second performance challenges this notion. There are still Aborigines living in Australia and they still practice their cultures. These cultures have not stayed static – indeed it would have been shocking had they done so given the radical changes that the white settlement in Australia caused. Not only did Aboriginal culture react to the incursion of a new group of people on the island, but it continued to grow and change as technology and the forces of globalization continued to shape modern and contemporary Australia.

The mixing of various cultures Casey describes in the second performance is not exactly the same as the hybridity of the Caribbean examples above. In fact, Casey specifically rejects the notion of "hybrid" in the closing lines of her essay. Within the Caribbean hybridity, the idea is that the hybrid elements have fused together in some fashion and become "Caribbean." The performances Casey describes is transcultural rather than hybrid. It demonstrates the idea that separate, distinct cultures have circulated around the world, sometimes blending and mixing, but often maintaining their distinctiveness. What the second performance "frames" for its audience is an aboriginal response to living in a global society.

Casey also resists the binary between traditional and contemporary, noting that European modernity is not the only way to approach the modern world. Casey insists that scholars, critics, and performance venues should frame performances – however theatrical they may become – as part of living cultures. The idea of a living culture is intuitive, simple, obvious, and not always applied in discussions of indigenous cultures the world over. In simplest terms, a living culture is one that changes over time. Theatrical practices shift, performance practices change, society's response to these practices alters. I have specifically resisted the social Darwinist use of the word "evolve" here, because the idea of a living culture is not a value judgment. The culture is definitely changing, for better or for worse (and how would we decide "better" or "worse" in any event?).

Casey's take on culture provides a new set of questions to apply to intercultural theatre, to ritualized theatre, and to any theatre that is treated as representative of a given culture. To what extent is this performance framed as historical – representing a culture as it was? To what extent does this performance attempt to stage something "authentic" about the culture? Is this authenticity a contemporary, living authenticity, or is it a historical notion of the authentic? To what degree are the intercultural elements of a performance hybridized? To what extent are they left as foreign? What is the overall relationship between the two cultures in this piece?

Extract 4.4 Selections from "Performing for Aboriginal Life and Culture: Aboriginal Theatre and Ngurrumilmarrmiriyu"
Maryrose Casey

[Editorial note: The article below was initially about two different productions, but this excerpt only includes one: after the first paragraph, I have changed singular to plural where necessary without marking these changes.]

Since colonisation, the tensions between the intentions and meanings of Indigenous performers and the cross-cultural framing and reception of their performance have been part of the complex relationship that exists between Indigenous and non-Indigenous peoples in Australia. In the eighteenth and nineteenth centuries, Indigenous-controlled performances drawn from their own historical cultural practices were a focal point of cross-cultural exchange and engagement. Within the colonial exercise, the Euro-Australian and European attitudes towards, and framing of, these performances as a lower form of practice were an important part of containing and colonising Indigenous cultures and the land. Since the 1970s, there have been many transitions and movements shifting the terms of reception and providing the basis for a more respectful engagement with Indigenous performance. However, the notion that Aboriginal historical practices represent primitive or simple cultural forms has continued as traces in the reception of performances that draw on traditional pre-contact practices.

Examinations of performances that derive from traditional or historical Aboriginal performance practices are usually divided into ritual and oral histories as authentically Aboriginal forms, and performances for cross-cultural entertainment or communication as, at best, 'hybrid'. This type of division and epistemic violence shapes and limits the cross-cultural reception of a performative dialogue that includes traditional or historical practices that are not ceremony or oral history. Though the last decades have seen the development of new ways of understanding and interrogating Indigenous performance aimed at recuperating colonised people's agency, the basic premise that continues to cast a shadow of imperialist assumptions over performances is the blindness to, or lack of value attributed to, both historical as well as contemporary, culturally specific performance practices for entertainment.

This [excerpt] examines the performative dialogue between Indigenous and non-Indigenous Australians presented in [one] performance from remote communities in the Northern Territory, one from the 1960s [...] *Aboriginal Theatre* was performed and toured in 1963 in the context of campaigns for land rights and against slave-labour working conditions.

Aboriginal Theatre is from three language groupings, including the Yolngu community at Yirrkala [...This community was] formed around Methodist missions with similar histories of forced creation in the twentieth century. This show is the focus here because it comes from a community that is largely externally acknowledged, and internally identify, as following traditional Law. It combined historical performance practices for fun with, as Magowan terms them, ancestral dances; it was created through Indigenous and non-Indigenous collaborations, with the Indigenous participants aiming to communicate the living cultures of their communities to cross-cultural urban audiences. It seeks [...] to communicate the impact of — and to counter — legislative and commercial interventions into their lands and lives.

In 1967, a group of Yirrkala dancers was featured in an episode of the television show *Skippy*. The episode 'Be Our Guest' (1968) follows a storyline where the Aboriginal people, without English, rescue a lost white Australian. Clancy is lost in the bush and the Aboriginal people find her drinking at a contaminated waterhole and lead her to clean water, give her food and guide her home. Clancy is initially scared of the Aboriginal people and, to conquer the language barrier, they communicate through drawings in the dirt. The episode was written in 1967, the same year as the Referendum to change the Constitution to enable Commonwealth jurisdiction over Aboriginal people and remove anomalies in the collection of the Census data. In this context, after a ten-year campaign against racist legislation as it existed under State Governments, the episode presents a tongue-in-cheek view of expectations and fears of Aboriginal people that were habitually represented in literature, film and the media. Their first appearance is through the often-used image of the 'native' face peering through the foliage. When Clancy learns that they are eating snake, she sets the food aside. The programme presents the Yirrkala as the classic noble savages. Given that producer Lee Robinson had an 'absolute respect' for Aboriginal people as a result of his years of working with Aboriginal individuals and communities in the Northern Territory, it is not unreasonable to interpret the episode as intentionally parodying widespread non-Indigenous views of Aboriginal people.

In the first half of the twentieth century, the Aboriginal peoples of northern Australia, particularly Arnhem Land, were an important focus for constructions of Australian indigeneity by both Indigenous and non-Indigenous Australians because of recognition of their ongoing connection to and practices of traditional Aboriginal Law and culture. The *Skippy* episode was one of the results of a tour — beginning with the Festival of Perth in 1967 — of a show titled *Festival of Aboriginal Theatre*. Aboriginal people living in remote areas were still under the control of mission and government authorities at the time. The tour to Sydney prompted the conception of the episode and enabled the performers to be available for the shoot. The production was a remounting of a show called *Aboriginal Theatre* produced in 1963 by the Australian Elizabethan Theatre Trust (AETT) and the Northern Territory Administration Welfare Branch. The production brought together performers and performances from Tiwi people of Bathurst Island, Murinbata and Ngalkbun people from Port Keats near Daly River, and Yolngu people from Yirrkala in eastern Arnhem Land in the Northern Territory. Posters advertising the show presented it as *Aboriginal Theatre* with 'full blood Aborigines from Arnhem Land'.

[...] Though largely initiated and produced by non-Indigenous people, these performances were to a large extent controlled by the Indigenous communities and performers. The communities had the knowledge of the dances and control over what they offered and, as documented in the case of the Yirrkala, control over who was chosen to perform. According to Edgar Wells, superintendent of the Yirrkala Mission at the time, decisions were made at meetings without representatives of either the Territory Administration or the AETT and all 'nominations were in the hands of the voting Aborigines, and only Aborigines voted for the names'. Elders who owned sections of the performances met and decided what they would permit to be performed.

The show, *Aboriginal Theatre*, included sections of ceremonies, public Dreaming stories and topical performances, intended to educate white Australia about Indigenous culture. Historically, performance events of song, dance, mime and story can be divided into events associated with ceremonies that are sacred and private, and events associated with entertainment and social negotiations that are public. These performances can be based on the adventures of ancestral beings; magic and power; totemic songs; hunting; dramatic songs and epics; fighting songs; topical events and everyday life. Within Aboriginal cultures, there is no clear division between sacred and ordinary stories; rather, sacredness is a matter of degree. Within this continuum of connection to the sacred, Indigenous performance can be divided into three major types: ceremony; public performances based on Dreaming stories; and performances based on topical issues for entertainment. The only events usually acknowledged in writings about Indigenous performance — within studies of ritual and ethnographic studies of elements of performance such as song or dance — are either those related to ceremony or public performances based on Dreamtime stories. This focus overlooks a major segment of Indigenous Australian performance: performances created for fun.

The Yirrkala performances included a number of Dreaming stories and a 'Mokoi' or Spirit Dance. The programme also included performances created for entertainment following historical practices such as the

Tiwi 'Darwin Impressions', which included Aeroplane Dances and performances based on motor cars, urban life and cowboy films. From the Yirrkala, there were comedy sequences, such as two men playing a husband and wife whose bickering and complaining at each other is overwhelmed by a swarm of flies; the Sick Man Dance, a comedic take on a man finding himself alone and sick in the desert and his troubles returning to his kin; and a Monkey Dance based on observations of chimpanzees. These performances — as humorous creations for entertainment — immediately challenge premises that frame all performance as ceremony or oral history. To frame this work as oral history not only misrepresents it but reduces the meaning of oral histories. In a context where the presumption is that 'authentic' Aboriginal performance is ceremony or oral history, work such as this — because it does not fit — is largely ignored.

Haag and Chief Welfare Officer Edward Evans, who managed the tour, are quoted as working to ensure the 'authenticity' of the performances. Reviews reiterated this, either by speaking of the show as being 'completely authentic' or by focusing on the 'primitive' qualities of the performance in contrast to contemporary urban life. The show was credited as conceived and staged by Haag; his main input was in the design of the mise-en-scene, which included a series of projections of landscape or seascape to indicate the performers' homelands. The other main element of his conception was the use of a white Australian narrator to introduce each segment. In 1969, Haag wrote a report explicitly stating his understandings about Indigenous Australian cultures and their relationship with Euro-Australian cultures:

> We must accept that pure ethnic Aboriginal culture ... can only exist in traditional tribal living and is therefore doomed ... the individual is therefore faced with either a void or the complete adoption of an alien culture — our culture.

The frame of authenticity was focused on the performances that drew on ceremony and Dreaming stories, with headlines such as 'Stone Age for City Footlights'. The presence of sequences for entertainment within the show —representing contemporary Indigenous cultural practices and lives, such as the 'Darwin Impressions' — were not acknowledged or engaged with in publicity, the reviews, or Haag's conception — except by implication as something impure.

The erasures of contemporary Aboriginal life are multifaceted. Haag's comments clearly reflect assimilation policies and arguments. Even though the material context of the performers' lives is not acknowledged, there is a level on which the show challenged these erasures, not only by the embodied counter statements of contemporary life within the entertainment sequences and the commitment to Law, but by the circumstances that the people from the remote communities, such as those from Yirrkala, were dealing with prior to and at the time of the tour. The three-month tour of major cities by *Aboriginal Theatre* began in October 1963 — in the same month that a Federal Parliamentary Select Committee of Enquiry into the Grievances of the Yirrkala Aborigines arrived at Yirrkala. The twenty dancers left for the tour after meeting with the Select Committee. In 1963, the Yolngu people from Yirrkala were campaigning to protect their traditional lands and their cultural lives. The programme notes for *Aboriginal Theatre*, about the people from Yirrkala, stated that 'the inhabitants have retained their culture, largely intact, to this day'. The final sentence notes that 'deposits of bauxite were discovered and are soon to be mined'. This little note is the only indication of a major campaign against the mining by the Aboriginal people at Yirrkala.

[...]

In the late 1950s Yolngu became aware of people prospecting for minerals in the area of the Gove Peninsula, and shortly after, discovered that mining leases had been taken out over a considerable area of our traditional land. Our response, in 1963, was to send a petition framed by painted bark to the Commonwealth Government demanding that our rights be recognised.

However, despite the attention it garnered, the petition was unsuccessful in securing recognition for Yirrkala Land Rights or protection of their land. When attempts to influence politicians failed, the Yirrkala took their grievances to the courts in 1971, in the case of Milirrpum vs Nabalco Pty Ltd, the Gove Land Rights Case. The High Court ruled against the Yirrkala people and in favour of Nabalco's bauxite mining projects. The judge's decision relied on the doctrine of terra nullius to deny the Yolngu rights to their land: 'The Aborigines belong to the land, but the land does not belong to the Aborigines'.

The Yolngu had not been consulted, or even formally told, that large sections of the mission they were restricted to was about to be excised for mining. The decision was made in an agreement with the Methodist Mission, the Federal and State Governments and the Gove Mining Corporation. In 1963, the Northern Territory Government and the mission were seeking to discredit the Yolngu opposition to the mining, claiming that it was 'Mission officials who had swayed the natives against bauxite development', that 'the people were not disturbed at the proposed mining development' and that 'the signatories were not in a position to speak on behalf of the whole of the people'. In this context, the tour of *Aboriginal Theatre* looks like a nexus of different political agendas. The hierarchy of the Methodist Mission and the Northern Territory Government were engaging in a public relations exercise to dispel concerns for the remote Aboriginal communities that were widely discussed in the press and this may well have influenced their decision to approach the Elizabethan Theatre Trust. The community at Yirrkala were also actively engaging with urban media and organisations to publicise their campaign to save their lands and gain recognition for their traditional rights and living culture. As a result of the Yirrkala and other Aboriginal campaigns, the indirect outcomes of the 1963 tour included a campaign with Actors Equity to gain award wages for the Aboriginal performers and arguments for direct payment rather than to mission- and government-controlled trust accounts.

Haag may have claimed credit for conceiving and staging *Aboriginal Theatre* but it was the communities and dancers who decided what to perform. This performance of both ancestral dances and contemporary practices for entertainment was a series of performative statements bearing embodied witness to living cultures, and the practices and rights that were part of those cultures. As Dwight Conquergood observes: 'Subordinate people do not have the privilege of explicitness, the luxury of transparency, [or] the presumptive norm of clear and direct communication'. Despite the challenges of a production aimed at fulfilling and supporting government and church policies to present urban audiences with 'authentic' Aboriginal practices and the focus on ceremonial performances, the inclusion of comedic contemporary work clearly acts to give a richer picture of continuing cultures and to challenge images of being frozen in time. The performers combined work that presented a vibrant living culture that not only stretched back in time but exists in the present.

Work such as *Aboriginal Theatre* is usually framed in scholarly writings as problematic because the lack of cultural context and information results in the show's being a process of inscription of a Western view on the dancers' bodies. I would suggest that there is another layer to this practice of inscription on the dance and dancers. In general, the framing of Indigenous performance has been an example of Emmanuel Levinas' notion of the 'violence of categories'. Categories and conceptions of Aboriginal culture as expressed by sociologists, such as Durkheim, only recognise ritual or ceremony as cultural performance. In this view, 'rituals and "dramatic performances" embed and reproduce the cultural system in collective and individual actions'. Everything else is categorised as oral history or as being contaminated and inauthentic in some way. Within this frame, the lack of information about the cultural context and historical performance practices allows a slippage between Dreaming stories and performances for entertainment, such as the 'Darwin Impressions' that is unacknowledged. This slippage acts to erase what is actually being witnessed.

As I have argued elsewhere, dominant narratives about the Australian nation such as those expressed in the policies of assimilation have shaped and limited the terms of reference for Indigenous performance. Within these narratives, as articulated by Haag, traditional practices are a thing of the past — museumised representations of the primitive. The performance choices made within *Aboriginal Theatre* foreground both traditional and contemporary culture and life. This embodied performance of people who live these lives unsettles the a priori assumptions and performances for entertainment that are part of the continuum of historical pre-contact practices such as the 'Darwin Impressions', directly challenging locked notions of authenticity. The performances for entertainment demonstrate that Aboriginal cultures are neither passive nor static. In some ways, it is no wonder that historical practices for entertainment based on topical issues have been largely erased or seen as inauthentic when they always present a challenge to reductive narratives.

[...]

Since Aboriginal cultures are among the most performance-based in the world, it is not surprising that performance has been an important part of cross-cultural exchange and communication. Equally, the framing of that performance has been a central part of the reception and understanding of those cultures within European social and political narratives. The terms of reception of these performances have changed over time but there continue to be traces of past racialised narratives that allow no room for living cultures. Regardless of the breadth of scholarship focused on the recognition of cultural difference and the positive aims of critics and audiences, the 'authenticity' of cultural production by minority cultures continues to be received as 'something independent and external, removed from any possible relation to praxis'. The reception and framing of Indigenous performance operates within the context and language established by a palimpsest of current and past notions of authenticity.

The notion of Aboriginal practices being frozen in time, only authentic if they are demonstrably pre-contact, continues to inform reception of contemporary work through the lack of recognition given to historical and contemporary performance practices for entertainment. In the show discussed here, contemporary culturally specific performance practices for entertainment are a crucial part of the poetic politics. The 'fun' performances add a significant layer to what is being communicated to cross-cultural audiences. Almost like a state of exception in itself is the continuing lack of recognition of living cultures as expressed in practices of contemporary entertainment except as derivative, hybrid or inauthentic.

Questions to ask about theatre and culture
Culture, tradition, resistance, and revolution

Western critics and intercultural theatre practitioners have tended to treat culture as a matter of choice and affiliation – something that someone does. Culture can be traded, gained, lost, and translated. It may grow and change. In societies that have been subjected to colonization almost all of these understandings of culture can be problematic. If culture is a choice, and changing cultures is a choice, this is often considered to be at odds with the idea that culture shapes identity. If culture shapes identity, then the loss of a culture changes or destroys identities. Controlling culture might be a means of controlling people: marketing culture might be a way of marketing people. In these cases, culture isn't simply an action someone takes. It is a deep system of meaning and it requires a context. The idea of translating cultural elements or borrowing cultural elements doesn't make sense – moving costumes from Chinese opera to Western theatre isn't borrowing a part of Chinese culture because Chinese culture is a web of related signs and signifiers. The split between Western theory and theories from around the world is not an absolute. Outside of the theatre world, cultural anthropologists like Clifford Geertz write about webs of culture. In Japanese theatre, Suzuki Tadashi talks about interculturalism and choice in a way that is relatively consistent with the Western theories discussed above (although his practice is radically different). Figuring out exactly what counts as culture and how one might interact with culture is a major question for theatre practitioners.

Whatever the relationship between the theories in various parts of the world, it is rare to find world theorists who are not deeply concerned with the nature of "culture" in their discussions of intercultural, national, or postcolonial theatre (and, indeed, it is rare to find theatre artists from the mid-twentieth century onwards whose work does not actively identify with some variation of these camps).

The idea that culture can be colonized is a repeated refrain in postcolonial studies. Ngugi Wa Thiong'o's *Decolonizing the Mind* (1986) argues that African literature must be written in African languages because European languages carry European culture with them. Chinua Achebe argued that he could create a new English that was "capable of bearing the weight" of African experience. The two modes of decolonizing literature can be seen in the theatre world as well. On the one hand, some artists argue that a return to traditional theatrical techniques updated for a contemporary context displays a freedom from European influence. Other artists argue that tradition is part of an old order of the world, and that the artist has a duty to create something new for the new culture that has emerged. While Buenaventura focuses on whether the idea of culture is compatible with politics and reaches the conclusion that theatre should be about experiences and not about official notions of culture, the debate in the African and

Caribbean context focuses more heavily on *which* culture might be effective at generating political resistance.

Casey figures culture in yet another way – not as political resistance, government, edict, or identity, but rather as an artistic process that can be framed and reframed to alter its meaning. Casey works to shape the way people perceive culture, particularly by making them aware of multiple aspects of the culture in which they are participating. The idea that one could be blind to parts of one's own culture, and that such parts might need interpretation is an interesting one. Casey is concerned with figuring out how to understand and interpret them before and beyond the need to express them. The idea of repeatedly needing to reframe culture – to interpret it in new ways – or to keep multiple frames in mind at the same time is also provocative. It gives Casey's culture a fluidity that can sometimes fade into the background with other discussions of culture.

The theorists in this chapter remind us of the multiplicity of possible ways of conceiving of culture. Even if we discuss resistant cultures, the type of resistance can vary. It is far too easy to collapse all world intercultural theatre into a single category – "The Empire writes back" idea discussed in Chapter 8. Looking at the ways in which the disparate writers in this chapter deal with the idea of cultural blending suggests that any one-size-fits-all model of resistance simply doesn't work.

The place of ritual

Quite aside from interculturalism and multiculturalism, issues of culture in world theatre must also deal with *intra*cultural issues. This is particularly noticeable in modern and contemporary theatre that tries to remain connected to the past. Casey's negative description of a piece that tries to portray a static notion of an authentic cultural past is a good reminder of how tricky this can be. How can the rituals, traditions, and lifestyles of people be put on stage without it becoming a quest for authenticity?

Walcott talks about how the rituals he imagines or discusses are no longer the rituals that they were – how the dark past remains dark and unknown. He states that neither he nor his current theatre colleagues are in touch with the meaningful roots of the rituals that their ancestors practiced. Without the immediacy, without the spiritual beliefs, these rituals become empty performances. They are imitations of the past, not reclamations of it. This seems to be an argument for leaving rituals behind entirely, or for adopting contemporary rituals. At the same time, Walcott's poem-essay seems unwilling to leave the past behind completely. The past continues to inform the present. Walcott's theatre must be in touch with its ritual roots without trying to reproduce them and it must be in touch with the present situation.

Walcott's theatre does not recreate traditional rituals, but it does have ritualized elements. Ritual is not just a marker of the past, of tradition:

rituals are actually performed in order to generate certain results. Rituals tap into larger (often spiritual) forces. Walcott's theatre may not reproduce traditional rituals, but it certainly has this mystical component, a feeling of watching people participating in something sacred, albeit tarnished. Since Walcott is writing in a poetic manner, it is unclear the extent to which we are supposed to take the mystical nature of what he writes as literal. It may be that he is just expressing the fact that theatre can be powerful when it is done well. On the other hand, Walcott's theatre does have a spiritual quality to it, albeit an evasive one that is hard to pin down.

In contrast, for Buenaventura ritual is simply something that has been co-opted by the government and made into a tourist attraction. This is similar to what Casey describes as part of the worst practices of "indigenous" theatre. When Walcott discusses the Caribbean's "African" phase, he is treating ritual in the same way – as something that belongs in a museum that is recreated to make tourists happy. This is always a danger of representing ritual rather than enacting it. There is a fine line between celebrating a culture and making that culture into a static object for other people to consume and critique.

The early part of Werewere Liking's work provides a third option, strongly endorsing ritual. She doesn't duplicate rituals on stage, but, instead, recreates them. She explores their meanings, their modes of expression, and their purposes and figures out a way to make her theatre do all this. She is, effectively, creating new rituals as she goes. The idea of a new ritual is, of course, a bit of an oxymoron, given that rituals imply repeated action. Of course, almost all theatre consists of repeated action (rehearsals and performances) so perhaps new theatre rituals are possible. Obviously, they are possible, given that Werewere Liking's work is effective. The mental exercise of trying to figure out how new rituals are created, or if they are even possible is worth pursuing. So too, however, is the realization that sometimes forms of theatre exceed our ability to logically process them. This becomes more true as we move further from our home territories – the "logic" that we practice isn't always the same as the "logic" of other places.

A long-standing argument between Wole Soyinka and Femi Osofisan serves to combine all these various threads of ritual and tradition into a single contentious debate. Wole Soyinka argues that Africa has a distinct world view and that this world view is both stable and assimilative. It is able to incorporate new experiences. Soyinka explains this world view in terms of Yorùbá deities. Soyinka describes the quintessential moment of tragedy as a man alone in a spotlight, feeling his isolation and his severance from society, from god, and from all frame of reference. This tragic gulf can be bridged, and Soyinka describes the ritual energy that society contributes to help the lone man rejoin the community. This description is mystical, mysterious, and enigmatic. Soyinka's theatre (like Artaud's – myth and magic infuse portions of Western theatre too) claims to point to something higher and more mysterious than immediate reality.

While Soyinka is arguing for a supernatural understanding of theatre and the world based on the Yorùbá pantheon, he is also using a basic argumentative structure that clearly and directly references Nietzsche's *Birth of Tragedy* which uses Greek gods as metaphors for artistic development. This could suggest that Soyinka's work is also not taking the supernatural elements it discusses in a completely literal way. Whatever the place of the supernatural, it is absolutely clear throughout Soyinka's writing that his recourse to the Yorùbá world does not exclude hybridity with Western culture, theory, and theatrical form. Of course, this makes sense, given that Soyinka argues that the Yorùbá world view can assimilate new experiences without fundamentally changing.

Femi Osofisan has rejected Wole Soyinka's work, with its focus on myth, as being counter-revolutionary. Simply put, Osofisan argues that if theatre is going to have real effects, it must be grounded in reality, not in the supernatural. Indeed, Osofisan wrote *No More the Wasted Breed* as a pragmatic response to Soyinka's mythic theatre in *The Strong Breed*. Soyinka's play can be read as suggesting that a communal ritual can solve the problems that the play presents. Osofisan's play can be read as showing the failure of the gods to intervene on behalf of mortals. A focus on myth, according to Osofisan, decreases the potential for individual action and responsibility: if you are waiting for the gods to save you, you will not take personal responsibility for your place in the world around you. Osofisan has designed his theatre to have immediate, concrete political and social effects – to spur the audience into thought and action. Both Badal Sircar and Femi Osofisan argue that folk theatre is stagnant – not speaking to real oppression.

While Osofisan rejects Soyinka's mythopoetics (use of mythology and ritual as a primary source of structure), his work is nonetheless grounded in traditional African performance. In this way his work is similar to that of Ngugi Wa Thiong'o and Zakes Mda, both of whom argue that one of Africa's greatest tools for advancement is the strong communal nature of African traditional societies. Many of Osofisan's plays show an explicit blending of the African and European (e.g. *Tegonni*, an adaptation of *Antigone*). For Osofisan, the return to African storytelling techniques is not a rejection of European traditions, but, rather, a tool that can be used in a specific political moment.

Global vs specific: universal vs particular

When dealing with theatre that specifically positions itself in terms of multiple cultures, the question of the universal comes up. On the one hand, claiming that all humanity shares certain characteristics can lead to ideas of equal treatment for people around the world. Things like slavery, genocide, religious wars, and the underlying racism, sexism, classicism, and xenophobia would be much more difficult to maintain if people firmly believed that there was more that united humanity than divided it. This is the idea of the universal in its positive form.

The same idea has a negative form as well, one that is inextricably bound to the positive aspects. Once people start trying to figure out what all humans share, it is a short step to the idea that all humans *should* share certain characteristics. The savage, the primitive, the uncivilized – these are labels for people who get left out of the universal. As Chinua Achebe vehemently points out, the word universal is generally synonymous with the word Western, and, as such, it almost always acts to the detriment of any non-Western culture. The idea of the universal is much less common in world theatre theory than it is in Western theatre theory.

The same liberal impulse that leads to the idealistic vision of the universal described above also leads to a celebration of distinct, individual cultures as having unique things to offer to the world. The idea of particularity, however, can slide into the same type of negativity as the idea of the universal. Valuing cultural difference can easily become a fetishizing of the exotic – a valuing of something simply because it is new and different without considering its place within its own culture. An insistence on difference can also lead to constructions of hierarchy – if two things are different, perhaps one is better, older, more cultured than the other. This leaves the intercultural practitioner in an awkward place, forced to negotiate between two ambivalent options.

Time plays a factor in the debate between universality and particularity. Werewere Liking and Derek Walcott talk about emergent cultural practices (whereas Maryrose Casey talks about emergent understanding of long-standing cultural practices). Part of Wole Soyinka's argument about the universality of African theatre is rooted in its timelessness, in its connection to eternal matters. The idea of emergent cultures or cultural practices, given that it suggests change rather than timelessness, seems to be aligned with cultural particularity rather than cultural universalism. In other words, for something to be universal, it must be somewhat stable – otherwise it could not be shared around the world. Thus, these new practices described by Liking must, almost by definition, belong not to the universal but to the particular.

Rather than thinking about the universal and the particular as binaries, the theories in this chapter suggest that both these categories have something to offer. Considering where elements of a given piece of theatre fall on the scale of universality and particularity could be informative. Furthermore, figuring out the political project of a given concept of the universal or the particular can shape an interpretation of the piece. Wole Soyinka's idea of timeless, unchanging truths is not the same as Western colonial notions of the universality of humanity.

The hybrid

Unless they are extraordinarily well-hidden, there is not a single culture on earth that has not interacted with multiple other cultures. In fact, most cultures are made up of bits and pieces from a variety of sources. Sometimes they took these pieces in a violent manner – sometimes these pieces were violently forced upon them. Sometimes these cultural exchanges happened through economic pathways, sometimes through marriage, and sometimes in the spirit of intellectual exchange. Theatre, then, as a part of culture, is always a mixture. Some types of theatre draw attention to this mixture.

When faced with a piece of theatre that is obviously commenting on the relationship of two or more cultures, it is worth noting that there are a number of different possible cultural interactions.

Hybridity refers to combining two forms to create something new. While one might argue that a totally new theatre could be created without reliance on prior forms, I have yet to locate a theorist whose theorization of "new" work was not explicitly hybrid. Hybridity offers the advantage of versatility, the ability to take the best of multiple worlds. On the other hand, if theatre reflects ideology, a hybrid theatre would likely generate some degree of hybridity in its political statements. If the goal of a theatrical endeavor is to create a strong political intervention aimed at forging a new national identity, then hybridity might be a poor option. Each of these intellectual options is compelling, and each has been advocated to one extent or another by theorists around the world. Curiously, however, hybridity sneaks its way into all these arguments in some fashion or another. As much as theatre can shape ideology, it is also shaped by ideology. Globalization is a fact of contemporary life: even the most fiercely nationalistic groups find themselves in constant relationship with portions of other cultures.

Both Soyinka and Osofisan address hybridity as a secondary factor in their theatre. For Badal Sircar hybridity is a core theatrical concept: it is the most effective form to reach his political aims. Sircar says that city theatre has "fine advanced ideas" but does not require the audience to act on them. The folk theatre has the potential for action, the city theatre has the themes that might inspire action. Sircar talks repeatedly about communication and the fact that this communication must reach the villages and rural spaces. He juxtaposes this discussion with various mentions of social problems. The implication, here, is that theatre, as a communicative medium, can actually help to solve these problems. It is precisely the blending of the concerns of the city and the country that allow theatre to accomplish its social and communicative messages. What is created in Sircar's Third Theatre, like Soyinka's theatre, is something greater than its component parts. Both Sircar and Soyinka start with an intensely local focus and move out from there. Soyinka ultimately claims to be defining an African world view, and suggests that this view could usefully be adopted in Europe. Sircar's expansiveness stops within the borders of India.

When viewing a piece of culturally mixed theatre, it is important to consider the extent to which the cultures remain separate and the extent to which they blend. Each of these choices have possible political ramifications. Is one culture taking over another? Are two cultures learning to exist in harmony? Are two cultures becoming one new culture? Is it good that these two cultures are becoming one culture? Are the two cultures discovering that they actually had more in common than they might have appeared to? All of these are possibilities in theatre.

Performance and choice

All of the above questions are fraught with political and cultural disagreements, disagreements about which people feel passionately. While the ideas of hybridity and interculturalism are full of possibility, colonial and postcolonial theatres also carry with them a fear that none of the new identities or the old identities, the new techniques or the old techniques, the new stories or the old stories will be able to capture the essence of colonial life. The argument here is that the colonial subject has so long been pulled in multiple directions that the postcolonial subject remains a stranger to himself. This subject cannot rest comfortably in any of the identities open to him because he does not fully belong to any of them. While philosophers and theorists from Jean-Paul Sartre (who claims that the condition of the native is always a nervous condition) to Paul Gilroy (who claims that one cannot simultaneously be black and British and therefore must develop a double-consciousness) have explored this concept, theatre seems uniquely suited to such discussions.

Within the theatre, the actor is generally asked to assume a role, a role that is foreign to the actor. This basic supposition of performance is that part of our identity is performed and that the techniques of the actor might have some bearing on life. If the postcolonial subject is forced to choose and perform certain identities, then studying such performance in theatre might yield insights into the function of such performance in life. This particular deployment of theatrical performance as similar to performances in life is most commonly discussed in the Caribbean context where the idea of life as a performance is prevalent.

To what extent does the idea of performance imply choice? To what extent does the performance become real? To what extent does the fact that identity is performed imply that there is not real identity? Is there a certain performance technique or combination of techniques that might yield a more stable identity? Is stable identity the goal? Is the traditional Western style of performance and acting specifically linked to a specific notion of identity? If so, should this tradition be shifted to reflect other modes of identity? Or perhaps the goal is to shift the postcolonial societies so that they function in the same mode of identity as the Western society (not the same identities, but the idea that identity is constructed in similar ways in both cases)?

Conclusions

Is revolution a world phenomenon, a national phenomenon, or a local phenomenon? Should revolutionary theatre be for the world, the national, or a given local circumstance? This is a question of the audience of the theatre, but it is also a question of the theatre's form. At times, revolutionary theatre seeks to create a national identity to stand against the remnants of colonialism, the threat of dictatorship, fears about advancement, or unity in the face of an external foe. To do this, the theatre must find a way to communicate with the entire nation. Since "nation" signals a shared culture, national theatre is often helping to create the nation to which it is directing its messages. National theatre focuses on unity, but other revolutionary theatre celebrates diversity by blending elements of theatres from all over the world. This type of revolutionary theatre suggests connections among groups that might have formerly struggled with each other. On the other hand, hybrid theatres and the ever-present encroachment of Western theatrical practices can also be viewed as threats to traditional cultures, as a form of cultural imperialism. Finally, some movements, like the community theatre movement or socialist realism, suggest that they have found a theatrical practice that is the appropriate mode for revolution wherever revolution is needed. Such theatres are often based on the idea that the workers around the world share a common set of needs and goals. These are not mutually exclusive options, and often theatres will try to move among these various modes. To do this, theatres must negotiate issues of language, hybridity, and nationalism.

What is the place of traditional theatre practice in revolutionary theatre? What is the place of traditional belief in world theatre? Can postcolonial theatre be hybrid? Must postcolonial theatre be hybrid? These questions are complicated ones in world theatre. The spread of modernization and the spread of colonialism went hand-in-hand in many places around the globe. One aspect of this expanded global contact was access to Western-style theatre. In the postcolonial era, after Europe had given up its formal colonies in Africa and Asia, many of the new governments were based on European models. It makes sense to suggest that any resistance to these new governments should not adopt the theatrical form that came along with these governments. Western theatre might not be the most effective way of resisting Western-style government, given that theatrical structure can reflect ideology. On the other hand, traditional theatrical styles were designed to address a different set of issues. Even if this was not the case, the nations once subjected to colonization were, and continue to be, invested in the idea of advancement and progress. It would be odd for the vehicle of progress to be a return to the theatrical structures of a (potentially fictionalized) past.

Note

1 http://globetoglobe.shakespearesglobe.com/archive/2012/

Chapter 5

Identity / the actor

Case study: Japanese bunraku theatre

The aesthetics chapters explored some of the characteristics of nō theatre, one of the major Japanese traditions. This case study looks at bunraku, a Japanese style of puppet theatre. One of Japan's great playwrights, Chikamatsu Monzaemon, worked in an early version of this style of theatre (among others). Bunraku contains music, puppets, puppeteers, and chanters. In some styles of performance there will only be one chanter who gives voice to all the characters. In other styles, multiple chanters will take on roles. The chanter also takes on the significant task of narrating the play. The tradition of narration is strong enough in Japan that Tsubouchi Shoyo, a translator and theatre critic, remarked that Shakespeare's scripts were much improved by the addition of such narration.

It seems obvious that one cannot have theatre without actors, but what exactly is an actor? A simple generic Western definition would be a person who adopts the characteristics or mannerisms of another person for purposes of performance. By this definition, not all theatres in the world have actors: neither the chanters, musicians, puppets, nor puppeteers are actors in this sense. The chanter may shift vocal patterns to match the character in question, but he is not performing this role – there is a puppet doing the movement, and a puppeteer controlling the puppet.

The simple Western definition of the actor is actually a somewhat modern innovation, perhaps emerging as recently as Stanislavski. The idea of one actor performing one role says something about the nature of the individual. There is a self distinct from other selves. That self has stable characteristics and is reasonably complete. To say that I will play the role of Hamlet is to say that there is a Hamlet-shaped "I" that I can step into, and that this "I" is distinct from any other "I." It is not hard to imagine, as a number of playwrights and novelists have done, Hamlet showing up in other texts.

With puppet theatre, locating this sort of "I" is impossible. We can clearly see a puppeteer pulling the strings. This "I" is not autonomous. Not only is someone pulling the strings, but someone else is speaking for the puppet. What is this style of theatre saying about the nature of the "I"? What constitutes good "acting" in puppet theatre. A "realistic" portrayal of a character is obviously not the goal, unless, of course, there is a conception of the "I" as being composed of various interactions with other people. Maybe the Western idea of the unique, isolated, self-contained individual is the wrong notion of "I" for this theatre. Perhaps the notion of identity and character is completely foreign to this style of theatre. Maybe this is more akin to storytelling. Even if this is storytelling, however, we can judge stories by the degree to which their characters captivate. Maybe this is a theatre that, like a painting, seeks to establish a particular response, mood, or feeling. In that case, "acting" seems foreign to the discussion of the effect.

Introduction

This chapter explores theories of acting in relation to theories of identity. Generally speaking, theatre involves living bodies on stage (puppet theatre being an obvious exception). This body interacts in some way with a notion of identity. In contemporary Western realism, the body is assumed to have psychological depth, to be distinct from other identities, and to be acting autonomously (to have agency, the ability to choose actions). This idea of what the body on stage is depends upon the idea that people are in fact autonomous beings with their own distinct identities and agency. Some masked forms of theatre, like Italian *commedia dell'arte* decrease this idea of the autonomous, unique individual identity in favor of character types. Scholars have argued that Greek tragedy actually connected the bodies on stage to communities of people rather than focusing on the idea of individuality.

The theories in this chapter address two related sets of questions. First, what is the actor on stage meant to do? What does this actor represent / present / or otherwise perform? What manner of craft and training might prepare the actor for such work? Is the actor practicing his craft in isolation? In connection with other actors? In connection with the audience? In connection with spiritual beings? In connection with the Earth? Second, what is the relationship of the actor's craft to the world? Is the actor representing an individual? If so, what is the concept of "individual" at play? Is the actor representing a community? If so, what does the word "community" mean in this context? Are there certain types of beings / individuals / communities that are not represented in a given theatre or that this theatre cannot represent?

In all other chapters, the various definitions of the terms used shift. The aesthetics chapter, for instance charted various uses of the term "aesthetics." Even finding the basic words that bind the material in this chapter together is more difficult. Is the body on stage necessarily "acting" or an "actor?" Does saying "individual" necessarily imply distinction from "community?" Given the radical differences underpinning ideas of "acting" and "individual," I will be focusing more on clarifying each of the distinct theories below than on an explanation of the little that binds them together. It might be worth considering that many theatrical advances have come from reconsidering the nature of the actor. The diversity of ideas about acting and the individual below certainly suggest a bright future for theatre – in any given context, there are many possibilities yet to explore.

Definitions of identity

When looking at one discrete body, what is it that we are seeing? For lack of a better term, what is the "identity" of this body? Rather than providing a singular definition of identity, this chapter looks at many different modes of identity. These modes tend to be chartable on a series of scales resulting from debates around the concept.

The first such scale is the degree to which identity is related to the divine – any being, concept, or force beyond mankind. Identity might be figured, as in Christianity, as related to the purpose which God created man for. Identity might be explained in terms of progress along a path toward enlightenment, as in Buddhism, where layers of self are stripped away in the journey. On the other extreme of this scale, there is a functional definition of identity, like that presented by Marxism or Maoist socialism. Each body is recognizable as having an identity relative to the work it performs. The divine is replaced by pragmatic concerns.

The second scale involves the interiority or exteriority of identity. How much of a given identity can be seen? On one extreme we have psychoanalytic and psychological modes of identity (often referred to by the term "subjectivity") in which the external attributes of identity are only reflections of a deeper interior life. In contrast, while Mao's brand of socialism does police individual thoughts, many understandings of Marxism focus on action rather than thought.

The next scale involves the degree to which identity is individual or communal. Returning to psychoanalytic notions of identity, many postcolonial theorists (e.g. Frantz Fanon from the Caribbean, or Achille Mbembe from Nigeria) have argued that the system of colonization creates a psychology within both the colonizer and the colonized. In this way, group psychology is a more useful explanatory tool than individual psychology. Marxism, in all its forms around the world, similarly focuses on the group. As for the other extreme, traveling outside of the U.S. and the U.K., one quickly encounters the idea that much of the rest of the world is shocked by the intense focus on the singular, discrete individual found in American and British media, art, culture, and society.

The final scale deals with issues of consistency or change. Identities may be very stable – discourses about genetic determinates of personality, god-given talents, or *iwa* (the unchanging spirit of a person in the Yorùbá culture) are examples of this. On the other hand, identity may be flexible. The development of the *bildungsroman* (novels about growing up), the journey motif in literature, or even the self-help book deal with the idea that characters can evolve and change.

Each of these scales contains the idea of agency embedded within it. Agency refers to the ability of the individual to make meaningful choices in an autonomous way. In its most extreme form, having agency means that you make meaningful choices that substantially impact your life and that you do so completely free of outside influence. In terms of the divine, the question of agency might be re-termed "free will." In terms of interior and exterior our own psychology or the material conditions of our existence might limit the choices in front of us – or force our hand in choosing. In terms of community, our place within a communal group might either be the thing that allows agency or restricts it.

Each of the above dimensions of identity can give rise to radically different schools of acting. The basic task of the actor shifts depending on what the core conception of identity is. This is complicated still further by the fact that any given mode of acting might choose to challenge a given identity instead of affirming it. Whether the acting is erasing or embracing a given type of identity, it is important to distinguish between the modes of identity that underlie a given performance.

Western notions of identity and acting

Debates over acting in the West are frequently also debates over the nature of identity. August Strindberg (1849–1912) makes a similar point in his preface to *Miss Julie*. Strindberg is attempting to define "naturalism" in theatre – a way of presenting the empirical (observable and measurable) world on stage in a concrete manner. In this essay, he makes some specific distinctions between naturalism and realism – naturalism presents only what it needs to in order to communicate its empirical reality, whereas realism (in Strindberg's use of the idea) attempts to completely realize the world on stage. In order to explain naturalistic acting, Strindberg looks at the definition of character. He says that the word has been used to discuss someone's moral character (e.g. he is of a high moral character and would not do anything that would hurt others). He also notes that the same word has been used to designate a type (e.g. a "character" role like a clown, the dirty old man, etc. – these were common in Italian *commedia dell'arte*.). Character is also used to refer to someone's uniqueness (e.g. "he is such a character – so strange"). Strindberg notes that these uses of the word "character" are all static – assuming that the person in question is one thing consistently. He argues that the modern character must be fluid, flexible, and constantly changing. Strindberg's actors are required to present all the aspects of these characters sequentially. This "presentation," however, is different from attempting to represent or embody the whole character.

The above idea might make some intellectual sense when studied in detail, but it is extraordinarily difficult to actually do what Strindberg suggests in a theatrical production. Indeed, Strindberg's ideas on naturalism did not launch a theatre movement. Their influence, instead, comes from Strindberg pointing out the different conflicts inherent in acting styles and ideas of what people are. He explores the roles of emotion and continuity in created people and then considers the ways in which these ideas might be staged. Directors have tried hundreds of techniques to address these same issues, for example, character-masks, neutral masks, constantly shifting characters, roles split between multiple actors, choral roles, actors split between multiple roles, and declamatory acting that separates emotion from the role.

The tension that Strindberg's work emphasizes involves the connections between acting styles and the psychology of the individual. A similar debate emerges as U.S. theatre practitioners take up the work of Stanislavski. Stanislavski created the first systemized training program for actors (based on the work of other theatre practitioners). He borrows the idea of observable, measurable behaviors from naturalism and trains his actors to become more fully aware of themselves and their range as human beings. His acting style is not about becoming someone else, but, rather, fully recognizing the potential of your individual body as a dramatic instrument. This distinction is lost by the time his system makes it to America, where it becomes "method acting" (a term which has, itself, meant several different things). Method acting picks up on the realistic threads of Stanislavski's work, suggesting that the actor attempt to inhabit a space as similar to the character as possible. To perform the character, one must become the character. This distinction between being the character or being yourself suggests a conflict between the idea that mankind is all of a similar type – my happiness and your happiness are similar things – and the idea that each of us is a distinctly unique individual, in which case my happiness and your happiness might have nothing to do with one another.

Despite this disagreement over the universality of mankind, both method acting and Stanislavski agree that characters have both physical and psychological aspects. Actors must be in command of both of these realms.

Bertolt Brecht explicitly critiques the idea of the psychologized character, returning, as he does so, to older Western styles of acting, and to Asian performance styles (or at least his interpretation of both of these things).

While the above examples focus on modern and contemporary Western thought, these debates are not new. Plato and Aristotle are both concerned with the moral effects of pretending to be something on stage. Medieval English theatre is similarly concerned about the ability of a man to portray a god or even a prophet on stage, which suggests the idea that the actor must, in some way, inhabit the role he intends to play. Western theatre has consistently wrestled with the nature of the individual and the appropriate way of placing this individual on stage (or not).

World notions of the actor and identity

The above references to psychology assume a theory of psychology, which, in turn, can lead to a theory of acting. What other types of acting might be located when theories of identity are different?

Suzuki Tadashi's physical acting style might be related to conflicts over the Japanese concept of *shutaisei*, which is a particular type of subjectivity that emerged as a subject of debate in post-war Japan. During this time, Japanese people were struggling with their individual and collective responsibility for the war. Was the emperor to blame? If the emperor spoke for Japan, was all of Japan to blame? Was each individual to blame for individual actions? Had the emperor been manipulated by strong individuals who should accept the blame? These new questions required new words in the Japanese philosophical lexicon, just as ideas of the emperor's relationship to individual Japanese people had required the development of a set of new terms before the war. If new concepts of identity required a new language to discuss them, it is hardly surprising to see new acting styles developing alongside this. Perhaps the madness and physicality that shows up in so many of his productions is somehow produced by the above conflicts.

Gao Xingjian similarly articulates a new acting style in which the physical "neutral actor" can be seen. This is the physical self of the actor, separate from his everyday self and separate from the character. It is, in some sense, the container (my word, not Gao's) that these other identities inhabit. The idea of the body as a container for identity resonates with various performances that function on the idea of possession, where one identity takes over the body that belonged to another (e.g. Egungun masquerades in Nigeria). Indeed, a focus on the body of the actor is one thing that Western theatre claims to find inspirational in Asian theatre (albeit older Asian forms).

Wole Soyinka articulates the place of the self in the Yorùbá worldview, as isolated from the gods and from other humans. He says this is the fundamental condition of the human. This unites humanity in their shared condition even if that condition is one of isolation. He does not directly connect this to a theory of acting, but he does note that the actor must draw spiritual support from the audience. This idea of one's personality being supported or shaped by the community also emerges in Ngugi Wa Thiong'o's work with community theatre in Kenya in which each role was shaped by the input of several people. His theatre and the roles within it literally would not exist if it weren't for a group effort.

Each of the scales mentioned above functions differently in different regions around the world. To understand the nature of acting and the individual is to understand an entire set of philosophical, religious, or social ideas. This creates an exciting world for theatre in which there are innumerable ways of considering what the actor is. It also makes summative statements about these styles of acting as a group almost impossible.

Augusto Boal: discovering the I in and beyond class

Augusto Boal was imprisoned, tortured, and eventually exiled from Brazil after the 1964 military coup. During his time in exile, he wrote about his theatre of the oppressed. While his theatre had been experimental since his schooling, his more radical theatrical endeavors developed during his exile.

Boal's theatre is often considered to be leftist or socialist in character, particularly with regard to the national government. In general, left-wing nationalism aims for social equality through popular government. Right-wing nationalism often accepts social inequality as a part of life. Both sides of the political spectrum have extreme elements who have abused the fundamental principles of each viewpoint. Inasmuch as Brazil has a large gap between its wealthiest and poorest citizens, it is not surprising that some degree of popular left-wing politics would appeal to the nation. Such politics are undeniably disruptive. They set out to change the way things are. Simply put, those in power are often distressed by changes to the way things are. As an advocate for left-wing politics, Boal was dangerous to those in power.

Boal's theatre functions on a series of basic presuppositions, many of which are shared by other Marxist theatre. In Boal's system, inequality requires that the oppressed cooperate with their oppressors. To gain this cooperation, the oppressed must have little voice in politics and they must believe that their voice does not matter. The system must limit what the oppressed can imagine for themselves and provide them just enough of this imagined life to keep them from open revolt. The system must encourage passivity: your actions won't matter anyway, so why take an action.

Based on these assumptions about the way the system of inequality works, Boal's theatre seeks to promote individual thought, action, and voice. First, the oppressed must realize the extent of their oppression. Second, they must realize they have some ability to speak and think about the problems facing them. Third, they must realize they have the ability to act. Fourth, they must believe that these actions can change the current social conditions.

Boal provides a polemical, if convincing, account of Aristotelian theatre, in which he argues that Aristotle wants to influence a passive audience into believing things that promote the current social order. An audience that sits and accepts what it is told is exactly what the system wants. Boal creates a theatre in which the "spect-actors" actively participate in the performance. The quintessential moment in Boal's theatre is the staging of a problem and then the invitation to the audience to step into the roles and generate solutions to the problem. While the idea of stepping into a role and solving a problem seems somewhat intuitive from a privileged Western standpoint, Boal's theatre carefully lays out a series of steps to help his "spect-actors" reach a point where they too feel they can take such actions. Chapter 14 details a basic exercise designed to help the oppressed see the world in different ways. Boal also experiments with providing the oppressed access to different modes of language to help them express their own voices. He works with photographs and physical languages to accomplish this.

Boal's theatre was undeniably effective as a political tool. In fact, Boal was elected to city office and developed a mode of theatre by which voters could suggest legislative policy. Variations of Boal's work have been adopted by governmental bodies in various countries in Europe and North America as well. If Boal's theatre has begun to be used by those in power, does this mean his project has succeeded or that it is succeeding? Boal's theatre began as an attack on the current system, but it became a part of a system. Is Boal's theatre inherently revolutionary in the sense of being against all systems? Is it revolutionary in the sense of seeking equality for the broadest group of people? Once this equality is achieved, can the system work to reinforce itself? Would this reinforcement of the system take a similar form to Aristotle's theatre against which Boal reacted?

While Boal's work certainly would have fit in the chapter that questioned the political efficacy of theatre structures, it is significant that the primary focus of change for Boal is the actor as an individual. Rather than treating actors as cogs in a theatrical machine – which would mirror the inequitable system's treatment of peasants as cogs in the political machine – Boal encourages individual experimentation and voice. Each individual has the power to create. At the same time, however, in Marxist fashion, these individuals do speak from within a specific social class. This is not a radical individualism in which each person approaches every issue from a completely different vantage point. It is an individuality where each person adds his voice to a collective project. Why would Boal's theatre insist simultaneously on the individual's voice and on the individual as part of the group? What are the dangers of radical individualism? What are the possible benefits? What would a theatre of the oppressed look like if it included radical individual elements?

Extract 5.1 Selections from *Theatre of the Oppressed*
Augusto Boal, translated by Charles A. and Maria-Odilia Leal McBride

How Aristotle's Coercive System of Tragedy Functions

The spectacle begins. The tragic hero appears. The public establishes a kind of empathy with him.

The action starts. Surprisingly, the hero shows a flaw in his behavior, a hamartia; and even more surprising, one learns that it is by virtue of this same hamartia that the hero has come to his present state of happiness.

Through empathy, the same hamartia that the spectator may possess is stimulated, developed, activated.

Suddenly, something happens that changes everything. (Oedipus, for example, is informed by Tiresias that the murderer he seeks is Oedipus himself.) The character, who because of a hamartia had climbed so high, runs the risk of falling from those heights. This is what the *Poetics* classifies as peripeteia, a radical change in the character's destiny. The spectator, who up to then had his own hamartia stimulated, starts to feel a growing fear. The character is now on the way to misfortune. Creon is informed of the death of his son and his wife; Hippolytus cannot convince his father of his innocence, and the latter impels his son, unintentionally, to death.

Peripeteia is important because it lengthens the road from happiness to misfortune. The taller the palm tree, the greater the fall, says a popular Brazilian song. That way creates more impact. The peripeteia suffered by the character is reproduced in the spectator as well. But it could happen that the spectator would follow the character empathically until the moment of the peripeteia and then detach himself at that point. In order to avoid that, the tragic character must also pass through what Aristotle calls anagnorisis — that is, through the recognition of his flaw as such and, by means of reasoning, the explanation of it. The hero accepts his error, hoping that, empathically, the spectator will also accept as bad his own hamartia. But the spectator has the great advantage of having erred only vicariously: he does not really pay for it.

Finally, so that the spectator will keep in mind the terrible consequences of committing the error not just vicariously but in actuality, Aristotle demands that tragedy have a terrible end, which he calls catastrophe. The happy end is not permitted, though the character's physical destruction is not absolutely required. Some die;

others see their loved ones die. In any case, the catastrophe is always such that not to die is worse than death.

Those three interdependent elements (peripeteia, anagnorisis, catastrophe) have the ultimate goal of provoking catharsis in the spectator (as much or more than in the character); that is, their purpose is to produce a purgation of the hamartia, passing through three clearly defined stages:

First stage: Stimulation of the hamartia; the character follows an ascending path toward happiness, accompanied empathically by the spectator. Then comes a moment of reversal: the character, with the spectator, starts to move from happiness toward misfortune; fall of the hero.

Second stage: The character recognizes his error — anagnorisis. Through the empathic relationship dianoia-reason, the spectator recognizes his own error, his own hamartia, his own anticonstitutional flaw.

Third stage: Catastrophe; the character suffers the consequences of his error, in a violent form, with his own death or with the death of loved ones.

Catharsis: The spectator, terrified by the spectacle of the catastrophe, is purified of his hamartia. [...]

The words "Amicus Plato, sed magis amicus veritas" ("I am Plato's friend, but I am more of a friend of truth!") are attributed to Aristotle. In this we agree entirely with Aristotle: we are his friends, but we are much better friends of truth. He tells us that poetry, tragedy, theater have nothing to do with politics. But reality tells us something else. His own *Poetics* tells us it is not so. We have to be better friends of reality: all of man's activities — including, of course, all the arts, especially theater — are political. And theater is the most perfect artistic form of coercion.

[...]

Experiments with the People's Theater in Peru

[...]

In any country the task of teaching an adult to read and write poses a difficult and delicate problem. In Peru the problem is magnified because of the vast number of languages and dialects spoken by its people. Recent studies point to the existence of at least 41 dialects of the two principal languages, besides Spanish, which are the Quechua and the Aymara. Research carried out in the province of Loreto in the north of the country, verified the existence of 45 different languages in that region. Forty-five languages, not mere dialects! And this is what is perhaps the least populated province in the country.

[...]

All idioms are "languages," but there is an infinite number of languages that are not idiomatic. There are many languages besides those that are written or spoken. By learning a new language, a person acquires a new way of knowing reality and of passing that knowledge on to others. Each language is absolutely irreplaceable. All languages complement each other in achieving the widest, most complete knowledge of what is real.

Assuming this to be true, the ALFIN project [a national literacy program in Peru] formulated two principal aims:

1) to teach literacy in both the first language and in Spanish without forcing the abandonment of the former in favor of the latter;

2) to teach literacy in all possible languages, especially the artistic ones, such as theater, photography, puppetry, films, journalism, etc.

[...]

We tried to show in practice how the theater can be placed at the service of the oppressed, so that they can express themselves and so that, by using this new language, they can also discover new concepts.

In order to understand this poetics of the oppressed one must keep in mind its main objective: to change the people — "spectators," passive beings in the theatrical phenomenon — into subjects, into actors, transformers of the dramatic action. I hope that the differences remain clear. Aristotle proposes a poetics in which the spectator delegates power to the dramatic character so that the latter may act and think for him. Brecht proposes a poetics in which the spectator delegates power to the character who thus acts in his place but the spectator reserves the right to think for himself, often in opposition to the character. In the first case, a "catharsis" occurs; in the second, an awakening of critical consciousness. But the poetics of the oppressed focuses on the action itself: the spectator delegates no power to the character (or actor) either to act or to think in his place; on the contrary, he himself assumes the protagonic role, changes the dramatic action, tries out solutions, discusses plans for change — in short, trains himself for real action. In this case, perhaps the theater is not revolutionary in itself, but it is surely a rehearsal for the revolution. The liberated spectator, as a whole person, launches into action. No matter that the action is fictional; what matters is that it is action!

I believe that all the truly revolutionary theatrical groups should transfer to the people the means of production in the theater so that the people themselves may utilize them. The theater is a weapon, and it is the people who should wield it.

But how is this transference to be achieved? As an example I cite what was done by Estela Linares, who was in charge of the photography section of the ALFIN Plan.

What would be the old way to utilize photography in a literacy project? Without doubt, it would be to photograph things, streets, people, landscapes, stores, etc., then show the pictures and discuss them. But who would take these pictures? The instructors, group leaders, or coordinators. On the other hand, if we are going to give the people the means of production, it is necessary to hand over to them, in this case, the camera. This is what was done in ALFIN. The educators would give a camera to members of the study group, would teach them how to use it, and propose to them the following:

We are going to ask you some questions. For this purpose we will speak in Spanish. And you must answer us. But you can not speak in Spanish: you must speak in "photography." We ask you things in Spanish, which is a language. You answer us in photography, which is also a language.

The questions asked were very simple, and the answers — that is, the photos — were discussed later by the group. For example, when people were asked, where do you live?, they responded with the following types of photo-answers:

A picture showing the interior of a shack. In Lima it rarely rains and for this reason the shacks are made of straw mats, instead of with more permanent walls and roofs. In general they have only one room that serves as kitchen, living room, and bedroom; the families live in great promiscuity and very often young children watch their parents engage in sexual intercourse, which commonly leads to sexual acts between brothers and sisters as young as ten or eleven years old, simply as an imitation of their parents. A photo showing the interior of a shack fully answers the question, where do you live? Every element of each photo has a special meaning, which must be discussed by the group: the objects focused on, the angle from which the picture is taken, the presence or absence of people in it, etc.

To answer the same question, a man took a picture of the bank of a river. The discussion clarified its meaning. The river Rimac, which passes through Lima, overflows at certain times of the year. This makes life on its banks extremely dangerous, since shacks are often swept away, with a consequent loss of human lives. It is also very common for children to fall into the river while playing and the rising waters make rescue difficult. When a man answers the question with that picture, he is fundamentally expressing anguish: how can he work with peace of mind knowing that his child may be drowning in the river?

Another man photographed a part of the river where pelicans come to eat garbage in times of great hunger; the people, equally hungry, capture, kill, and eat the pelicans. Showing this photo, the man communicated his awareness of living in a place where ironically the people welcomed hunger, because it attracted the pelicans which then served to satisfy their hunger.

[...]

One day a man, in answer to the same question, took a picture of a child's face. Of course everyone thought that the man had made a mistake and repeated the question to him:

"You didn't understand; what we want is that you show us where you live. Take a picture and show us where you live. Any picture; the street, the house, the town, the river."

"Here is my answer. Here is where I live."

"But it's a child. . . ."

"Look at his face: there is blood on it. This child, as all the others who live here, have, their lives threatened by the rats that infest the whole bank of the river Rimac. They are protected by dogs that attack the rats and scare them away. But there was a mange epidemic and the city dog-catcher came around here catching lots of dogs and taking them away. This child had a dog who protected him. During the day his parents used to go to work and he was left with his dog. But now he doesn't have it any more. A few days ago, when you asked me where I lived, the rats had come while the child was sleeping and had eaten part of his nose. This is why there's so much blood on his face. Look at the picture; it is my answer. I live in a place where things like this still happen."

I could write a novel about the children of the barrios along the river Rimac; but only photography, and no other language, could express the pain of that child's eyes, of those tears mixed with blood. And, as if the irony and outrage were not enough, the photograph was in Kodachrome, "Made in U.S.A."

The use of photography may help also to discover valid symbols for a whole community or social group. It happens many times that well intentioned theatrical groups are unable to communicate with a mass audience because they use symbols that are meaningless for that audience. A royal crown may symbolize power, but a symbol only functions as such if its meaning is shared. For some a royal crown may produce a strong impact and yet be meaningless for others.

[...]

It is easy enough to give a camera to someone who has never taken a picture before, tell him how to focus it and which button to press. With this alone the means of photographic production are in the hands of that person. But what is to be done in the case of the theater?

The means for producing a photograph are embodied in the camera, which is relatively easy to handle, but the means of producing theater are made up of man himself, obviously more difficult to manage.

We can begin by stating that the first word of the theatrical vocabulary is the human body, the main source of sound and movement. Therefore, to control the means of theatrical production, man must, first of all, control his own body, know his own body, in order to be capable of making it more expressive. Then he will be able to practice theatrical forms in which by stages he frees himself from his condition of spectator and takes on that of actor, in which he ceases to be an object and becomes a subject, is changed from witness into protagonist.

The plan for transforming the spectator into actor can be systematized in the following general outline of four stages:

First stage: Knowing the body: a series of exercises by which one gets to know one's body, its limitations and possibilities, its social distortions, and possibilities of rehabilitation.

Second stage: Making the body expressive: a series of games by which one begins to express one's self through the body, abandoning other, more common and habitual forms of expression.

Third stage: The theater as language: one begins to practice theater as a language that is living and present, not as a finished product displaying images from the past: First degree: Simultaneous dramaturgy: the spectators "write" simultaneously with the acting of the actors; Second degree: Image theater: the spectators intervene directly, "speaking" through images made with the actors' bodies; Third degree: Forum theater: the spectators intervene directly in the dramatic action and act.

Fourth stage: The theater as discourse: simple forms in which the spectator-actor creates "spectacles" according to his need to discuss certain themes or rehearse certain actions.

Suzuki Tadashi: we have been, therefore I am

Along with Ninagawa Yukio, Suzuki Tadashi (b. 1939) is one of Japan's best-known contemporary theatre directors. He writes in both English and Japanese. Along with Wole Soyinka and Gao Xingjian, Suzuki is also one of the most prolific world theatre theorists. He created "The Suzuki Method of Actor Training" that focuses on the physical body of the actor and on the actor's relationship to the text. This stands in marked contrast to Stanislavski's psychological focus.

Providing an overview of Suzuki's work is almost impossible given its variety and plentitude. Broadly speaking it belongs to a modern movement in Japanese theatre that moves away from Western-style realism and experiments with intercultural production, non-linear development, fragmentation of text, and manipulation of actor's bodies. This Japanese movement is often linked to modernism, the Western avant-garde, or postmodernism (three literary, theatrical, and philosophical movements emerging from the West), and certainly there are commonalities between Jerzy Grotowski, Antonin Artaud, Bertolt Brecht, Samuel Beckett, and these Japanese works. Each of the Western movements grew out of a particular Western backdrop, rebelling against particular aspects of Western philosophy and artistic practice. Thus, even the elements that appear in common amongst these various writers might actually be pointing to different influences, given that Japanese philosophical and literary history is quite different from that found in the West.

One of the major turning points for twentieth century Japan was their defeat in World War II. While Suzuki would have only been six at the end of the war, Japan's foreign and domestic policies changed radically. The role of Japan's emperor, which had increased and decreased in strength throughout its history, was strictly limited by the new Japanese constitution. This constitution also prohibits Japan from having a standing army. The new government of Japan had to rebuild the nation and they took this opportunity to shift Japan's feudal society (many peasant farmers living off land owned by the wealthy) into a thriving capitalism that has now become one of the world's three largest economies. Within the span of a few years, technology advanced and became widely available, social practices changed, many people moved to urban areas.

Given these changes, it is not difficult to understand Suzuki's concerns in the essay below. He writes about ways in which communal experiences shape individuals, and how this might be presented on stage. He characterizes these experiences as universal in the sense that everyone might have them (and, indeed, must have them in order to mature). These experiences will inform the physical movements of the actors – no amount of training can substitute for life experience. The individual must have experiences which are shared with the group. The individual then becomes part of the community and can speak for and with the community.

Within his examination of experience, Suzuki looks at changes in society and changes in theatre. He says that theatres mature alongside societies. Both are structured on a set of rules designed to cope with the reality of their moment. When the moment changes, the old rules crumble, leading to the need for a new set of practices. He writes about the relationship between the old and the new with a certain fatalism – all things will crumble – but also an excitement about what new possibilities may lie ahead. Whether exuberant or nostalgic, Suzuki notes that the Japanese situation (presumably like all situations) is unique and that imported sets of rules will not work.

While Suzuki does not go into detail about his training techniques in this essay, they involve helping the actor inhabit his or her physical body. These bodies are always figured in connection to something else – specifically the ground (the earth or the floor) in the first steps of Suzuki's training. By exploring a range of physical movements, the actor is able to accumulate a certain type of experience which then forms a toolbox for later theatrical work. Despite Suzuki's insistence on cultural and temporal specificity, his acting style focuses on a set of movements as part of a universal (somewhat akin to Eugenio Barba's pre-expressive – a set of movements that exists before cultural differentiation). The tension between the specific and the universal is something that Suzuki frequently addresses both in his productions and in his theoretical writing, and his answers remain enigmatic.

The relationships of individual to community, of past to future, and of unique experience to universal experience are found throughout contemporary Japanese philosophy and criticism. Different theorists have taken different stands within this set of issues, but these are the pressing issues with regard to the question of individuality as it relates to theatre. How does the individual relate to the group? To what extent is the individual (nation or person) similar to the communal (or world)? How completely has the place of the individual changed in the world? What elements of prior notions of the individual may be brought forward? What performance practices reflect the answers to these questions about individuality?

Extract 5.2 Selections from "Human Experience and the Group"
Suzuki Tadashi, translated by Thomas Rimer

Whatever the problems involved, every individual—regardless of his age, his sex—from his birth until his death, faces all issues on the level of personal experience. What interests me now is to discover in what form personal experiences can be incorporated into the structure of a group. National experience is woven from the commonality and diversity of all individual human experiences. To put it another way, what are the means by which the commonality of mankind's experiences can be passed on to the next generation? How is this process carried on? The contemporary means employed are radically different from those used in former times; in this regard, Japan has made a particularly strong break with the past in comparison with other cultures. [...] Looking at specific cases involving the transmission of culture, various difficulties become apparent: problems with the organization [...] of young versus old or men versus women are conceived of in contemporary and specific terms, and with an implicit and specific mandate to resolve them. For example, since the traditional Japanese performing arts are particularly involved with problems of youth and age, the theatre itself is conceived of in terms of such polarities, and the passing on of a commonality of vision must be ensured. Until the end of the war, there were many in the Japanese theatre who denied this traditional commonality altogether, branding the traditional art forms as feudal, premodern. Yet, examining the supposedly feudal period, an age that seems so different from our own, one actually finds an approach strikingly similar to ours toward the problems of age and youth revealed quite clearly in the traditional performing arts.

Traditional attitudes demand that respect be paid to the depth of human experience, the value of which can be determined by the extent to which those experiences are held in common. Such experiences extend beyond the spiritual occurrences shared by everyone. That is not to say that the regular course of a lived life—birth, childhood, youth, and the bodily changes that we experience as we grow weaker with old age—should merely be set aside. But in the world of the theatre in particular, the value of experience comes from determining how changes in age and body can be put to use. Relevant experience must be developed by the actors through their own self-consciousness of those changes. Therefore, the talents of a mature performer are naturally more fully developed than those of a youthful actor. An old actor, by drawing on his objective sense of the richness of his own personal human experience, can reach the fullest flowering of his talent. Human experience, then, requires development over an extended period of time. This attitude is most prevalent in the nō theatre, in which it continues to be assumed that artistic possibilities increase as an actor grows older. In the nō, an actor of about twenty may well be praised for his youthful sensibilities—what Zeami called "the young blossom." But he must also come to realize that he will grow older in terms of his physical means of expression. What then becomes most important is the way in which he takes control of these changes, and the manner in which he deals with them. The strength of his art comes from the value he places on the skills developed in his own body. From this point of view, an actor's skills develop fully only in his older age. So it is entirely reasonable that the older actor, who has completed the process of physical and psychological change, will naturally lead a privileged existence in the midst of his troupe.

In the traditional performing arts, and particularly in the nō, such considerations have always been particularly clear. The nō stage, for example, is the one place where all of the beauty and richness of human experience are given focus, and the changes brought about by human experience are made palpable, through the troupe's skill in representing mankind's commonality. To a certain extent, the attitudes embodied on stage can be considered representative of the feudal past; still, it seems altogether natural that a nō or kabuki actor can only become the Real Thing as he grows older.

[...]

When the transition from one generation to another takes place as a natural process in the traditional performing arts, the connections between those restrictions and conventions, when involved in a traditional sense of commonality, function in terms of an organizational psychology. However, should the substance of the system collapse, then such a way of life, the kind of spiritual and physical devices that were created in response to fixed conditions and restrictions, will be turned upside down in terms of the structural relationships, inevitably political, between the controller and the controlled. They will be improperly used.

On the other hand, many young people who have gone to study in Europe wish to abandon any such communal control, and are quick to point out and condemn the existence of such structures. It was out of just such rebellion, of course, that the idea of a modern theatre in Japan was born. It seems to me that the major battle of the Japanese theatre in our century, a struggle involving both the traditional and the modern theatre, has focused and must continue to focus on the vital matter of how to establish a useful connection between the natural process of aging and the universality of human experience. The struggle also involves deciding which aspect of the relationship should receive the emphasis. The choice, conscious or unconscious, of where to place that emphasis vitally affects the very concept of the theatre that is created. Such assumptions have affected the kind of stage to be used, the role of the director, and the style of acting. In the end, the modern theatre movement in Japan has been Romantic in nature, and so has valued the outpouring of youthful individuality, the potential flowering from within the individual.

[...]

If one looks at the various theatrical devices employed in the nō —the use of the stage, the various fixed patterns of performance, the use of hereditary professional names—it may seem on the surface that distinctions between young and old performers are maintained. In fact, however, such distinctions simply do not apply; rather, the distinction maintained in the ensemble is between performers who are free and those who are not.

The initiation I mentioned above does not function to separate adults from children. Rather, there is an assumption as to the relative profundity of an actor's experience in relation to the communal experience; this distinction is really no more than a code of behavior affirmed by all. The level of deliberately created communality has no reason to depend, then, on distinctions between youth and age, adults and children. To put it another way, in this system children are conceived of only as small adults. The essence of the matter lies in the creation of a communal sense of what individuals have lived through, what has come to be called "experience." What is at stake is the depth of that experience. It is not a question of merely dividing humans by a quantitative standard of chronology, of age. In terms of performance, the piling up of years does not automatically convey artistic adulthood; only the depth of experience through which the actor has lived in the troupe is of value.

[...]

Suppose, for example, an extraordinarily precocious performer of twenty appears. His talent surely arises from his family situation, from the nature of the human relationships in which he has been involved. Another, because of his family upbringing, may know nothing. The difference between them has nothing to do with their relative ages; it arises from their personal life experiences.

Although not all aspects of ordinary life were so tightly regulated up until the modern period, the positive aspects of these older ways of thinking did make themselves felt in the area of the traditional performing arts. From a contemporary vantage point outside the system, such attitudes may appear formalistic and quantitative, but I believe there were actually considerations of quality involved as well. In the modern period, however, quantitative considerations have come into importance. The concept of time now dominates, making questions of youth and age very important.

As I mentioned above, a freedom from the distinctions between youth and age based on the linear passage of time is attained in the traditional performing arts through a process of initiation that does away with time as a series of linear moments. The preservation of this artistic reality has been achieved through the use of fixed patterns of performance. These fixed forms of ensemble performance provide a means to prove the communality of the experience involved: if patterns can exist, then there must lie behind them a genuine spirit of the group.

Therefore, the fundamental structure of a traditional arts ensemble is not based on individuals; rather, its assets accrue from the wisdom passed on by the group, the vision created from the communal experience of a whole family of actors. In our century, those "families" are no longer created by ties of blood but are based on the economic necessities of performance, without considerations of any spiritual bond. Nevertheless, those families have created a particular approach to performance. A close examination of that approach employed by an ensemble makes it possible to understand at once whether a young actor is able to match his experience to that of the group. In order to transcend questions of age, in fact, the concept of chronological age is dispensed with by using such strategies as casting a hitherto minor actor in an important role, or granting the family name to a young actor not necessarily related by blood.

[...]

These days, excuses disguised as ideology are invoked when a drama company is dissolved. None of the real reasons—"I can't get along with the troupe;" "I can't deal with the culture of the young;" "you're too old and I don't want to work with you any more"—are articulated. Even when the reasons are emotional—the real generation gap, the problems of older directors and younger actors getting along—those who quit always say, "I can no longer agree with the principles on which the troupe is being run. So I resign."

Up until my generation, all theatre people described their actions in this fashion, as if ideological warfare were the definitive manifestation of their real feelings. Presumably, all those who belonged to groups motivated by politics behaved like that. Everything was put forth as a matter of principle. The front they put on and their ulterior motives differed considerably, however.

Trouble over the ages of actors and the difficulties between actors and actresses seem most likely to erupt in modern theatre troupes. Presumably this is because there exists an unarticulated assumption that the difficulties arising from such distinctions should not be expressed openly. It is difficult to understand how such beliefs have become implanted, yet they now appear somehow fundamental. Perhaps a kind of modern humanism has brought them into being. In any case, theatre people talk on and on, insisting that good human relations must be established for the benefit of communication and a communal vision. Yet they insist that no distinctions of sex or age should enter into forming such a communal vision, particularly in a group conscious of its real artistic identity. The same belief is held by those who organize theatrical groups along political lines.

Yet when any such communal principles are actually put into practice, there follows a rejection of any succession of bloodlines or families, and so no means are provided by which a group dedicated to a certain set of ideas can assure its continuity. Before the modern period, when it came to such matters as social position or the differences between the roles of men and women, all groups were strongly molded by societal forces. [...]

It must be remembered that any modern theatre troupe that seeks to reproduce itself must have been constructed in terms of modern ideas of independence and equality in the first place. The establishment of any special relationships that might be seen as "feudal" will be obvious at once. Modern theatre people will condemn these attitudes and see them as revealing a lack of modern consciousness.

Since individual skills cannot be passed on to the next generation, then what about artistic experience? Those in charge are more or less forced into accepting the principles of a one-generation artistic effort. There seems to them something pure and righteous about such a quick dissolution, and there remains a romantic Japanese quality in such an attitude. Of course this does not apply to those groups that seek only profit. Modern theatre troupes founded on artistic principles, holding the basic attitude that through artistic skill, imperfect human relationships can somehow be rendered spiritually rich, are driven to the conscientious conclusion that their troupes ought to cease to exist after one generation.

One would suppose then, that those men and women wishing to form a group based on modern perceptions of human relationships must be ready to weary themselves with the problems of evaluating their experience so as to continue their efforts, and then to identify the means to ensure succession for a meaningful period of time. But on the other hand, such concerns seem to cause them to feel that they are somehow conservative, even reactionary, but certainly not truly modern. They may feel intimidated by such matters. Since modern troupes see no value in turning theatrical experience into communal succession, it follows that the stream of present-day Japanese theatre troupes represents the culture of youth: they have broken with the troupes that preceded them. And since those older troupes have only thought of their work in terms of one generation as well, they too are incapable of bringing forward something new. Their members can only grow old together as a group. When something new appears, they can find no way to make use of it; they see it as something outside themselves, only an "exception." Such is the situation in which the modern theatre troupes in Japan find themselves, it seems to me.

My own purpose is to create a kind of work unrelated to matters of age or gender. Who wouldn't strive to develop a theatrical conception capable of transcending such distinctions? Yet we live at a time when the tendency toward a rupture between the generations is pronounced, when a youth culture is strong, when things are not going smoothly. Any effort to establish communication through the sharing of individual experiences seems to have disappeared; only an externalized communality, based on the fleeting popularity of something on television or on some best-seller or other, seems to exist.

What is missing is the healthy sort of communication that develops when we have had the opportunity, based on our ages and life histories, to consider the depths of our own personal experiences, both in their unique and their common aspects. Joint experience, after all, begins with a consciousness of personal experience; one compares one's own development with that of others, examines the differences and locates the common factors, which may include the kinds of connections one has with one's family, what one has read, and so forth. These various life experiences can then be objectified in terms of mutuality, so that a genuine communication can begin to develop. Such issues as the status of the sexes and the differences between the generations will form a part of this communality; but in order for a group to develop in this fashion, it must resist the hard, monolithic surfaces in favor of a many-sided, open vision.

In the actual conduct of contemporary Japanese theatre companies, the biggest problem today seems to involve a lack of an appropriate standard of dedication. For example, an actor in rehearsal may suddenly announce, "My mother's coming up to town today, so I have to pass up this practice. I'll be leaving now." This kind of behavior is not "up to standard," and what is more, the whole idea of a "standard" that could even consider condoning such an attitude is highly suspect. To speculate on this kind of behavior further, let us assume that the person who asked for time off knew from the beginning that the request was inappropriate, but just wanted to check to see how far he could go. What are the standards he is "checking" against? This kind of problem arises in managing an established company on a day-to-day basis which is maintained on the principle of joint experience.

[...]

In my view, the most important work of a theatre troupe does not involve any simple spreading about of its message, whatever that may be. The group must instead take charge of expressing a felt responsibility for finding a means to pass along the unique experiences that the group has undergone. This is because, in practical terms, individual judgments can and must be questioned. However, as I mentioned above, since the theatre involves an expression of the relations among living human beings, it is quite possible that the methods chosen to communicate experiences will reveal elements of an older thinking mixed in with them. After all, Japan maintains a number of premodern attitudes; contemporary human relations still reveal certain feudal aspects. Because of this, often no attempt is made actually to explicate any methods developed by a group. Until now, no troupe has as yet thought through the issues to this extent. [...]

A theatre troupe that rejects the family model and seeks to perpetuate itself through the individual development of its members can today only hope for change through sentimental and emotional factors. Groups that center on ideas will in the end be destroyed, since the moment must come when their ethics can no longer be trusted. At that point, each time an issue comes up, the response to it must be based entirely on the individual's emotional state—"do I like it or not?" The general level of ethical thinking thus ultimately drops to the level of individual preference. Society is indeed shot through with protestantism! The highest standard of ethics no longer consists of a belief in the truth shared with others. The situation has become very serious.

I am convinced that ethics can only play a part in human relationships if man believes in a universality outside himself. These days, however, little concern is shown for the truth expressed by another. The very concept of an objective truth itself does not develop. Truth has come to be regarded as a kind of deception. And because human relationships are now conceptualized in terms of psychology, anomie has become a reality. In this environment, individual distinctions of sex and age have now become all the more strikingly evident. The old now merely see themselves as old, and feel an obsessive inferiority to the young. The young are merely young, and nervous about their difficulties in communicating with their elders. When people meet on the level of "male" and "female," men bring an entire complex of sexual feelings to their dealings with women. Thus, while distinctions in the social system seem to be breaking down, the real differences are becoming all the more obvious. All of these distinctions now manifest themselves in physiological ways, spontaneously, even on our very faces.

In such circumstances, when thinking about the formation of a theatre group, the only possibility may seem to be to put things together on the basis of likes and dislikes, on a foundation of sentimentality. That seems to me to sum up the problems encountered in attempting to work together.

The kind of troupe I envision would not come into being along those lines. The emotional bond I seek would not be that of some Nazi-like group. Such devotion to a group can only, after a time, give rise to an emperor, a dictator. The vital element should be not a sense of devotion itself, but the manifestation of another quality, one that grows out of that devotion, a sense that there is a certain level of regulation necessary for the sake of the group, a sense of the need for rules and prescribed ways to pass on experiences. Of course, all this can be

> carried out in a frivolous spirit; I am afraid that today, in fact, there sadly remain only two impulses in the theatre—one, a determination to be frivolous, and the other, a desire to make rules.

Jiao Juyin: realism and ideology

Jiao Juyin (1905–1975) is one of the twentieth century's most important Chinese directors, although his work has seldom been translated into English. He was involved in the foundation of the Beijing People's Art Theatre, which went on to stage works by rising stars of Chinese playwriting (including Gao Xingjian) alongside classic works of Western theatre.

Each of the theorists above considers the actor as a subject – as a human being who is part of a community and has the potential to take action. In Jiao Juyin's writing, the actor becomes a tool by which characters are presented. Characters are presented to express the artistic and ideological ideas of the playwright and the director.

Jiao was writing and directing at a time when ideology was a subject of much debate in China. Jiao Juyin argues that his ideological principles involve consideration of the working people. In this regard he is similar to Boal who is concerned with the poorer members of society. While Boal is specifically trying to remind his spectators that they can actively change the word, Jiao Juyin focuses on the mechanisms of creation and the role of the director in shaping the performances of actors. It is possible that, by showing all of the constraints on the actor, Jiao is asking the audience to consider the extent to which material conditions are damaging parts of Chinese society.

Jiao Juyin wants his actors to relate to life, but he claims that the director must teach them how to do this, although he does mention that the director should also encourage actors' creativity. He praises his actors for the organic unity of a combination of mind and body. Much of Jiao's work explicitly references Stanislavski, a figure who was hotly politically contested in China. Chinese theatre critics and political theorists debated whether the presence of the individual in Stanislavski made him inherently anti-socialist or, instead, if the focus on the body and the material conditions surrounding the actor – the realism of Stanislavski – made him inherently socialist. Jiao's focus remains on explaining a system of acting and, for the most part, he only incidentally addresses the political implications of a given acting style.

In Jiao's system, the actors must be mentally engaged with their characters. The physicality will come from this mental engagement, and not from a formulaic set of rules. At the same moment, Jiao insists on his own style of realism, which is, itself, a set of rules. After saying that the characters will develop mental images of the characters through rehearsals, Jiao then proceeds to lay out his own mental images of the characters in the play and discuss the ways in which the actors met these expectations.

Jiao Juyin's focus on the material conditions that shape the realities of the characters seems at first to contrast with his focus on mental images: in other words, if the hardships that a character has suffered and the current lifestyle a character leads are more important than the character's thoughts (or produce a character's thoughts), then why is the actor approaching the role by thinking about it? The mental image is the way by which an actor can come to understand the material conditions of a character. The image is constructed of pieces of the actor's concrete lived experience, shaped and interpreted by the director, in accordance to the demands of the script.

Curiously, in Jiao's writing on nationalizing theatre, he discusses the fact that the audience should be involved in creating the piece of theatre. This is an odd move given that his discussion of the mental image focuses on the internal life of the actor. How can the internal life of the actor be important if theatre is communally created? How does the community create the individual? What kind of individual is that that is created?

Extract 5.3 Selections from "On Directing"
Jiao Juyin, translated by Shiao-ling Yu

1. Emphasize the ideas of the play script

The work of the playwright is the first creation; the work of the director is the second creation. The tool the playwright employs to create lifelike characters and realistic subject matters is language. With a few well chosen words and deftly executed strokes, the playwright can sketch out various images which can arouse readers' imaginations and evoke sympathetic responses in their thoughts and emotions. When the director tries to reproduce these images on the stage, his tool is not language, but the animate human body and the inanimate sound, light, color, points, lines, surfaces, and volumes, as well as rhythms and atmospheres. The director cannot make the audience see the characters and their lives with their imaginations, but make them see and hear them with their eyes and ears. When he tries to convey the theme, style, and characters of the original script to the audience through more concrete stage images, his method is different. In other words, he must create a second time. But the educational effect of this second creation on the audience must be the same as the original script and even more lively. Therefore, the director's work is not imitation, not copying word for word, but a highly creative work.

However, the director's creativity is not developed aimlessly. His creative process must unite with that of the playwright; he should have a deep understanding of the spirit, ideas, feelings, and style of the original play, and have a firm grasp of the playwright's "inner motivating force" for creating his characters, and apply the same force to stage the play. The director's basic responsibility is to realize the playwright's intention and portray the characters as seen by the "spiritual eyes" of the playwright. (The characters seen by the "spiritual eyes" may not be completely the same as those appearing on the written page.) Furthermore, the director should endeavor to express the playwright's ideas and feelings to the fullest. The playwright's ideas and feelings must live in the mind of the director and become his own; the original play's theme, life, and characters must be what the director fervently wishes to create and bring to life.

Only this way can the performance on stage become real, captivating, and full of life; otherwise, it is only a recitation of the play script with makeup. If the director is merely interested in showing off his directing techniques, he could even distort the meaning of the play and cause harm to the characters in the play.

Lao She's play *Dragon Beard Ditch* (*Longxu gou*) is a work with a high degree of integration between ideology and artistic quality. It therefore requires the director to first elevate his own ideological level before considering how to stage this play. It is also a work of distinctive artistic style, without any vulgar clichés, tedious descriptions, slogan-like dialogues, and fantastic plots; it is all about everyday life—the thoughts and feelings of a group of real, living, and breathing people. This requires the director to learn from life, and from his deep understanding of life to grasp the fine character of the working people and their thoughts and feelings under different political conditions. Lao She is very familiar with the working people; he loves and respects them, as well as the people's government and the Chinese Communist party. That was why he was able to combine his political zeal with artistic skill to produce this tribute to them. As for myself, I have the same political zeal as the playwright and the same intimate knowledge of the working people, having grown up among them when I was young. My love and respect for these people not only become one with that of the playwright; my thoughts and feelings are inseparable from the working people. This was reflected in how I handled the play script. Even though there are quite a few differences between my stage script and Lao She's original play, they are not entirely due to the technical demands of the stage; rather, the changes are made mainly to conform with Lao She's requirements, with my requirements based on my own life experiences, and with the requirements of our shared "inner creative force" to breathe life into the characters and their thoughts and feelings. I, the playwright, and the characters form a trinity. This is probably the source of creativity of the new realist director.

I felt honored by Mr. Lao She's praise that I did not change the character of the characters he created. This shows how important it is for the director to understand and respect the playwright, and also to understand and respect the working people just as the playwright does. Furthermore, the director should become one with the thoughts and feelings of the working people so that in his adjustments to the stage production, he will not lose the direction set by the playwright, distort the theme of the original play, and cause harm to the characters.

With his superlative craftsmanship, Lao She can vividly portray a person's character, thoughts, and feelings with just a few words. He says modestly that he is not familiar with stage techniques. Based on my personal understanding, it is not necessary for a writer to be familiar with stage techniques. All the techniques, artistic rules, and regulations are derived from life and the dialectics of nature. Artificial artistic regulations divorced from life and the laws of nature are not real and a destruction of reality. If a writer stubbornly holds on to a set or several sets of stage techniques, they will restrict and stifle his creativity. The development of all things begins with content, vitality, and an inner motivating force; and in the process of development, regulations are produced. In other words, there are regulations in how things develop, but these regulations are determined in the process of development of the inner motivation force clashing with its opposing force. Things definitely do not come into being because of regulations. Therefore, an artistic creation with content, ideas, vitality, and developmental potential will manifest its own regulations, but these regulations have a unique life of their own, and are in agreement with materialist dialectics; they cannot be expressed by the mechanical and fixed techniques of any other play. Every play has its own character; it must be treated with a technique suitable for it. This is the technique of new realism. Many writers, in the process of writing a play, consciously and excessively employ certain performance techniques, and the directors are supposed to follow these fixed techniques, which may not be suitable for the play. As a result, the skeleton of the regulations may be preserved, but the life of the play is smothered. Stanislavski asked us to learn from life, and to study carefully the script and the thoughts and emotions of the characters through the dialogues of the play. He taught me how to understand a playwright and how to handle a script. In my personal taste, I have a predilection for the kind of works such as Lao She's that are clear, simple, and lively, without any long-winded idle words—they seem to come from the mouths or pens of the working people themselves. This is also why I admire the plays of Chekhov, Gorky, and Xia Yan, and became so enamored with Lao She's *Dragon Beard Ditch* that I fell into his "inner creativity" and became one with him.

2. Emphasize the actors' creativity and collective creativity

The duty of the director is not mechanically prescribing the actors' actions and positions on the stage and arranging the scenes; if it's only these, the actors themselves can handle it just as well. Far from these, he has a much more important duty than directing the actors how to raise their hands, move their feet, talk, walk, and make facial expressions; the scenes, the characters' actions and speeches, and the atmosphere and rhythm of the performance are the results of his achieving his more important duty. The director's important duty is to guide the actors to live the lives of the characters they will portray. Through analysis, explanation, persuasion, and actual examples from life, he guides the actors to learn from life, to affirm certain attributes, and to reject the others, so their thoughts and feelings gradually become one with the characters they portray. The actors lose their own identity and become living characters on the stage; the dialogues in the play script become what the actors want to say in their own hearts; the actions of the characters become what the actors themselves want to do. The duty of the director, therefore, is to give full play to the actors' creativity.

Regarding the performance technique, the director consistently opposes formalism and following formulas, and pays great attention to understanding the essence of "rehearsals." Some actors do not realize that from experiencing life to performance is a continuous creative process, and that rehearsal is also a process from experiencing life to creating characters. Therefore, some of them ask the director to set definite rules at the beginning of the rehearsal regarding their positions on the stage, their postures and actions, the pronunciation of certain words, and even the character of the characters. This is formalism and sticking to formulas in artistic thinking. The actor's experiencing life before rehearsal and "entering into the character" are only a preparation. The "mental image" of the character he will portray has not formed yet.[1] Even if he has experienced life in Tianqiao and along the stinking ditch,[2] he has not experienced life in the condition specified in *Dragon Beard Ditch*, and with the characters in the play. As for myself, as a student of new realism, I definitely insist on my own method. At the beginning of the rehearsal, I never give any specific assignment, but ask the actors to rely on their own mental activity to make their body act in the "specified conditions." I do not assign them positions, do not look for scenes on the stage, do not approve or correct the way they read their lines and their small movements. Why so? Because only the external actions that come from the actors' mental activity can produce feelings, and only when they mentally react to the "specified conditions" and other characters can their feelings become genuine. Genuine feelings in turn can modify their way of thinking, and only then can the characters they portray develop fully in their mind, their mental and external actions gradually transform into the characters', and the lines they speak on the stage transformed into the characters'.

Not only is the director's creation inseparable from that of the actors, actors' creation is also inseparable from all the characters in the play. Performance is not only the director's creation, it should also include the creation of all the stage workers. Performing a play is a collective artistic creativity; it cannot be accomplished by a single individual. Therefore, in directing *Dragon Beard Ditch*, I consistently emphasize the collective spirit of "unity is strength."

3. Images of the characters in *Dragon Beard Ditch*

In this second staging of *Dragon Beard Ditch* by Beijing People's Art Theater, actors definitely put in a great deal of creative energy into establishing the images of the characters on the stage. Even though the characters depicted by Lao She have not been fully realized on the stage, the characters created by the actors already have a certain foundation. The "seeds" of the characters have already developed in the mind of the actors, or are in the process of developing. These "seeds" or "nuclei" will continue to develop and finally transform the actors into flesh and blood characters.

The great majority of the actors of *Dragon Beard Ditch* are young people with relatively little life experience and stage experience. Based on the level of artistic creation in general, their accomplishments are only preliminary, but viewed from their original foundation, their accomplishments should be considered very great. Compared with their past performances, this performance made great progress. This was possible because of their political zeal, exhaustive research, and sensitivity to the current situation. In their creative method, they begin from life, learn from life, and experience life by combining the theme of the play script, the specific condition in the play, and the thoughts and characters of the characters. At the same time, they experiment with how to transform the thoughts and feelings of the characters into artistic images through stage performance.

During this second performance of *Dragon Beard Ditch*, everyone had some praiseworthy story to tell. Let me comment on a few actors for the reference of our audience.

Comrade Yu Shizhi is one of the promising young actors. He meticulously created a well-developed image of Mad Man Cheng. From the character he embodied we can see the crime of reactionary government that drove kind-hearted people to insanity. This character has a typical appearance, and from his appearance we can also see his mind. To combine mental activity and external action into an organic unity is Yu Shizhi's major achievement in his performance.

Comrade Ye Zi's Ding Si's Wife has a multifaceted personality. She is sometimes hot-tempered, sometimes depressed, sometimes calm, and sometimes impetuous. On the whole she is a straightforward person who has suffered a great deal in the old society. Even though she often scolds her daughter and quarrels with her husband, we can see that she cares a great deal about them. This woman Ding portrayed by Ye Zi appears real. Her cheerfulness after the Liberation also has a realistic basis from the political point of view.

Cheng's Wife is the most difficult character to portray in the whole play. What she suffered in the old society made her physically weak and emotionally distressed, but she forces herself to be energetic in order to make a living. If we show too much of her pain and depression, the working people's indomitable spirit will be weakened; if we stress too much of her toughness, she will appear cold and ferocious. In creating this middle-aged working woman, Comrade Han Bing spent a great deal of effort in striking a right balance to bring out an appropriate portrayal of this character.

Comrade Zheng Rong's old bricklayer Zhao is a likeable fellow. Before Liberation, he was a laborer with a strong sense of social justice; after Liberation, he became an activist. This kind of character is also difficult to handle; the performance can easily become dull and boring. But the actor not only gave this character a fitting concrete image, but also abundant feelings. Old man Zhao appears as a lively and developing character on the stage.

From the image of Ding Si created by Comrade Yang Baocong we can see the professional characteristics of this character as a laborer and also his personal characteristics.

The actor's effort in presenting both sides of this character is laudable. People like Ding Si who are warm and cold by turns, leaning to the left one moment and leaning to the right another moment are found in real life and in all walks of life. The stage image of this character rings true.

Elder Woman Wang is cautious, timid, and conservative. These traits are not entirely inborn, but the long suffering people's reactions to life. Comrade Li Ping grasped the essential features of this character and created the image of a hardworking and likeable woman, making her one of the most welcomed characters by the audience.

I must mention the contributions of the extras. In the performance of *Dragon Beard Ditch* this time, with the exception of three former actors, all the others were new recruits. They realized the responsibility of every actor in the production as a whole and put in no less work than the principal actors. They were fully prepared and participated in the complete creative process: analyzing the play script, acquiring a good grasp of the theme of the play, experiencing life, experiencing the characters as defined in the play, and creating stage images in combination with their own professional training. Even actors without a single spoken line took their roles and artistic creations seriously. As a result of their effort, crowd scenes are lively, realistic, and true to life. Everyone in the crowd, without the help of any speech, can make the audience recognize his profession, such as cart driver, mover, blacksmith, bicycle repair man, or assistant in a coal shop.

Major questions

To some extent the scales that form the definition of identity above also provide the set of questions that close this chapter. In all their variety, notions of identity can be thought of as existing on several different spectrums: the degree of relationship to the divine, the degree of consistency, the degree of individuality or community, the degree of interiority or exteriority, and the degree of agency. Essentially for each piece of theatre, one must consider what the basic unit of identity is and how it functions. Figuring this out might involve studying other related theatre, theatre theory, history, or sociology.

While the basic parameters of these scales may be relatively consistent, the meaning of the words may change rather dramatically. The "community" of Marxism is not the community implied by Egungun masquerades. Thus, while it is important to ask questions of community in socialist China and in Nigeria, the questions that we will ask will be different in both places. Again, to understand what the individual is in a given setting requires research – the above scales are only useful after they have been contextualized.

After determining what the basic unit of identity is, the problem then becomes finding the relationship between acting style and this unit of identity.

How is the performance working toward undermining or supporting this unit of identity? It is easy to imagine a theatre working against the current system. Boal, for instance, rejects the idea that the oppressed should be passive. He is attempting to create a new type of identity with his theatre, not to perform an identity within the existing framework.

Notes

1 "Mental image" (*xinxiang*) is an important concept in Jiao Juyin's theory of directing. Jiao wanted his actors to develop images of the characters in their mind before performing them on the stage. Mental image serves as a bridge between real life and stage performance. For a more detailed explanation of this concept, see Shiao-ling Yu trans. "A Chinese Director's Theory of Performance: On Jiao Juyin's System of directing," *Asian Theatre Journal*, vol. 20, no. 1 (Spring, 2003): 25–34.
2 This is a slum area in Beijing where the play takes place. Shortly after the Chinese Communist government came to power, it launched an urban renewal project to clean up this area. Lao She's play portrays the lives of several families who share a courtyard compound near the ditch.

Chapter 6

Modernity and theatre

In many ways, this chapter is a culmination of the prior chapters. When scholars around the world talk about modernity, they talk about culture, tradition, subjectivity, structures, aesthetics, and politics. Like aesthetics, modernity is a term that is challenging to define for any one context, and is subject to a great deal of variation around the world. There is even a debate about whether there is a single modernity or whether each nation / region / culture produces its own modernity. Thankfully, to understand the ways the concept of "modern" has been used to shape theatre around the world it is not necessary to determine whether this modernity is one thing or many things. Each of the theatres in question in this chapter have treated modernity in distinctive ways. Broadly speaking, modernity refers to the cultural response to modernization: the manner of art and society that is produced when humans are subjected to technological innovation. Modernism most frequently refers to a specific movement in Western art from the late nineteenth through the mid-twentieth century. Other locations experienced periods of modernity at different times (before and after Western modernity).

Given that modernity, by definition, involves greater contact between countries around the globe, it is not surprising to see both a great deal of overlap and a great deal of tension in the various manifestations of modernity. Each modernity must find its own way of incorporating the past and tradition into modern life. Some traditional elements might serve to reconnect a society with a sense of self that was destroyed by the rapid pace of modernization. On the other hand, tradition might hold a society back from embracing what modernity has to offer. As a set of contacts between cultures, modernity forces nations to consider their relationship with the rest of the world. Modernization would not have been possible (in the form it took) without the exploitation of colonized people around the globe, which puts a negative spin on cultural contact. On the other hand, modernist art frequently incorporates elements from a variety of locations in a way that enhances its artistic potential. Modernization is the celebration of the mechanization of the world. At the same moment, however, the modern human must find space for humanity amidst this modernization. Science fiction is both our fantasy of what technology might do and our fear of the same. Finally, as with any rapid change, modernity brings with it a sense of dislocation. Variations of the question "Who am I?" are ongoing themes of world modernities.

Rethinking the prior case studies in terms of modernity is a useful project. Why is the adaptation and critique of Western theatre a critical part of world modernity (as seen in Aime Cesaire's work)? Why does modernity require new theatrical forms and how do these forms reflect the status of modernity (in terms of the three Chinese operas)? Why do so many modern theatres return to the human body and a simpler setting as focal points (as per Badal Sircar's production of *Spartacus*)? Why does the same blurring between the "I" and the "he" of bunraku theatre reemerge in several different modern contexts? These questions have no absolute, set answers, but they exemplify the central concerns of modernity in theatre around the world. The questions one poses about modernity can be usefully, if judiciously, applied to any period where a nation or region saw particularly rapid change, but it is also useful to consider the industrialization in the early twentieth century as a distinctive period of modernity.

What are modernism and modernity?

It is difficult to discuss modernity without reference to modernism, the Western literary and artistic phenomenon. As is evident in the work of Gao Xingjian and Hirata Oriza below, Western modernity is a direct influence on many parts of world modernity. That being said, even a cursory familiarity with Western modernity shows that it is equally reliant on an understanding of other parts of the world (or, at times, a misunderstanding). Brecht, Artaud, Proust, and others shared an obsession with Asian arts and theatre. Visual artists experimented with the simplicity of African designs as a way of generating an art-for-art's-sake. This section, then, provides some loose parameters of the artistic questions posed in many modernities around the world.

The relationship between art and the world is a major question for modernity. Frequently, this comes down to a struggle against realism and romanticism. Realism sought to recreate the world in art. Romanticism sought to generate a sublime effect by magnifying certain aspects of the world. In the Romantic definition of sublime, man was to recognize the overwhelming effect of nature and, in doing so, recognize his own small place in the world. Realism's world might be equally overwhelming, but the response to it is often to realize that one does not fit in the world at all. While realism does mark the beginning of modernism in Western theatre, as the world changed around modern artists, some began to question the need for art to connect to the world in any direct way. Many modern painters, for instance, began to create non-representational art, often using geometric or seemingly random patterns. In the later parts of Western theatrical modernity, there was a quest to find a purer, more streamlined way of relating the actor to the world. Brecht experimented with presentational rather than representational forms. Artaud experimented with pure pantomime. Whatever the case, modernity contains within it a question about the status of art within a rapidly changing world.

Modernity is also a resistance to master narratives. In other words, modernity is a period of time in which everything people thought they knew about the way the world works came under question. One major source of order for the West prior to modernity was a conception of God. In this conception, God had created the earth and he had a plan for it. God is unknowable, mysterious, and all-knowing. The powerful outside force giving order to the universe (sometimes, but not always, God) can be seen in the Romantic notion of the sublime. As confidence in this mysterious God faded in parts of the population, confidence in science grew. A new conception of the world emerged and this world was subject to a set of specific, observable rules. It could be tested and it could be known up to the limits of man's capacity to know. Realism and naturalism are both ways of depicting this "testable" world.

Despite the testability of the world, there would always be things man did not know: these were not unknowable, just unknown. This recognition of the unknown also prompted a recognition that many of the things we thought we knew were false or limited (Newtonian physics, for instance). It was a short step from this recognition to the question of whether anything we claimed to know was fully "factual" or if it was all subject to change again. This constant questioning of received wisdom on every topic is what is known as a mistrust in master narratives. In art, this resistance to master narratives is, not surprisingly, easiest to see in the modern novel. Multiple narrators, epistolary form (novels written as a series of letters), non-linear narration, unreliable narrators, and other similar features emerged. Some modern theatres brought back the narrator and many found ways of violating the Aristotelean unities of the neoclassical world (the idea that plays should have a unity of time, action, and place: taking place in the span of one day or a few hours, having a unified plot, and having a single setting). This was a way of disrupting the unity of the theatre and allowing for alternative voices to be heard.

The rejection of master narratives also meant that each human had to find his or her own place in the world. The idea of the modern woman, for instance, was a rejection of the Western stereotypes of womanhood. Henrik Ibsen's *A Doll's House* is a theatrical expression of one form of the search for selfhood. Other playwrights, like Luigi Pirandello and Jean Anouilh, began to experiment with the line between character, actor, and sometimes audience. Theatre became a space in which the audience could watch individuals struggling to figure out who they were – and what it meant to "be."

Theatrical movements like biomechanics (a physical system of acting developed by Vsevolod Meyerhold in the 1920s in Russia that focused on the human body's physical / mechanical potential) emphasize the dual fascination with rapidly evolving science and the desire to understand this science at a human level. As noted above, traditional art forms often came to be associated with this more "human" level, although these traditional techniques were used in novel ways to address the modern condition. Modernity is a struggle to find the place of tradition within a new world.

Strindberg insists on a definition of character that includes both psychology and physiology. While we retroactively read Greek tragedy and Shakespeare in terms of psychological realism, Strindberg considers his treatment of psychology to be novel. The modern era saw the advent of modern psychology through the work of Sigmund Freud, and this changed the way people conceived identity and selfhood. Strindberg's attempt to redefine character on stage, to insert a flexibility and ambiguity into the concept, corresponds to this larger impulse toward exploration of humanity.

Strindberg's repeated references to fate are an indication of his status as a transitional figure, someone ushering in a new modern theatre. Modernity is suspicious of master narratives, and fate is a quintessential master narrative. It comes from a higher power and can be used to explain all aspects of someone's life. Strindberg's overall belief in fate doesn't fit well with the direction modernism would later take, but he also implies that man can take some degree of control over fate. This is a nod toward the fracturing of a master narrative, albeit one that remains covert in Strindberg's early work.

Above all, Strindberg is concerned with removing things that might distract from the central conflict of the play. He suggests hiding the orchestra, getting rid of footlights (and, indeed, when was the last time you saw a production with footlights?). It is the class conflict that Strindberg considers to be modern, and the rest of the stage techniques provide a method for emphasizing this conflict.

Western theatrical modernism has its roots in realism and naturalism, whereas in both the literary and visual arts, modernity functions more as a rejection of the prior realistic mode. While Ibsen may be the father of modern theatre, he, and many of those who followed quickly moved away from realism, seeking closer and deeper connections to reality (see prior chapters on Brecht and Artaud). The other issue faced by Western playwrights is that the "reality" that their realisms might have tried to represent was growing increasingly hard to comprehend. The absurdist movement (e.g. Eugene Ionesco 1909–1994) was a radical attempt to present this new sort of reality. In one of his most famous works, Ionesco has a number of his characters transform into rhinoceroses on stage as a way of representing the callous, bestial nature of the modern man. Obviously transforming a man into a rhinoceros is not "realism" in one sense, but this transformation pointed to the feeling of a reality that was otherwise difficult to express. Western modern theatre persistently tried to figure out what to represent, the degree to which this representation related to any sort of reality, how such a reality was defined, and what mechanism theatre could use to highlight the relationship. When the term "experimental" is applied to theatre, it is often this set of questions that is at the center of the experiment.

World modernities: Westernization and anti-Western sentiments

Every single culture represented in this book has produced theorists who have actively discussed the status of modernity within their countries. The range of ideas covered in these discussions are far too wide to do justice to here, but there are several general trends.

Some modernizers have actively adopted Western philosophies as a starting point for their own modernities (e.g. Hu Shih, Lu Xun, Nishida Kaitaro). Others (e.g. Achille Mbembe, Roberto Schwarz) have insisted that their countries' modernities require their own sets of analytical techniques. The tension between rejection and adoption of Western methods can be seen in Aime Cesaire's theatrical practice, which incorporates Western work in order to critique the West. Suzuki Tadashi incorporates Western ideas in order to express something he considers to be at once universal and Japanese. Gao Xingjian and Wole Soyinka have both harshly criticized the West's reliance on various "isms" to explain its cultural progress and both have created theatres that reject such periodization in favor of a more unified approach. Given that our current era of modernization was sparked by colonialism, world modernity must address its relationship to the West in some fashion or another.

As with the West, there is more writing about literary modernity than there is about theatrical modernity. The great theatrical modernists (e.g. Ibsen, Strindberg) are often mentioned, but, as with the Chinese New Culture Movement, the stories of the plays are often extracted from their theatrical venue. In other words, China was concerned with the ways in which Nora might or might not have been successful at leaving her husband in *A Doll's House* – and not with the nature of theatrical realism.

It is not uncommon, particularly in East Asia, to have countries equate modernity and literary realism. Both China and Japan developed new modes of narration in novels and new modes of theatrical production in an effort to duplicate the Western realism that they saw as part-and-parcel of social advancement. On the other hand, realism's focus on the "I" was heavily critiqued in both China and Japan, which led to an exploration of the tenets of socialist realism and other Marxist literary forms. By the latter half of the twentieth century, a new avant-garde began to develop in both China and Japan which reincorporated (and sometimes celebrated) the "I." In Japan, the *angura* theatre movement, an underground movement coming from universities, dedicated itself to finding alternatives to theatrical realism. This movement was specifically interested in modernizing Japanese culture, and it did so in distinctly non-Western sorts of ways.

Thus, over the space of a few years, "modern" meant realistic, socialistic, and then anti-realistic. What then qualifies as modernity? This question is answered differently in each context. What is the role of interculturalism in this modernity? What is the role of tradition? What is the role of realism? What is the place of the individual? All of the questions from the prior chapters can be reapplied here alongside the discussions of modernity that emerge in each context.

Hirata Oriza and the modern Japanese self

Even if one only looks at playwrights and theorists whose work is well known in Western circles, the variety of approaches to questions of modernity is immediately apparent. There were experiments with updating kabuki and nō, with updating Japanese theatre with Western techniques, and with creating a completely new Japanese theatre. The aesthetics of these theatres varied from intense, grand spectacle to quiet slow motion with limited dialogue. These movements all shared the idea that something needed to be changed to help Japanese theatre more closely reflect, enhance, alter, or comment on contemporary life. During the 1970s there was a strong progressive slant to the government, which is to say that Japan experimented with socialist principles. Socialist ideas are often associated with questions of the relationship between art and the people. Soviet socialist realism, for instance, rejected the overly ornate theatres of the bourgeois (middle class) in favor of theatre that focused on the concrete material existence. In Japan, the progressive impulse in government led to an era of expanding art criticism and experimentation. During the 1980s, as the socialist tendencies of the 1970s receded, many artists turned to vibrant spectacle, claiming that this spectacle captured the essence of life in a thriving hyper-modern Japan. Later practitioners, like Hirata Oriza (b. 1962), attempted to find a theatre suited for a later period with a less robust economy.

Oriza's work falls into two broad categories. While he developed the "quiet theatre" he describes below throughout his career (and continues to do so), he has also experimented with robot actors. These robots serve to make the audience question the role that technology plays in everyday life, the extent to which electronic interactions have replaced human ones, and, indeed, the nature of humanity.

The above questions are central to any discussion of modernity broadly, and, given the rapid pace of Japanese modernization, particularly relevant in this context. For Hirata, the question of humanity's place in the world (and the Japanese subject's place in Japan) comes down to a question of how the current societal and technological facts of our existence limit and expand our interactions. Hirata argues that the relative isolation of Japan through much of its history shaped the development of the Japanese language in a certain way. There are whole types of interactions that the Japanese language excels at and other types that are extremely hard to produce.

If we exist through our interactions with other people and language shapes these interactions, it makes sense to focus on language in any theatre that seeks to reflect contemporary life. By focusing on language Hirata rejects both the focus on spectacle and the political focus of earlier modes of Japanese theatre. This is not to say that Hirata's work is apolitical, merely that any politics one might find grow out of the linguistic interactions.

In practice, this means that many of Hirata's scripts contain overlapping dialogue delivered in a naturalistic way (with actors sometimes facing away from the audience). There is not a traditionally structured plot in many of his plays, although settings (e.g. a museum) are particularly important in shaping dialogue.

Hirata's work raises a number of questions. What does it mean to be a contemporary Japanese citizen / subject? What is the impact of contemporary society / technology on these people? How are these selves related to their historical context? How is art shaping these selves? How is art representing these selves? What other modes of representation could art employ to alter these selves or more accurately represent them?

These questions can likely be applied to the context of modern theatre around the world. As seen from the diversity of answers Japan has supplied to these questions, there is no single path, even in a single context, toward an answer.

Extract 6.1 Selections from *Introduction to Theater*
Hirata Oriza, translated by Hiroko Matsuda

Is Theme Necessary?

Before we go on with playwriting, there is one point we need to make clear. That is, whether we should decide the theme beforehand when we write a play or not. [...] In my course, what to write is never discussed. Only how to write is. Please make no mistake. I'm not saying you don't need the theme, the subject you would like to write about. Of course you have something you want to write about. What I'm saying is that it should not be linked to the skills of writing plays. Further, I believe that to have a presiding theme/subject can be obstacle to playwriting.

You should not consider the theme before you start writing a play. The conventional playwriting method may find this odd but from my viewpoint, it is the conventional method that is odd. Far more so. Say you are drawing a picture. You don't first consider the theme and then go and find the landscape to suit it. You come upon a certain landscape, feel the urge to depict and express the scene, which drives you to draw the picture. I understand there are painters who first have the theme but I take that they are rare cases. In other words, your themes are already in your mind. The desire to draw is evoked when the inner theme or the impulse to express matches the subject matter. In still other words, we do not create to express the theme but we express to give some shape to our chaotic image of the world.

What is Modern Theater?

Let's have a further look at the issue of theme a bit more. The greatest difference between the so-called conventional modern theater and the contemporary theater I'm aiming at may be, as it is clearly seen in the playwriting methods, whether the theme should precede the expression or the other way around. [...]

[In modern theater] there is world/human in the center, with creator (expresser) on one side and receiver (audience) on the other. The most typical characteristic of modern art and theater is that the creator has, from the beginning, a certain theme (in other words, doctrine, claim or ideology) they want to communicate to the audience. There is a theme and the creator's intention to convey it. The theme is projected to the world or to the characters for the audience to receive. This is the basic structure of modern art. Here, the world is a mere jumping-board for theme.

The comparison of this model to that of the pre-modern times when there were not yet clear distinctions between religious rituals and art explains why the model is characteristically "modern." Before the modern times, I'm sure they didn't have to argue like, "This year, the theme of our festival should be 'No to War'." "No, let's make it 'End the Discrimination'." Pre-modern communities did have themes but they were never-changing, like cornucopia and safe home. And they were something that needed to be confirmed from time to time and not ideal to communicate to others. The act of conveying the author's personal theme and thoughts to many through art is truly characteristic of modern art.

You find the same "modern" approach in high school and college entrance exams too. Questions like "State what the author intended to say in this piece within 25 words." and "Excerpt the passage that most expresses the theme of this piece within 30 words." are almost always on the contemporary Japanese exam. In this modern approach, a good author conveys the piece's theme subtlety and well and a good reader/audience member notices the theme keenly.

What is Contemporary Theater?

The most distinctive characteristic of contemporary art and theater, I think, is that it has lost this something to communicate, or the themes, compared to the modern art which has things to convey to the audiences. There are mainly two aspects to this.

One is that the theme has indeed been gone. The present de-ideologizing age has seen the Berlin Wall fall, the Soviet Union disappear and the Cold War come to an end, of a sort. On the other hand, the already shaken standard values were being further more diversified, thanks to phenomena such as AIDS and frighteningly rapid computer development, and now it was completely meaningless to try and solve complicated problems sticking to one mighty ideology. The thought to communicate to the others itself was hollowing out, so to speak. Of course Japan was not outside this magnificent tide. The situation is chaotic, with the Liberal Democratic Party and Socialist Party of Japan forming a coalition government and the Communist Party and conservative parties jointly submitting a no-confidence motion against the Cabinet. We have entered an era in which presenting a massive story or ideology doesn't mean a thing.

The other aspect is the shift of the social role expected for art. We artists would like the task of changing political and economic systems — that is to say society we live in, narrowly defined — to be borne by politicians, mass media and universities. It's no longer art's commitment to state simple doctrines and claims.

Once theatrical pieces were an important medium for the illiterate. And it had been a powerful tool, before the films, to spread a thought to many people simultaneously. I don't mean only high thoughts. Chikamatsu Monzaemon promptly made a current incident into a play. It was an efficient journalistic tool when Chikamatsu chose a double suicide of passion in Osaka as the subject of his play and showed the vivid re-creation as if he had seen it himself in front of the Tokyo audience, who learned not only what happened but also the culture and manners of the far away western part of the country.

But now theater has become the slowest, most cumbersome of the journalistic media. There are plenty other effective ways to deliver doctrines and claims. To deliver the antiwar thought or opinion, theater loses to 24 hours a day broadcast by CNN of the refugee children in Bosnia and Herzegovina. [...] Theater no longer is a media or means of propaganda. Contemporary theater starts from the thorough recognition of this fact.

Desire to Express

"I say in contemporary theater there is nothing to communicate to the audiences" and am often met by reproachful "Then what are you doing your artistic expression for?" To that I always answer, "I have nothing to communicate but much I would like to express."

As I stated before, to have nothing to communicate means that there are no longer any doctrines or values to communicate to the audience. But with nothing to convey to the audience, the exuberant desire to express is definitely inside me. The desire is, in other words, the impulse to give a shape to the chaotic thoughts in my mind about what the world is and what us human beings are and show it to the world outside. I want to depict the world.

However, the world here is not a philosopher's conceptual world, or the objective matter. The world I say is "the world for me," "the world I recognize it to be." My "desire to express" is a simple and violent wish to capture the world I am looking at and listening to. I want to take that world in my hands and depict it as is as theatrical expression. I want to turn my brain inside out and show it to the world, so to speak.

We selectively discard or integrate various pieces of information our brains directly recognize so that our lives are bearable. We forget inconvenient incidents or regard that we never encountered them to begin with. As we grow older, we get less accepting of things outside the convention learned through experiences and try harder to live peacefully till the end of the time.

Art, however, calls a halt to the function to integrate, arrange and control, disregard common sense and rules of thumb for the time being and tries to present the world that reached our brain as is. Maybe it's more depiction or description than expression. I want to describe the world as is. That's my desire, nothing else. Naturally I think the role of contemporary theater is to be exclusively this: "to describe the world I see as is."

Contemporary theater should be free of existing values such as common sense and experience, or at least exclude as much of them as possible and describe the world as is. To achieve this goal, it also needs to make an effort to acquire the suitable style. This is the overall framework of contemporary theater for me.

[...]

Writing Dialogues

Of the various spoken words, theater depends most on dialogues.

[...] To first give you simple definitions, a dialogue is an exchange of new information with a stranger. It doesn't have to be a total stranger. By "stranger" here I mean someone you don't really know yet.

On the other hand, a conversation is a chat among people who already know one another, a daily conversation at home, work or school.

In English these two are clearly distinguished but the difference is very vague in Japanese. This can be a pitfall in writing a play in Japanese. Many of my playwriting students write conversations instead of dialogues but conversations alone cannot make a play script.

Why is dialogue the most important element in modern theater?

If you have read this book thus far, you may be already aware of the answer. As I explained in the section about the place, there is little information valuable to the audience in a daily conversation. A family can keep on talking and the audience get no idea what the father's occupation is.

To let the audience easily follow the storyline, a play needs someone similar to the audience, the absolute strangers, and that is the outsiders who create dialogues on stage.

[...]

Generally speaking, the successful incorporating of the outsiders is absolutely necessary for a script or scenario to be good. Inexperienced writers tend to stick to everyday conversations here and fail. Or, contrarily, they omit the everyday conversations all together and start writing "public address"-like, explanatory lines.

[...]

Absence of Strangers

Writing dialogues seems to be especially difficult for high school students. Likewise, high school actors are often very poor in distinguishing the difference between conversations among friends and dialogues with strangers. The reason is obvious. High school students today have little opportunities to encounter strangers. As schools are ranked according to the academic levels, students in one school are all alike, and even among them, they only talk to their buddies in the classroom. The skills for carrying on dialogues would never grow in such an environment.

But it is not really about the decline of communication skills among the younger generation. In Japan, the collective of village societies, were never used to having dialogues in the true meaning. I believe that the absence of strangers may be a historical characteristic of the

Japanese language. A language with so many speakers and its own advanced culture to have stayed unaffected by other languages for such a long time is a very rare case.

The Japanese letter-writing culture dawned with the incursion of Chinese characters but after the Japanese alphabet was established, so-called "national culture" became prominent and they stopped sending envoys to the Chinese dynasty, and linguistically Japan entered into practical isolation around 10th century, shutting herself from the cultural influence from overseas, even in the Age of Geographic Discovery (I won't talk about the pros and cons of it now).

For a thousand years, up until mid-19th century, the country was never conquered by foreign nations and the language kept on developing on its own without being significantly affected by outside cultures. This must be one of peculiar examples in the world's history. Especially in the 300 years starting from Azuchi-Momoyama Period (late 16th and early 17th centuries), the Japanese society as a whole was extremely low in fluidity. Most of the population never went out of their native clan all their lives. They had no chance to experience the cultures of other clans, let alone foreign countries. In such a society there would be no need for "dialogues" as throughout their lives they live without encountering strangers. All they should be concerned about is how to get along with the village people who they know well. Conversations facilitate assimilation whereas dialogues admit differences. It is no wonder their language developed conversation strategies but not those for dialogues.

[...]

The Japanese language is not suited for dialogues. Not suited, or history never demanded it to be so. In that sense it is extremely different from European languages and cultures which have been refined by undergoing conquering and being conquered in wars, affecting and being affected by other cultures.

In a highly fluid society, people naturally have to explain who they are, what they love and what they hate to people who know nothing about them. European languages were developed to serve such purposes through dialogues. I'm not saying which is better or worse, but it is a fact. What is important for theater creators, however, is that what we are to create falls mostly in the framework of Western "modern dialogue plays."

Dialogues in "Sanshiro"

How is it in Japanese? Of course there would be regional differences and I have a hunch more people would say "Yes, I talk to a stranger" in western Japan than eastern. This is another digression but in my short experience of living in Kyoto, I found the taxi drivers there are the most talkative in Japan. Kyoto is full of sightseers and that obviously means more opportunities to encounter strangers and different cultures.

The most notable conversation on a train in literature for me is the opening of Soseki Natsume's "Sanshiro." Sanshiro Ogawa, the protagonist, has graduated a Kumamoto high school and is on the train to Tokyo to enroll at the Imperial University. He happens to sit with a woman

[...]

"Will we reach Nagoya soon?"
"I suppose so."
"Do you think we'll be behind the time?"
"Are you getting off at Nagoya too?"
"Yes, I am."

From this conversation, in several hours' time, they will be staying overnight sharing a room in a Nagoya inn. I wonder if the author's intention is behind it or it was a common practice in the 41st year of Meiji Era when the story takes place.

[...]

When it took more than 15 hours on an express from Kobe to Shinbashi (Tokyo), I suppose it was impossible to exchange no words with someone seated in the same booth. Eventually they begin a little more meaningful conversation. The man who might be a teacher comments on the Western couple passing by "Oh, beautiful." "How beautiful the Westerners are!" and then adds "We are miserable." "Look at our faces. And we have no strength. Winning the Japanese-Russo War and becoming the first class nation have done us no good." Sanshiro, a naive country boy, replies in defence, "But Japan will be prosperous, gradually." The man's calm and prompt answer "It is doomed" surprises him even more. It is an excellent introduction suggesting Sanshiro's wandering journey of soul in Tokyo.

"Sanshiro" is my favorite among the numerous masterpieces by Soseki Natsume. I have read the novel more than 20 times but each time this introductory passage gets me excited.

Okay, let's go back to talking about dialogues. Soseki Natsume was totally different from the preceding Japanese writers in that he depicted dialogues. In this opening scene of "Sanshiro" people belonging to different social classes talk to one another. Such semi-public situations had seldom been portrayed in Japanese novels. Changing times may be one reason behind it. Toward the end of the Meiji Era, the modernization of Japan was about to reach its final phase and these semi-public spaces and times were finally entering into the lives of ordinary people. People who would never have met in the feudal Edo Period now easily encountered each other, converse, have dialogues, however poorly, and then part again. In that sense too, "Sanshiro" is a literary work that symbolized the new age.

But, unfortunately, Japanese literature, after Soseki Natsume, doesn't further develop this form of dialogues. I think playwrights are also largely responsible on this matter. Play scripts, along with novels, should have pursued the style of dialogues.

[...]

Is a Dialogue Drama Possible?

As I stated before, what we generally call theater has the modern Western framework to start with. And this modern Western theater is based on dialogues. I believe I have clearly and logically explained this in my earlier passages about creating drama.

On the other hand, the Japanese language unfortunately has yet to acquire the structure for dialogues. This might seem hopeless. Based on this speculation you may syllogistically reach the conclusion that modern theater is impossible in Japan. Quite natural, assuming that modern theater is based on the "dialogues" in modern Western society.

It may not be an exaggeration to say that the difficulty of theater in Japan, or the difficulty of talking about theater in Japan, can be distilled to this one thing. We pursue what the new contemporary theater should be, but the modern theater to be overcome has not been established in Japan.

Of course we could nullify the syllogism itself by declaring "Western" and "modern" are not universal and ignoring these irrelevant and "peculiar" aspects. But, like it or not, the modern Western framework is already in our lives and culture. And in theater too. Aware or not, we cannot think of theater in this framework, just like in cases of "democracy," "market economy" and "science and technology." Then, it will not be totally useless to clarify now the distance between modern Western theater and the Japanese language, focusing on dialogues. Whether we would enhance the modern Western theater or demolish it, I think we should start with the recognition that modern theater is difficult to establish in Japan.

It is a difficult task to establish dialogue drama in Japan. But is it impossible? I don't think so. I believe there is hope somewhere. Dialogues are not the forte of the Japanese language or the Japanese people. It is precisely why we have been carefully looking for the places and backgrounds where the Japanese people who are not good at carrying on dialogues have to encounter and talk with others in this book.

The playwriting methods I have explained are at the same time procedures to create dialogues. I cannot deny that Japanese has some downside on producing dialogue drama. Depicting Western style dialogues in Japanese might be an impossible task and that is the reason we cannot help thinking "It is theoretically understandable but we Japanese don't talk that much," when we see theater performances, especially translated dramas.

The bright side of us Japanese not being used to dialogues might be, however, that we can consciously deal with dialogues. New cultures, arts and expressions are bound to originate in the outland. The Western reservoir is undoubtedly great but it comes with serious stagnation. It's always the outlanders who feel uncomfortable with the reservoir and try to innovate it that break the stagnation. So, the Japanese theater, marginal to the Western theater, may be able to strike back and give some impact.

[...] Playwrighting in present Japan means seeking the forms of dialogues for the future, as well as searching the forms of dialogues suited for the Japanese people.

Gao Xingjian: the potential of theatre

The Nobel Prize cemented Gao's status as one of the premier playwrights of the twentieth century. He had left China for France in the 1980s after criticizing the Chinese government in various writings. When he won the Nobel Prize, the Chinese government congratulated France on the victory. By the 1990s Gao was writing in French as well.

This politically motivated change of countries and the resultant shift in language and question of Gao's nationality is, in many ways, characteristic of modernity. Modernity is not limited to a single geographic region. Indeed, the modern world is a world of increasing globalization. Artists must figure out where they fit in this larger landscape.

Gao's argument for a total theatre – a theatre incorporating all manner of gymnastics, song, dance, dialogue, and performance techniques – suggests an approach to a unified modern art that transcends any particular cultural boundary. The techniques of theatre may have developed in different cultural venues, and each culture may have something to contribute, but Gao sees the potential of theatre as residing in the ability to mix all of these elements together. Gao, like Suzuki, speaks about "theatre" without an adjective denoting a region. This is markedly different from writers like Walcott or Zeami who insist on the specificity of particular types of theatre. This is different again from Barba's arguments about the pre-expressive – the idea that there is a theatrical form that preexists cultural differentiation. Gao is looking at culturally diverse theatres as the building blocks for his new total theatre. This manner of bricolage (collection of different artifacts into a single work of art) is characteristic of modernity.

Gao's theatre is selective, despite its desire to mix elements from a variety of sources. There are aspects of Western theatre Gao directly criticizes. In this regard, he does have an idea of what makes theatre into the art form that it is. He refers to this as "theatricality," a term that stays somewhat enigmatic in his writing, but seems to suggest those aspects of theatre which could only exist in the theatre. At no point does Gao refer to this "theatricality" as a distinct feature that emerges from his experience with Chinese theatre, or with French, or European theatre. "Theatricality" is a factor by which all theatre may be judged and can be used to decide which elements from a diverse array of cultures make it into the total theatre Gao discusses.

It is not just a mix of cultures in Gao's work: temporalities are mixed as well. While the Cultural Revolution in China actively rejected many aspects of traditional life, Gao actually brings some of these back as appropriate for a modern theatre (which is perhaps not surprising, given that he left China due to pressures from the Cultural Revolution). By the same token, however, Gao also embraces many aspects of modern theatre – as long as they contribute to theatricality. Other parts of modern theatre – those that lose the narrative thread provided by the playwright – Gao rejects as unsuitable for the theatre he envisions (although he leaves space for these to be considered their own mode of artistic production). For Gao, modern theatre need not be wholly new, as long as it is good theatre.

The connections between cultures and temporalities are also mirrored in connections between people. Gao spends an extensive amount of time discussing the different ways he employs pronouns in his plays. "I," "you," "he," and "she" mix together, with actors sharing lines and playing multiple roles. Even when an actor is playing a single role, the audience is aware of the three levels the actor is existing on: the character, the actor himself, and the neutral physicality of the actor that stands between the two. Gao has written about the neutral actor – the moment when the actor is free of both role and daily life – but the concept remains enigmatic from a Western perspective although it is more easily observed than written about. The complex mixing of characters, actors, and audience reflects the fact that Gao's theatre is not the theatre of the individual. This is to say that American interpretations of Stanislavski often stress the psychological nature of each individual on stage, acting separately from one another. Gao's theatre begins to explore the ways in which our psychological realties are shaped by people around us. He does not erase the individual, but, instead, changes the concept of what it means to be an individual. The "I" in Gao's work is not the same type of thing as the "I" in a Chekov play.

The acute awareness of the multiplicity of possible ways of forming identity that comes from living in an increasingly cosmopolitan world informs Gao's idea of the actor as well. Gao divides the actor into three parts, noting that all three parts are necessary for a solid performance. In the West, we traditionally draw a line between the actor and the role.

Extract 6.2 "The potential of theatre"
Gao Xingjian, translated by Mabel Lee

In modern and contemporary theatre the director's position far outranks that of the playwright. The directorship system emerged at the end of the nineteenth century, and through the twentieth century the director gradually took over the lead role from the playwright in contemporary theatre creation. European theatre prior to that was the theatre of the writer. Established patterns for actor performance existed, and whether a footstep should be light or heavy was decided entirely by the playwright; new topics, fresh ideas, and theatre forms all came from the script. However, traditional Asian theatre was the theatre of the actor, and what people saw was the superb performances of actors. The scripts were invariably traditional plays, and these were seldom changed. When the Western director system emerged, to begin with here too it was performance that was valued, so the technique and profession of acting became a consummate art.

Following the Second World War, the appearance of absurdist plays gave impetus to the rise of avant-garde theatre. Then by the 1960s the director's position became progressively more important, whereas the playwright's became progressively insignificant. This was because it was mainly the director who had completely redefined the aim of performance art, of the theatre, and even of theatrical art as a genre. Technical innovations in stage equipment, sound, and lighting also greatly helped the director's recreation of the script, and whether a classical or contemporary work was chosen, it would be staged according to the director's formula. The search for performance form meant that any literary text that arrived in the director's hands could be brought onto the stage. So if playwrights fail to produce some fresh ideas about the art of theatre or to find new forms of theatre expression, it seems as though they will simply be reduced to supplying literary plays in the same way scriptwriters do for films.

The playwrights of the present who want to restore vitality to the domain of theatre creation must reacquaint themselves with this ancient art form as well as search for new possibilities from within the internal mechanisms of theatre, and this is the very topic I wish to address.

[...]

My searching in theatre, however, begins from a different background. [...] I do not refute traditional theatre, and though I fully endorse the premises of traditional theatre, I set out to reacquaint myself with possibilities inherent within this art itself. First, I pose the question What is theatricality? Because it is on this basis that theatre constitutes an independent art form. The traditional understanding was that a play must have at least one connected series of movements. Contradictions and conflicts arise between a number of characters, resulting in a stream of incidents that build to a climax and then a conclusion: a single story threads through the whole play. This is the case in the plays of ancient Greece, as well as in China's traditional opera and Japan's noh and kabuki. The singing or chanting of songs and poetry without a connecting story would not be theatre but simply a series of performances.

An even fresher understanding came about when the idea of theatre as action evolved into that of theatre as a process. It was the French playwright Antonin Artaud who first proposed this after seeing Balinese opera from Indonesia. The Polish playwrights [Jerzy] Grotowski and [Tadeusz] Kantor afterwards emphasised this idea and, moreover, realised it on the stage with their creations. They mostly started from the perspective of the director, embodying it in the performances that they presented.

Playwrights who also have this sort of understanding will discover a new realm for writing plays. In fact, any movement looked at in slow motion or magnified will be a process. If a play is written solely about a certain process, there will be no need to create conflicts or construct events and even subtle psychological activities—as long as the process of these activities can be performed on the stage— can constitute theatre. Such an understanding greatly expands the subject matter and expressive potential of theatre. For example, when approaching death, a person's mental activities at this critical juncture will be enough to write a play about. Such states of mind and even certain situations can be theatre, as long as these can be presented as changing within a flow of time.

Following this line of thinking, it can then be found that change may also be theatre. Change from one state to another, stretching and going slack or rising and falling, likewise, also possesses theatricality. Furthermore, contrast can construct theatricality: two different factors, two unrelated characters, and two series or two groups of events can possess theatricality without constructing conflict, and they can even move in tandem or intersect. My *Wild Man* is this type of piece. A scholar's research on the ecology and the media's investigations on the wild man intersect and move forward without the two constructing any conflicts, yet theatrical tension is sustained throughout.

Theatre can also be discovery or surprise. When the piece of red silk is lifted, the egg has turned into a hen, or when the gun is fired, the woman in the box vanishes. Magic is fun and rich in theatricality, and public performances excite even when audiences know what will happen.

By reacquainting myself with theatricality, I was able to confirm that theatre was movement and this led to the understanding that theatre is process, change, contrast, discovery, and surprise, all of which are intrinsic to the art of theatre but which have often been overlooked and forgotten in contemporary plays. Instead of wearing oneself out to introduce nontheatrical methods in order to bring about theatrical innovations, one would do better to reexplore what is inherently vital to this ancient art.

There is no need to reiterate that theatre is art in the theatre. But what is theatricality? However, to ask this question again—and, moreover, to confirm it—raises new issues for the creation of contemporary plays. Theatre does not need to replicate real life on the stage: authenticity is unnecessary on the stage. Audiences go to the theatre to see actors present a performance, and performance in itself is not reality; moreover, naturalist performances are not particularly interesting but are in fact usually dull and boring.

The stage is essentially a specifically constructed environment. On the stage the actors do not need to present portrayals of real life: it is the performance that the audience comes to see. Theatricality does not attempt to conceal that it is the actor's public performance in the theatre. Both Italy's impromptu comedy and Asia's traditional opera rely on public performances to attract audiences. Theatrical art has always been like this, but the realist plays that emerged at the end of the nineteenth century and the beginning of the twentieth century completely blurred this understanding of theatre. If instead of relying solely on stage words, modern theatre mobilised all available performance techniques and included in theatre creation the performance methods of song, dance, masks, face make-up, magic, and acrobatics, it would be wonderful theatre. This full affirmation of theatricality would of course lead once again to a form of omnipotent theatre and would require omnipotent actors.

[...]

This reacquaintance with theatre, of course, broke through the confines of lounge-room theatre and also liberated theatre from the narrow framework of imitating scenes from real life. There is no reason why contemporary theatre cannot broaden its thinking and look back to epics and myths.

[...]

Unlike in fiction, the narrator in a play must rely on performing before an audience and both narrate and perform. There is no need to conceal the storyteller's status as actor, and the narrator is also a character in the play. It was Brecht who reintroduced the narrator into modern plays, and the alienating effect of his narrative plays was ideologically driven to arouse a socially critical consciousness in the audience. In Lao She's *Teahouse* the storyteller is written into the play with a role, and he both presents the story to the audience and moves amongst the characters. The narrator can create distance between the stage and the audience, as well as establish direct communication between the two, depending on how it has been arranged in the play and by the director. Narration can be transformed into a powerful device in theatre, and there can be many new ways to reintroduce narration into the play that can lead to yet another kind of performance. I will discuss this in detail further on.

[...]

The ancient art of performance is generally acknowledged to be a dual relationship constructed by the actor and his role. Playwrights from Diderot to Stanislavsky and even Brecht, all believed this to be so, even though each had different theories and methods for dealing with that relationship. The prevailing realist performance demands that the actor strives to live in his role to the smallest detail, and this is represented by Stanislavsky's method. The expressionist method is another. Taken by Brecht to its greatest heights, this method emphasised that the actor on the stage acting his role was expressing his role. So of course the actor did not have to be the same as the character, and it was possible to use all sorts of exaggerated performance strategies.

[...]

Before the actor emerges in the role there is a process that is usually overlooked. If one analyses traditional Chinese opera performances, this can be seen with greater clarity. In the actor's daily life he has a voice, intonation, and bearing that he is accustomed to, so before entering the role he must first purify himself by cleansing himself of his usual voice, intonation, and bearing and focus his energies on preparing to enter his role. Of course, in realist performance this process often escapes detection, but it becomes clear by observing at close range a Peking Opera performer, especially when it is a man acting the role of a woman. Take, for example, the Peking Opera performance artist Mei Lanfang acting a young woman or an imperial concubine even after he has turned fifty. As he applies make-up, warms up, and practices his singing, he is purifying himself, ridding himself of his male status and entering the state of mind of the neutral actor. The process is similar to the preparation of athletes at the start of a race; consciousness of self is discarded as the athlete enters a combative mode and listens for the pistol to fire. When the actor warms up by walking around backstage before going onto the stage, he is cleansing himself of his habits in daily life and entering a neutral state. At the sound of the gongs and drums, he walks onstage to the beat, but the process of his change of status is not completed until he faces the audience, strikes a pose, and speaks with the status of the character. It is only at this point that he is in the role before the audience. The striking of a pose is of utmost importance, because it is the first time the actor communicates face to face with the audience. Aided by his physical and psychological movements, the communication conveys meaning, namely, "I of this instant am here to make this role presentation of this character for all of you to see!" A talented actor is able to conquer the audience because he is fully aware of his own performance and is able to control it.

[...]

With the establishment of the status of the neutral actor on the stage, the precondition exists for posing new questions regarding dramaturgical methods and performance methods. Generally, the creation of characters in plays depends mainly on the words spoken on the stage: dialogues and monologues all come from the mouths of the characters and are always spoken in the voice of the first-person I. Now if what is spoken onstage is changed to the third-person he—both in dialogues and monologues—everything is transformed into a narrative, and the connection between actor and character is immediately established. The actor on the stage will also of course be able to talk about his character, whether or not he is acting, and he will be able to enter or exit his role with great ease.

[...]

If the method of writing a play is merely a technique, an idea, a clever trick, it cannot serve as a model. However, if the method of writing a play derives from a writer's life experiences, it is a kind of understanding, and even if it is a framework and form for artistic creation, it is still interesting. A playwright's search for theatrical forms derives from his understanding of life.

Waiting is a situation regularly encountered in life. Nightmares are similar, and no one can escape them. And life can often suddenly become like a nightmare if a person becomes trapped in a difficult situation and there is no hope of escape. *Nocturnal Wanderer* deals precisely with this issue. Everything is going all right for this person when his act of kindness rains calamity upon him; threatened and controlled, the more he struggles, the deeper he sinks. Kafkaesque nightmares in actual social life are in fact very real. Although the protagonist is walking in his sleep, the human relationships he encounters all around are quite real. Indeed, this allegory is a fairly universal portrayal of modern humanity's existential predicament.

Reemphasising the hypothetical nature of the stage and the fabricated nature of performance is not only manifested in performance and directing arrangements but is also written into the play. In other words, theatre is restored to being fully theatre—that is, omnipotent theatre. The stage is purged of the trivia of daily life that does not need to be imitated and is also purged of assorted clutter, so that maximum space is left for performance.

[...]

A character's inner mind experiences have been transformed into visible stage images, mental images have been transformed into the scenery of the play, anxiety and bewilderment have been transformed into movement, and through the performance of the actor, the hypothetical and theatrical nature of theatre have been confirmed; nonetheless, even if the play is a total fabrication, audiences will be convinced, provided the play has captured people's authentic experiences.

Plays were originally for the entertainment of adults. When children play games they are always imitating adults, but when adults entertain themselves, there is no need for them to imitate children. Setting out to replicate real life on the stage will always be a sham, but if the function of theatre to entertain is retrieved, the art of theatre will provide entertainment and aesthetic fulfilment.

[...]

Art is ennobled by virtue of its creation, and new concepts, new forms, and new methods generally have been proposed in two ways. One of these is rebellion, rebelling against tradition, overthrowing antecedents, and travelling on an antagonistic road to bring about change. In the twentieth century, which has just passed, such art revolutions were so frequent and familiar that many art historians wrongly thought that art innovation was possible only through revolution. However, I maintain that art creation has another more universal law, one that is not an overthrowing and overturning. It instead requires probing deep into a genre's history and the basis for its existence, exploring what possibilities can be discovered in this art form and proceeding to develop these possibilities by injecting fresh perspectives and providing new content and new forms.

It is only by using another perspective to observe that it is possible to discern unusual aspects that are hidden in something. The artist cannot be the Creator and create a new world, but he is capable of forming his own unique understanding of the world and moreover of finding a suitable form for presenting it.

[...]

From the theatre of ancient Greece to modern theatre, outstanding playwrights have struck deep chords in the complexities of human nature and the many dilemmas of human existence, and as thinkers of their times, they have used theatre to voice thoughts that could not be openly expressed. In fact, they have all been thinkers of their times.

However, compared with their philosopher contemporaries, playwrights may be said to possess an additional dimension of artifice, or one might say they have the advantage of being able to cast aside political and ethical taboos by speaking through their characters on their understanding of society, the times, and life. The political authority, morality, and fashion of those times and places may have long vanished, yet in a different time and place the vitality of their plays remains undiminished, and the plays can be endlessly repeated on stage. Moreover, entrusted to the images of the characters, the thinking in the plays remains vivid and cannot be matched by religious preaching or direct propaganda. Whereas for later generations the writings of philosophers have significance only as intellectual history, these works of drama continue to move different generations of audiences.

Indeed, playwrights and plays that can withstand the test of time are like needles in the ocean, but those works that can be salvaged are gold. I believe this to be the quest of all playwrights committed to the creation of serious theatre, although not all of them will necessarily achieve this goal. Nevertheless, what harm is there in striving, and even if a work is not transmitted to later generations, at least it will win the pleasure of being spoken on the stage in front of people, and it will be much more interesting than speeches at political gatherings.

Questions to ask about modernity and theatre

Total theatre

Both of the above pieces come from Asia. Both emphasize a form of total theatre, as do a number of Western modern practitioners (e.g. Ibsen or Strindberg, albeit in different ways). How does this move toward a total theatre, one including a variety of performance techniques, relate to the fracturing of the master narrative? Are there other modern movements that inform theatre? How do the above discussions relate to the idea of modernity?

Traditions and modernity

Earlier chapters have noted the role of tradition as resistance to cultural imperialism. This chapter also points out that tradition might enhance or hinder modernity. How does the desire for the new or modern relate to the desire to retain indigenous traditions? If tradition is significantly reworked to fit into modernity is it still "traditional?" Is it possible to use traditional structures in a modern context without losing their significance? Is it even desirable to do so?

Hybridity

Both of the above examples, and, indeed, many of the theories in this book, look at theatre as a hybrid medium that merges multiple cultures together. Is this hybridity a necessary part of modern theatre? To some extent, every culture has resisted the hybridization of modernity. The idea of the nation as a political entity having its own distinct identity is a product of the modern world. All nationalisms are, to some extent, resistances to hybridization. Are there modern movements where cultures retrench themselves and resist such hybridity (perhaps the Cultural Revolution in China)? What manner of theatre do these cultures produce?

Multiple modernities

Modernity can be explained as the spread of capitalism around the globe. Capitalism demands that certain nations become richer while others remain poor (there are a limited number of resources and capitalism is about the accumulation of these resources). Capitalism demands technological innovation so that humans can produce more value with their limited amount of time (aka profit). Disagreements about the nature of modernity can be explained as differences in perspective depending on which part of the system one is in. Modern capitalism looks substantially different from a penthouse in an Abu Dhabi hotel than it does from a trailer in Alabama. This idea is often called "singular modernity." There is one modernity to which we are all subject. Different cultures respond to this modernity in different ways depending on their relationship to it.

On the other hand, the "alternative modernity" movement suggests that, while there is a global flow of capital, each nation's response to this flow is not part of a general modernity, but, instead, is a unique cultural experience. The model of alternative modernities gets around the idea that some nations are further along the path of progress than others (which is both implicit and often explicit in the singular modernity arguments).

When examining the diverse terrain of modern theatre around the world, it is worth considering what historical and cultural forces the theatre is responding to. Are these forces related to other nations? If so, can the same theoretical models explain both theatres? Are the contexts different enough that the same forms might be doing different things?

To some extent, the structure of this book leans toward an alternative modernities model, insisting that both the differences and similarities between world theatre theories be examined. By rejecting Western theory as the primary explanatory tool, I am, effectively, rejecting the idea that a singular modernity has shaped all cultural response. Inasmuch as this book celebrates theoretical pluralism, however, I still consider the idea of a singular modernity an interesting tool for framing questions about cultural difference.

Chapter 7

Toward a theorization of gender in world theatre

> I find it unacceptable to be categorized as a feminist. I am a writer with the consciousness of a woman; I cannot escape my gender, but it is not my sole identity. My women characters live in a troubled, patriarchal world, but they are strong and capable of speaking and acting for themselves. But that does not make me a feminist
>
> *An Interview with Poile Sengupta*, Anita Singh.

Case study: Griselda Gambaro, *Antigona Furiosa*

During 1986, mothers in Argentina marched in the capital, protesting the fact that their children had been "disappeared" by the government. The mothers marched, in part, because they could not perform other grieving rituals without the bodies of the deceased. Many of these mothers continue to march once a week even in 2016. In 1986 in Buenos Aires, Laura Usem directed Griselda Gambaro's *Antigona Furiosa*, which is an adaptation of Sophocles' *Antigone*. This production is described in Marguerite Feitlowitz's English translation of the play.

The audience is seated on all sides of the performance space. The lights come up. Antigone is hanging, dead, from one of the bars of her pyramid-shaped cage. She does not exit this cage for the duration of the play. The cage is surrounded by café tables, where the chorus-leader sits. A large polyester suit consisting of a torso, arms, and a helmet is also visible on the stage. Later in the play, an actor will put on this shell to portray Creon, but the shell will also be used as a puppet and as a shield. There are only three actors in the play: the chorus-leader, Antigona, and Antinous.

The play opens with the chorus-leader making paper flowers and comparing Antigona to *Hamlet*'s Ophelia. Antigona and the chorus-leader discuss the fact that Creon has forbidden anyone from burying Polynices, Antigona's brother. Antigona defends her actions by saying

"My Mother lay down with my father, who was born of her belly, and thus we were begotten. And in this chain of the living and the dead, I will pay for their wrongdoings. And my own." Antigona is referring to Oedipus, her father, who slept with his own mother to conceive Antigona. She claims to bear the weight of this misdeed.

Later in the play, after Creon has sentenced Antigona to death, she discusses her near-marriage to Haemon, which has been called off on account of her crime. She says she will marry only death and refers to her tomb as a wedding chamber. She also says she is pleased to die a virgin. In the final moments of the play, the chorus-leader and Antigona discuss the fact that she will *always* act in this way, always defy the law, and always bury her brother. Antigona then kills herself and the play ends where it started, with her corpse hanging in the cage.

Gambaro is an Argentinian writer who deals with the subject of violence in many of her plays. She is also one of the few female playwrights from the world context who has gained a following in the West. Why would a female writer from Argentina choose to adapt a classical Greek text? What is she commenting on in this production? Why does Antigona never leave her cage? Why compare Antigona to Ophelia? Does this relate to the idea that Antigona will "always" make the same choices? What is the connection between this Antigona and other Antigones? Is this connection part of the "always?" Why is Creon represented by a shell rather than an actor? Given the context of mothers-in-mourning that surrounds the play, are any of the production elements commenting specifically on gender-related issues? To what extent is it productive to think of this play as specifically written by a woman? By a South American woman? Is this concern about gender-related issues something that Western scholars can add to the text or are such gender issues brought up in the local context as well?

Introduction

The fact that only four female theorists are included in this volume is indicative of the fact that there are not many women from the world (as defined in this book) working in the field of theatre *theory*. To be sure, there is a rapidly expanding, although still small, pool of world female playwrights and theatre practitioners gaining international prominence, but very few of these explicitly theorize their work in writing. Of course, both men and women write about gender, but, in contrast to the West (where gender is an academic growth field), while gender is absolutely a concern for theorists writing about African, Asian, Middle Eastern, South American, and Caribbean theatre from other locations, fewer critics *from these locations*, male or female, write at any length about gender *in the theatre*. Fewer still address lesbian, gay, bisexual, transgender, and queer (LGBTQ) issues in relation to theatre.

Many readers have likely responded negatively to the preceding paragraph. Gender, gender identity and sexuality are important issues to critics all over the world. When speaking about theory outside of theatre, theorizations of gender in theatre emerging from Western scholars, or gender issues in theatre practice as opposed to written theory, there is a profusion of works that could have been included. There is simply a scarcity of *world theories of theatre* related to gender and LGBTQ issues. Indeed, at time of writing, I was unable to locate any sustained theoretical writing of this sort addressing LGBTQ issues.

The above statements are unfortunate, and should not be downplayed, particularly given the brilliant work by Western scholars in these fields and the sociological work being done around the world that addresses both LGBTQ topics and gender. With regard to Latin American female playwrights, Margo Milleret says that there is "scholarly work done on women's theatre, but not Latin American women; on Latin American women writers, but not women dramatists; and on Latin American theatre, but not women dramatists." She goes on to note the thousands of plays written by female dramatists, making it clear that a scholarly absence is not the same as an actual absence. While her topic is different from the concerns of this book, just as she charts a constellation of ideas around the central topic she wishes to discuss, there are a number of pieces of scholarship related to the idea of gender in theatre, even while there are not very many pieces of theory from the world on this topic. There are general theorizations of gender in the postcolonial setting (e.g. Gayatri Spivak, Anne McClintock, Mary Louise Pratt), discussions of gender in minority theatres in the West (e.g. Daphne Lei, Annemarie Bean), analyses of theatre by women all around the world emerging from world contexts (e.g. Yvette Hutchinson), the still somewhat limited category of Western theorizations of gender in world theatre (e.g. Siyuan Liu, William H. Sun), and a similar, if more limited, constellation around LGBTQ issues. As with the other chapters, the materials that should be included in this chapter are discussions of a theoretical issue (gender) in a theatrical context emerging from the specific region in question.

Every time I make the above statement in a public setting, I am bombarded with dozens of names (many of whom are mentioned in either the bibliography or the chapters of this book). People want there to be world theorizations of gender in theatre. By the same token, most scholars would agree that we have not achieved gender equity in access to the means of production in the theatre, representation in theatrical canons from any location (either in terms of the division between roles on stage or in terms of works appearing in anthologies), or in the general structure of the academy. My highlighting of the lack of world theatre theory related to gender should be read as pointing out another similar area of concern, while simultaneously noting that other parts of the world have other priorities.

For the moment, this chapter is shorter than other chapters because of the lack of material that has thus far been produced in the regions in question. As late as 2014, David Damrosch has pointed out that Western scholarship re-inscribes the division between the artistic production of the world and the West's theorization of this production: that the postcolonial world has produced much of the literature that the West has theorized is certainly true, but there has been a gradual recognition that theory has also emerged from the world, and that such theory offers its own ways of "knowing." It is, however, currently the case in many parts of the world that women are producing the theatre that men – primarily European and American men – are theorizing. Theatre theory is still a heavily male game. It is my hope that economic and social conditions will shift over time in such a way as to make this statement false.

What are gender and feminism?

In contemporary Western theory, gender is defined as a social construction related to, but often not fully dependent on, the biological differences between birth sexes. Modern and contemporary Western society has tended to treat gender as a binary distinction between man and woman, but there is a growing awareness of a more diverse array of options. Judith Butler has characterized gender as a forced performative reiteration of social norms. This means that gender is performed – it is something we do, rather than something we are. To say that gender is performed is not to say that we have freedom to choose or create any gender identity we wish. There is a powerful normative force at work that shapes our performances, even in the case of gender-bending performances like drag, which often rely on the same set of gender conventions that they begin to unseat. In addition to these performed differences, some scholars, like Mary Daly, have argued that there are substantial differences in women's ways of perceiving and thinking and that the world needs to be reshaped to allow for these differences. So, gender is a social performance related to biological difference that leads to (or is caused by) substantial differences in ways of perceiving the world.

The components of the above definition are subject to constant challenges and revisions within the Western world, and other societies have had different conceptions of gender. Three-part divisions between man, woman, and intersex / non-binary are common around the world and, indeed, in Western history as well. Some societies adhere to a strong biological essentialism, assuming that the qualities of men and women are an inherent part of their (often divinely created) biology rather than social constructs.

Feminism has meant a number of different things in Western history and continues to evolve as a concept: in broadest terms, it seeks to adjust the relationships between women and men and between women and the world. Radical feminists, like Andrea Dworkin, defined the problem as one of patriarchy in which male domination in all areas of life had resulted in the wholesale oppression of women. To combat this problem, they separated themselves from men and created women-only campaigns, which focused on the effects of male violence, rape, and pornography. Marxist feminists linked male domination with class exploitation, arguing that equal rights for men and women wouldn't improve the lot of poor women. They have worked for things like equal pay. Liberal feminists placed the emphasis on change from within society rather than revolution by putting forward positive role models for girls, establishing equality in their own relationships, and lobbying parliament for legislation on equal rights. There have been multiple waves of feminisms in Europe and in the U.S. and each of these waves have changed its goals, tactics, and its suppositions about gender in significant ways.

Broadly speaking, postcolonial feminists claim that Western feminism tends to assume a shared sisterhood among women – that the category of woman is equivalent across contexts. Furthermore, the critique claims that Western feminism assumes that women share a set of common goals, and thus societies and individuals can be judged in terms of their distance from these goals. Postcolonial feminists claim that this is a narrative of progress that fails to recognize the diversity of different ways to exist as a woman and the diversity of different goals feminism might have. Aside from critiquing the homogeneity of Western feminism, postcolonial feminists also note how much of the colonial system relied on specific conceptions of the female body. Postcolonial feminists have worked hard to make this reliance visible and to explore its ramifications. If European modernity is based on colonization and colonization required the female body to be treated in certain ways, what happens to European modernity as the woman changes conceptions of her body?

The various waves of feminism have inspired new techniques in literary criticism. In keeping with the idea that women might perceive the world in distinct ways, several critics, like Julia Kristeva, Helene Cixous, and Luce Irigaray, have explored ways in which women's literary production might be different based on the unique female perspective. This line of argument is particularly attentive to the meaning behind traditional literary structures. For instance, linear, causal narratives could be considered phallic (male-centred, reproducing male logics) because reading follows the trajectory of a male orgasm (toward a point of "closure"). In contrast, women's narratives could be cyclical rather than linear with multiple points of climax. Other feminist writers have used traditional writing techniques to challenge the patriarchy. It is important to note that feminist literature and theatre can do more than simply present women in a positive light: it can challenge the structural assumptions that underlie such literature.

Gender and theatre in Western criticism

Theorizing gender in theatre, then, is thinking about socially constructed relationships about gender as a performance, about the biases in theatrical structures, and about equality of representation. When applied specifically to women, these concerns fall under the broad category of feminism.

Sue-Ellen Case wrote one of the most widely cited books on gender in theatre, *Feminism in Theatre*. This book addresses (primarily female) gender, sexuality, and feminism as concepts that might be used to read theatre and theatre history. Case traces the major types of critical studies involving these topics in the theatre world. First, Case examines studies that detail the relative absence of women on stage (and often in scripts) through theatre history. These studies often deal with the fact that men have played women's roles.

Case then explores specific genres of theatre that have tended to have a larger space for women. One of these is what Case calls "personal theatre," which deals with domestic issues in domestic spaces: Case specifically examines the salon (a French word for a space of intellectual meeting, often in a private residence). She goes on to explain various modes of performance art that deal with the place of the female body in society. This is a third trend in gender scholarship within theatre – examining the specific structures and forms of theatre that are foreground issues of gender. These sorts of critiques often examine the formal elements of theatre (its use of language, its assumptions about the bodies of the actors, the place of the director, etc.) in order to figure out how feminist theatre alters these conventions.

The final section of Case's work looks at the concrete effects of various types of feminist theatre – on how it has changed theatre, society, or politics in specific ways. Case divides this section by different types of feminist arguments, each one seeking to enact a particular kind of change. The diversity of argument here is a useful reminder that Case's study is not exhaustive – that it points to some ways that theatre might be feminist and / or deal with gender, but does not claim to catalogue a full range of possibilities. While Case does bring up racial components of feminism within the Western world, albeit briefly, she does not address the concerns of postcolonial feminism discussed below, but her careful delineation of various types of Western feminism leaves space for consideration of other modes of gender and feminist studies as well.

Since Case's work there has been a renewed interest in ideas of performing sexualities (e.g. Jill Dolan) and in gender in theatre more broadly. This discussion of women's bodies has led to a number of artistic and theatrical expressions (e.g. Candace Brietz). The pieces of art and performance are acts of theorization as surely as academic prose is. As Case reminds us, the logocentrism of Western theatre is often associated with phallocentrism – language has a masculine bias. Similarly, language-based theory likely carries with it certain masculine biases that practice-based theory might not share.

By privileging written theory, this book may, in fact, be recreating a form of gender bias (and then complaining about this bias). Case also provides a template for engaging with such practices as theory, but this engagement requires a different mode of interpretation that is beyond the scope of this book. Another way to consider the relative scarcity of scholarly theoretical texts dealing with gender in world theatre is to consider the idea that other forms of text are being used to communicate ideas that cannot fit within the biased forms of "traditional" theory.

Western theorizations of gender in world theatre

This section does not have analogous repetitions in other chapters. In those chapters, I have specifically not written about Western commentary on issues of structure, modernity, identity, etc., as they occur in world theatre. The point of this anthology is to provide a forum for the rich, often ignored voices in theoretical fields that emerge from around the world. Because issues of gender are less often discussed in these regions, I have included a brief overview of Western research on gender in African, Asian, and Latin American theatre. This section emphasizes the diversity of comments on gender being made and the openness of world theatre to gender-based criticism.

A great deal of critical attention has been paid to men-playing-women in Asian and African traditions. Theorists have attempted to distinguish these performances from Western drag, to determine what ramification these sorts of performance have for the study of sexuality in each specific location, and to trace shifts in these performances as ideas of gender have changed in the regions in question.

There are also types of theatre that have been all-female or female dominated (e.g. *Kutiyattem*, a type of Sanskrit drama, and *otome-bunraku*, a female version of Japanese puppet theatre). It is not easy to find analogues of such performance traditions in the West, and so theorists have attempted to determine what place these female-led performance styles had in traditional society, what these performances might teach us about redefining our conceptions of theatre, and how these traditions have interacted with other traditions to shape contemporary ideas of gender.

Henry Spiller and others have also begun to research ideas of masculinity in performance around the world. This is a logical progression of gender studies in the world theatre context. If postcolonial feminism's mistrust of "universal" definitions of feminism is founded, then a redefinition of masculinity is a necessary part of understanding the way any gender dynamic functions in contexts around the world. At the most basic level, this line of research stops scholars from overlaying Western ideas of gender roles onto plays from other locations where the stereotypes and preconceptions about gender roles can be substantially different.

Each of these lines of study has yielded fascinating results, although such results are often framed in terms of the critical concerns of Western theory. It would have been possible to flesh out this chapter with the above materials, but this would have done exactly what postcolonial feminism objects to and treated Western theorizations of the world as speaking for the world (instead of about it, as the above theorists rightly claim to be doing). That being said, there are some world critics who theorize the place of gender in theatre, and their work forms the rest of this section.

Between the writing and the publication of this book, I encountered the work of Denise Stoklos, a performer from Brazil. While her work is often discussed in terms of performance art rather than theatre, her *Essential Theatre*, which has not yet been fully translated into English, would have been an important addition to any number of sections in this book. This oversight is partly a result of my own linguistic skills (I don't read Portuguese), but partly a result of the way scholarship and criticism more broadly tends to treat writing by women. Denise Stoklos has gained a following in New York, but she remains relatively under-discussed in Brazil. Thankfully, Diana Taylor and others have been diligently working to make sure that Latin American female performers get the academic attention their work deserves.

Roma Potiki: myths and stories

Roma Potiki (b. 1958) is one of New Zealand's premiere playwrights and theatre critics. While Werewere Liking's work uses traditional culture to effect immediate change in the modern world, Potiki's work focuses on re-establishing / revitalizing a traditional Maori culture. She is particularly concerned with articulating the place of women within this larger culture.

Potiki laments the fact that many Maori cannot speak their own language. She talks about bringing myths and stories to the present to revive the Maori culture. While she is interested in traditional myths, she also wants to make sure that the stories presented portray women in a variety of ways. This is a curious desire to update and change as well as to preserve.

There is an elegant straightforward quality to Potiki's theoretical work that is reflected in her theatrical endeavors as well. She is reviving a storytelling culture and, unlike esoteric Western artistic practices, the purpose of such theatre is communication. To say that something has a simplicity to it is not the same as claiming that the ideas are any less complex. Potiki is writing in a simple manner, but is doing so to touch on major issues in a way that communicates these issues to a wider audience. This mode of theorization might be related to feminist claims about different writing structures or it might be related to Maori tradition more broadly.

Potiki does discuss and celebrate the woman's part in the larger Maori culture, but its stated aims are not "feminist" in the manner described above. Potiki does use inclusive language ("herstory") and does consider the place of the woman within the family unit, but she does not elaborate on these moves. The choice to address gender as part of another issue might be read in a feminist manner. The underlying assumption is that women are a part of society and can be discussed when society as a whole is discussed. This assumption stands in marked contrast to the imagined white male that forms the implicit or explicit subject of much other theorization in this book and more broadly.

The above speculation on the place of feminism within Potiki's work, however, is externally applied – it is my reading (or at least a possible reading I see). Given the directness of Potiki's writing style, such external readings that go well beyond what is said run the risk of obscuring the meanings of the piece. Ought we to read her piece as engaging with gender critique simply because of the gender of the author and her inclusive language? Is something like Werewere Liking's description of the place of the priestess in many of her created rituals engaging with gender more / differently? If neither of these theorists specifically ask to be read in the context of gender theory, what are the costs and benefits of doing so?

Extract 7.1 **Selections from "A Maori Point of View: The Journey from Anxiety to Confidence"**
Roma Potiki

Maori drama is about Maori people being able to tell their own stories. The heart of Maori drama is in this storytelling. In the majority of Maori plays I have attended over the last thirteen years one of the most important aspects for the Maori audience is that they can see themselves. They can recognise the stories and identify with the people in them. No-one else can do that for us.

Maori theatre offers an arena in which we can nurture our spirit, intellect, and emotional well-being by focusing on ourselves so we can get out the stories that our communities need to see and hear.

I want to say also that it is about being able to do this in a very contemporary and sophisticated sense. And in a sophisticated space which we will call theatre.

Maori theatre is about learning to communicate with ourselves and our own people. It is about deciding what to show, working on it and then sharing it with Maori and others. It is about re-claiming the distant and recent past by telling what we remember.

And in looking into our memories of Maori drama one of the things we have lacked is the people to record in the written form what has happened.

It is hard to establish oneself in the mainstream of a society dominated by Pakeha systems when you don't have a recorded his/herstory. Of course we have oral tradition, but the mainstream, which has the powerbase of buildings, money and resources, is defined by a written tradition, and more recently by video and film. Both of which cost an enormous amount of money to produce and edit.

Quite a number of Maori plays have been performed and toured but have no recorded script, nor video record. A lot of Maori his/herstory has not been put down on paper. I have been linked with Maori theatre since 1978 and there are many people before me. Yet I cannot go into any library or place of research in this country and easily get access to articles, a book or theses on the development of Maori theatre. So perhaps in recording anything at all we take a small step to see that Maori theatre *whakapapa* is not lost. (And I hope that some Maori people will decide to do a thesis on the subject.)

The process of colonisation has been very thorough. It has penetrated so deeply as to dislocate many of us even from our own culture. This dislocation causes a lack of confidence in ourselves and our opinions, a pervasive anxiety. [...] And perhaps the central questions for some of the writers are 'Who am I?', 'Where do I come from?' Where do I belong?'. Unfortunately questions not only of identity but also of place are still a very legitimate struggle for many of us.

One of the exciting things that Maori theatre and playwriting can do is that through it we start to delve into our anxieties and expose our confidences. And then in becoming confident with the form 'Maori Theatre' we also learn to debunk myths. Myths that not only Pakeha people have built around us, but also the ones we uphold about ourselves. These myths in some ways have been a kind of false protection, which we have also supported to varying degrees in coming out of our colonised recent past.

Specifically in terms of theatre, I am referring to the myth of rural life as being idyllic and somehow more noble and spiritually 'pure', closer to our roots than city life. That life lived in the city or in an urban dwelling is inferior to a country life.

[...]

At its best Maori theatre is a politicised form of self-awareness that goes well beyond the bounds of propaganda or 'worthy' theatre into the area of the human heart.

This type of theatre will tell the truth of stories that pertain to a wide range of Maori people. It will be conscious of what has really happened, not presenting a sanitised, repressed or idealised view that we may have wished were the truth. Maori theatre should have the power and conviction to both disturb, heal and celebrate.

Poile Sengupta and new males, new females, and the gender continuum

Unlike every other theorist-playwright in this volume, much of Poile Sengupta's (b. 1948) theatrical work was written for children. Inasmuch as persistent stereotypes about women's roles pervade discourses of gender around the world, it is interesting that one of the most prominent women from Asia to theorize issues of gender in theatre writes for children as well. Much of the critique of feminism emerging from postcolonial studies in the West took travel writings and other genres associated with women as its starting point because the evidence in these areas was more copious: travel writing is a genre associated with women. Theatre, on the other hand, has largely been written by men. Children's theatre, when written at all, is a genre traditionally associated with women. One significant difference between Sengupta's work and the travel narratives analysed by Mary Louis Pratt and others is that Sengupta is subverting expectations about the genre of children's theatre in order to accentuate its social relevance. Sengupta's challenges to expectations about children's literature are, more broadly, challenges to conceptions of what roles women should play and the value of such roles.

In the 1993 Hindu-Madras Players competition, her play *Mangalam* won the award for the most socially relevant theme, which shows that Sengupta's work goes beyond any limited notion of children's literature.

Sengupta was educated in the U.S. and in India, and her work – newspaper columns for children, theatre criticism, and plays – written primarily in English, has gained critical attention and popular praise in both countries.

As Anita Singh notes in her headnotes to the interview that is reprinted in this volume, many key female leaders in India have rejected the label of feminist, just as Poile Sengupta does. This has to do with the different notions of what feminism might mean (discussed above). Sengupta's work deals candidly and movingly with the place of women in contemporary Indian society, avoiding stereotypes and creating balanced, imperfect male and female characters. In this interview, Sengupta discusses the impulses toward positive portrayals of women as stemming from a theatrical, rather than feminist, impulse – three dimensional characters are simply more interesting.

What is perhaps most interesting about Sengupta's discussion of gender is that she links advances for women to changes in perceptions of masculinity. Much gender criticism focuses on redefining either masculinity or femininity without explicitly discussing the concept that these two ideas are linked and that a change in one might require a change in both.

Sengupta is also very specific about a link between her particular performance style and gender issues – the play in question isn't just about women, it is structured in such a way as to make gender issues visible to the audience. Specifically in *Mangalam*, Sengupta uses "alienation" in order to show that "the world of domestic oppression and pain knows no socioeconomic boundary and [extends] across time."

Not only does this idea link theatrical practice to gender directly, but it also emphasizes the type of potentially global sisterhood that other postcolonial critics have called into question. It might be worth considering the ways in which Sengupta's ideas are different from (or the same as) those presented by other feminist writers. What is at stake in her disavowal of feminism?

Extract 7.2 **An Interview with Poile Sengupta**
Anita Singh

Interview, 4 April 2011

AS: I begin with a hackneyed question. How did you gravitate to writing plays in English? Has it been a disconcerting choice, as the common perception about English theatre is that it is a gratuitous fizz? Also added is the whole question of the [Indian] audience, who find it difficult to come to terms with English as the language of performance. And theatre as a genre is not something that women settle [in]to so easily. Moreover you have been a short story writer, and as Shashi Deshpande rightly said in the introduction to your collected plays Women Centre Stage . . . [it is] universally acknowledged for short story writers to move on swiftly to writing novels. What fascinated you [about] this [dramatic] genre?

PS: English is the language of my thoughts, of my creative effort. So when I began to script plays, I naturally used English. I had written for children regularly since the 1960s and periodically [wrote] short stories for adult readers as well. Writing for the stage was an exciting challenge, partly because I was already an actor, but also because *The Hindu*, in 1993, announced its play scripts contest. I decided to enter and wrote *Mangalam* in about ten days. It is true that writing for the stage, and in English, is an unusual choice, and what Shashi Deshpande has said is largely true. I am not certain what pulled me towards drama, but one of the factors that challenged me was that writing for the stage is essentially the writing of dialogue, of conversation, of authentic, direct speech. There was an additional challenge for me: How many Indians normally speak in English, and where do they use it without self-consciousness? Normally I would have had to create characters who were urban, educated in the English medium, and working and living in an environment in which English was the only language of communication—where no other common language was available. This was a severe restriction. It is true that my audiences would very likely be that same urban, English-educated Indian [represented in such a play]. But why should I confine my writing to portray only this small segment of my countrymen and not touch on the vast expanse of humanity that India is? To be able, therefore, to break the rules of the English language, not for comic effect but for authentic-sounding speech patterns, was enormously exciting.

AS: Poile is an unusual name. Can you explain why you chose it as a pen name?

PS: Actually, I was born in Ernakulam, and Gopalakrishnan is my surname at birth. Ambika was and still is my formal name. The name that I am known by amongst family and friends, and now for all my writing, is Poile, which comes from the Bengali word Poila, in Hindi *pehla* (translated as "first" in English). Hope this explains.

AS: Can you tell us about your experience and familiarity with multiple languages?

PS: Malayalam is one of the languages I speak (the state language of Kerala). I also speak Tamil from my parents' side. And I do speak Bengali, my husband's language, Hindi, Kannada, and English. Knowledge of multiple languages has helped me to have a more comprehensive view of the Indian milieu and create a wide variety of authentic characters [like Mrs. Nandan and Mrs. Pandu in the same play (*Inner Laws*)].

[...]

AS: A lot of women are uncomfortable with defining themselves as being feminist. [...] Do you feel inclined to categorize yourself and your work as feminist?

PS: I find it unacceptable to be categorized as a feminist. I am a writer with the consciousness of a woman; I cannot escape my gender, but it is not my sole identity. My women characters live in a troubled, patriarchal world, but they are strong and capable of speaking and acting for themselves. But that does not make me a feminist. In *Mangalam*, I also depict the emergence of the new Indian male, Vikram, who on page 3 [feature section] of newspapers would probably be called the metrosexual male.

AS: The 1970s saw a spate of prominent dramatists like Tanvir, Sircar, Tendulkar, Mohan Rakesh, Elkunchwar, and Satish Alekar, among others. Women in their plays were found to be in a "no exit from the trap" situation. They stopped short at romanticizing pain. In your work people are trying to find a way out. How do you react to this?

PS: Gender ideology became important to me as my own plays began to take shape. From my perspective as a woman and my observation of women across socioeconomic groups, I found that self-survival and nurturing are strong motivators. Their [women's] circumstances may be extremely adverse and often cruel, but many women have reserves of strength that make them fighters. Now, with an increasing number of women in urban and semi-urban

India becoming financially independent, there is greater hope for them. However, caste violence, political neglect or harassment, and unmitigated poverty still exist, and these seriously affect not only women and children, but men too.

AS: However, your plays never quite break out of the proscenium format. Were you never tempted to do a kind of total theatre? Can we classify your theatre as bourgeois proscenium sort of "talking on stage" kind of theatre? Also can we reimagine site-specific theatre?

PS: A play script is the idea of the play; the execution/production is in the hands of the director. Some playwrights, myself included, put in suggestions for sets, sound, and other inputs; others may not do so. In each of my plays I have placed emphasis on different aspects of theatre craft—in *Mangalam* on sets and stage management, in *Inner Laws* on costumes and props, in *Alipha* on lights and costumes, in *Thus Spake* on makeup and sound. But all of them except *Thus Spake* allow the director to interpret the dramaturgy of the play as he or she wishes; like most writers, I would prefer that my text is left intact. In *Thus Spake* I have given specific stage directions because the device of makeup and costume changes in full view of the audience is integral to the play. Actually that play can well be tried in open air jatra format, or in the wooden O. My recent play *Samara's Song* can be considered to be total theatre; all aspects of theatre, including the physical, get importance. It can certainly be done outdoors too. But such theatre is expensive. I have not written site-specific drama though.

AS: A personal question if I may ask. Most of your plays are directed by your husband, Abhijit Sengupta. Do your plays transform into a director's play or remain a writer's play?

PS: A script has two parents, one biological, the other the foster parent. Nowadays, increasingly in India, the dramatist is also the director; perhaps she or he is forced to stage her or his own work. I do believe a creative director does bring fresh insights and adds further nuances to the text. As for Abhijit, he has always helped me with our theatre group Theatre Club, which is now a not-for-profit trust to support Indian theatre, and he and I are able to work together on production issues. (I hope that as a playwright I do not ever have to deal with a *Caucasian Chalk Circle* kind of crisis; I have heard of a college in Chennai doing just the first act of *Mangalam* for an intercollege competition, without any permission and thinking that the first act made a full play!)

AS: Your play *Mangalam* makes a strong statement about the defenselessness of women across all strata of society. It's all about family politics. It's about domestic violence and sexual abuse. Its portrayal of women is quite horrifying. Was this bleak setup deliberately done? Or do you see it as symptomatic of women's predicament?

PS: I am not sure I understand the question. *Mangalam* is about serious issues, but the alienation devices that I use—the play within a play and the poetry—and the character of Vikram saves it, I think, from it becoming bleak or horrifying. Vikram is the new Indian male, sensitive and willing to accept gender equality. The last poem in the play expresses my conviction that women are the protectors of civilization.

AS: You see an inspiring way out of this conundrum in women coming together to find support and strength amongst themselves. Are you advocating Adrienne Rich kind of "Lesbian continuum"?

PS: The coming together of the women in *Mangalam* and *Inner Laws* is in comradeship. But I have not said, as Rich proposes, that women should move away from men and from heterosexual relationships. My women are able, even happy—as with Radha in *Inner Laws*—to include men in their lives. Just as being heterosexual cannot be compulsory, neither can being homosexual. Ideally, heterosexual relationships need not be corrosive; they can be sustaining.

AS: *Mangalam* has been a much applauded play and rightly so for its use of a dramatic device [play within a play] which coheres integrally with the intent of the play. How did you arrive at such a fusion?

PS: The technique of alienation that I used in *Mangalam* was part of the basic design to indicate that the world of domestic oppression and pain knows no socioeconomic boundary and [extends] across time. The technique of distancing actually allows the fusion of the two worlds of the play. It also was to provide a challenge to the actors as each of them had to play two characters.

AS: *Mangalam*'s tenor was serious but *Inner Laws* offers a lighthearted satiric view. Have you used comedy as a strategy to highlight the oppression and objectification of women in society? Do you believe women have a different sense of humor than men? How do you respond to the assertion that has been made repeatedly over the years that women "don't have a sense of humor." This statement has been made most frequently by men. However, this same assertion has, at times, been leveled (often in an accusatory manner) by women toward other women.

PS: *Inner Laws* appears to address the serious issue of women's antagonism towards women in a lighthearted way. However, the lightheartedness is at the superficial level. The play is actually savagely satirical about the absurdity of this antagonism and other societal issues—our education system, the beauty business, the obsession with materialistic possession, and pseudo-Freudian practices. Many of these issues are not gender-specific. Yes, I do believe women have a delightful sense of humor, but it is usually kept hidden because the male of the species is often the target.

AS: *Thus Spake Shoorpanakha, So Said Shakuni* is an ambitious work [in which] you target two maligned characters from two of our great epics, *Ramayana* and *Mahabharata*. What was the whole idea behind conflating these two epics?

PS: *Thus Spake* is a modern play that deals with conflict that is timeless. The two protagonists suffer because they belong to oppressed communities; they are also forgotten by Valmiki and Vyasa [authors of the *Ramayana* and *Mahabharata*, respectively] themselves after a point. Though each of them trigger[s] the Great War in the respective epics, neither is given much attention after the battle lines are drawn. My play brings them center stage, as the marginalized should be, and brings their suffering forward to our times. The play was prophetic; the day before it premiered, the world saw the horrifying images of the destruction of the twin towers in New York City.

AS: The overriding question in *Keats Was a Tuber* is in Damini's words "if I write a poem 'Upon Howarh Bridge,' will it be included in the English syllabus?" Is the play then on the impact of the English curriculum and English usage on cultural constructs of "new colonialism."

PS: *Keats Was a Tuber* confronts the issue of an Indian writing in English without forfeiting his or her Indian identity. It is indeed difficult to express India in English, and that is what the play says. Within that larger context, the play does examine the poor quality of English that is taught in India today. To the extent that this is a part of our own new colonialism it is perhaps valid. But most important here was a personal world. As I have said in my introduction to the play in Women Centre Stage, in *Keats Was a Tuber*, I allowed myself to explore my own relationship with the English language and to express unabashedly my deep love for it.

AS: How has being an actor helped you in being a playwright?

PS: I believe that coming to theatre as an actor before writing for the stage was extremely important for my writing. I understood the dynamics of the stage, the effect provided by sound and light inputs, the way the sets contribute to the visual excitement, and how choreography and music can add another dimension to the script. I have been able to appreciate the actors' needs and the director's viewpoint when writing a play. Most important for me as a writer was the use of language. I realized how important it was to give specific tones and speech patterns to characters so that they do not speak the same way, so that their thinking itself is particular to them. This distinctness makes for sharpness in character delineation.

AS: In terms of theatre, who has exerted the greatest influence upon you?

PS: There have been many theatre influences in my upbringing. I have been told that my great-grandfather was the first to have translated Shakespeare into Malayalam, but the manuscripts are not to be found. My father, based in Delhi, was actively involved in Malayalam theatre, with greats like Omchery [great Malayalam playwright], and my mother took me to see Tamil plays. My husband has been passionate about theatre all his life and much of my close knowledge of theatre comes from him. I also learnt from my seniors at Bangalore Little Theatre.

AS: How far do you think your plays invite the audience to view the underside of patriarchal culture through women's eyes? And finally, can I have your comments on fresh ways for women to do theatre so that it does not become ossified and does not become a mere entertainment event?

PS: I have always felt it unfair that women writers are so consistently asked to see the world through "a woman's eyes" and to comment on gender politics. All creative people are artists and craftspersons first. There are notable exceptions, of course, like Mahashweta Devi, whose activism is integral to her creative work. As for me, I believe that a readership, an audience, ask to be engaged in the creative construct that is before them. Entertainment need not be mindless or empty of thought and intent. To my mind, a novel or a play that is disturbing has fulfilled something of what the writer would want; that which is boring is dead. In this context, you may like to look at *Samara's Song*, the last play in my book, which, if I may say so myself, has been prescient. The play is about a flawed and corrupt political leadership of a dictatorial "democracy" against which the people rise in rebellion. Barely weeks after it premiered, we saw the turmoil in Tunisia, Egypt, Libya, Yemen, Syria. . . .

Major issues raised: questions to ask of gender in world theatre

What counts as feminism? What are the definitions of gender at stake? What interventions is the structure of theatre making into discussions of gender?

The diversity of Western feminism and the postcolonial feminist critique serve as reminders that not all "feminist" projects are the same. Sengupta's insistence that she not be labelled a feminist emphasizes this point even more. There is no "one-size-fits-all feminism." Some playwrights are concerned with the types of roles women are given in scripts. Other theatre theorists are concerned with the dynamics of production within the theatre world and the amount of power given to the men or women. Other playwrights and theorists are concerned with dismantling the structures of a phallocentric theatre to leave space for women. Still others wish to challenge the very notion of "woman" and its distinction from "man." All these projects might fall under the broad umbrella of feminism.

It is important to recognize the differences between ideas of feminism without assuming that one is universally better / more appropriate. Potiki, Liking, and Sengupta insist on the specificity of what they are doing to the contexts in which they work. Advancement for women will look different depending on where women are at a particular moment in time and space. This advancement does not necessarily follow a single linear, causal (phallocentric) notion of progress. One does not have to move though the same stages in the same order to reach some preconceived notion of enlightened feminism.

Thus with each new text, it is important to consider the array of possible goals suggested above to determine what statement about gender the play is trying to make. Answering this question well requires firm attention to the specific definitions of gender in the specific context of the play and the relative position of men and women in the society in question. Oppression takes many, many forms, and feminism has a distinct response to each of these forms. What gender concepts (about men or women) are being fought for or against in this particular play? Are these economic, social, sexual, literary, performative, or something else entirely?

After answering this question, it is necessary to consider what techniques – in plot, in structure, in character – the play is using to get across these points. The plight of down-trodden women might be shown in order to elicit a particular response, and in contrast strong independent, successful women might be shown to elicit a response. Linear plots might be altered, collaboration might be emphasized, or language might be restructured. Knowing the specific goals of the play allows all aspects of the text to be read as potential avenues of resistance to or reinforcement of gender norms.

Part II
Cultural and literary history

Chapter 8

Latin America and the Caribbean

> They have no language of their own . . . they have no idea of country, and no pride of race that the Caribbean is a non-place with non-people.
> Anthony Trollope, a British novelist, speaking of Jamaica in 1859

Critics characterize Latin American literature and Caribbean literature, separately or collectively, as resistant (to the West, to hegemony or normalization of any kind). Placing these two distinct literatures and cultures next to each other allows for finer distinctions to be made about what exactly is being resisted, how this resistance functions, and what "positive" (in the sense of affirming something rather than resisting something) aspects of these literatures emerge. It is far too easy to apply an easy wash of postcolonial theory – e.g. every formerly colonized writer is concerned that language might carry something of empire with it – without recognizing the multiplicity of techniques used to address similar (although not nearly identical) circumstances.

As with most of the regions in this book, the various nations contained in this region could be part of larger or smaller groupings – or, indeed, other groupings depending on what aspects of history are the subject of debate. The Caribbean has direct connections to Africa and Europe. The politics surrounding indigeneity vary throughout Central and South America. In terms of spatial metaphors, Caribbean literature and literary theory tends to focus on ideas of islands, while borders are much more prominent in Latin American work. On the other hand, the colonial histories of both parts of this region overlap. Languages, people, and cultural practices move in an ever-changing mix throughout the region. There is a tendency, when looking at a given location, to take for granted the way things worked out there, e.g. of course the response to colonial oppression is to do whatever this location did in terms of language usage, literary development, cultural hybridity, etc. The contrasts between the cultural and literary life in Latin America and the Caribbean highlight the extent to which similar histories may lead to substantially different conclusions.

The names of these regions give some indication of one challenge faced when writing about their history. Spanish America refers to the land from (roughly) present-day Mexico to the Southern tip of Chile and Argentina, much of which was colonized by Spain. Latin America refers to the same geographic region, but recognizes that the Spanish no longer maintain colonial control. Neither name for the region takes into account the Incas, Mayans, or Aztecs who lived there prior to European colonization. The Caribbean is named for the Carib people, one of several groups who lived there. Of course, the Caribbean is also referred to as the West Indies, which serves as a reminder that Christopher Columbus' European discovery of this land shapes its history. Because so much of what we know about both regions comes from the colonial era and later, it is easy to forget the long, if relatively undocumented, pre-Colombian history.

Latin America is home to the legacy of the Incas, Aztecs, and Mayans who developed powerful civilizations long before European colonization in the fifteenth and sixteenth centuries. During the colonial era, the Spanish firmly dominated in the region, although the Portuguese, the British, the Dutch, and the French all had some degree of power at one point or another. At various points in history different regions have become the crossroads for trade for many major powers, and the Caribbean served such a role from the fourteenth century to the sixteenth century, acting as an entry point to most of the Americas. Its culture and its history reflect this variety of influences: common factors in this history include trading, exploration, colonization, slave trade, and enslavement of indigenous peoples. Like the Middle East, traces of all the cultures that have trade routes through the Caribbean are visible alongside indigenous cultures.

Major historical threads

Compared to many other indigenous peoples in North America, relatively little is known about the history of the Caribs, the Tainos, or the Arawak (indigenous groups in the Caribbean) in part due to the degree to which their culture was wiped out by Columbus and other Europeans. Much of the history that does survive was written by Europeans during the colonial era, and it is full of obvious racial and ethnic biases. We are not even certain about the degree to which these three names reflect actual differences in ethnicities on the islands as opposed to Europe's ideas about the native inhabitants. The idea of cannibalism (which contemporary anthropology dismisses as not having been a standard practice in any society), for instance, emerges strongly in European writing about the Caribs. Unhelpful Amerindians on the islands were referred to as "Caribs," and Caribs were assumed to be cannibals. While there is no evidence that cannibalism was practiced on the islands, this bit of "history" is one the islands still struggle to correct. All three groups are likely related to Amerindians from the mainland, although the nature of the relationship is unclear (e.g. exiles, emigrants, explorers, etc.). Based on scant archeological evidence, the Caribbean islands are considered to have been inhabited by humans only relatively recently (late Neolithic or sixth millennium BCE), but information from before the thirteenth century is scarce.

In the long history of Europe improving and expanding its trade routes, it was inevitable that they would reach the Caribbean; and geographic factors insured that, once Columbus landed, these islands became regular ports of call for traders, explorers, and conquerors headed to the mainland. From the late 1400s through the early 1500s the Spanish settled on a few of the larger Caribbean islands. Similarly, once "discovered" the Americas themselves had to be explored, and the Spanish rapidly colonized from the Atlantic coast to the interior of Latin America. The colonies used Amerindian labor to produce agricultural products to supply sailors and for export. The islanders proved remarkably susceptible to European germs and, alongside the harsh conditions imposed on them by the Spanish, these germs led to the near extinction of the island Amerindians. The Incas and the Mayans actually mounted armed resistance, which, while ultimately unsuccessful, protected some of their legacy. On the islands, Spain cynically coped with the loss of its workforce by importing Africans, and on the mainland, the subjugated peoples worked in poor conditions (notably the silver mines, which subjected miners to harsh conditions and poisonous chemicals used in the mining and processing of silver).

Indigenous groups in Latin America also suffered at the hands of the colonists, but more records of these civilizations survive than do of the Caribbean. The Aztecs, from central Mexico, initially allied themselves with the Spanish, but the Spanish later violated the alliance. Nonetheless, the period of cooperation led to a significant portion of Aztec culture surviving to the present day, and, indeed, being incorporated into mainstream Mexican culture. Further to the south, the last major Mayan city fell to the Spanish in 1697. The Mayan culture survives in large communities, but these communities are relatively isolated from political and social life in their respective countries, except when economics bring them into conflict (e.g. the use of the rainforest). The Inca, in Chile and Peru, were decimated by the Spanish, and while many descendants of the Inca live in poverty today, the Incan culture and language are still readily visible.

While struggling with and / or eradicating the natives, Spain also had to fight off its European rivals. The naval aspects of this struggle grew particularly heated. Both the British and the Dutch contested the islands, notably with the raids instigated by England's Sir Francis Drake. While Spanish is still the dominant language in Latin America, parts of the Caribbean use English instead of, or in addition to, Spanish.

In the Caribbean, the largest threat to Spanish power came from the hundreds of violent uprisings of the enslaved people. In 1804, famously, Haiti became the first – and, indeed, still the only – nation to see a slave revolt that led directly to a new government and to the end of slavery in that nation. While historians term it the only "successful" slave uprising, this is somewhat misleading as it implies that all other slave resistances have "failed" – that they haven't accomplished anything. Whatever the case may be, Haiti's revolution stands as a historical marker. Other Caribbean countries gained independence in the years following Haiti. The groups who claimed this independence were varied. In some cases, there was a large group of Spanish settlers who were part of the independence movement. In other countries, like Haiti, the movement was led by enslaved Africans. In others, the movement was hybrid. As with Africa, a large majority of Caribbean countries gained their independence in the 1960s, more than 100 years after their neighbors in Haiti.

Latin American independence, like American independence, was largely the former Spanish fighting the Spanish, rather than the enslaved peoples rising up. In Brazil, the Prince Regent of Portugal actually managed to be named the emperor of newly independent Brazil in 1822. The wars of independence took place in the late 1700s and early 1800s, with Bolivia's independence in 1824 being the last (although Bolivia first declared independence in 1809). The wars are marked with a number of hero figures who form a large part of the popular historical narrative. For example, the Mexican War of Independence lasted from 1810 to 1821 and Jose Maria Morelos was a Roman Catholic priest who united various armed groups against Spanish rule. Francisco de Miranda (1750–1816) fought for Venezuelan independence and attempted to create an independent, unified Latin America. Similarly, Simon Bolivar helped in multiple fronts of the Latin American wars of independence, assisting in the liberation of Venezuela, Colombia, Ecuador, and Peru.

The modern histories of the Caribbean and of Latin America are more substantially different than their colonial histories. Latin America had a "boom" period in the mid-twentieth century, when economies and culture were doing relatively well. The Caribbean has remained largely economically depressed throughout the twentieth century.

Both Latin America and the Caribbean have had no shortage of charismatic leaders who might also be called dictators (although many writers use such labels with skepticism in that they are impacted by how the U.S. views the politics of a given leader): Castro, Papa Doc, Juan Peron.

During the 1960's boom period, Latin American literature gained an international audience. This also corresponds to the growing influence of Latin America on world culture more broadly. The 1970s, particularly in Brazil but across the region, saw some of the above-mentioned dictators institute harsh censorship policies. This, combined with a series of economic difficulties curtailed the literary boom.

While the Caribbean has stayed relatively free of large-scale conflicts in the later part of the twentieth century, Latin America has had a series of military events ranging from full-scale wars to semi-secret American operations.

From 1974 to 1983, Argentina's military government conducted what has become known as the Dirty War in which the military systematically hunted down and killed or incarcerated people with communist ties. Mexico had its own Dirty War during the 1960s and 1970s during which a number of students were killed. In Nicaragua, the U.S. government funded the Contras, a loosely organized network of rebels fighting against the Sandinista government. The Sandinistas, as a large political party, had many factions, but broadly speaking, they were anti-U.S., pro-Marxist, and pro-education. Armed conflicts over drugs in Colombia have been ongoing through much of the twentieth century.

In many of these conflicts, the ideological differences over communism play a role. The Zapatistas (who made their first public declaration in 1994), and the Zapatismo movement more generally, is also characteristic of another major thread in the modern history of Latin America and the Caribbean. The Zapatistas are a revolutionary group in Mexico seeking to overthrow the current government and replace it with a government more supportive of the workers. Zapatismo as an idea has also spread to many other parts of the region, either formally or informally – there is a struggle between what might broadly be referred to as communism or socialism and dictatorship and / or democracy. In some cases, like Cuba, a dictator also shared some of the same communist aims as the Zapatistas. The relationship of the government to workers remains a point of contention in almost every country in the region, either in terms of active cooperation or heated antagonism.

Despite these conflicts, the Latin American economy, as a whole, has stabilized in the later part of the twentieth century. And crime rates in several major cities have dropped substantially. Both Latin America and the Caribbean have rapidly expanded their tourist industry and are actively marketing themselves to the world as resort destinations with a rich history.

General literary and cultural theory

Hybridity, multiculturalism, and the nation

Latin America and the Caribbean both contain within themselves a number of different ethnic groups, but they have very different ways of conceptualizing the place of these groups within the nation. In brief, the Caribbean tends to focus on hybridization – the merging of cultures into a single, new form. Latin America tends to focus on mestizaje, in which cultural elements of a variety of cultures are incorporated into the dominant culture. In both these cases, there is some idea of national culture and an insistence on the distinctive features of this culture.

In many parts of the world, various ethnicities have fought against each other, conquered each other, and worked hard to peacefully coexist. There are a variety of multicultural practices out there. Some countries argue that each culture should be accorded respect and, as such, tend to celebrate differences. Other versions of multiculturalism tend to shift the focus to what is shared in common. In its history, each Caribbean nation had to decide how to go about dealing with the various groups that had settled there. African, European, and Amerindian influences are all part of the islands. Rather than establishing an idea of multiculturalism that kept things separate or focused on what was already in common, the Caribbean chose to create and is celebrated for a new, hybrid culture that was made up of parts of all of these cultures and influences. On some islands, like Cuba, the hybrid culture has formed into something distinctly Cuban and relatively stable. In other places, like Martinique, cultural identity is still relatively flexible. Regardless of the degree to which the current culture is flexible, there is a general trend toward celebrating hybridity and the many pieces that make up a given culture in the Caribbean.

The Caribbean is marked by hybridity and ethnogenesis – it has created a set of new cultures by blending the old. In the epigraph that opened this chapter, Trollope denies the idea that newly created cultures can have value, dismissing the Caribbean as a non-place filled with non-people. During his Nobel Prize acceptance speech, Saint Lucian author Derek Walcott, one of the best known Caribbean writers, celebrates precisely the same qualities that Trollope claims negate the Caribbean, noting the freedom and creativity that springs from such a situation. For Walcott, being linked to many places but bound by none allows the writer creative space. These same threads continually reemerge in the history below – a history of tragedy and regrowth: a loss of identity and a creation of new identities. The Caribbean was part of the new world – full of exciting possibilities, indescribable in terms of the old, and, at the same moment, perpetually pushed toward being a colonial duplicate of the old world.

V.S. Naipaul (b. 1932), a Nobel Prize-winning Trinidadian novelist, writes about this idea in terms of the fluidity of the absent presence. In other words, he finds some cultural freedom in the fact that the Caribbean is figured negatively – as not nation, not people, not ethnicity. While all of these "nots" are attempts to dismiss the Caribbean, they also don't subject the region to the limitations imposed by a specific national identity. On the other hand, the Caribbean shows a strong sense of regional and national identity in much of its writing. C.L.R. James (1901–1989), a journalist and historian writing at an earlier moment of heady independence comments that "[t]he good life is that community between the individual and the state; the sense that he belongs to the state and the state belongs to him [...] the citizen's alive when he feels that he himself in its own national community is overcoming difficulty" (James 1965, p. 6). In between Naipaul's anti-nationalistic stance and James' optimism, figures like Édouard Glissant call for a reconceptualization of identity to move the concept of nation toward the lived experiences of the masses and away from the private lives of the elites. One manifestation of these alternative notions of identity was the brief existence of the West Indian Federation, which, like the pan-African movement, attempts to find extra-national modes of affiliation and identity.

As Trollope was writing about the lack of identity in the Caribbean, most of Latin America had regained its independence from Europe and was taking some of the same cultural features found in the Caribbean and reshaping them into new national identities. Unlike the Caribbean, Latin America has had a long-standing dominant culture, based in Spanish traditions. Through most of the twentieth century, Spanish remained the preferred language for literary endeavor and also provided a unity across the region, despite the presence of a number of other (European, African, American) languages in the region.

While the Spanish culture may have been dominant, it did not remain static. Mestizaje, like Caribbean hybridity, refers to the blending of multiple cultures and multiple biological features into a single culture. As the independence movements started, this idea of mixture was seen as a way of making Spanish culture Latin American rather than European. Jose Marti (1853–1895), a revolutionary and writer, specifically points out that all elements of Latin American culture (specifically indigenous ones) should be included in this mixture. Nonetheless, recent writers have begun to worry about this assimilative nature – incorporating cultural difference into official culture reduces the autonomy of said culture. Unlike the Caribbean context, which has an ongoing fascination with its own fluid hybridity, mestizaje tends to have an "official" connotation, suggesting formal policies and static attitudes toward mixture. This is the subject of an ongoing debate and the above statements can provoke a rather intense reaction depending on one's current analysis of mestizaje.

Part of this debate lies in a discomfort with the idea of nation as a whole. While the independence movement proudly declared its nationalism, later writers became concerned that the newly formed nations were, in fact, limiting the Latin American people. Carlos Mariátegui wrote in 1928 that "The nation itself is an abstraction, an allegory, a myth, that does not correspond to a constant and precise, scientifically determinable, reality" (1963). As Latin America struggled for its independence, nationalism was, however, a major thread in literature. After the struggles for independence subsided, writers like Mariátegui became critical of nationalism, and the criticism formed a backdrop for twentieth-century writing.

When looking at literature and art from Latin America and the Caribbean, what notions of culture are at play? Is culture a mixture of several groups? Is this mixture equal, or have some cultures been subsumed by others? Is culture a static, limiting notion or a fluid, free one – or, conversely, is culture strong enough to declare an identity or is it weakly fluid and incapable of forming a rallying point?

History from below, modernity from outside: Issues of time and identity

The issue of cultural blending within national identity is directly related to issues of history and the idea of the "modern." The Caribbean has made active efforts to reformulate the way history in general, and specifically the history of the nation, is written. Latin America, on the other hand, is invested in rewriting the ways in which nations become "modern" or participate in modernity. Since many of the actual technologies associated with modernity come from Europe, there is a marked tendency to treat other modernities as derivative. Latin American literature is often concerned with reclaiming parts of the modernist legacy as their own. The Caribbean rewriting of history and Latin America's rewriting of modernity are both ways of restructuring knowledge – or finding ways of thinking about the world that make sense in a given society. Knowledge is not a one-size-fits-all product.

With the exception of China and Japan, Western philosophy has often dismissed other parts of the world as being without "history." Indeed, even in this book, I have repeatedly noted that the early history of Africa, the Caribbean, and the Pacific Islands is not well known. The academy has tended to privilege a particular style of written history – prose-based, non-mythical, "factual," based on direct observation or credible reports – over other modes of history (oral, archeological, artistically rendered) and other ways of writing (e.g. poetic, mythical, fictionalized). It is thus important to note that one of the major threads of twentieth-century historiography (the study of how we write and think about history) started in the Caribbean.

This type of historical writing is often referred to as history from below or history of the people. C.L.R. James' work, *The Black Jacobins* (1938) tells the history of the Haitian Revolution and does so by attempting to take a variety of different viewpoints into account. His book is a reminder that history is not one-sided and that there is no "factual" location from which to report things in an unbiased manner. While James incorporates a variety of viewpoints, he focuses on the revolutionary contributions of the native Haitians, connecting the contribution to the French Revolution.

This book was part of a change in the way history was thought and written about. It was one of the first times a history had been written about Africans or Amerindians that treated these people as participants in a historical process rather than as objects of study. While the idea of a pluralized history that takes multiple viewpoints into account is accepted today, it would be hard to overstress the importance of C.L.R. James' revolutionary work in this arena.

In Latin America a similar issue emerges in the line between popular and official culture. For instance, "worker's theatre" was a phenomenon across Latin America in the latter half of the twentieth century. These were publicly performed, relatively straightforward plays designed to address the problems faced by the working class. They were plays directly connected to the people and often even devised (if not written) by people outside the traditional artistic sphere. Few of these plays were written, and, as such, they have fallen off the literary and theatrical terrain. On the other hand, more elite forms of theatre and literature have survived, partly because they were written and partly because many Latin American governments recognized the value of such literature. Much of the censorship discussed above was aimed at anything that could be considered art-from-below.

History and art-from-below are collective activities. Other forms of theatre are often written by a single person, directed by a single person, and potentially read in a solitary way when not performed. The tension between the two sides of artistic production is a tension between individual and collective, which is, itself, a marker of Latin America's debates over modernity. There is an inherent contradiction in early Spanish American literature that at once wanted to celebrate the individual and the glory of nature and lay out a firm plan for an ordered society. The tension between the individual and the group is visible all the way through to the twenty-first century, and it is amplified, along the way, by leaders like Peron who directly ask their people to sacrifice individual desires for the good of the nation. This tension also readily fed into political debates about the place of communism, capitalism, and socialism in the region.

The nation, as a marker of modernity, requires a collective identity. On the other hand, part of what ushered modernity into Latin America is the idea of a Romantic, rugged individualism. The list of war heroes mentioned previously is an indication of this strand of individuality. Modernity in Latin America is torn between resistant individuals and participation in a collective.

Who is constructing Latin American and Caribbean theatre? How is power shared in this construction? How is knowledge created and disseminated by these theatres?

Tidalectics, borders, and new literary forms

It is a central premise of this book that each region has created a variety of theatres and that each requires their own approach. Both the Caribbean and Latin America have written theories about why their literature and theatre might be distinctive. In both cases, geographic issues arise. In the Caribbean, the idea of the island emerges as a way of explaining the distinctive features of the literature. In Latin America, the idea of borders (and later checkpoints) emerges as an explanatory metaphor. The idea that the physicality of a region might influence its literature is an interesting one and certainly suggests that strict attention be paid to the physical setting of novels and plays in this context.

The idea that a unique location would require a unique way of thinking about history has shaped much of the fiction of the Caribbean as well. The idea that space and the organization of space might influence writing is not unique to the Caribbean context, but it is an overriding artistic concern there.

Jamaica Kincaid, Kamau Braithwaite, and Derek Walcott have all written about the ways in which island culture has shaped their creative output. Islands are isolated, cut off from other things by water. At the same time, the Caribbean islands were hubs for trade – the same water that isolates them connects them to everything else that touches an ocean. On a small island, one is forced to be aware of the rhythms of the ocean.

One quintessential type of story in Western narrative and theatre involves the journey of a hero, often a young hero growing up. There is something about taking a journey and growing as a person or progressing as a group that is linked artistically in the Western tradition. Caribbean authors wishing to address the theme of growth or progress must find different metaphors given the limited travel space available on the island. When Kamau Braithwaite discusses "tidalectics," the artistic ways of dealing with living on an island, he is referring to these sorts of issues.

This leads to a discussion of the idea of exile and return. If islands are both isolated and connected, then it makes sense that there would be contradictory impulses to leave and to stay. To leave an island, however, is to expose oneself to a wholly different world with different spaces, different languages, and different literary and social traditions. If one returns to the island after such a trip, the island will seem different by virtue of having seen other parts of the world. These logics of exile, departure, and return can be found across parts of Caribbean writing.

It is interesting to note that the image of the island cuts both ways. In 1944 Jorge Manach wrote about the *"conciencia de isla"* or insular consciousness that Cuba must develop in order to have an identity. Cuba must become aware of itself as an island – as separate from Spanish (and later U.S. and Soviet) influence. On the other hand, Antonio Pedreira refers to the tragic isolation of his island as the cause of its slowly developing culture. The idea of "island" literature, culture, and society is absolutely a part of Caribbean identity, but what precisely the "island" means has changed over time and between islands.

The metaphor of the island as an explanatory device is almost omnipresent in Caribbean literature. The idea of the border in Latin American literature is not quite so widespread. Often, it is the border between the U.S. and Mexico that receives the most attention (both politically and as metaphor), but the various checkpoints, border crossings, and disputed boundaries across Latin America certainly make borders an issue elsewhere as well. Gloria Anzaldúa has written eloquently on the idea that every border is actually a fluid space of transition. Rather than thinking of borders as a line, she thinks of them as their own space / place. Since the border exists between two worlds, people on the border are not governed or protected by either set of rules. The border is a space of possibility. At the same time, however, the border also forms a clear (if somewhat permeable) line that limits the movement of people and ideas.

As with the Caribbean claim that island theatre is different from other theatres, Latin America has a number of genres that are particularly concerned with issues of borders and border crossings. For instance, costumbrista, which might loosely be translated as travel writing, was big in the 1830s and exhibits the tension between a modern, scientific study of the world and a simultaneous fetishization and fear of the natural world and the indigenous peoples that the writers associated with this natural world. These narratives range from heavily scientific to more journalistic in style, but all involve travelling to and documenting of a new location. They are different from the epic journey narrative mentioned earlier inasmuch as they are not focused on events but instead, on cataloguing difference.

There is a profusion of different genres that are unique to Latin America. Some, like costumbrista, are clearly related to geographic concerns. Others may take shape for other reasons. When considering spatial metaphors as a way of approaching literatures, it is important not to use these metaphors to erase differences. Instead, this idea should be used to pose a specific question about what metaphorical value that setting of a given piece might have, if any, and then to consider the geographic conditions of the production of the text as well.

In what ways are the specific geographies of the region worked into theatre? Do performances treat these geographies as something to be resisted or embraced?

Languages and orality

The issue of language is one that arises in Africa and India as well, but it takes a distinctive form in the Caribbean. In most sub-Saharan African countries there are dozens of languages spoken, and there is a tension between "imperial" languages (like English), dominant native languages (like Gikuyu in Kenya), and minority native languages (like Khana in Nigeria). Similarly, India has a profusion of languages spoken in different regions by different groups of people. South Africa, India, and other countries have chosen to adopt multiple official national languages, choosing from among the vast array of possibilities. Other countries have a single national language despite the array of languages spoken by their populaces.

The Caribbean has treated language differently. Kamua Braithwaite describes a general recognition that European languages share syntactical structures which differ from the African and Native Caribbean linguistic structures that are also present in the Caribbean. Rather than seeing a tension between the languages, however, Braithwaite describes the Caribbean process of developing a voice as one of picking and choosing elements of each language that suit the needs of the Caribbean.

Creolization refers to the process of mixing and blending (in this case of languages). The various Creoles spoken in the Caribbean are explicitly not "dialects." A dialect refers to a minor variant of a language, generally spoken by a minority of the people. Dialects always exist as secondary manifestations of a language. Braithwaite and others insist that the creolization of language in the Caribbean has created a new language – one that may have taken bits of other languages but is nonetheless independent from these languages.

Braithwaite is particularly vehement in insisting that Creoles are not "bad" English, but represent a new set of rules, syntaxes, and artistic possibilities. This is important as many Creoles adopt the vocabulary of the "imperial" language but use syntaxes of the native languages (or invented syntaxes). Thus an English or French speaker would be able to understand much of what was said in a Creole, but would find the grammar unfamiliar. To say that a Creole is not "bad English" is to remind readers that these languages have their own, stable set of rules.

Creoles raise interesting questions when it comes to translation. Since many of the words are already in "other" languages, they don't require direct translation, but, as seen by Braithwaite's arguments against the idea of "bad English," readers might assume something about the sophistication of the writing if it is left in the Creole. On the other hand, translating a Creole into English loses the hybridity that is so important to Caribbean identity and language use.

These Creoles exist side-by-side with languages like English and Spanish that are readily associated with "official" discourse even when the government recognizes a multitude of languages. Even English and Spanish, however, do not function in exactly the same way. Braithwaite has developed a theory of "nation language" and argues that:

> Reading is an isolated, individualistic expression. The oral tradition, on the other hand, makes demands not only on the poet but also on the audience to complete the community: the noise and sounds that the poet makes are responded to by the audience and are returned to him. Hence we have the creation of a continuum where the meaning truly resides. And this total expression comes about when people live in the open air, because people live in conditions of poverty, because people come from a historical experience where they had to rely on their own breath patterns rather than on paraphernalia like books and museums. They had to depend on immanence, the power within themselves, rather than the technology outside themselves.
> (Braithwaite 1993, p. 273)

A national language is one that the government has declared to be the language (or one of the languages) of official business. The "nation language" on the other hand suggests a "total expression" in which cultural elements shape and are shaped by language as it is used by people. This sort of language might go beyond national borders or exist in smaller communities within those borders. "Nation" in this sense signals the idea of a shared set of values and not the boundaries of a legal state.

The idea of translation is also key to many aspects of Caribbean literature. Since many of the citizens of the islands are multilingual and code-switch between various languages within a given sentence as needed, the idea of translation is somewhat different in this context. It is not a matter of attempting to move the content and form of a text from one language to another language, but, instead, a process of figuring out how best to express this content in the array of possible languages. As Gustavo Perez Firmat points out, this sort of intralingual translation does not necessarily seek fidelity to the original, and, indeed, is often celebrated for its novel ways of expressing ideas.

Criollismo is the broad term for literature that celebrates writing in "nation languages" or the distinctive Creoles of a given location. In its early forms (e.g. Jose Antonio Ramos or Jorge Manach in the 1920s and 1930s), this mode of literature often focused on themes of man's engagement with nature. Scholars are now identifying a critical resurgence of criollismo that is also used to critique traditional cultures and to question the nature of modern life. As with many of the movements discussed here, the use of Creoles in writing can alternate between celebration and critique – or even be both at once.

In contrast, Latin America is dominated by the Spanish language, which was the language of the colonizers. Spanish is the official language in most of the countries and is, therefore, a language of power, whatever other purposes it might be put to. The native languages still exist, although they are not as commonly spoken and are even less frequently used in contemporary artistic production. There are several pieces of orature (orally transmitted literature) that survive from the precolonial days, but these are often left out of discussions of contemporary literary development.

The *Popol Vuh*, for instance, is an orally transmitted Mayan sacred text that is actually structured, in part, as the retelling of the actions of a performance. Some theatre histories mention this as an early piece of theatre, but then leave it relatively unconnected to later theatrical developments. A line can be drawn between the oral transmission of the Mayan text to contemporary performance, including dances, religious rituals, mime, and other spectacles. Such performance is often associated with the indigenous people, whereas theatre is strongly associated with the former colonial powers. Certainly one can speak about theatre and performance in India or Africa in the same way, but Latin American writers accentuate the tension between these categories more prominently. Curiously, however, many of the Latin American festivals include theatre among their other elements. While there may be an intellectual and historical tension, the practical distinction can at times recede.

Unlike Australia and New Zealand where there has been an upsurge of indigenous writings recently, the indigenous literature from Latin America is largely in the distant past (although given the concept of mestizaje, it could be argued that all of Latin America still expresses the indigenous parts of its heritage). That being said, since the 1990s, there has been a Mayan theatre movement, albeit one that has yet to draw extensive critical attention (due, in no small part, to the fact that little of it is translated into Spanish and even less into English, thus severely limiting the number of potential readers).

The difference between Latin America's and the Caribbean's use of language is striking given that both regions have connections to Africa, to Europe, and to native culture. Both were colonized. Both resisted colonization. Both value some version of blending. When these two language situations are considered next to India, South Africa, or Nigeria, the vast array of choices made (or forced upon) cultures in terms of their language usage becomes apparent. Playwrights and performers in all these regions can manipulate these language politics to a variety of effects.

The empire writes back

Unlike the other sections in this chapter, this one will only address the Caribbean. The idea of "the empire writing back" in these terms originates with Salman Rushdie, and not in the Caribbean, but the Caribbean has been particularly concerned with its relationship to creative and academic pursuits of the former colonial powers (primarily France, Spain, and England in this case). The idea of an ongoing, somewhat antagonistic, relationship to Europe can be seen in the "translation" or adaptation of various European texts by Caribbean writers in which the writer uses the adaptation to critique European ideas. As importantly, the former empire also writes back in terms of theory, insisting on not only their ability to produce literature and theatre, but also on their ability to analyze this artistic production. For instance, in several essays in *Roots*, Kamua Braithwaite insists that European methods of criticism have not, thus far, been able to deal with Caribbean literature. He argues that Europeans have an idea of culture as a single, monolithic thing rather than a fragmented, diverse thing, and, moreover, that they have a single concept of history into which they insert this idea of culture. Since, as discussed above, Caribbean literature and theatre explores fracturing, multiplicity, hybridity, and plurality, this literature will always seem strange when viewed through European lenses. He argues that not only is Caribbean literature worth studying, but that the theoretical writings produced by Caribbean authors are worth considering. This is an insistence on not just being an object of study but, instead, an active participant in this study.

While this idea has been in circulation in the Caribbean context since the 1980s, there is still an imbalance in the use of Western and world criticism. Many scholars treat Western criticism as universally useful and, if they deal with world theory at all, treat this theory as only relevant to its specific context and in need of supplementation from Western theory.

Like Wole Soyinka's insistence on the distinctive qualities of African theatre, this Caribbean insistence on the idea that Caribbean literary criticism requires Caribbean theory is a move that accentuates difference. The Caribbean seems not to have gone through the mimicry of European styles that subtends some African and Asian cultures in the mid-twentieth century. It always insisted on its own difference in a way that distinguishes it from other postcolonial contexts. To be sure, these other contexts also insist upon their difference, but that insistence is also often mixed with the remnants of a colonial, imitative desire.

Significant playwrights / movements in the Caribbean

One trend in Caribbean literature is the adaptation of classical Western texts. Aime Cesaire (Martinique, 1913–2008) is one of the few Caribbean playwrights to become part of the canon of Western theatre. His adaptation of *The Tempest* forms one of the case studies in this book. Félix Morisseau-Leroy (Haiti, 1912–1998) translates Sophocles' *Antigone* into Haitian Creole. This work is "closer" to the original than Cesaire's work is to *The Tempest*. In 1975, several years after Cesaire's *A Tempest*, Patrick Chamoiseau, also a Martiniquan, wrote an adaptation of *Antigone*, which, like Cesaire's work, is critical of French colonialism, but which also emphasizes the revolutionary potential of small actions taken by the people of Martinique. In doing so, it paints Antigone as a heroic figure. Jean Rhys (1890–1979) is from Dominica and is best known for her critique of colonial influences in her adaptation of *Jane Eyre*, *Wide Sargasso Sea*. These four writers represent part of the range of possibilities of adaptation and translation that color the hybrid terrain of Caribbean theatre.

Derek Walcott (Saint Lucia, b. 1930) won a Nobel Prize for his poetry and drama. Walcott's work is expansive enough to be difficult to characterize, although many of his plays celebrate the hybrid culture of the Caribbean through an examination of myths, landscapes, and languages. He founded the Trinidad Theatre Workshop, which produces both new and canonical plays from around the world.

Eugène Dervain is a Martiniquan with Ivorian citizenship, in other words someone from the Caribbean who immigrated to the Ivory Coast in Africa. Both his theatre and his biography serve as a reminder that the Caribbean maintains connections to Africa (as well as the European connections discussed above). Elie Stephenson (French Guyana, b. 1944) incorporates the idea of hybridity in his theatre with the characters in *O Mayouri* shifting back and forth between French and Creole. Indeed, it would be challenging to locate a piece of Caribbean theatre that did not, in some fashion, address the issue of hybridity and intercultural contact in some manner (e.g. critical or celebratory).

The Cambridge Companion to Africa and Caribbean Theatre provides a brief sketch of the life and works of the most prominent playwrights from each island, only a small handful of which have been discussed here. This chapter is certainly not exhaustive, and it leaves out the creative work done by actor-director-producers (a common category in the Caribbean) like Yvonne Brewster (Jamaica, b. 1938) who have shaped contemporary staging practices and popularized the work of European, African, and Caribbean playwrights. Gertrudis Gomez de Avellaneda (Cuba, 1814–1873) is one of the first female dramatists to gain widespread recognition in any of the regions discussed here, and her work receives relatively little recognition in scholarship.

Frantz Fanon (1925–1961) is the Martiniquan founder of postcolonial theory. His writings shape the way generations of scholars have thought about language, identity, and nation in the postcolonial world. While his writing is not literary theory, it is, nonetheless essential for gaining a more detailed understanding of the world in which Caribbean literary theory exists.

Roberto Fernandez Retamar (b. 1930) is a Cuban poet, essayist, and literary and cultural theorist who addresses contemporary issues. In one essay, he returns to the Caribbean fascination with the process of adaptation and uses Caliban as a metaphor for the assumptions Europe makes about the absence of Latin American culture. He refers to a pride of place among the working class people of Cuba and a strong identification of culture with political struggle.

Significant playwrights / movements in Latin America

Internationally, Latin American literature is frequently associated with magical realism. The term "magical realism" is often misused to refer to any literary deployment of fantastical elements. Argentinian Jorge Luis Borges (1899–1986) wrote a number of short stories and essays on literary theory. His discussions of magical realism lay forth a set of specific criteria, some of which are enigmatic. Broadly speaking, the magical elements in this genre should be expansions of the real – they take elements of reality that are strange and push them to a new level of strangeness. The general world remains in the realm of mundane reality with only a few elements shifted. While there is some critical debate over this, it has been argued that magical realism does not create estrangement through its strangeness, that, in fact, it is a way of coming to terms with the distinctive nature of the contemporary Latin American world, and that people living in this world would recognize their reality even in the strangeness (in contrast to works like Kafka's that use magical elements to demonstrate that man has become disconnected from his world). Two primary examples of magical realism are Isabel Allende (Chilean American, b. 1942) and Gabriel Garcia Marquez (Colombian, 1927–2014).

Magical realism is one of the modernist moves in Latin American literature, although one more associated with novels than with plays. Within theatre in Latin America, the modernist movement begins with writers like Florencio Sanchez (Uruguayan, 1875–1910) who experiment with both realism and naturalism. By the time of Xavier Villaurrutia (Mexico, 1903–1950), modernism had become more experimental, incorporating variations of absurdism and other "non-realistic" techniques.

While literary theatre continues to be a dominant form around Latin America, Brazil specifically has challenged this trend by developing a distinctive set of comic genres. The Brazilian Comedy Theatre (founded 1948) performs all manner of distinctive comic plays, sketches, and acts. Brazil's ongoing privileging of comedic genres over others places it in a somewhat unique category in terms of world theatre, where tragedy is often the most visible mode. Oswald de Andrade (Brazil, 1890–1954) incorporates many aspects of popular ritual into his staging, including some bits and pieces from African traditions.

Many Latin American playwrights express political arguments in their plays – regardless of the form of the play. Jose Ignacio Cabrujas (Venezuela, 1937–1995) is an example of one playwright who doubts the rosy nationalism of the post-independence era.

Many playwrights from this region have gained international prominence (e.g. Manuel Puig (Argentina), Ariel Dorfman (Chile), and Aristides Vargas (Ecuador)). The UK's CASA Latin American Theatre Festival is a great resource for tracking current developments in the region.

Chapter 9

Sub-Saharan Africa

As I have travelled through Africa over the years, I am repeatedly struck by how massive and diverse it is. Books addressing the continent will always start with the shocking statistics about the size of Africa compared to Europe or America – and yet, despite its geographic and cultural range, ideas of pan-Africanism have remained strong. The idea of "Africa" as a whole is a modern one, but from its earliest known history Africans traded with one another across great distances. There is a curious tension between this desire to conceive of Africa as an interconnected whole and the various ethnic tensions that have led to so much violence on the continent. The decision to include the portion of Africa that is north of the Sahara Desert in the Middle East section is emblematic of this tension. To what extent do these identities overlap? Books like Stewart Gordon's *When Asia was the World* (2009) make arguments about the history of trade and interconnections between and among Africa, the Middle East, and Asia. These connections are useful when figuring out how ideas were developed and circulated, but it is equally important to place each of the theorists in question in this text in a local context as well.

Major historical threads

Current archeological evidence suggests that human civilization existed in Africa before it existed anywhere else in the world. Whether or not this is the case, African history predates both written and oral records. Until roughly 650 CE we have only archeological evidence about what happened in Sub-Saharan Africa, and our ability to interpret this information is limited. We do know that there were three major bands of civilization, each of which has its beginning long before we have historical records and each of which continues to the present day.

The Sahelian trade empire made use of the rich grassland just south of the Sahara Desert. The largest African empire, the Songhai of the fifteenth and sixteenth centuries was in this region. Both coasts of Africa had massive trade networks as well. On the eastern coast, this trade network was characterized by the spread of the Swahili language, which is now one of the most common modes of communication between various ethnic groups in Africa. As a language of trade, Swahili is heavily influenced by many major world languages including Arabic, English, and German. The developed trade routes on the west coast would eventually facilitate the transatlantic slave trade.

Central Africa is a diverse region south of the Sahel and inland from the coastal trade routes. Within Central Africa, a number of empires rose and fell, connecting the people of what would become a number of different modern countries. Central Africa remained more isolated than the other two regions, although trade was still a vital part of its survival. Further south, Southern Africa saw the development of agricultural and herding practices, although not sprawling empires.

Europe began to colonize Africa in the 1500s and this reshaped longstanding empires, cultures, and economies. The colonial powers sought to grow rich from the natural and human resources in Africa and, at the same time, attempted to determine what relationship Africa would have with Europe. Colonization carries with it the idea that Africans – the founders of some of the planet's oldest civilizations – were primitive savages in need of spiritual and cultural guidance from Europe. By the end of African colonization in the 1960s, Europe had divided Africa up into most of its present nations. Europe did this based on its own design, ignoring historical connections, placing warring ethnic groups within the same nation, and dividing ethnic groups between nations.

Contemporary Africa is still struggling with the legacy of colonization. Nigeria, for instance, contains people who speak more than 250 different languages. The three largest cultural groups, the Yorùbá, the Igbo, and the Hausa-Fulani have struggled with each other for political dominance. Many countries, including Nigeria, have had civil wars in an attempt to work out internal differences. These wars have resulted in attempted genocides. On the other hand, economies in Africa continue to grow, standards of living are rising, and many African nations are developing their own, distinctive democracies.

General literary and cultural theory

Unlike many parts of Asian literary theory, which trace their intellectual roots back for millennia, African literary and theatrical theory tends to focus on contemporary issues and the connection of these issues to Africa's cultural past. These movements as a whole have been characterized by concerns with authenticity of cultural production and the relationship between African and European cultural production. African literary theory is frequently overtly political. The overtly political nature is not surprising given the strong Marxist tendencies of many of the artists, critics, and philosophers in question. The material conditions of Africa demand a response, and the movements above reflect this pressing need. Theatrical and literary movements in many countries can be usefully thought of in two phases: nationalism (leading up to independence, focused on European influences) and disillusion / post-nationalism (after independence, focused both on the remnants of colonization and on the failures of new African governments).

While nationalism is a useful term in thinking about Africa's drive for independence, many of these movements were actually transnational in scope. The Negritude movement (which was prominent in Northern Africa and the Caribbean as well) is related to the idea of Afrocentrism, inasmuch as both assert an independent African culture. Negritude is a literary movement focused on the development of a distinct African aesthetic that could be used to challenge colonial thinking. Léopold Senghor, Léon Damas, and Aime Cesaire are three major writers from the movement, and they indicate the pan-African (if francophone) nature of the Negritude project. Jean-Paul Sartre characterized Negritude as *"racisme antiraciste"* (antiracist racism) inasmuch as Negritude emphasizes the distinctiveness of black culture and the detrimental effects of white European culture on black culture. In francophone Africa in the 1970s and 1980s there was a "culturalist movement" that sought to connect African theatre to its own performative roots. A similar movement in both South Africa and anglophone Africa was labeled "nativist." This movement is related to the Negritude movement inasmuch as both sought to find value in traditional African culture. Both the nativist moment and the culturalist movement adapted texts from Europe and made them African (Shakespeare, Sophocles, and Euripides were popular source materials).

Playwright theorists like Kenyan Ngugi Wa Thiong'o (b. 1938) argued that such work was best accomplished in African languages rather than European languages, and the issue of language remains central to African theatre in the twenty-first century both in terms of translating and adapting European work and in terms of African theatrical production. On the one hand, translating great works of Western theatre into African languages serves as a marker of these languages' status as important on the world stage. On the other hand, an insistence on African language as the appropriate medium for African theatre and literature suggests that Africa does not always need to concern itself with the world stage – that, as the Negritude movement asserts, Africa has its own value.

Another transnational movement is pan-Africanism. While it has manifested itself differently at different moments, it is, at core, a belief that there is a connection between all people of African descent, regardless of geographic, national, and ethnic differences. Marcus Garvey and Malcolm X advocated this idea as part of their civil rights platform in the United States. When Kwame Nkrumah became the leader of Ghana in 1951, he was both one of the first leaders of an Africa rapidly moving toward independence, and a fierce advocate for the rights of other Africans. The pan-African movement is often connected to Afrocentrism – an insistence on both the historical and cultural centrality of Africa in the world. While Africa has not, to date, reached the level of economic and social interconnectivity that Nkrumah envisioned, the pan-African movement was successful in providing working-class Africans in Africa and in diaspora (away from their native country) with a firm idea of their own human rights and history.

While part of the purpose of pan-Africanism and Negritude is certainly to resist the hegemonic influence of Europe and America, these movements are primarily focused on the creation of a new Africa or a new concept of Africa. Other writers in the nationalistic period were explicitly anticolonial. They wanted to fight colonization. Frantz Fanon is an anticolonial critic who explains the ways in which black identity has been erased by a mask of whiteness. He talks about race as a performance, subject to learned mimicry. In the theatre world, anticolonial works often took the form of stark realism – direct presentations of the brutality of colonial processes. F. Abiola Irele and Njabulo Ndebele both write about ideas of performance and literature in an anticolonial sense.

Theatre for Development (TfD) is a label that has been applied to a range of artists in both nationalistic movements and in the period of disillusion that followed these movements. TfD refers to a range of community artistic practices designed to empower the community together at a local level. The movement is characterized by relatively simple scripts with straightforward, immediate, pragmatic arguments: scripts about government corruption and a people's revolution, scripts about resisting oppression, or scripts about the rights of women. Ngugi Wa Thiong'o from Kenya and Zakes Mda from South Africa are two major names in this movement. The TfD movements are significant inasmuch as they are "popular" theatre: TfD is created by the people for the people in local, specific ways.

Both the Negritude and pan-African movements were heavily influenced by African ideas of Marxism. Nkrumah repeatedly compared himself to Lenin. For Nkrumah, Marxism provided a means of reconciling the technology of modernization with the human values he espoused. Marxism was a complex pattern of social relationships, and not, perforce, a revolution. In Africa Marxism was not a new arrival in longstanding systems, but, instead, a new philosophy in newly independent countries. Marxist governments in Africa embarked on large-scale public works projects and actively taxed the populace. In other words, these governments, at their best, made attempts to provide all citizens access to resources, but perhaps the most enduring legacy of African Marxism is the idea of cultural and historical materialism. African leaders have again and again reminded the world of the material circumstances (many stemming from colonization) that created the present problems and successes of Africa. Artistically, the South African protest theatre movement bears some formal similarities to doctrines of socialist realism and has strong Marxist sensibilities.

In terms of large-scale cultural production, Nollywood – the Nigerian film industry – has a gigantic footprint. Currently Nollywood claims to be the second largest film producer in the world after India, although, given the highly unregulated nature of the business, gauging the exact quantity of output is challenging. These films range in subject and genre across a wide spectrum, although romantic comedies and romances have been popular in the first half of the 2010s. These films have generated their own distinct acting style, their own special effects techniques, and their own (largely pirate-based) distribution networks across Africa and in immigrant African communities around the globe. Few of these films have gained popularity with other viewing publics, but, in that they are frequently released straight to home video markets, which allows for repeated reviewing, they have become touchstones of contemporary anglophone African culture. With the rise of film, stage productions in Nigeria have become less common and less well-funded.

Nollywood films often have intricate dialogue, reflecting the richness of African languages and African English. The idea that, without a large number of written languages, African culture might have a rich linguistic heritage was brought to world-wide attention by Ngugi Wa Thiong'o and others who insist on the importance of oral culture – orature rather than literature. In Nigeria, for instance, family and communal praise poems are passed down for generations. Proverbs are exchanged in rapid-fire discussions on the street. Travelling through cities and towns in Nigeria today, one would be hard-pressed to go a week without someone offering you a copy of a self-published book of poetry, novel, or other piece of writing. Be it orature or literature, Africa produces a vast quantity of sophisticated, commonplace, and ritual language. The plays mentioned in this volume represent a small fraction of the best of this production.

The above descriptions of literary theory in Africa have focused primarily on Africa's relationship to its colonial past and its contemporary political struggles. While this is certainly a dominant thread in African literary and theatrical discourse, it is important to note that there is a thriving literary critical scene in Africa that deals with a wide array of other topics. The breadth of South African Lewis Nkosi's (1936–2010) work is exemplary in this regard. He writes on the nature of realism, the development of genre, political issues, culture issues, sexuality, and a stunning array of other topics. It would be a mistake to consider African literary and theatrical theory as purely a byproduct of colonial and postcolonial struggles.

In many African countries, theatre and literature often are connected to popular culture in ways that defy contemporary European conceptions of theatre and literature as "high culture." Some of the earliest theatrical endeavors in Nigeria were a form of travelling popular theatre. This is similar in many regards to the Ghanaian concert party movement (a comic travelling performance), to Kenyan community theatre, South African township theatre, and a number of other movements. Such productions tend to be simple in structure, often containing musical or dance elements. They deal with themes like economics, marriage, oppression, and morality that are of immediate interest to the general population. They might be performed in theatres, schools, churches, vacant lots, or in any space where the community could gather. It is a rare country in Africa that does not have some sort of popular theatre tradition like this.

Even playwrights whose work is more formally complex often retain a flavor of popular theatre in their work, which is part of what makes contemporary African theatre accessible to a wider audience: it is immediately concerned with concrete aspects of the human condition. This is something that Wole Soyinka says separates European and African theatre: European theatre tends toward the abstract following of theatrical trends while African theatre stays in touch with its human roots. Obviously such a vast statement is an overgeneralization, but it is also a reminder that the simplicity of many African plays is a stylistic choice made for aesthetic reasons, and not a lack of sophistication.

Aside from Wole Soyinka and Femi Osofisan, whose work is in other chapters of this book, the most significant theatre figures in Nigeria are Ola Rotimi (who wrote many history plays, some absurdist comedies, and *The Gods are not to Blame*, which is an adaptation of *Oedipus Rex*), J.P. Clark-Bekederemo (who resituates the tropes of Western tragedy in an African setting), Wole Oguntokun (who familiarized the West with Soyinka's work and managed Terra Kulture, one of Nigeria's premiere theatres), Tess Onwueme (whose post-modern work shuttles back and forth between African and American contexts), and Zulu Sofalo (whose work often incorporated mythic elements to address contemporary problems). Other writers like Stella Dia Oyedepo (who writes fable-like plays with clear morals) are incredibly popular within Nigeria, but haven't garnered much attention in the West.

Like Nigeria, Ghana has a rich array of theatrical traditions ranging from its vaudevillian concert party tradition – which mixed music, dance, and theatre – to storytelling to literary drama. Ghana has one of the best known female African playwrights, Ama Ata Aido, whose work moves fluidly between fables and contemporary materials. Joe de Graft (1924–1978) and Efua Sutherland (1924–1996) both worked to found a national Ghanaian theatre at the Ghana Drama Studio. Having a national theatrical tradition that is distinct from other traditions is a mark of national identity and raises questions about the degree to which "African" theatre can be discussed. That being said, both Efua Sutherland and Joe de Graft wrote plays that were explicitly pan-African in nature, suggesting that Ghana's national identity might be able to include a conception of Ghana's position within Africa.

South Africa has a stunningly rich array of theatre practices ranging from experimental post-dramatic forms to hyper-realistic protest theatre. Athol Fugard is the most accessible entry point given that he writes in English, has attracted a great deal of critical attention in the West, and that his plays are widely available. His work includes "township plays" which focus on black life in poor urban areas, autobiographical pieces about his life in the theatre, experimental adaptations of Greek tragedy, collaboratively written pieces, and documentary theatre. Fugard's style has a great deal in common with European literary theatre. In contrast, writers like Maishe Maponya create literary versions of TfD and protest theatre. Maponya's work is realistic, direct, and clear, often presenting a series of vignettes focused on social problems.

This concern with immediate social conditions is characteristic of what has been termed "protest theatre." Such theatre tends to adhere to a straightforward realism, but other politically active theatre, like the work of Yael Farber, Jane Taylor, or William Kentridge, uses more experimental techniques. Other South African playwrights whose work has drawn international attention include Susan Pam-Grant, Pieter-Dirk Uys, and Paul Slabolepsky. As is true across the world, many, many performances, theatre, and artists in South Africa are not represented here because their work is not published. The Grahamstown Theatre Festival provides a venue for experimental and established techniques alike. Namibia, which was formerly controlled by South Africa, has a theatre scene that has been largely ignored by contemporary scholarship. Dorian Haarhoff's plays often use multiple languages in ritualized settings to foreground the complex issues of identity in Namibia as it deals with German, Dutch, South African, and British influences. Vickson Tablah Hangula, Kubbe Rispel, Norman Job, the Bricks Theatre Company, and Boli Mootseng are also underexplored Namibian playwrights.

Despite his twenty-year exile, Ngugi Wa Thiong'o's name is one of the most recognizable of Kenyan dramatists. Ngugi, like his fellow Kenyan playwrights Mirce Githae Mugo and Samuel Soko Osebe, is associated with the TfD and community theatre movement. This theatre tends to be written in collaboration with oppressed, impoverished people. It deals with everyday situations in direct, straightforward ways. Like South African protest theatre, this branch of Kenyan theatre is significantly different from Western literary theatre and, perhaps for this reason, is not often anthologized or performed outside of its original context.

Zimbabwe is an interesting case inasmuch as it, like South Africa, was a settler colony. There was a thriving white Zimbabwe (Rhodesia at the time) theatre scene before independence that tended to produce extremely sentimental theatre (e.g. William Fitzsimmon and Arthur Cripps). These works stand in contrast both to traditional performance and the black theatre scene in Zimbabwe which includes Stanley Makuwe. Notable playwrights from Uganda include Atwine Bashir Kenneth and Angella Emurwon.

As John Conteh-Morgan has argued, the Ivory Coast is a representative model of theatre history in francophone Africa. Curiously, despite France's own avant-garde theatre scene, it encouraged its colonies to reproduce theatre that had a neoclassical aesthetic (a formal proscenium arch, Aristotelian unities, and a general move toward realism) in the French language. Despite a vibrant storytelling tradition and a number of other performance styles across francophone Africa, anticolonial theatre, and to a lesser extent postcolonial theatre adhered to this model. French is still the primary language of theatre, although the last decade has seen a resurgence of African languages (albeit in work that is seldom translated and disseminated beyond its national boundaries). This resurgence is particularly evident in theatrical trends that seek to reinstate traditional performance as a part of modern theatre, like the works of Dieudonné Niangoran Aboubacar Touré, which utilize many aspects of traditional storytelling in modern ways. These trends toward traditional performance in theatre exist side-by-side with neoclassical and avant-garde theatres that utilize these forms in novel ways in their African context. Important Ivorian playwrights include Werewere Liking (who is one of the few female playwrights in this list and whose work stages Bassa rituals in innovative, often shocking ways), Bernard Zadi Zaourou, Souleymane Koly, Bernard Dadié, and Koffi Kwahulé.

While Ivorian theatre may provide some insight into the rest of francophone Africa, this insight is by no means complete. Discussing the history of theatre in the Congo is complicated by the ever-shifting boundaries of the various nations that take "Congo" as part of their names. The Democratic Republic of Congo, the Republic of Congo, Zaire, and Congo have all, at various times, referred to overlapping geographies containing a multiplicity of ethnic groups. This constant shifting of national identities provides a caution about too easy categorization of any aspect of African theatre. This tumultuous region has produced some of Africa's most famous playwrights, including Sony Labou Tansi whose plays have often been studied in terms of modern African theatre's ability to effect political change; Sylvain Ntari Bemba whose work, including an adaptation of *Antigone*, explores the intersection between traditional performance and modern African and European theatre; and Tchicaya U'tam'si whose work spans across both the pre- and post-independence eras.

Outside of the Ivory Coast and the Congo, other significant francophone writers include Kossi Efoui (Togo), Koulsy Lamko (Burkina Faso), José Pliya (Benin), Michèle Rakotoson (Madagascar), and Sierra Leone's Dele Charley and Yulisa Pat Amadu Maddy. Senegal has traditionally focused more attention on the art-house film and the novel than on theatre, although Cheik Ndao wrote several plays alongside his other work. Ethiopian theatre has received little critical attention outside of Africa although it has a history stretching back to Tekle Hawariat (whose first major work was in the 1920s). Theatre development accelerated when Haile Selassie officially began to support it in 1930. As Jane Plastow argues, the colonial days of Ethiopian drama were shaped by the indigenous elite's desire to demonstrate high culture, and thus remained divorced from traditional performance. More recently, the works of Tsegaye Gabre-Medhin stand out as bridges between traditional performance and Ethiopian theatre. Bole Butake's work from the Cameroon highlights the issues faced by women in Africa and she has worked tirelessly to promote the visibility of African women's writing.

Chapter 10

North Africa and the Middle East

As the book *When Asia was the World* (Gordon, 2009) so vividly argues, much of what we currently consider to be the Middle East was culturally connected to East Asia; to Greece, Italy, and Spain (and to a lesser extent other parts of Europe); and to Africa. This region is vital to cultural, economic, and religious exchange and has an incredibly diverse, complex, rich history that goes well beyond the scope of Islamic-focused historical narratives. Francophone North Africa has close links to anglophone North Africa – and both of these share cultural bonds with the Middle East and their sub-Saharan African neighbors. The Mongols, the Turks, the Greeks, and the Romans all controlled large portions of the Middle East at various times. Present-day Israel shares tense borders with a number of countries in which Islam is a majority religion.

Choosing to position North Africa with the Middle East in this chapter privileges a certain religious and cultural narrative (the story of Arab and Islamic culture and its related conflicts) at the expense of others (e.g. the history of the Ottoman Empire, the dissemination of Greek and Roman thought, the Mediterranean world, Jewish culture, or the Asian world). Including Iran, for instance, in the Asian history, or even European history would create a very different narrative. While this region is by no means homogenous, it does share some salient literary and cultural elements which inform the theatrical theory that follows. In other words, there is a story to tell about the development of the Arabic world and Arabic theatre.

Some terminology

Islam is a religion that was founded in the 600s CE. This, along with Christianity and Judaism, is a major religion in the Middle East.

Arab is an ethnic and / or cultural marker. Many people speak Arabic who claim other ethnic heritages. There are many different varieties of spoken Arabic (although officially only one variety of written Arabic). Many Arabs practice Islam, but not all do. Many Arabs live on the Arab peninsula (present-day Saudi Arabia and surrounding countries), but many do not.

Major historical trends

Egyptian civilization is one of the six major "original" civilizations – civilizations which developed largely independently of one another at roughly the same period. While there is archeological evidence of earlier settlement, records of a cohesive civilization date from 3150 BCE. Egypt went through a period of dynastic change and internal conflicts, many of which are marked by pyramids and statues that survive into the present day. By 1069 BCE Egypt's golden era had passed and they were invaded by a series of foreign powers, notably the Assyrians, the Persians (Archaemenids), the Greeks (fourth century BCE), and the Romans (first century BCE).

Egypt's history shows a trend that is relatively common throughout the Middle East. Groups developed strong identities and bonds within a community and often acted aggressively toward other groups. Over time, the boundaries between these groups shifted, with cultures merging, blending, disappearing, and remerging at various times. Religion, culture, and geography were markers of identity, but this identity was fluid over time.

The Zoroastrian faith, a messianic faith focused on humanity's ability to freely choose to follow a supreme being, was one that emerged in the sixth century BCE and, while it was the semi-official state religion of the Persians, it spread through the lands they conquered and through trade routes. Pieces of this faith have been reabsorbed by other religious practices, notably Islam. The idea that a whole state could follow a religion and then have this religion shift and change, eventually almost completely disappearing, suggests that the way we currently construct identity is not the way identity was always constructed. Things did not necessarily have to be binary – us / them, either / or. As with many African cultures, cultures across the Middle East exhibited some ability to create "both / and" societies in which contradictions could coexist.

The Persians and the Romans had an extended conflict that ranged across the region, and several Persian dynasties rose and fell during this time. Both groups eventually ended up back in the boundaries of their original territory (modern Iran and Italy). Both still claim connections to their many thousand-year-old histories, but, in the ever-changing contemporary nations, different parts of this heritage are stressed and ignored at different times.

Until the Islamic Revolution in 1979, Iranian history focused on the military and diplomatic conquests of the Persian Empire. After the revolution, the focus shifted to a history of the Islamic world, implying a connection between groups of people that had been on opposing sides of many of the conflicts as they were told in "Persian" history.

Specifically, this Islamic history begins with the sixth century CE birth of Prophet Mohammed and foundation of Islam which led to a concentration of power in Arabia – in Arab, as opposed to Persian, Roman, or Jewish hands. Unlike many other religious figures, Mohammed led militarily, spiritually, and politically. Upon his death, the caliph system was established in which a leader would be appointed. After his death, there was a period of struggle eventually leading to the founding of the Abbasid caliphate which began a steady integration of Persian and Arab culture. Converting to Islam did not make one "Arab" and the Arabs had held power since the foundation of Islam. Once the Persians gained power, Islam took on a more international character. By the eleventh century, the Muslims had regular contact with the Turks on their Eastern borders. This contact became increasingly aggressive as the Islamic empire began to show weakness. Despite this aggression, many Turks actually worked within the Arabic military.

The empire fell apart as the Mongols invaded. By the early 1200s, the caliphates had been demolished and a new order began to be established. As with the early formation of civilizations in the region, the history of the first millennium CE is one of ever shifting affiliations and definitions. The current dominant narrative, which characterizes Middle Eastern history in terms of the rise of Islam, is only one of the possible ways to construct a narrative of the region. The rise and fall of Egyptian, Persian, Roman, and Abassid empires, for instance, paints the story in a different light. From a colonial standpoint, one might focus on the history of Jewish displacement or conquering of territories by foreign occupiers (who often remained long enough that the colonial history was all but forgotten). The history of religious conflict between Judaism, Christianity, Islam, and, to a lesser extent, Zoroastrianism would be another way to approach the region, particularly from 1299 to 1918 when the Turkish Ottoman Empire had power.

The year 1798 is often marked as the beginning of the modern era of Arab culture. After Napoleon's conquests in North Africa, Egyptian leaders began to work toward creating a modern nation. They reformed education, poured money into sciences (particularly sciences with military application), and began a program of translation into Arabic from European languages.

While many Middle Eastern countries followed this trend, some held firmly to their Islamic roots, insisting that modernization could be accomplished without sacrificing core elements of traditional culture. The Islamic Revolution in Iran is one example of an extreme response to European-style modernity. "Islamist" refers to someone who believes that all law and governmental principles should be drawn directly from the Qur'an and later commentaries. Iran was one nation to adopt such principles.

Another ongoing political move in the Middle East is Arab nationalism. Arab nationalists seek to create a unified Arabic state out of what they see as the various fractured parts of Arabic civilization. In its more militant form, Arab nationalism has clashed heavily with Israeli nationalism.

All of these overlapping historical narratives, when combined with the partitioning of the globe after World War II, account for the present-day boundaries of the modern nation-states in the Middle East. From World War II, sentiments in various nations in the region have shifted from pro-communist, to pro-capitalist, to anti-American, to secular, to religious.

As with each region in the book, any blanket characterization would be incorrect – and this bears repeating in terms of the Middle East given that contemporary Western society has strong stereotypes of the region.

Issues in literary and cultural theory
Islam and representation

Islam is a major factor in the development of culture in this region. Islam is not a singular, unified set of practices, but all branches of Islam are monotheistic and utilize Abrahamic thought (the same Abraham discussed by Christianity and Judaism) as part of what forms their beliefs. They also share a reverence for the words, thoughts, and personage of the prophet Mohammed (circa 569 to circa 632), who is hailed as the last of God's prophets. Like Judaism, Islam is generally a scholarly religion, with many, many volumes of studied, careful analysis of the words of the prophet and Abrahamic thought. While the Qur'an is considered to be the literal word of God (when written in its Arabic form – translations are changes to the word of God), these additional volumes of studied interpretation, along with the *Hadith* – the collected sayings and stories from the life of Mohammed – are exceptionally influential and can explain many of the differences between contemporary branches of Islam.

When talking about the relationship between Islam and culture, then, all scholars are either performing their own interpretation of Islam or selecting from the existing, well-accepted interpretations. It is commonplace in scholarship to say that Islam is hostile to representation – visual representation in art and theatrical representation (and to a lesser extent, written representations). It is absolutely true that, through much of its history, much of Islam was hostile to various forms of literary and theatrical representation. It is equally true, however, to note that Islamic scholars are largely responsible for the survival and transmission of the texts of key literary and theatrical figures like Aristotle. Beyond the transmission of scholarly texts on representation, there are various modes of storytelling, puppet plays, narrative poetry, rituals with narrative components, and other cultural practices that are unmistakably "representational" in nature in historical and contemporary Islamic culture.

The degree to which Islam is hostile to representation – and what types of representation fall under this restriction – is a matter of ongoing debate. Regardless of the conclusions of this debate, the idea that Islam has shaped cultural practice is clear. The general interpretation of several very straightforward passages in the Qur'an specifically forbid the representation of the prophet Mohammed, his immediate family, and his close followers. Beyond this, the *Hadith* and many *tafsirs* (interpretations) assert varying degrees to which all representation of humans is forbidden and the degree to which these prohibitions affect various modes of performance. Traditional Islamic art tends toward geometric patterns, and this long-standing tradition is often taken as an indication of the complete anti-iconism (rejection of any form of representation of humans or the divine). To say that Islam forbids all representation of humans and the prophet, however, is immediately and clearly untrue inasmuch as the *Hadith* is a literary representation of the prophet, as would be most speech. If linguistic representation (in some contexts) is permitted and visual representation is not, this leaves theatre in a curious position as both a linguistic and visual medium.

There are a number of narrative performance traditions that are often linked to the development of theatre in the Islamic world, and each of these is representational in some fashion.

It is probably best to approach this as a question about theatre from the region – what is the status of representation in a given piece? This question does not exhaust the possibilities of a given piece of theatre nor will it be universally productive when applied to theatre in the region. It is, however, a place to begin investigation.

Is this play particularly attentive to issues of representation? Does it contain ekphrasis (the representation of other art within itself)? Does the structure of the play call attention to the limits of representation (e.g. actors taking off or putting on masks, actors breaking from character, actors declaring that they are creating representation)? Are different issues / topics in the play subject to different modes of representation (e.g. does the play shift in and out of realism)? If representation is an issue in the play, what is it that can't be directly represented? Is the play attempting to find ways to represent the unrepresentable? Based on the use of representation, what argument is being made about the status of representation or the topics / issues / people being represented?

Arabic poetry

Depending on how one defines literature, Arabic literature before 1800 consisted almost entirely of poetry (with one set of epic stories). Western scholars have historically tended to dismiss Arabic poetry as lacking in formal sophistication, while Arabic scholars have argued that the classical age of poetry (500–1250 CE) stands as one of the world's great literary achievements. To some extent this is a matter of taste and depends on how one defines "good poetry." In keeping with the idea of world theatre theory, rather than attempting to make Arabic poetry fit into a preconceived framework, it is useful to consider what it is that this poetry does.

Poets like Imru' al-Qays (d. 542) may have taken bits of ideas or even words from other sources and combined them in novel ways to create their own poetry. The ability to create an innovative collage of other people's work is prized in Western postmodern art, but this same skill may have been a feature of classical Arabic poetry. Love, revenge, and traveling are common themes during the classical era and poets often wrote about these in the qasida form (akin to English odes). After the foundation of Islam, poetry was also used as a form of devotional writing in which one could express the glory of the prophet. It is curious to note that, despite the prevalence of poetry in Arabic culture, few verse plays have gained critical attention. This suggests that poetry and theatre exist in at least partially separated categories from one another in Arabic culture. This may have something to do with the relative newness of some types of theatre on the Arabic landscape. In terms of contemporary poets whose work is available in translation (to English), Mahmoud Darwish (Persian) is one of the best.

Literature, philosophy, autobiography, travel narrative, and religious writing

At various points in history Western writers have distinguished between what counts as literature and what does not. Certain genres or styles of writing are thought to be more or less "literary," which might refer to the craft involved in writing them, to their subject matter, to their fictitious (or not) nature, or to their place within culture. These definitions are not absolute – even within the Western tradition they continue to change. Thus, the above statement that Arabic literature consisted almost entirely of poetry before the 1800s is a bit misleading. Within the Arabic tradition, poetry shared a similar category with philosophy, autobiography, travel narrative, and religious writing. Whether we choose to call this category "literature" or not, these philosophical writings certainly shaped contemporary Arabic theatre and literature.

Issues of language, tradition, and the avant-garde

There is a profusion of languages in the Arab world. The Arabic language is, however, along with European languages, one of the largest forces in the region. The language of the Qur'an is the official form of written Arabic. Not only are the general orthography (spelling and alphabet) and grammar supposed to remain consistent, but the actual literary style of the Qur'an is considered to be the ideal form of written Arabic. Spoken Arabic, on the other hand, contains enough variation to make comparison across linguistic borders almost impossible in some cases.

As Arabic theatre developed, there was debate about the appropriate language. Could European languages be used? Could vernacular / spoken styles of Arabic be used? Should all Arabic drama use formal written Arabic – and if so, how should this formal written language be "translated" on the stage? For instance, Ya'qub Sanu (1839–1912), an Egyptian Jew, wrote in vernacular Egyptian languages instead of formal Arabic. This move is sometimes credited with starting modern drama in the Arabic world. In general, this early period of drama was dominated by adaptations of Western works into Arabic (linguistically and culturally) in the mode of realism.

Audience response to this theatre was mixed. Some, who were in favor of European-style modernity, embraced this new realism. Others – particularly those who took a "defensive" stance – felt that this non-participatory theatre had no place within Arab culture. Theatrical events prior to the mid-1800s had tended to involve the audience in discussion, often rewriting that text as the performance progressed. Scholars actively debate the extent to which these styles of performance "should" count as theatre. As with the Australian material, considering something as "theatre" gives it a certain status, but this consideration can also distort the uniqueness of the form as well if our definition of theatre is too narrow.

As a part of the same issues raised by the language debate, playwrights also experimented with traditional storytelling (al-hakawati), puppetry, and traditional music performance. One branch of Arabic theatre continues to merge the best aspects of both worlds together. Rather than choosing between the styles and languages available, this group sought to create a theatre for a society where all these ideas were already mixed. Because of the linguistic density and the performative nature (which is hard to write down), few of these productions are available in English-language books.

Yet another branch – most notably Tawfiq al-Hakim (1898–1987) – sought to revolutionize European-style drama rather than simply adapting this drama to the Arab context and language. Tawfiq al-Hakim's writing mixed Arabic spirituality with postmodern techniques, traditional narrative practices, and modern situations and themes. His work is sometimes classed as "theatre of ideas," but this label undercuts the dramatic tension of his texts even while pointing out the challenges they present.

The Nadha

Nadha is both a general term for revolutions in Arabic thought and culture and a term that designates a specific renaissance in the late nineteenth and early twentieth centuries (mainly in Egypt, but expanding outward). Islam is a religion in which hundreds of years of commentary have been incorporated into the canon of religious texts, although this commentary certainly does not approach the status of the Qur'an. There is a sense in which Islam is a constantly evolving religion, with a theology that is specifically designed to shift and apply itself to the changing world.

The Nadha is particularly interesting in this regard. It has three major threads. The first was a group of scholars and activists who felt that Islam was holding back the Arab world and sought to disentangle government and law from Islam. The second group of scholars, clerics, and activists thought that Islam had failed to keep up with the world and that it needed to be revolutionized. The third group – which contained members of both the first two groups – felt that the ideal way to begin any revolution was to include women in political, social, and religious discourse.

These three movements generated a profusion of scholarship, art, creative writing, and theatre. European materials became more readily available, and debates over the relationship of the Middle East and Europe became more pressing.

It is interesting that, almost 100 years after this period, the Arab Spring occurred. This was a primarily youth-led, internet technology-fueled movement for social and governmental change. In many cases, the very groups that had gained power in the first Nadha were ousted by another revolution that espoused many of the same principles as the first.

The cyclical nature of renaissance and rebirth is an interesting part of Arab culture and certainly flies in the face of any stereotypes of "traditional Islamic culture."

A brief note on Israel

Israel has produced a great deal of literary and theatrical criticism. To a large extent, this has been incorporated into the Western academy and does not require special treatment here. Despite this academic actuality, the choice to consider Israel as part of the West, in contrast to the Middle East, with which it shares a history and a geography, has a number of uncomfortable political resonances. It suggests an "us / them" mentality which positions the Western academy and Israel on one side and the Arab Middle East on the other. Leaving Israel out might also be read as a statement about the lack of importance of Israeli scholarship. On the other hand, Israeli literary and theatrical criticism positions itself, to a great extent, as part of the Western academy, and thus its inclusion would have been out of place here – and it was this principle that guided my selection process.

Of course, having a brief note on Israel and not addressing the Armenian culture or any of the other minorities in the Middle East also creates a false binary (to say nothing of the fact that there are Arab Jews and Islamic people with Jewish ancestry). Middle Eastern theatre scholarship is a rapidly expanding area, both in terms of Western awareness and publication within the region itself. By the time you read this passage, it is quite likely that multiple new scholars, perhaps from these minority groups, will have become obvious as people who should have been included here.

Chapter 11

Australia and New Zealand

A quick look at a map will indicate a relatively short distance between Australia and New Zealand: indeed, they are part of the same (mostly submerged) continent of Oceania. The same map will also suggest just how far both these islands are from most of the world's population centers. What the map does not suggest, however, is the patterns of initial settlement. Australia's first settlers came from Melanesia (North and North West of Australia, around present-day Fiji). While the Lapita people who colonized Polynesia (to the East and North East of New Zealand) and eventually New Zealand also have their roots in / near Micronesia and Melanesia, they had developed a unique culture by the time New Zealand was discovered. Not only were these islands settled by two very different groups of people, they share little direct history in terms of trade or politics after this settlement. It was not until European colonization that similarities in culture began to develop, at least among the colonists. While both have a rich performance tradition, neither has an extensive pre-colonial theatre history. Maryrose Casey and Diana Looser have demonstrated that many native performance traditions have theatrical elements and could be considered theatre. Indeed, I have included Casey's examination of this issue as a marker that, while this book considers what is currently part of theatre theory, there are arguments about what *should* be included in such theory.

Including both Latin America and the Caribbean in a single chapter shows how similar situations can lead to radically different theatres and cultural traditions. In many ways, this chapter is a demonstration of the opposite. Despite their initial differences, there are a number of similarities in contemporary theatre theory and cultural practice in Australia and New Zealand (and, of course, some differences). Were this a book of performance theory and practice, Australia and New Zealand would need their own chapters, but, in terms of theatre, they have much in common.

Major historical trends

Early Pacific exploration started in 50,000 BCE, but it was not until 1200 BCE that people arrived in Micronesia and Polynesia. In 1300 CE Polynesian settlers discovered New Zealand and settled there. Some archeological evidence remains from this period, which indicates strong navigational abilities and also confirms that the island was the last major landmass to be colonized by humans. Aside from this, few records exist for the next 400 years until the 1770 voyages of James Cook. Cook was an explorer (the first European to visit many parts of the Pacific) whose voyages opened the door for a long, often violent, history of colonization and settlement. In what became a rather trenchant debate for nearly 200 years, Cook's records pose the question of where the Maori people (the native New Zealand people) had come from. Two major theories were that the Maori were actually the lost tribe of Israel who had come to the island by way of Egypt or Greece. By the mid-1800s this theory had been replaced with the idea that the Maori were actually from India. It was not until the turn of the twentieth century that scholars working with Maori oral narrative put forth the theory that the Maori were from Polynesia. This is an active and ongoing area of research. It may well be that the current theory is also incorrect (although likely not so dramatically wrong as the idea of the lost tribe of Israel). It is interesting to note that the origin of the Maori people is a subject of national concern, attention, and pride for New Zealand. The country's identity is currently built on the idea of brave seafarers setting out in canoes across the uncharted waters that separated Polynesia from New Zealand. This version of New Zealand's history, however, has only been the accepted version for a handful of decades. People alive today remember alternative national narratives.

It is also important to note that the Maori are not a culturally homogenous group, despite their likely shared ancestry and relatively recent immigration to New Zealand. The multitude of creation stories the Maoris have is a reminder that some portions of the Maori perceive themselves as having a different history from others, however united by current political debates they may be.

Wherever the aboriginal people in Australia and New Zealand came from precisely, they had developed societies before European colonization. The colonial powers marginalized, ignored, and even attempted to wipe out indigenous cultures and people. As is generally the case, the era of colonization was preceded by an era of "discovery" and exploration. The first European to record his voyage to Australia was Willem Janszoon in 1606. New Zealand was first sighted by European sailors in 1642. New Zealand's various Maori groups signed a treaty with the British in 1840, the terms of which remain a matter of debate. The British interpreted the treaty as giving them sovereignty over New Zealand, but protecting the land ownership of the Maoris by giving them the rights of British subjects. In the British interpretation, the Crown also had power to buy land from the Maoris. By the beginning of the twentieth century, European countries had bought up much of the arable land, often on relatively unfair terms. Australia followed a similar pattern, although it was first established as a British colony in 1788.

The idea that Australia was entirely settled by criminals is misleading. First of all, many of the settlers had been convicted of minor crimes (the equivalent of unpaid speeding tickets in the contemporary world). They had been given the option of utilizing their skills in a new colony, receiving a full pardon for their crimes, and, often, a reasonable amount of financial assistance in starting up a new life. This population made up slightly more than half of the first group of settlers to arrive (in 1788). Most of the rest were military, but a number of scientists and laborers also chose to go. Later waves of colonization included many Irish "dissidents" who had protested over land rights in Ireland. In practice, different waves of colonists were treated differently. Later convicts arrived to find themselves put in almost slave-like conditions. By 1825 the line between convicts and other settlers had begun to blur, and did so with increasing speed as more outposts were founded.

In both Australia and New Zealand, the official narratives of history – the ones found in books, on websites, etc. – are relatively silent on the treatment of the aboriginal people. The histories talk about aboriginal culture and then about European colonization, sequentially, with very little transition. Australian colonial history, particularly, is written in terms of a struggle to survive in an environment that was alternately hostile and bountiful. It is only relatively recently that the respective governments and mainstream scholars have begun rewriting history to consider what happened to the people already living in these nations when Europeans arrived. Even the official histories agree that the aboriginal people in Australia were treated poorly. For instance, in 1835, the British declared that all the land in Australia belonged to the Crown, and it redistributed this land, ignoring current occupants or treaties.

By the late 1880s, both nations had a majority European population, and both strongly identified with the British, expressing fears about an influx of Asians, specifically Chinese. By 1901 there was an official policy promoting a "White Australia" and banning the migration of non-white people, which, given its proximity, was targeted primarily at Asia. This policy was officially altered, softened, and reinstated a number of times before being pronounced "dead" in 1973. Despite the end of the official policy, and Australia's adoption of a rhetoric of multiculturalism, elements of fear of immigration remain strong in the country. The mixed response to the Hmong immigration from Laos in the 1970s is an indication of the ongoing struggle over immigration.

After the discovery of large quantities of gold in Australia in 1851, relationships with Britain became strained. There were a few military clashes, but, through largely peaceful means, Australia transitioned into a commonwealth in 1901. In this case, the nation retained a close relationship as part of the British Commonwealth (later the Commonwealth of Nations a group formerly synonymous with the British Empire and currently functioning as an alliance of nations that share common goals and values), while gaining independent rule. In the 1840s in New Zealand, several of the Maori people mounted armed resistance against the settlers. Like Australia, the settlers negotiated with the British and secured independence in 1907, although New Zealand has maintained varying degrees of connection with the UK since this time. It is currently a member of the Commonwealth of Nations.

The twentieth-century governments of Australia and New Zealand tried a number of different strategies to improve upon relationships between aboriginal people, the state, and the majority. Many of these strategies, by contemporary standards, seem rather harsh. For instance, in 1909 to 1969, aboriginal children were taken from their families and sent to live with white foster parents "for their own good." Many of these children never saw their families again: they are referred to as the "Stolen Generation." Australia's current constitution is interesting inasmuch as it has removed all negative references to the aboriginal people, but it does not offer them any special protections. Australia's multiculturalism is predicated on an idea of equality (treating everyone precisely the same) rather than equity (treating people in a way that takes unique historical circumstances into account). Many people argue that seeking equality over equity is a way of avoiding facing Australia's historical and ongoing poor treatment of the aboriginal population. At the same time, however, the Australian government formed the Council for Aboriginal Reconciliation, which has proposed several treaties that would provide the aboriginal people with some limited land rights. All forms of this treaty have been rejected by one or both sides. The word "reconciliation" is different from "restitution" or "justice," inasmuch as it suggests that the eventual goal is the rejoining of the various parts of Australia into a single united entity – of course, this goal of "reconciliation" implies that there was once a unified body that Australia seeks to reincorporate the aboriginal people back into. This is obviously not the case, but, like most of the world, Australia continues to struggle with the legacy of colonization and the relative rights of different parts of its national demographic. Australia's aboriginal people have an even greater diversity among themselves than those of New Zealand, which further complicates any effort at reconciliation – there are many voices that need to be heard.

New Zealand's government has adopted a number of well-meaning policies that specifically target Maoris. Maori is one of two official languages in New Zealand, which means all official services must be available in both English and Maori. The Ministry of Education has a separate Maori education initiative to close the performance gap between Maori students and students of European descent. At the same time, however, immigration statistics suggest that New Zealand is attempting to manipulate demographics to create a state with a greater white majority. It can be argued, in fact, that the prevalence of special laws designed to help the Maori actually has increased the tensions between groups rather than promoting equality. That being said, New Zealand and Australia have adopted very different strategies and both display the same sorts of race-based difficulties in their countries (or even outright racism at times). Dealing with the problems caused by the collision between native cultures and European settlers – especially in cases when the settlers stayed on in the country after colonization ended – will likely continue to be an issue in both countries, and this issue shows up in many modern and contemporary works of literature and theatre.

Literary and theatrical history

As with many of the places discussed, the history of theatre in Australia and New Zealand is often presented as starting with European colonization in the relatively recent past. Unlike many of the other locations in this book, theatre is not a traditionally privileged form in either Australia or New Zealand. Indeed, New Zealand's government-approved encyclopedia refers to theatre as being treated like the "step-sister" of the arts, implying that it hasn't attained the status of film, television, novels, or poetry. Nonetheless, there are important and emerging issues in the literary and theatrical history and theory of Australia and New Zealand.

In the case of New Zealand, Hone Kouka, Diana Looser, and others have pointed out that many indigenous performance traditions closely resemble European theatre. In fact, many scholars argue that the specifically communal aspects of New Zealand's contemporary theatre stem from its Maori roots. This argument seems to have little impact on the way most histories of New Zealand theatre are written. When Maori performance comes up at all, it does so only in the context of a distinct tradition that has had little impact on European-style theatre in New Zealand. This is one of the first sets of questions that presents itself when experiencing a new piece of theatre in New Zealand. What is the history of this piece? What history does the production or playwright claim for itself? What is the place of the various cultures involved in this history? Are there multiple histories? What is the relationship between these histories? Often these questions are research-based, requiring a careful study of various oral and written archives, but, in a growing number, this issue of multiple histories is directly written into plays as well.

Current scholarship on Australian theatre has a slightly different argument with the standard theatre histories in Australia. Most volumes claim that Australian theatre began with Ray Lawler (b. 1921) despite recognizing that several scripts and performances existed before this. The histories claim that, when Lawler won the 1955 Playwright Advisory Board Competition he inaugurated an era of distinctively Australian theatre that would gain international recognition. While the issue of ignoring indigenous performance and theatre traditions is certainly still notable in Australia, critics have also pointed out that a woman, Oriel Gray, won the same prize in the same year. Whether the issue is the contributions of indigenous theatre, the contributions of women to theatre, or as discussed later, the contributions of LGBTQ people, theatre history is always selective in what it tells and what it leaves out (including the history you are currently reading). Histories make stories out of events and therefore must be selective (unless you want to spend ten years reading the history of ten years of theatre that has literally not left a single event out). If the author of the history is up front about selection criteria, this allows the reader to be aware of what is left out, which is the first step toward considering whether the story that can be told by including this material is deeper / richer / more interesting / more useful / more relevant (of course including more historical material will make the story more accurate) than the story that does not include the missing material.

When the things left out of a history consistently erase certain groups of the population, this can often point to contemporary biases – reading history can be as much about the current state of affairs as it is about the events recorded. Maryrose Casey, whose work on indigenous theatre appears in Chapter 4, refers to this as an issue of creating frames – deciding what context provides the appropriate information to best interpret the theatre one is experiencing, but also considering how the context shapes the experience of the theatre.

Aside from the interest in history, Australian theatre also deals heavily with identity. Constructions of race, gender, class, and sexuality vary radically across Australian drama. One interesting development, in this regard, is the concept of "wogboy" as performance style, "wog" being a term for non-Anglo immigrants (frequently, although not exclusively, Middle Eastern and Mediterranean). The stereotype of the "wog" included ideas of primitive, uncivilized people who were not accustomed to the cultural norms of Australia. Rather than challenging this stereotype directly, performers chose to amplify aspects of it and create a unique style. This is a high-energy style of performance with a great deal of physical movement. It is often said that theatre mirrors life or that life mirrors theatre. In this case, theatre is self-consciously expanding on an idea of life – not actual life – in order to make a political point.

Another interesting trend in New Zealand literary and theatrical criticism is the incorporation of traditional Maori practices. Hone Kouka (b. circa 1970), a Maori playwright, explicitly argues that the Maori culture isn't one in which the "sole critic" could exist because it assumes that no one individual should have complete knowledge of something or power over it. As noted in the introduction, theory may take many forms, and some of the communal performances act as a sort of theatre theory. Kouka discusses ritually consulting with the elders, the *kaumatua*, as he writes and creates his theatre. There is a strong community theatre movement in Africa, but in New Zealand, the idea of community extends to the interpretation of the piece as well as its creation. While Kouka made this point several years ago, determining the nature of a communally derived theatre theory is still an ongoing project.

Australian literary criticism, like that found in the Caribbean, is particularly interested in space and geography. "The Antipodes," like "the Orient," conjures up a number of cultural stereotypes and geographic ideas. In rough form, these ideas include the following: Australia is an isolated island, on the bottom half of the world, and the customs there are all slightly reversed from their counterparts in Europe. Alongside this set of ideas, Australia does have limited land that is conducive to settlement, and, as such, has had a series of displacements of populations in its history. These ideas of difference and displacement show up in a great deal of criticism. Joanne Tompkins, a contemporary critic whose work is internationally known, discusses the idea that the settlement of Australia was a displacement of British populations and a displacement of aboriginal populations and that theatre can actually bring up these unsettling images. She goes on to note that the Australian landscape is often characterized as an "absence" or inconceivable. She considers how theatre might utilize space to generate discussion about absence and displacement. From the political works of Mudrooroo (b. 1938) to the mysticism present in Louis Nowra's (b. 1950) plays, these themes are clearly important in Australian theatre.

Much of the early history of New Zealand theatre involves foreign touring troupes (many from Australia). It was not until the 1980s that New Zealand playwrights, like Anthony McCarten, who would later go on to be recognized by the Academy Awards and the British Academy of Film and Television Arts, made New Zealand's own theatrical tradition more apparent to the world. Indeed, this shift from theatre to TV and film has unfortunately characterized many contemporary New Zealand dramatists' paths (e.g. Warren Ambrose Dibble (1930–2014), Ken Duncum (b. 1959), and David Geary (b. 1963)).

Most of the above discussion has focused on the writing of the former European colonists – and, indeed, a high percentage of the best-known playwrights are of European descent. The rate of theatrical production among aboriginal people and Maori has increased dramatically over the past 25 years however (and seems to be poised for even more growth). Maori playwrights include Hori Aphene and Hone Kouka. Riwia Brown, a woman of mixed descent, published *He Reo Hou*, a collection of Maori drama. In Australia, major indigenous playwrights include Jack Davis, Eva Johnson, Richard Walley, and Bob Maza.

There is a significant distinction to be made between aboriginal Australian drama and Maori drama. To a great extent, aboriginal theatre takes place within the same spaces and utilizes the same basic conceptual framework as "white" theatre in Australia. Maori theatre, on the other hand, which emerged as a named movement in the 1980s, is immediately and clearly involved in a different project. As with the idea of communal criticism, Maori theatre demands the participation of its audience, frequently employing a number of traditional performance techniques to do so. Productions can incorporate singing, chanting, and even offerings to the gods. The Maori playwrights noted above write English plays, but the communal form of Maori theatre is, by definition, in the Maori language, and, I am told (as someone who cannot read or speak Maori), often deploys this language in a deeply idiosyncratic, complex way. As such, the barrier to entry for non-Maoris (*Pakeha*) is particularly high. While scholars have traced the general parameters of this movement, little specific work on particular productions has been circulated in the Western academy.

Much of the work that has been done focuses on a problem presented by this sort of theatre. Incorporating traditional rituals into contemporary theatre can lead to fascinating theatrical innovation. The problem is that these traditional rituals are often active, sometimes sacred (or at least important), parts of Maori life. On one hand, the incorporation of Maori culture into contemporary theatre acts as a means of transmitting this culture and celebrating it. On the other hand, placing important culture elements on stage makes them a spectacle. It cuts them off from their initial meaning. It can make something that is a vibrant part of life into a spectacle for other people to look at. This is a problem faced by many indigenous cultures around the world – preservation of ways of life often takes the form of generating a museum-style spectacle of that way of life, which robs it of some of its meaning. Culture is never static, but figuring out which evolutions are helpful or harmful to a given culture is a daunting task.

Chapter 12

East Asia

East Asia, which generally refers to China, Taiwan, Korea, Japan, and Mongolia (and culturally, if not also geographically, to Vietnam), is a region of contrasts. While traveling through China and Japan, it is difficult not to be struck by the juxtaposition of the ancient and the modern. From the relative isolation of the Mongolian steppes to the large population (and economy) of Tokyo, but also city-block by city-block within Kyoto, the nature of the East Asian experience changes. Buddhist temples next to Shinto shrines, Confucian meditations under the portrait of Mao Zedong, the latest of fashions and traditional outfits – all of these things stand side by side.

Major historical threads

Without downplaying the neocolonial influences at work in East Asia, it is important to note that, historically, this region has often been controlled by China. In fact, China maintained a tribute system in which the vassal states owed both allegiance and tribute to China. Of course, the precise nature of this "China" changed over time, as the borders of China expanded and contracted and as various "foreign" groups gained power and became "Chinese." By the late nineteenth century, Japan gained the upper hand and established its own variation of the tribute system.

After World War II, the West, particularly the U.S., has maintained its interests in East Asia. The Philippines, for instance, has often been accused of being an unofficial colony of the U.S. While these islands are further south than China or Japan, they do provide the U.S. with a foothold in the region.

While the civilizations in East Asia trace their roots considerably further back, our first written records are of the Xia Dynasty in China in circa 2100 BCE. This dynasty was followed by a long series of different dynasties during which the boundaries of China continued to shift. Confucius, whose philosophies would later be adopted as core principles of Chinese governance, wrote during the fifth century BCE. There was a general trend toward expansion and unification culminating in the Qin dynasty's conquests in the third century BCE. The Qin Dynasty was followed by the Han Dynasty, which was succeeded by the Three Kingdoms era during which China was split into multiple parts.

Korea followed a similar pattern of unification and fragmentation in its history, although it also had to defend itself from Chinese incursions from the north. China was similarly aggressive toward Japan, although in neither case did China gain extensive territory. China did, however, establish a tribute system by which Korea and Japan paid China as a protector and adopted many Chinese practices.

Buddhism arrived from India during the Han Dynasty. Buddhism did not replace Confucianism or the other religions in China, but instead existed alongside them. Buddhism, Taosim, Shinto, and Confucianism continue to exist in one form or another across East Asia. The changing dynasties of each East Asian country had radically different attitudes toward these various religions and so the place of each has risen and fallen over time.

Since the long-standing Western stereotype of the East includes the idea of spirituality, it is also important to note that the Chinese, and later the Japanese, were technologically advanced. The printing press, for instance, invented in China in 1040, had a massive impact on the place of writing in Chinese culture. Other inventions like gunpowder speak to China's consistent conflicts. The Manchurians, who would later become the Qin Dynasty and rule China, the Huns, and eventually the Japanese all threatened China at one point or another.

Japan's history is significantly different to that of China and Korea inasmuch as the Yamato Dynasty managed to retain control from the seventh century BCE until the present, although the scope of this control varied from imperial to provincial. The continuation of the dynasty, however, should not be confused with consistent governance. While the imperial family has been on the throne for more than a thousand years, the shoguns (military rulers) and rival families held real power for much of this time. The fifteenth and sixteenth centuries, particularly, saw a fragmentation of Japanese politics.

It is strange to think that in China, Japan, and Korea, ways of governance and life that had been around for centuries collided with modernity in the form of Western incursions. Russia's influence in China led to the Cultural Revolution of the twentieth century. China had experienced civil war and the Republic of China that emerged from this conflict had heavy communist influences. These influences culminated with Mao Zedong taking power. Mao attempted to help the workers in China by following (and recreating) the ideals of socialism and communism. He went so far as to change the Chinese written language to make it more accessible to the common people. While many of Mao's projects were admirable in their goals, his methods for achieving these goals were often violent. Mao was succeeded by the current government of China which is more open to contact with the rest of the world and has adopted some capitalistic principles.

After the famous incidents surrounding U.S. Admiral Perry's ships off the coast of Japan in 1854, the nation was forced to open its borders to a variety of trade. This led, in turn, to militarization. Japan was at war with China in 1894 to 1895 and then with Russia in 1904 to 1905. Japan fought with the allies in World War I and emerged from this war as one of the major political powers in the world. Its fortunes changed with its defeat in World War II. After World War II, Japan, under the supervision of allied powers, adopted a new constitution which forbade them from having a standing army. Under this new constitution, Japan has become a major world economic and cultural power.

The history of East Asia is one of dynastic struggle, coexistence of religions, Chinese regional dominance and China's fall from power, Western incursions (although not colonization), Japanese militarization, and rapid modernization.

Major literary and theatrical figures, trends, and issues

The nature of language

One of the most enduring myths about the Chinese language (and the Korean and Japanese given that they share some characters and history) is that it is pictographic – that each of the Chinese characters used to make words acts as a small illustration of the concept in question. This myth was popularized by modern European writers seeking artistic inspiration and ways out of the limitations of the logocentric West. Just as in the English alphabet, a limited number of Chinese characters do actually attempt to illustrate an idea, but, as with the English alphabet, the pictographic quality of symbols is not generally the primary function. When Japan adopted Chinese characters as a tool for writing its language, it almost completely separated many of these characters from their initial meanings and used them to represent sounds. As with comparison between any set of languages, there are things one can say in Chinese that can't be said in English (or at least not without a great deal more effort). Unlike much of Africa, which developed its orthography (written version of a language) during the colonial era, Chinese, in both written and spoken forms, predates Western contact. All translation should be approached with caution – all translation is inexact – but this is particularly true with East Asian translations given the linguistic and cultural distances involved.

There is also what is known as a translation gap between East Asia and the West. While much of what is written in English is translated into Chinese and Japanese, a far smaller percentage of Japanese, Chinese, and Korean works are translated into English.

The four books and the five classics

From roughly 200 to 1905 CE, China had a system of examinations to qualify for civil service. These exams required detailed knowledge and understanding of a set of nine texts including the I-Ching (a mystical guide to divination), books on ancient rites, poetry, historical speeches and documents, *The Analects of Confucius* (see Confucius below), and other collections of Confucian thought. These texts comprised a library that anyone wishing to be considered educated would have known from the twelfth century onward.

Confucius (circa 551–479 BCE)

Confucianism is one of the three major overlapping belief systems in China. Inasmuch as Confucius was required reading, his system of morality shows up in virtually every piece of Chinese writing (although, since the end of the Cultural Revolution, his centrality in literature has gradually waned), either as a positive or a negative force. Confucius stressed individual virtue within a communal context rather than focusing on the metaphysical, spiritual, and supernatural beliefs that shaped Chinese morality. Confucianism also advocated knowing one's place and speaking in a manner appropriate to this. While this Confucian modesty was used by various rulers to keep unruly populations in check, Confucius also suggests that rulers must lead by example, with gentle instruction taking the place of more overt forms of punishment. The Confucian system of virtues is incredibly precise, so much so that generations of commentary have developed to try to determine how best to live according to these Confucian principles. The trope of Confucian novices learning appropriate modes of life is common in Chinese literature.

Buddhism

Buddhism exists in hundreds of different forms around the world, and has a handful of prominent forms within China. It came to China by way of India in the first century BCE, and has more of the qualities of what the West considers "religion" than Confucianism. For instance, many Buddhist sects revere not only the teaching of Gautama Buddha (circa fifth century BCE), but his personage as well, although still not treating him as a deity precisely. The Buddhist "Way" involves considering the ways in which one fits within the world and the ways in which one might fit in the next world. This consideration often leads to a decreased focus on individual autonomy: many strands of Buddhism suggest that you have to leave your self behind in order to reach transcendence. Even these vague outlines of Buddhism, however, are points of contention between the various sects.

Four (pre-modern) classics of Chinese literature

The four books listed below are often considered novels (as opposed to the four works of philosophy that are part of the four books and five classics of the exam system), although each has a highly poetic structure and the relationship between these texts and concepts of history, religion, and nation are certainly different from what one expects from a novel. These books are certainly precursors to the modern Chinese novel, but can also be considered as distinctly Chinese literary forms. *Journey to the West* is a sixteenth-century piece that explores Buddhist principles through a narrative that focuses both on the morally ambiguous, powerful Monkey King and the young, pure, righteous Xuanzang. This book is notable for the poetic, choral moments that are inserted into and between the vignettes that make up the plot. The other three classics are *The Red Chamber / Story of the Stone, Water Margin,* and *Romance of the Three Kingdoms.*

Censorship

Twentieth-century Chinese literature bears the mark of intense censorship – a censorship that was enforced on the bodies and the texts of authors. Even before Mao came to power, China's tense relationships with Japan laid the groundwork for charges of treasonous activities against a number of Japanese-educated writers. Going abroad for education was common, and when writers returned, it could be difficult to determine which portion of the material they returned with was useful to the growth of China and which was potentially dangerous political propaganda. While Lu Xun argues vehemently for the adoption of foreign ideas (and a reshaping of these ideas), many other writers ended up censored or jailed for making similar cases.

Science fiction and romance

In general, Japanese literature has not had the firm divisions between "literary fiction" and "genre fiction" that organize the bookstores and course syllabi in the West. The eleventh-century novel (or what was later classified as a novel), *The Tale of Genji,* is somewhat unique among the canon of classical literature in any society inasmuch as it was written by a woman. Murasaki Shikbu (there are certainly other female writers before the eleventh century, but none as well known) used her novel to expose the hypocrisy of Japanese court life. This novel contains a surprising alternation between courtly poetry and rather straightforward discussions of sexual indiscretions.

Science fiction and romance, if well-written, can be just as respected as any other mode of writing. *Genji* is, to some extent, a romance, while *Taketori Monogatari* (tenth century) deals with space travel. Both these texts generated a set of stylistic conventions that are still visible in aspects of Japanese literature today. In the chapter on aesthetics, I discussed the idea that one way of judging theatre is to consider how well it does what it sets out to do. This ability to find artistry in any piece of work that utilizes or violates a set of conventions in an effective way is a major characteristic of Japanese literary criticism, a characteristic that allows for a much more expansive idea of what counts as "culture" than we have in the West.

Chikamatsu Monzemon

On the subject of elevating an art form to the realm of "culture," Japan's canonical seventeenth-century playwright wrote his work, in part, for a form of puppet theatre. Many of his simple plots retold famous love stories, often involving suicides. He took familiar forms, forms that had often been associated with common folk theatre, and made them popular with a wider audience. He is often referred to as Japan's Shakespeare, but this diminishes the cultural significance of both Chikamatsu and Shakespeare in Japan.

The modern and the postmodern

In both China and Japan, there have been periods during which writers and philosophers of all types were explicitly concerned with the idea of "the modern." In China, the New Culture movement (1917–1923) was committed to figuring out what style of literary writing was most appropriate for modernizing China. China had just come out of a bloody civil war in 1912 which had divided China from Taiwan. This war left China open to a Japanese invasion, which, in turn, led to China signing an unfavorable treaty that left many citizens feeling humiliated. The writers of the New Culture movement, and, indeed, of the Cultural Revolution, were convinced that China needed to grow or change in some fashion to return it to its former greatness. The slight sense of contrast in the last sentence is intentional. China wanted to grow and change while also somehow desiring a return to the past. Part of this growth was accomplished through contact with other cultures, but Chinese writers of the period were also proudly "Chinese." These contrasting impulses are part of Chinese modernism and often manifest themselves in deep ambivalences in the fiction, poetry, and theatre of the period. Hu Shih (1891–1962), Zhou Zouren (1885–1967), Chen Duxiu (1879–1942), Yu Dafu (1896–1945), and Lu Xun (1881–1936) are several of the important writers from this period.

Japanese modernism and postmodernism tend to be more experimental (relative to both traditional Japanese literature and European traditions) than China's modern writing. Japan's modernism was inspired, in part, by a desire to keep pace with the rapid changes in society immediately before and after the World Wars, although some writers from before this era certainly showed "modernist" tendencies. Natsume Soseki (1867–1916), Mori Ogai (1862–1922), and Yasunari Kawabata (1899–1972, who won the Nobel Prize) are notable figures in Japan. While their styles vary, they are all concerned with figuring out how individuals can make their way through the complex philosophical, geographical, and social landscape of modern China.

Adaptation

Both Japan and China have made active attempts to incorporate Western-style literary traditions into their novels, theatre, and poetry. Lu Xun introduces the idea of "Grabbism" to explain the importance of China continuing to borrow (or "grab") other traditions, focusing on China's need to modernize. First-person narration and spoken drama were both developed in specific ways as responses to Western literature. China also translated great Western works, including Shakespeare. Japan likewise considered Western traditions, although much of the later period of Japanese modernity and postmodernity was concerned with how such traditions could be made Japanese.

Chapter 13

India

Major historical threads

Scholars used to say that the first bits of recorded Indian history appear in documents created during the reign of the Persian emperor Darius (circa 520–486 BCE). Darius' empire extended into the Indus river valley which runs from the Arabian Sea along the border of Pakistan and India up to China. This same stretch of Northern India has been continuously occupied since roughly 3000 BCE. Indeed, written records are not our only source of history, and archeological records from this time also provide some idea of what was happening. A group now known as the Harrapans occupied India during the Bronze Age and they left records of arts, laws, systems of weights and measures, and architectural innovations.

One of the patterns set in the Bronze Age period of India's history continued for the next 2000 years. At some point in India's early history a group of people (maybe a new ethnicity, maybe a social class, maybe a loose affiliation of several groups) who would eventually be referred to as Aryan (meaning "pure") entered the Indus valley. It is unclear in what ways they interacted with the Harrapan, or, indeed, the differentiation between the two groups. There was some sort of struggle between the Sanskrit speaking Aryans and the Dravidians (another group who spoke a Dravidian language rather than Sanskrit). The Dravidians themselves had likely come to India from somewhere else. Different histories and legends paint the Aryans as invaders forcing out the Dravidians, or the Aryans as bringing civilization to the Dravidians. There is little enough direct evidence or enough scholarly argument to prevent easy conclusions. This difficulty in figuring out the relationships between groups does suggest an assimilative nature in India. Whatever the initial relationship between groups was, there was an eventual blending of cultures, and a flexible – albeit tightly held – notion of cultural identity has characterized much of Indian history.

While it didn't write documents that were initially considered to be "history," the late Bronze Age provided us with the *Vedas* (circa 1200 BCE), some of the world's earliest holy books. These books and the commentary on them form one pillar of classical Indian civilization and actively shape contemporary Indian life. Alongside hymns and praise poetry, the *Vedas* tell stories which have been passed down and retold for thousands of years. One such story talks about Manu, the survivor of a great flood from whom a new group of people were descended. This story shifts over time, with Manu eventually becoming elevated to a god-like status in Hinduism. The *Vedas* were written in Sanskrit, a language that is to India as Latin is to Europe – a progenitor from which other languages diverged. The *Mahabharata* and the *Ramayana*, two of India's classical epics, are also written in Sanskrit. These two documents provide additional information on the history of India before Alexander's incursion.

Depending on the chronology one chooses, it is possible that Buddha lived before Alexander the Great came to India. Because Buddha's life is dated by an entirely different system than the chronology we have assigned to Western events, it is difficult to match the two. We date Alexander as living 500 years before Christ. The *Vedas* provide a very precise set of dates, and it is possible to figure out Buddha's relationship to these dates. The issue is figuring out the relationship between Vedic dates and Christian dates. As a number of Indian historians have pointed out, if we chose one of the Vedic dates for our world system, Alexander's "precise" moment in history would be unclear.

Whatever the dates might have been, Gautama Buddha provided his followers (and generations around the world) with a series of lessons on enlightened living. In its inception, this was compatible with the Vedic practices, Hinduism, Janism, and later even with Sufism. As with Indian culture more broadly, religious and spiritual beliefs proved assimilative, with Hinduism picking up elements of these other practices as it went along. So, when historians claim that we have no history of India before Alexander, this diminishes the fact that India had already composed great epics, holy books, and two major world religions.

While we talk about Alexander's incursions into India, Indian troops had also made forays into the Persian Empire. Ultimately, the Archaemenid (early Persian) time in India was limited, and while some aspects of the cultural encounter remain in India, Indian history moves on to one of its greatest leaders, Ashoka (enthroned 268 BC) who was a member of the Maurya Dynasty. He is known for establishing a ruling system based on dharma – living in harmony with the universe. Some consider him to be the first Buddhist ruler of India. While the Maurya Dynasty continued after Ashoka, it dwindled in power under pressure of constant invasions from the Asian plains. The dynasty, which had reached through much of Northern India, crumbled.

In 320 CE, the next great dynasty, the Guptas, arose, uniting most of Northern India and moving further south than the Mauryas. This was a golden age for India in which the people had a high standard of living. It is important to note that while Buddhist, Hindu, and Janist practices still circulated, Hinduism was not a fully established religion with a set of doctrines at this moment. During much of the Gupta reign, the people were left free to practice whatever faith or combination of spiritualties they chose.

The Gupta dynasty was followed by a long period of dynastic struggle and invasion by the Huns. This period of struggle left India vulnerable to the military and diplomatic influences of the Islamic empire which shared a border with India by 700 CE. The border remained relatively stable until the thirteenth century, when the Delhi sultanate was installed in Northern India, cementing Islamic domination. As with earlier incursions of various people and ideas, there was certainly violence involved in the spreading of Islam, but India also continued to assimilate new ideas. Islam quickly became mixed with Hindu and Buddhist practices. Various sultans ruled parts of India until 1336 when Southern India's resistance led to the formation of the Vijayanagara Empire. The Vijayanagara Empire did not succeed in driving out all of the sultans, but they once again united India, this time focusing power in the south.

The flourishing sciences of the Vijayanagara Empire paved the way for the Mughal Empire's great economic (and architectural) successes. The Mughals came from the north, repeating a long pattern of border crossings followed by cultural assimilations, and by 1600 had consolidated their hold over most of India. The empire endured in one form or another until the 1730s (with 1739 marking a major defeat), by which time various rival powers within India had succeeded in expanding their powers and claiming large portions of land.

The British (and to a lesser extent the Dutch and Portuguese) had been trading with India and gradually settling there since the 1490s. As the Mughal Empire crumbled, the British took on more and more power. In 1757 large-scale violence broke out in Bengal, which ended with the British in control of the region. It is important to note that, unlike many other colonies, it was the British East India Company and not the British Crown that was taking over India: a commercial enterprise with few pretentions of being anything else controlled most of India by 1857. In 1857, members of the company in India decided to rebel against the company's share-holders in England, and, while the rebellion was quickly put down, it led to the British throne seizing power in India.

The British ruled from 1858 to 1947, during which time there was widespread if ineffective and scattered resistance. It was not until Gandhi and other leaders organized the Indian independence movement in the 1920s that the scattered acts of rebellion became unified. There are several reasons why Indian resistance to colonization took a distinct form. Unlike many other British colonies, the British actually recognized many of India's own leaders, giving them real power. Many Indians retained or expanded their fortunes during this period. At the same time, widespread famine killed large segments of the population (between five and ten million over the course of two years), which numerically weakened popular support for independence. Finally, various factions within India, primarily the Muslims and Hindus, found it difficult to agree on a course of action.

Gandhi's non-violent revolution was successful in gaining India's independence in 1947 (earlier than most of Africa). Despite India's long history of assimilation of a variety of cultures, the newly independent sub-continent was immediately partitioned into (predominately) Muslim Pakistan and (predominately) Hindu India. This partition led to widespread migration and violence: relationships between the two countries remain tense. In its modern history, India has conflicted with China. Perhaps this conflict is not surprising, given that both India and China are among the world's largest and fastest growing economies.

The details of India's history are fascinating, but there are several general patterns that also prove important for understanding Indian literary and theatrical texts. The notion of cultural assimilation discussed above emerges frequently in various pieces of art and literature. The historical difficulty in separating Persian, Dravidian, Chinese, Aryan, Harappan, and other influences suggests the extent to which "India" has adopted and adapted elements from a wide range of cultures. The idea of India as a crossroads between China and the Middle East (providing a ground for disseminating several spiritual and religious practices) stands in marked contrast to the fact that the Himalayas cut India off from most of the rest of the continent. Both the idea of separation and connection are important and can be seen in the rise and fall of various Indian empires as new forces entered the sub-continent.

Major literary movements, playwrights, performance styles, and theatre practices

Many accounts of the history of theatre in India suggest that the formal elements of dance and music came together in the distant, unrecorded historical past of India. Indian theatre then developed through various regional rituals which contained dramatic elements. These accounts contain the inevitable reminder that India is a massive, varied place and that no single elements of any ritual, theatre, or artistic practice can stand in for all of India. As accounts of Indian theatre move closer to the modern era, they pass through major performance forms like Kathakali, wherein dance is used to tell mythical stories. They note the close association of religious and spiritual movements with theatre. After colonization, scholars often divide Indian theatre into anglophone and non-anglophone groups, noting that, unlike other literary production, a majority of modern and contemporary Indian theatre is not in English. This basic outline contains many of the major issues and debates in Indian theatre: issues of diversity; of language;

of religion; of connection to traditional modes of performance; and of connection to ritual.

Classical Sanskrit drama

Even if one ignores the evidence of dramatic elements in early ritual and dance and focuses instead on items that closely match the European definitions of drama, the history of Indian drama dates back to at least the third century BCE, which makes it roughly contemporary with ancient Greek drama. Bharata Muni was theorizing Indian theatre at roughly the same time Aristotle was theorizing Greek theatre (although the precise dates of Bharata's composition and, indeed, even his existence as one individual writer are subject to some debate). Bharata's dramatic theory discusses both the spirituality and entertainment value of theatre. This theatre relied heavily on dance.

Sanskrit, one of the world's oldest languages, is the primary language of classical Indian drama. Between the fifth century BCE and the eighth century CE, Bhasa, Ashvaghosa, Kalidasa (considered to be the greatest Sanskrit dramatist), Bhavabuti, Shudraka (whose *Little Clay Cart* is one of the most readily available Sanskrit dramas in translation), and others wrote some of the oldest surviving dramatic texts in the world. The playwrights based a number of their plays on the great Hindu literary epics.

These literary, theatrical adaptations of Hindu epics existed side-by-side with other forms of theatrical activities (the devotional and folk theatre discussed below) that could be performed in a variety of local or regional languages.

Bengali, Kannada, and Marathi writing

Among the diversity of languages in India, three, aside from English, have most notably shaped the landscape of India drama from the nineteenth century onwards. During the nineteenth century, India was subjected to British colonization, and, as might be expected, a number of writers used literature as a means of resistance. These theatres are often grouped according to the language in which they are written.

As a Nobel Prize winner, Rabindranath Tagore (1861–1941) is perhaps the best-known Bengali writer, although his theatre garners less critical attention than his other literary and theoretical writing. It is Girish Ghosh (1844–1912), however, who is credited with figuring out a technique of melding the various religious and historical themes into theatrical scripts that were political, modern, and still connected to traditional theatrical forms. Utpal Dutt expands on the political, spatial, and traditional aspects of Bengali theatre for modern purposes.

As with many of the Indian language theatres, Bengali theatre exhibits the complex interplay between a newly introduced form – Western theatre – and a rich, vibrant tradition of all manner of performances. There is a sense of freedom and exploration in Bengali theatre in the twentieth century that is rare in the theatre world. There was no one "correct" way of doing things and each playwright and theatre troupe forged their own path through the possible combinations of materials.

This ability to create novel combinations is also characteristic of Kannada theatre, which has its roots in translating and adapting Shakespeare and Sanskrit drama during the colonial era. While generally less political than Bengali theatre, playwrights like Bellave Narahari Sastri (1882–1951) have had a major impact on contemporary Indian theatre.

Among the Marathi playwrights, Vijay Tendulkar, Satish Alekar, Marhesh Elkunchward, and P.L. Deshpande are some of the most significant. Alas, aside from some of Tendulkar's and Elkunchward's work, most of the modern and contemporary Marathi drama remains untranslated (at least into English).

A small but growing number of Indian playwrights are following Tagore's lead and translating their own works into English. Girish Karnad is perhaps the best-known of the contemporary figures in this category.

The anglophone Indian novel

While there are relatively few plays written in English in India, the same is not true for other genres. Indeed, there are several well-known anglophone novelists. In terms of the English novel in India, writers often self-consciously identify as cosmopolitan. Salman Rushdie, for instance, has talked about the idea that national identity is a story and that we, as a unified humanity, must find a way to stop fighting over such stories.

Despite this move toward cosmopolitan writing, the works of Arundhati Roy, Salman Rushdie, and Amitav Ghosh are all grounded within the cultural frameworks of their locations (frequently India, although the characters, like the authors, often travel). The Indian novel is a diverse form that ranges from postmodern non-linear narratives to more traditionally structured novels.

It is worth noting the amount of scholarly attention paid to the Indian novel relative to other aspects of Indian art and literature. Something about this form appeals to Western academics. Determining the reason for this is impossible, but I will present a hypothesis. As noted above, many types of Indian theatre involve the rich Indian performance traditions. It is possible that the Western attention to the novel has something to do with the recognizable form that the novels often take. On the other hand, this distinction might simply have to do with the privileged place of the novel within the Western academy more generally.

The Hindu epics: devotional and folk theatre

Almost all varieties of Indian theatre have made use of pieces of ancient Hindu literature (written in Sanskrit) at some time or another. The Hindu epics, collections of Hindu praise songs, and other books of the Hindu tradition do not fit easily into Western categories. They are works of literature, guides for living good lives, histories, and sacred books all at once. For theatrical purposes, the *Rig Veda, Bhagavata Purana, Mahabarata,* and *Ramayana* are the most significant. Each of these traces the life of one or more of the major figures of the Hindu faith, and the stories contained within show up regularly across Indian (and Western) theatre.

While these stories may appear in any type of theatre, there are several traditional modes of performance, broadly called "devotional theatre," that specifically present these stories. These performances tend to be in regional or local languages and are performed in more rural settings. They frequently include music, masks, and stylized costumes. The name "devotional" is somewhat misleading inasmuch as these performances are often part of larger festivals, serving to entertain as well as instruct.

Some forms, like Kathakali, use dance and music to tell these stories. Several varieties of puppet theatre with and without spoken text present many of the same epics as Sanskrit drama in popular forms. These puppets could be brightly painted three-dimensional wooden dolls attached to strings and controlled from above, or two-dimensional shadow puppets (either in black or multiple colors) that are manipulated by sticks from below. The *jatra* is a form of musical theatre in which a travelling group of singers present stories as they journey from place to place. While some contemporary *jatra* groups will perform an entire story at a given location, the form generally retains some idea of traveling or journey, requiring interested audience members to move along with the actors.

Dalit literature

Dalits are a caste of people in India, the caste sometimes referred to as "untouchable." Unlike ethnic or racial designations, caste was historically a marker of social class as well as lineage (obviously race and ethnicity are tied to social class, but race is not directly a class designation). Modern India has outlawed discrimination based on caste, but, as with racial discrimination in other parts of the world, caste-based discrimination continues. Issues of caste are part of modern and contemporary Indian literature. One genre, for instance, consists almost entirely of first-person narrations of the violence and degradation of everyday events in the lives of Dalits. Some of this literature is written by Dalits, while some of it is written by people adopting the Dalit point of view. Little of this genre is written in English, but echoes of it appear in works by the authors mentioned above.

The place of criticism

As numerous postcolonial critics have pointed out, there was a long period of time during colonialism and after where the colonies and former colonies produced literature and Europe produced criticism. This imbalance has gradually lessened over time, but many Indian scholars lament the relative scarcity of "Indian literary criticism." As with Japan, there is a question about whether such criticism should exist and exactly what such a school of criticism might look like.

Sri Aurobindo (1872–1950) was a dramatist who also worked to champion the cause of criticism in India. His *Future Poetry* lays out a course of action which has remained a topic of debate. His project is more about convincing Indian people to participate in criticism and less about "Indian literary criticism" as a distinct entity. As such, he discusses Shakespeare extensively. One of the debates about his work involves the relative importance of European authors in it. Is this the sort of criticism that Indian scholars should be aiming for?

Part III
Practical exercises

Chapter 14

Theory and practice

Theatre is active. While a great deal of knowledge can be transmitted through writing, this writing should never substitute for a connection to active theatre. What follows are a few activities to try out that relate to the theories anthologized in this book. Some of these activities are modifications of the actual practices of the writers in question. Others have developed from my own teaching and professional work. These should be viewed as active "discussion questions" and not as "training" in any of the techniques or styles discussed here. These are physical points of departure designed to explore some of the topics discussed in this book.

Theatre and semiotics

Several of the prior chapters asked questions about how theatre communicates what it does with its audiences. In Chapter 3 this was a question of the general structure of the theatre, whereas the acting and aesthetic chapters explored the ways that specific elements within a larger structure might communicate specific meanings. With "realism" still being the dominant mode of acting in popular Western theatre, it is difficult to imagine the rich language that can emerge from a series of developed, prescribed gestures. It is easy to imagine these gestures as hollow repetitions rather than as meaningful interpretations. For instance, there is a specific walk done by soldiers in various Chinese operatic traditions. Every actor playing a solider role knows what angle his feet should be at, where his overall mass should be balanced, the length of stride, the focus of the eyes, and every other aspect of this movement. Within a given school of a given type of opera in China, this motion is "set" down to its smallest detail. That being said, watching two performances of the same movement side by side, one can feel, if not always see, differences between two skilled actors. Within the formal framework of a language of gestures, these actors manage to make their own statements, just as two actors using the same set of words in English can offer different interpretations of these words without changing the "set" way in which they are pronounced or ordered.

Purpose:

This exercise helps actors to consider the value of precision in non-verbal language, and the potential for variance even in forms that might, at first, appear to be rigid. It is very loosely adapted for the Western classroom from training techniques common in several traditional Asian theatres.

Post-activity discussion:

1 Based on the case studies in this book or on other theatre you have seen, what are some examples of theatres that rely on non-verbal languages? What do these examples have in common? How are the examples different? How do they relate to other movement-based activities like dance, martial arts, or sports? Is there any way to distinguish between "theatre" movement and other sorts of movement?
2 To what extent does contemporary Western realism rely on non-verbal cues to communicate its messages? Imagine listening to a TV show without being able to see the images (or better yet, actually do this). How much do these sorts of programs rely on words? How much do they rely on actions? Does the same ratio hold true in theatre?
3 What are the relative strengths and weaknesses of logocentric theatre and movement-based theatre? What is each best at communicating? What are the limitations of each form? Is one form more advanced than the other? Can the two forms work effectively together?
4 Where does individual variation enter into a shared vocabulary of movement? What does having a precise movement associated with an emotion say about this emotion? Was the emotional content communicated effectively? What things did actors do to make the emotions more or less clear? If the movements ever bordered on parody or exaggeration, what factors contributed to this? What would the benefits of having such a defined language of movements be? What are the limitations?

Time:

40–60 minutes.

Requirements:

Multiple groups of three–four students each, four identical copies of a different "everyday" prop for each group (four sets of sunglasses, four iPhones, four cups of coffee, etc.).

Step 1:   Each individual should begin "playing" with a prop. Use this prop at different speeds. Use this prop in different postures. How might one breathe when using this prop? Where might one look? Is the body tense or loose? Find the full range of motions one might ordinarily take with this prop.

Step 2: Each individual should identify a *specific* emotional state. For instance, "sad" is a general state. The sort of sad that one feels when an ex starts dating someone new before you have started dating someone new is more specific. These emotional states should be common – everyone should hypothetically have experienced them or have known people who have experienced them. Each individual should write down this emotional state.

Step 3: Without telling anyone the emotional state in question, each individual should begin to experiment with the prop again. How would you physically use this prop when in the precise emotional state described? Consider every part of your body from head to feet. Consider your eyes, your breathing, your posture, your tension level. Consider your use of the space in the room.

Step 4: After finding a use of the prop that reflects the emotional state, "refine" this movement. Figure out exactly what your body is doing during it. By the end of step four, you should be able to repeat the movement precisely enough that a camera would detect no difference between cycles.

Step 5: Return to your group. One by one, each individual should perform with the prop. After each performance, the other members of the group should attempt to articulate the emotional state being expressed.

Step 6: The group should choose the clearest use of the prop and then be "trained" in this action. Each member of the group should be able to repeat the action precisely.

Step 7: Form new groups with one member of a different group using different props. Each individual in the group should perform for these new group mates.

Step 8: Discuss the emotional states in the new groups.

Step 9: Each individual should choose two emotional states and two props in the new group. The individual should then figure out a way of bridging between these emotional states and props. If each individual action with a prop was a word, actors should now try to create sentences.

Step 10: Multiple actors should share their experiments with the entire class.

Theatre and resistance

Different types of theatre acts as resistance in different ways. Several chapters have addressed the ways in which various theatrical structures can change the way the audience considers the world around them, and, by challenging a world view, challenge the political implications of that world view. Augusto Boal's theatre of the oppressed is a particularly active, visceral version of theatre as structural resistance. The following activity is adapted from the early training stages of theatre of the oppressed as it is currently practiced in various parts of the world. Inasmuch as Boal's techniques are active, his books provide extensive documentation on his training techniques – what follows is one, early, basic activity.

Purpose:

We have been trained to interact with the world in certain ways. These ways are, according to Boal, part of an ideological system. Our way of interacting with the world keeps us in our place. In this activity, actors are challenged to realize the limitations and boundaries of their interactions and then to expand these boundaries.

Post-activity discussion:

1 What are some moments when theatre – or literature and the arts more broadly – have shaped politics or society? If you cannot think of any, do you think theatre can shape society? If not, what stops theatre from having social or political effects?
2 How could theatre be more effective at changing the world? Is there a model presented by the theorists in this text that would be effective in your context? What pieces of theatre have you seen that come the closest to being effective?
3 What are the most appropriate social and political targets for theatre? What type of issues might it be best at addressing?
4 Should theatre even seek to generate political change at all? If not, what should the primary purpose of theatre be? Why "should" theatre do / not do these things (based on your own experience and the theories presented in this book)?

Time:

20–25 minutes.

Requirements:

A variety of toys or everyday objects, one for each participant with a few extras. Some of the objects may be duplicated, but greater variety is better. Examples include beach balls, cardboard boxes, hula hoops, and jump ropes. Avoid any potentially dangerous objects (nothing with sharp edges).

Special note: This activity works best if participants are not aware of the steps beyond their current step. The development of the activity should come as a surprise.

Step 1: Each participant should choose an object and find a space in the room.
Step 2: Give each participant a brief amount of time to "play" with the object.
    Question: How many of you used the object in its "intended" manner? (Generally, in the first instance, people will use the toys in traditional ways.)
Step 3: Encourage the participants to find one new way of using the object.
Step 4: Encourage participants to find another new way of using the object.
Step 5: Repeat until several participants appear to have "exhausted" the possibilities.
    Question: How many of you moved around the room? How many of you changed your body position in a significant way – lying down, for instance? How many of you interacted with another participant? How many of you engaged parts of your body other than your hands? How many of you engaged your voices?
Step 6: Encourage participants to find as many new ways of interacting with the objects as possible. Stop this step as the activity in the room crescendos, but well before participants begin to exhaust their new sets of possibilities.

Discussion:

What rules did you impose upon yourself? Where did these rules come from? What did it feel like to begin to break these rules? If you felt awkward, did that feeling subside over time? What were the consequences of breaking these rules? Are there other areas of life in which you impose rules on yourself? What are they? How might you begin to experiment with expanding these boundaries? What might the consequences of breaking these boundaries be? What might the benefits be?

Additional notes:

In discussion point out things like nervous laughter, copying of more daring students, reticence to experiment, and even potential resistance to this sort of "play" in an educational setting. All of these occurrences stem from particular ideological formulations: these are precisely the sort of behaviors that demonstrate the rigidity of ideology.

Collaborative ritual

Several of the theorists anthologized in this volume insist on the necessity of collaborative development of a piece. While Western models often have a director working from a preset script, this model of theatre is by no means the only one. The need for collaboration is particularly evident in ritual work like Werewere Liking's early plays. The steps listed below are not taken directly from any particular theory, but rather are designed to guide participants through a process of collaboration and ritual creation. This is a project that relies on experienced actors who are willing to experiment and push the boundaries of their beliefs. Rituals cannot help but touch on belief. In a circumstance where time or actor-willingness do not allow for completion of this activity, it is still worth considering the steps below as a way of discussing the idea of the creation of ritual.

Purpose:

This activity explores the potential of exploring a social issue without a director or a preset script. It is different from improv inasmuch as the piece that develops will be refined. The piece developed will have the quality of ritual in the sense that it is a defined set of actions with the intention of directly intervening in the material or spiritual condition of the world.

Post-activity discussion:

1. Can ritual ever change anything? Does it act on people's minds or can it generate a change in the world? If ritual doesn't change the world, is there another reason to continue practicing rituals?
2. Can newly-created rituals ever be useful? What aspects of the rituals you created were useful?
3. Can ritual enhance the aesthetic value of theatre? Can rituals make theatre better in some sense? Looking at the discussions of modernity in this book, why do you suppose so many of the modern Western theatre artists turned toward ritual to enhance their theatres?
4. What aspects of ritual in theatre have you encountered and what effects did these aspects have on you?

Time:

Multiple hours spread out over a week or more.

Requirements:

Requirements will vary.

Note: This activity will work best in classes containing more experienced actors. It is not as guided as the other activities in this chapter.

Step 1: Each group should agree on a "problem" they wish to address. This could range from the emotional (e.g. stress over finals), to the immediate concrete (e.g. treatment of minorities in the community), to the wider concrete (e.g. the California drought).

Step 2: Groups should discuss what power sources might be available to them (e.g. community, God, emotional support from parents and peers, energy from the natural world). Ideally they will reach consensus, but when this isn't possible, they should attempt to find compatibility and overlap within their power systems.

Step 3: The group should use some of the same techniques discussed above in the semiotic activity to develop a physical vocabulary related to their problem.

Step 4: The group should consider the systems of movement that already exist surrounding their power source(s).

Step 5: The group should begin combining these two physical vocabularies.

Step 6: After having played with these vocabularies, but before having "set" any particular moments, the group should "story-board" their ritual. This story-board should contain the most general outline of what they hope to accomplish (e.g. gaining the power to change things on their own, changing things with the ritual, having the power change things on its own) and how they hope to accomplish it (e.g. verbs like supplication, sacrifice, summoning, invocation).

Step 7: The group should consider what roles their ritual requires (e.g. officiant, offerant, supplicant).

Step 8: Students should begin to refine their physical vocabularies within their roles to set up a basic framework for their ritual.

Step 9: Students should consider what props, music, and setting might be most appropriate for their ritual (or whether their ritual requires such things at all).

Step 10: Rehearsal.

Step 11: Enactment.

References

Achebe, Chinua. "An Image of Africa: Racism in Conrad's *Heart of Darkness*." *Massachusetts Review*, 18, 1997.
Awodiya, M. P. *Excursions in Drama and Literature: Interviews with Femi Osofisan*. Ibadan, Nigeria: Kraft Books, 1993.
Barba, Eugenio. "Eurasian Theatre." In *The Intercultural Studies Reader*, ed. Patrice Pavis. New York: Routledge, 1996.
Barba, Eugenio and Nicola Savarese. *A Dictionary of Theatre Anthropology*. New York: Routledge, 1991.
Batra, Kanika. *Feminist Visions and Queer Futures in Postcolonial Drama: Community, Kinship, and Citizenship*. New York: Routledge, 2010.
Bharucha, Rustom. *Theatre and the World: Performance and the Politics of Culture*. New York: Routledge, 1993.
Boal, Augusto. *Theatre of the Oppressed*. London: Pluto Press, 1979.
Braithwaite, Kamua. *Roots: Essays in Caribbean Literature*. Ann Arbor, MI: University of Michigan Press, 1993.
Brecht, Bertolt. *Brecht on Theatre: the Development of an Aesthetic*, ed. and trans. John Willett. New York: Hill and Wang, 1964.
Brook, Peter. *The Open Door: Thoughts on Acting and Theatre*. New York: Anchor Books, 2000.
Chen, Xiaomei. *The Columbia Anthology of Modern Chinese Drama*. New York: Columbia University Press, 2014.
Dasarupa, Dhanamjaya. *Treatise on Hindu Dramaturgy*, ed. George Haas. New York: Columbia University Press, 1912.
De Mel, Neloufer. "Re/presenting African Theatre in Sri Lanka: A Casebook on Intercultural Transformations." In *(Post)Colonial Stages: Critical and Creative Views on Drama, Theatre and Performance*, ed. Helen Gilbert. Sydney: Dangaroo Press, 1999.
Dunn, Charles and Bunzo Torigoe (eds). *The Actor's Analects*. New York: Columbia University Press, 1969.
Dutt, Uptal. *Towards a Revolutionary Theatre*. Calcutta: Sarkar and Sons, 1982.
Gao Xingjian. "The Potential of Theatre." In *Gao Xingjian: Aesthetics and Creation* Amherst, New York: Cambria Press, 2012.
Gordon, Stewart. *When Asia was the World: Traveling Merchants, Scholars, Warriors, and Monks Who Created the Riches of the East*. New York: Da Capo Press, 2009.

Hirata Oriza. *Introduction to Theatre (Engeki Nyumo)*. Tokyo: Kodansha Gendai Shinsho, 1998. James, C.L.R. *The Black Jacobins*. London: Secker and Warburg, 1938.
James, C.L.R. *The Artist in the Caribbean*. Open Lecture Series. Mona, Jamaica: University of the West Indies Press, 1959.
Jameson, Frederic. *Marxism and Form: 20th-Century Dialectical Theories of Literature*. Princeton, NJ: Princeton University Press, 1971.
Kassab, Suzanne. *Contemporary Arab Thought: Cultural Critique in Comparative Perspective*. New York: Columbia University Press, 2010.
Kilito, Abdefattah. *Thou Shalt not Speak my Language*. Syracuse, NY: Syracuse University Press, 2008.
Liking, Werewere. *It Shall be Of Jasper and Coral and Love-across-a-Hundred-Lives*, trans. Marjolijn de Jager. Charlottesville, VA: University of Virginia, 2000.
Looser, Diana. "A Piece 'More Curious Than All the Rest': Re-Encountering Pre-Colonial Pacific Island Theatre, 1769–1855." *Theatre Journal*, 63:4, 2011, pp. 521–540.
Mariátegui, Carlos. *Siete Ensayos de Interpretacio de la Realidad Peruana* (Lima, 1963) quoted in Gwen Kirkpatrick "Spanish American Narrative, 1810–1920." In *The Cambridge Companion to Modern Latin American Culture*, ed. John King. Cambridge: Cambridge University Press, 2004.
Muni, Bharata. *Natyasastra*, trans. Manomohan Ghosh. Varanasi: Chowkhamba 1987.
Ngugi Wa Thiong'o. *Decolonising the Mind*. New York: James Currey, 1986.
Osofisan, Femi. "Ritual and the Revolutionary Ethos." *Okike*, 22, 1982, pp. 72–81.
Osofisan, Femi. "'The Revolution as Muse': drama as surreptitious insurrection in a post-colonial, military state." In *Theatre Matters, Performance and Culture on the World Stage*, ed. Richard Boon and Jane Plastow. Cambridge: Cambridge University Press, 1998.
Potiki, Roma. "A Maori Point of View: The Journey from Anxiety to Confidence." In *Feminist Voices: Women's Studies Texts for Aotearoa/New Zealand*, ed. Rosemary Du Plessis and Phillida Bunkle. Oxford: Oxford University Press, 1992.
Sengupta, Poile. 'An Interview with Poile Sengupta' by Anita Singh. *Asian Theatre Journal*, 29:1, 2012, pp. 78–88.
Sircar, Badal. *The Third Theatre*. Calcutta: Sri Aurobindho Press, 1978.
Soyinka, Wole. "The Fourth Stage." In *Myth, Literature, and the African World the Fourth Stage*. Cambridge: Cambridge University Press, 1976, pp. 143–148.
Suzuki Tadashi. "Human Experience and the Group." In *The Way of Acting*, trans. Thomas Rimer. New York: Theatre Communications Group, 1986.
Walcott, Derek. "What the Twilight Says: An Overture." In *Dream on Monkey Mountain and Other Plays*, New York: Farrar, Straus and Giroux, 1970.
Wannous, Saadallah. *Manifestos for a New Arab Theatre* (1970). Unpublished translation by Eyad Houssami (published in Arabic as *Bayanat li massak arabi jadid*, Beirut: Dar al-Farabi)
Zeami Motokiyo. *On the Art of No Drama*, trans. Thomas Rimer. Princeton, NJ: Princeton Library of Asian Translations, 1984.

Further reading

Works spanning multiple categories

Martin Banham and Errol Hill. *The Cambridge Guide to African and Caribbean Theatre*. Cambridge: Cambridge University Press, 1994.
James R. Brandon. *The Cambridge Guide to Asian Theatre*. Cambridge: Cambridge University Press, 1997.
Helen Gilbert. *(Post)Colonial Stages: Critical and Creative Views on Drama, Theatre and Performance*. Sydney: Dangaroo Press, 1999.
Stewart Gordon. *When Asia was the World: Traveling Merchants, Scholars, Warriors, and Monks Who Created the Riches of the East*. New York: Da Capo Press, 2009.
Samuel Leiter. *The Encyclopedia of Asian Theatre*. New York: Greenwood, 2006.

Postcolonial theory

Chinua Achebe. "An Image of Africa: Racism in Conrad's *Heart of Darkness*." *Massachusetts Review*, 18, 1997.
Homi Bhabha. *The Location of Culture*. New York: Routledge, 1991.
Frantz Fanon. *Black Skins White Masks*. New York: Grove Press, 1952.
Frantz Fanon. *Wretched of the Earth*. New York: Grove Press, 1961.
Ngugi Wa Thiong'o. *Decolonising the Mind*. New York: James Currey, 1986.
Jane Plastow. *African Theatre and Politics*. Amsterdam: Rodopi, 1996.
Edward Said. *Orientalism*. New York: Vintage, 1979.
Gayatri Spivak. *A Critique of Postcolonial Reason: Toward a History of the Vanishing Present*. Cambridge, MA: Harvard University Press, 1999.

Modernism

James Harding and John Rowe. *Not the Other Avant-Garde: The Transnational Foundations of Avant-Garde Performance*. Ann Arbor, MI: University of Michigan Press, 2006.
Dilip Gaonkar. *Alternative Modernities*. Durham, NC: Duke University Press, 2001.
Gerald Gaylard. *After Colonialism: African Postmodernism and Magical Realism*. Witwatersrand, South Africa: Wits University Press, 2006.
Pericles Lewis. *The Cambridge Introduction to Modernism*. Cambridge: Cambridge University Press, 2007.

Gender and world theatre

Kanika Batra. *Feminist Visions and Queer Futures in Postcolonial Drama: Community, Kinship, and Citizenship.* New York: Routledge, 2010.

Coralie Casassa. "Female Roles and Engagement of Women in the Classical Sanskrit Theatre Kutiyattam: A Contemporary Theatre Tradition." *Asian Theatre Journal,* 29:1, 2012, pp. 1–30.

Sue-Ellen Case. *Feminism in Theatre.* New York: Routledge, 1988.

Jennifer Goodlander. "Gender, Power, and Puppets: Two Early Women Dalangs in Bali." *Asian Theatre Journal,* 29:1, 2012, pp. 54–77.

Yvette Hutchinson and Jane Plastow. *African Theatre: Contemporary Women.* Martlesham: James Currey/ Boydell & Brewer Inc., 2015.

Margo Milleret. *Latin American Women on/in Stages.* Albany, NY: State University of New York Press, 2004.

Elaine Savory. "Registering Connection: Masking and Gender Issues in Caribbean Theatre." In *Postcolonial Stages,* ed. Helen Gilbert. Sydney: Dangaroo Press, 1999.

Poile Sengupta. *Women Center Stage.* New York: Routledge, 2010.

Henry Spiller. "How not to Act like a Woman: Gender, Ideology and Humor in West Java, Indonesia." *Asian Theatre Journal,* 29:1, 2012, pp. 31–53.

Western Theatre Theory (and its critics)

Eugenio Barba. "Eurasian Theatre." In *The Intercultural Studies Reader,* ed. Patrice Pavis. New York: Routledge, 1996.

Eugenio Barba and Nicola Savarese. *A Dictionary of Theatre Anthropology.* New York: Routledge, 1991.

Rustom Bharucha. *Theatre and the World: Performance and the Politics of Culture.* New York: Routledge, 1993.

Bertolt Brecht. *Brecht on Theatre: the Development of an Aesthetic,* ed. and trans. John Willett. New York: Hill and Wang, 1964.

Peter Brook. *The Open Door: Thoughts on Acting and Theatre.* New York: Anchor Books, 2000.

Latin America

Gloria Anzaldua. *Borderlands / La Frontera.* San Francisco, CA: Aunt Lute Books, 2012.

Erica Beckman. *Capital Fictions: The Literature of Latin America's Export Age.* Minneapolis, MN: University of Minnesota Press, 2013.

Augusto Boal. *Theatre of the Oppressed.* London: Pluto Press, 1979.

Stephen Boldy. *A Companion to Jorge Luis Borges.* Woodbridge: Tamesis, 2009.

Enrique Buenaventura and Joanne Pottlitzer. "Theatre & Culture." *The Drama Review,* 14:2, 1970, pp. 151–156.

Nestor Garcia Canclini. *Hybrid Cultures: Strategies for Entering and Leaving Modernity.* Minneapolis, MN: University of Minnesota Press, 2005.

Eladio Cortes and Mirta Barrea-Marlys. *Encyclopedia of Latin American Theater.* Westport, CT: Greenwood, 2003.

D.P. Gallagher. *Modern Latin American Literature*. Oxford: Oxford University Press, 1973.
Mike Gonzalez and David Treece. *The Gathering of Voices: the Twentieth-Century Poetry of Latin America*. London: Verso, 1992.
Roberto Schwarz. *Two Girls and Other Essays*. London: Verso, 2013.
Diana Taylor and Roselyn Costantino. *Holy Terrors: Latin American Women Perform*. Durham, NC: Duke University Press, 2003.
Diana Taylor and Sarah J. Townsend. *Stages of Conflict: A Critical Anthology of Latin American Theatre and Performance*. Ann Arbor, MI: University of Michigan Press, 2008.

Caribbean

Kamua Braithwaite. *Roots: Essays in Caribbean Literature*. Ann Arbor, MI: University of Michigan Press, 1993.
Stefano Harney. *Nationalism and Identity: Culture and the Imagination in a Caribbean Diaspora*. Kingston, Jamaica: University of the West Indies, 1996.
Gustavo Perez Firmat. *The Cuban Condition: Translation and Identity in Modern Cuban Literature*. Cambridge: Cambridge University Press, 1989.
Derek Walcott. "What the Twilight Says: An Overture." In *Dream on Monkey Mountain and Other Plays*. New York: Farrar, Straus and Giroux, 1970.
Nana Wilson Tagoe. *Historical Thought and Literary Representation in West Indian Literature*. Orlando, FL: University of Florida Press, 1998.

Africa

Shadrach A. Ambanasom. *Education of the Deprived: Anglophone Cameroon Literary Drama*. Bamenda, Cameroon: Langaa Research and Publishing, 2010.
Derek Attridge and Rosemary Jolly. *Writing South Africa*. Cambridge: Cambridge University Press, 1998.
Muyiwa P. Awodiya. *Excursions in Drama and Literature: Interviews with Femi Osofisan*. Ibadan, Nigeria: Kraft Books, 1993.
Christopher Balme. *Decolonizing the Stage: Theatrical Syncretism and the Post-Colonial Drama*. Oxford: Clarendon Press, 1999.
Kwabena N. Bame. *Come to Laugh*. New York: Lilian Barber Press, 1985.
Martin Banham. *A History of Theatre in Africa*. Cambridge: Cambridge University Press, 2008.
Martin Banham et al. *African Theatre* series. Martlesham: James Currey, various dates.
Karin Barber. *The Generation of Plays. Yoruba Popular Life in Theatre*. Bloomington, IN: Indiana University Press, 2003.
Ingrid Bjorkman. *Mother Sing For Me: People's Theatre in Kenya*. New York: Zed Books, 1989.
Catherine Cole. *Ghana's Concert Party Theatre*. Bloomington, IN: Indiana University Press, 2001.
John Conteh-Morgan. *Theatre and Drama in Francophone Africa*. Cambridge: Cambridge University Press, 2006.

John Conteh-Morgan. *New Francophone African and Caribbean Theatres*. Bloomington, IN: Indiana University Press, 2010.
John Conteh-Morgan and Tejumola Olaniyan. *African Theatre and Performance*. Bloomington, IN: Indiana University Press, 2004.
Neloufer De Mel. "Re/presenting African Theatre in Sri Lanka: A Casebook on Intercultural Transformations." In *(Post)Colonial Stages: Critical and Creative Views on Drama, Theatre and Performance*, ed. Helen Gilbert. Sydney: Dangaroo Press, 1999.
John Fage and William Tordoff. *A History of Africa*. London: Routledge, 2001.
Doris Haarhoff. *Goats, Oranges, and Skeletons: A Trilogy of Namibian Independence Plays*. Windhoek: New Namibia Books, 2000.
Werewere Liking. *It Shall be Of Jasper and Coral and Love-across-a-Hundred-Lives*, trans. Marjolijn de Jager. Charlottesville, VA: University of Virginia, 2000.
Martin Meredith. *The Fate of Africa: A History of the Continent since Independence*. Boston, MA: Da Capo Press, 2011
Michelle Mielly. "An Aesthetics of Necessity." In *The Original Explosion Theatre Created Worlds: Essays on Werewere Liking's Art and Writings*, ed. John Conteh-Morgan and Irene Assiba d'Almeida. New York: Rodopi, 1994.
Femi Osofisan. "Ritual and the Revolutionary Ethos." *Okike*, 22, 1982, pp. 72–81.
Femi Osofisan. "'The Revolution as Muse': drama as surreptitious insurrection in a post-colonial, military state." In *Theatre Matters, Performance and Culture on the World Stage*, ed. Richard Boon and Jane Plastow. Cambridge: Cambridge University Press, 1998.
Jane Plastow. *African Theatre and Politics: The Evolution of Theatre in Ethiopia, Tanzania, and Zimbabwe*. Amsterdam: Rodopi, 1996.
Wole Soyinka. *Myth, Literature, and the African World*. Cambridge: Cambridge University Press, 1976.
Terrence Zeeman. *New Namibian Plays*. Windhoek: New Namibia Books, 2000.

Middle East

Raymond Farrin. *Abundance from the Desert: Classical Arabic Poetry*. Syracuse, NY: Syracuse University Press, 2011.
Eyad Houssami. *Doomed by Hope: Essays on Arab Theatre*. New York: Pluto Press, 2012.
Suzanne Kassab. *Contemporary Arab Thought: Cultural Critique in Comparative Perspective*. New York: Columbia University Press, 2010.
Abdefattah Kilito. *Thou Shalt not Speak my Language*. Syracuse, NY: Syracuse University Press, 2008.
Margaret Litvin. *Hamlet's Arab Journey: Shakespeare's Prince and Nasser's Ghost*. Princeton, NJ: Princeton University Press, 2011.
Julie Scott Meisami and Paul Starkey. *Encyclopedia of Arabic Literature*. New York: Routledge, 1998.
Dwight Reynolds. *Cambridge Companion to Modern Arab Culture*. Cambridge: Cambridge University Press, 2015.
Saadallah Wannous. *Manifestos for a New Arab Theatre* (1970). Unpublished translation by Eyad Houssami (published in Arabic as *Bayanat li massak arabi jadid*, Beirut: Dar al-Farabi).

Australia

Michelle Arrow. *Upstaged*. Sydney: Currency Press, 2002.
Jonathan Bollen, Bruce Parr and Adrian Kiernander. *Men at Play: Masculinities in Australian Theatre since the 1950s*. New York: Rodopi, 2008.
Maryrose Casey. *Creating Frames: Contemporary Indigenous Theatre 1967–1990*. Brisbane: University of Queensland Press, 2004.
Maryrose Casey. "Performing for Aboriginal Life and Culture: Aboriginal Theatre and Ngurrumilmarrmiriyu." *Australasian Drama Studies*, 59, 2011, pp. 53–68.
Jack Davis, Eva Johnson, Richard Walley, Justine Saunders and Bob Maza. *Plays From Black Australia*. Redfern: Currency Press, 1989.
Helen Gilbert and Jaqueline Lo. *Performance and Cosmopolitics: Cross-Cultural Transactions in Australia*. New York: Palgrave, 2009.
Aileen Moreton-Robinson. *Talkin' up to the White Woman: Indigenous Women and Feminism*. Brisbane: University of Queensland Press, 2000.

New Zealand

Alan Duff. *Once Were Warriors*. New York: Vintage, 1995.
Diana Looser. "A Piece 'More Curious Than All the Rest': Re-Encountering Pre-Colonial Pacific Island Theatre, 1769–1855." *Theatre Journal*, 63:4, 2011. pp. 521–540.
Marc Maufort. *Performing Aotearoa: New Zealand Theatre and Drama in an Age of Transition*. Venice, Italy: European Interuniversity Press, 2007.
Roma Potiki. "A Maori Point of View: The Journey from Anxiety to Confidence." In *Feminist Voices: Women's Studies Texts for Aotearoa/New Zealand*, ed. Rosemary Du Plessis and Phillida Bunkle. Oxford: Oxford University Press, 1992.

China

Xiaomei Chen. *The Columbia Anthology of Modern Chinese Drama*. New York: Columbia University Press, 2014.
Pangyuan Chi and David Derwei Wang. *Chinese Literature in the Second Half of a Modern Century*. Bloomington, IN: Indiana University Press, 2000.
Rossella Ferrari. *Pop Goes the Avant-Garde: Experimental Theatre in Contemporary China*. New York: Seagull Books, 2013.
Gao Xingjian. "The Potential of Theatre." In *Gao Xingjian: Aesthetics and Creation* Amherst, NY: Cambria Press, 2012.
Charles Holcombe. *A History of East Asia: From the Origins of Civilization to the Twenty-First Century*. Cambridge: Cambridge University Press, 2011.
Jiao Juyin. "On Directing." In *Jiao Juyin lun daoyan yishu* (Jiao Juyin on the Art of Directing), vol. 2. Beijing: Zhongguo xiju chubanshe, 2005.
Colin Mackerras. *Chinese Theater: From its Origins to the Present Day*. Honolulu, HI: University of Hawaii, 1988.
Jo Riley. *Chinese Theatre and the Actor in Performance*. Cambridge: Cambridge University Press, 2006.

Japan

Karen Brazell. *Traditional Japanese Theater: An Anthology of Plays*. New York: Columbia University Press, 1999.
Richard Calichman. *Overcoming Modernity: Cultural Identity in Wartime Japan*. New York: Columbia University Press, 2008.
Charles Dunn and Bunzo Torigoe (eds). *The Actor's Analects*. New York: Columbia University Press, 1969.
Hirata Oriza. *Introduction to Theatre (Engeki Nyumo)*. Tokyo: Kodansha Gendai Shinsho, 1998.
Kojin Karatani. *History and Repetition*. New York: Columbia University Press, 2011.
Donald Keene. *The Major Plays of Chikamatsu*. New York: Columbia University Press, 1961.
Donald Keene. *No and Bunraku*. New York: Columbia University Press, 1990.
Nishida Kitaro. *An Inquiry into the Good*. New Haven, CT: Yale University Press, 1992.
Benito Ortolani. *The Japanese Theatre: From Shamanistic Ritual to Contemporary Pluralism*. Princeton, NJ: Princeton University Press, 1995.
Cody Poulton. *A Beggar's Art: Scripting Modernity in Japanese Drama, 1900–1930*. Honolulu, HI: University of Hawaii Press, 2010.
Robert T. Rolf and John Gillespie. *Alternative Japanese Drama*. Honolulu, HI: University of Hawaii Press, 1992.
Suzuki Tadashi. "Human Experience and the Group." In *The Way of Acting*, trans. Thomas Rimer. New York: Theatre Communications Group, 1986.
Zeami Motokiyo. *On the Art of No Drama*. trans. Thomas Rimer. Princeton, NJ: Princeton Library of Asian Translations, 1984.

India

Vasuda Dalmia and Rasmi Sadana. *The Cambridge Companion to Modern Indian Culture*. Cambridge: Cambridge University Press, 2012.
Dhanamjaya Dasarupa. *Treatise on Hindu Dramaturgy*, ed. George Haas. New York: Columbia University, 1912.
Uptal Dutt. *Towards a Revolutionary Theatre*. Calcutta: Sarkar and Sons, 1982.
Ananda Lal. *Theatre of India: A Concise Companion*. Oxford: Oxford University Press, 2009.
P. Lal. *Great Sanskrit Plays in Modern Translation*. New York: New Directions Publishing, 1964.
Bharata Muni. *Natyasastra*, trans. Manomohan Ghosh. Varanasi: Chowkhamba, 1987.
Poile Sengupta. 'An Interview with Poile Sengupta' by Anita Singh. *Asian Theatre Journal*, 29:1, 2012, pp. 78–88.
Mano Shovana Narayan. *Indian Theatre and Dance Traditions*. New Delhi: Raj Press, 2004.
Badal Sircar. *The Third Theatre*. Calcutta: Sri Aurobindho Press, 1978.
Rakesh Solomon. *Globalization, Nationalism and the Text of Kichaka-Vadha: The First English Translations of the Marathi Anticolonial Classic*. London: Anthem Press, 2014.
Amrit Srivivasan. *Approaches to Bharata's Natyasastra*. Delhi: Hope India, 2007.
M.L. Varadpande. *History of Indian Theatre*. Calcutta: Abhinav Publications, 2005.

Index

Achebe, Chinua 144, 148
al-Hakim, Tawfiq 260
Anzaldúa, Gloria 238
Artaud, Antonin 61–3, 93
Althusser, Louis 57–8
Aristotle 22–3, 52–3, 60

Basiouny, Dalia 94
Barba, Eugenio 107–9
Bharata Muni 35–40, 50–3
Boal, Augusto 91, 158–65
Borges, Jorge Luis 244
Braithwaite, Kamua 239–42
Brecht, Bertolt 61–2
Buenaventura, Enrique 110–18, 144–51

Casey, Maryrose 134–45, 267
Cesaire, Aime 101–2, 243, 248

Dutt, Uptal 73–6, 97

Fanon, Frantz 244
Farber, Yael 94
Fugard, Athol 94, 110, 251–2

Gao Xingjian 15–19, 157, 198–206
Geertz, Clifford 144
Glissant, Édouard 234

Hirata Oriza 189–198

James, C.L.R. 236
Jiao Juyin 99, 175–82

Kani, John 94, 110

Kouka, Hone 268

Lawler, Ray 266
Liking, Werewere 126–34, 146–51

Marx, Karl 57–8, 89
Meyerhold, Vsevolod 186–7

Naipaul, V.S. 234
Nietzsche, Friedrich 40–1
Ngugi Wa Thiong'o 90, 110, 144, 158, 252
Nkosi, Lewis 250

Osofisan, Femi 64–73, 89–100, 147, 149

Potiki, Roma 216–18

Sanu, Ya'qub 259
Sengupta, Poile 219–25
Sircar, Badal 54–7, 90, 149
Soyinka, Wole 40–9, 89–100, 146–50, 251
Stanislavski, Konstantin 175
Stoklos, Denise 216
Strindberg, August 155–6, 188
Suzuki Tadashi 157, 165–75

Valdez, Luis 94

Walcott, Derek 118–26, 146, 148, 234, 243
Wannous, Saadallah 76–100

Zeami Motokiyo 25–34, 50–3

Printed in Great Britain
by Amazon

47040675R00179